Building Data Apps with Streamlit

Create Dynamic Dashboards, Machine Learning Workflows, and AI Chatbots with Streamlit and Python

Siddhant Sadangi

www.orangeava.com

First Published: January 2026
Published By: Orange Education Pvt Ltd, AVA®
Address: 9, Daryaganj, Delhi, 110002, India

275 New North Road Islington Suite 1314 London,
N1 7AA, United Kingdom

ISBN (PBK): 978-93-49887-84-8
ISBN (E-BOOK): 978-93-49887-93-0

Scan the QR code to explore our entire catalogue

www.orangeava.com

Dedicated to

My Entire Family

About the Author

Siddhant Sadangi is a Developer Experience Engineer at neptune.ai, where he helps researchers and developers from leading organizations such as OpenAI, Samsung, and Poolside efficiently track their state-of-the-art machine learning workflows. With a career spanning more than a decade across developer advocacy, data science, and product enablement, he operates at the intersection of engineering, education, and community building.

Before joining neptune.ai, Siddhant worked as a Data Scientist at Reuters, where his machine learning pipelines and data products generated over $3 million in annual recurring revenue. His work focused on automating large-scale content systems, improving model precision, and designing predictive pipelines that directly influenced key business decisions. Earlier in his career, as an ETL Developer Consultant at Deloitte, he specialized in analytics automation, efficiency tooling, and process optimization.

Siddhant is also a recognized Streamlit Creator and Community Moderator, known for his active contributions to the open-source ecosystem. His Streamlit components and apps - downloaded more than 100,000 times and starred by developers worldwide - are widely used to simplify authentication, database integration, and workflow automation in Streamlit-based projects.

He has delivered talks at major machine learning conferences such as NeurIPS, speaking on experiment tracking and large-scale model monitoring. His technical blogs have been featured on Analytics Vidhya, Better Programming, the neptune.ai and Streamlit blogs, where he is known for bridging complex topics with practical clarity.

Through this book, Siddhant brings together his expertise in Python, Streamlit, developer experience, and community education to help readers transform their scripts into shareable and impactful web applications.

About the Technical Reviewers

Siavash Yasini is an ex-physicist turned full-stack data scientist and machine learning practitioner. As a technical lead, he works at the intersection of data science and software engineering, with a focus on production-ready pipelines, scalable architectures, and tools that make data easier to explore and act on.

A Streamlit Creator, Siavash has developed numerous Streamlit apps across both academia and industry, with several features in the Streamlit Gallery. He discovered Streamlit in 2019 at PyData, and has been an early power user ever since.

He is also deeply committed to knowledge-sharing, regularly writing technical articles on advanced Python techniques and data science best practices, while enjoying opportunities to teach, mentor, and help other data scientists and developers improve their craft. When he is not building things, he enjoys reading a good book, making coffee for friends, or getting nostalgic playing point-and-click adventure games.

Yuichiro Tachibana, known online as @whitphx, is a Developer Advocate at Hugging Face, and an active open-source software contributor. His projects span areas such as web development, browser technologies, and developer tools.

In the Streamlit community, Yuichiro created streamlit-WebRTC, a library that adds real-time video and audio processing features to Streamlit applications. Later, he developed Stlite, which enables Streamlit apps to run entirely in the browser through WebAssembly.

At Hugging Face, Yuichiro applied knowledge gained from Stlite to create Gradio-Lite, which is essentially to Gradio what Stlite is to Streamlit.

He has also developed Awesome Emacs Keymap, an extension that brings Emacs-style key bindings to Visual Studio Code. While different in focus from his Streamlit and Gradio-related work, it reflects his interest in improving developer experience across tools.

Yuichiro regularly participates in the global Python community, attending and speaking at events such as PyCon. He values these opportunities to exchange ideas, and stay connected with developers from around the world.

Through these projects and activities, Yuichiro has focused on making technical tools easier to use and more accessible, while contributing to communities that support open collaboration.

Souvik Roy has been deeply engaged with Machine Learning (ML) since the beginning of his career. He started out as an ML Intern at The Sparks Foundation, later contributing as a Streamlit Community Developer, where he focused on creating and optimizing automated ML models using Streamlit. Souvik completed his studies at the RCC Institute of Information Technology in 2024, before joining PwC as a Cybersecurity Engineer.

Over the course of his career, he has continued to explore the intersection of security and Artificial Intelligence (AI). Currently, Souvik is dedicated to developing ML-based SecOps solutions, and has also worked on deep learning-driven models, many of which are available on his GitHub profile. He is passionate about advancing secure, intelligent systems, and applying his expertise and experience to drive innovation in cybersecurity through machine learning.

Khuyen Tran is a data scientist, educator, and author focused on helping teams build clean, reproducible, and production-ready data workflows. She has worked across data engineering, Machine Learning (ML), and developer advocacy at both startups and established companies, improving documentation, tooling, and educational content for modern data, and forecasting workflows.

Khuyen is passionate about turning complex data and ML concepts into simple, accessible, real-world solutions that teams can apply immediately. She is the creator of *Code Cut*, and the author of *Production-Ready Data Science*, with more than 250 technical articles that have guided thousands of practitioners. Khuyen brings deep expertise in Python tooling, workflow design, and clear technical communication to the projects she supports.

Acknowledgments

This book was made possible through the support and encouragement of many people.

I owe deep gratitude to my parents, who taught me the value of knowledge, and to my wife, Priyanka, whose unwavering patience, insight, and love carried me through every late-night writing session, and who, with endless encouragement, became the very first reviewer of this book.

I would also like to thank those who directly shaped this book with their insights and technical expertise:

- Yuichiro Tachibana, for being the most comprehensive technical reviewer that I have had the pleasure of working with.
- Siavash Yasini, not just for the technical review, but more importantly, for being a mentor and a constant source of a different perspective.
- Khuyen Tran, for her technical review and for sharing her incredible knowledge with the community.
- Thiago Teixeira, for his thoughtful feedback, and for taking the time to write the foreword.
- Médéric Hurier, for stepping in with just the right help at the right time, making it possible to complete this book.

My heartfelt thanks also go to the Streamlit Creators Community and the Streamlit Team, particularly Jessica, for all their support and encouragement throughout this journey.

Foreword

- Thiago Teixeira
Co-founder, Streamlit

Say you have a data analysis you want to communicate with your team, or the management, or with the world, and you have a deadline. You need to build a web app to convey your results, but you do not have the luxury of spending time exploring the wide world of web development. You just have an itch to scratch.

I know the feeling. That is how Streamlit itself came about.

When we wrote Streamlit, our ambition was non-existent. We just wanted to make a web app for our data analysis (a data app), but every solution demanded constant fiddling with web programming. Instead, we just wanted to focus on the data. So we took a quick detour, wrote a comically primitive version of "Streamlet," and got our data app out. Next thing you know, all our friends wanted to try it, and their friends too. And one typo later, Streamlit was born (now with an "i").

Today, six years later, Streamlit still holds on to that north star: to get out of your way so that you can focus on the data. And we learned that the way we achieve this is not by removing complexity, but by starting from zero, rethinking the problem space, and adding only what is strictly necessary. As you use Streamlit, you may notice the fingerprints of this ideology at work – it is in everything we do.

Reading this book, I recognize those same fingerprints. A long-time Streamlit user and member of the Streamlit Creators program, Siddhant carries deep within him that same ideology of radical simplicity. This book takes you from a typical Python script to a basic Streamlit app, and then to a comprehensive, performant app in an effortless succession of steps.

That Siddhant came from our community makes a lot of sense to me. As our friends-of-friends started using Streamlit, a community of builders, innovators, and problem-solvers began to form, and that enthusiasm never went away, even as the Streamlit community grew beyond our imagination!

So, I hope this book will inspire you to join us. Stop by our forum, even just to say "hi." You will likely bump into Siddhant or myself there. Ask silly questions. Show beautiful apps. Comment on other people's work. Experiment. Break things. Push boundaries. Give us ideas on what to build. Streamlit and this book are here to give you more. So, let us build amazing things, and welcome to the future of data apps!

Preface

When I first encountered Streamlit, I was struck by how effortlessly it transformed data scripts into live applications. What began as curiosity quickly turned into a journey of open-source exploration, building, and teaching, and this book is a product of that journey.

The goal of this book is simple: To help Python developers and data practitioners create, share, and scale their ideas as interactive apps. You will find practical examples, reusable patterns, and complete projects - all leading up to building a Streamlit app that analyzes data, trains models, and integrates an AI chatbot.

Each chapter distills lessons from real projects and community experiences - from structuring multi-page apps to handling configuration, secrets, caching, and cloud deployment. More than code, it is about the mindset of delivering tools that others can actually use.

If you have ever built a Jupyter notebook, and wished you could share it as an app, this book is your bridge from analysis to application.

Get a Free eBook

We hope you are enjoying your recently purchased book! Your feedback is incredibly valuable to us, and to all other readers looking for great books.

If you found this book helpful or enjoyable, we would truly appreciate it, if you could take a moment to leave a short review with a 5 star rating on Amazon. It helps us grow, and lets other readers discover our books.

As a thank you, we would love to send you a free digital copy of this book, and a **30%** discount code on your next cart value on our official websites:

www.orangeava.com

www.orangeava.in (For Indian Subcontinent)

☑ **Here's how:**

Leave a review for the book on Amazon.

Take a screenshot of your review, and send an email to **info@orangeava.com** (it can be just the confirmation screen).

Once, we receive your screenshot, we will send you the digital file, within 24 hours.

Thank you so much for your support – it means a lot to us!

Downloading the code bundles and colored images

Please follow the links or scan the QR codes to download the
Code Bundles and Images of the book:

https://github.com/ava-orange-education/Building-Data-Apps-with-Streamlit

The code bundles and images of the book are also hosted on
https://rebrand.ly/h9ansz0

In case there's an update to the code, it will be updated on the existing GitHub repository.

Errata

We take immense pride in our work at **Orange Education Pvt Ltd,** and follow best practices to ensure the accuracy of our content to provide an indulging reading experience to our subscribers. Our readers are our mirrors, and we use their inputs to reflect and improve upon human errors, if any, that may have occurred during the publishing processes involved. To let us maintain the quality and help us reach out to any readers who might be having difficulties due to any unforeseen errors, please write to us at :

errata@orangeava.com

Your support, suggestions, and feedback are highly appreciated.

DID YOU KNOW

Did you know that Orange Education Pvt Ltd offers eBook versions of every book published, with PDF and ePub files available? You can upgrade to the eBook version at **www.orangeava.com** and as a print book customer, you are entitled to a discount on the eBook copy. Get in touch with us at: **info@orangeava.com** for more details.

At **www.orangeava.com**, you can also read a collection of free technical articles, sign up for a range of free newsletters, and receive exclusive discounts and offers on Print Books and eBooks.

PIRACY

If you come across any illegal copies of our works in any form on the internet, we would be grateful if you would provide us with the location address or website name. Please contact us at **info@orangeava.com** with a link to the material.

ARE YOU INTERESTED IN AUTHORING WITH US?

If there is a topic that you have expertise in, and you are interested in either writing or contributing to a book, please write to us at **business@orangeava.com**. We are on a journey to help developers and tech professionals to gain insights on the present technological advancements and innovations happening across the globe and build a community that believes Knowledge is best acquired by sharing and learning with others. Please reach out to us to learn what our audience demands and how you can be part of this educational reform. We also welcome ideas from tech experts and help them build learning and development content for their domains.

REVIEWS

Please leave a review. Once you have read and used this book, why not leave a review on the site that you purchased it from? Potential readers can then see and use your unbiased opinion to make purchase decisions. We at Orange Education would love to know what you think about our products, and our authors can learn from your feedback. Thank you!

For more information about Orange Education, please visit **www.orangeava.com**.

Table of Contents

1. Introduction to Streamlit **1**

Introduction 1

Structure 1

The Problem 1

The Solution 2

Introducing Streamlit 3

History of Streamlit 4

Industry Applications 5

Exploring Other Tools in the Domain 6

Streamlit 6

Gradio 7

Dash 7

Flask 9

Django 10

FastAPI 11

Conclusion 13

Points to Remember 13

Objective Questions 13

Answers 14

Subjective Questions 14

Key Terms 14

2. Setting Up the Development Environment **16**

Introduction 16

Structure 16

Local vs. Cloud-Based Development 16

Local Development 17

Cloud-Based Development 17

Local Setup 18

Installing Visual Studio Code 18

Installing Python 20

Creating a Python Virtual Environment 22

Installing Streamlit 24

Installing Git 25

Creating a GitHub Account and Repository 26

Creating a Streamlit Account 26

Cloud-Based Setup 27

GitHub Codespaces ... 27
Hugging Face Spaces ... 28
Lightning AI Studio ... 28
Conclusion ... 29
Points to Remember ... 29
Multiple Choice Questions ... 30
Answers ... 30
Questions ... 31
Key Terms ... 31

3. Creating and Deploying Your First Streamlit App ... 32
Introduction ... 32
Structure ... 32
Writing a Simple Data Analysis Script ... 32
Setup ... 32
Basic Script ... 33
Incorporating Streamlit into the Script ... 36
Executing the Streamlit Application Locally ... 37
Enhancing the Script with Additional Streamlit Widgets ... 39
Deploying the Application to Streamlit Community Cloud ... 43
Pushing the Code to GitHub ... 43
Deploying the Application ... 43
Conclusion ... 44
Points to Remember ... 45
Multiple Choice Questions ... 45
Answers ... 46
Questions ... 46
Key Terms ... 46

4. Exploring Streamlit's Flow and Architecture ... 47
Introduction ... 47
Structure ... 47
Automatic Application Reloads Triggered by Source Code Updates ... 47
Application Reloads Prompted by Widget State Updates ... 48
Unforeseen Consequences of Application Reloads ... 49
Understanding the Reset of Variables in Streamlit ... 50
Understanding the Behavior of Nested Streamlit Buttons ... 53
Understanding Streamlit's Client-Server Architecture ... 55
Influence of the Client-Server Architecture on Application Design ... 56
Server Capacity ... 56
Access to Files, Software, and Hardware ... 56

External Actions 56
Conclusion 56
Points to Remember 57
Multiple Choice Questions 57
Answers 58
Questions 59
Key Terms 59
5. Persisting Data and State Across App Reruns 60
Introduction 60
Structure 60
Introduction to Session State 60
Using Session State 61
Adding and Deleting Keys 61
Automatic Key Creation 63
Using Session State to Fix the Button-Click Counter App 64
Caveats and Limitations of Session State 67
Updating the Value of a Widget 67
Session State and Default Widget Values 68
Session State and Button-Like Widgets 70
Conclusion 70
Points to Remember 70
Multiple Choice Questions 70
Answers 71
Questions 72
Key Terms 72
6. Exploring Streamlit's Page Elements 73
Introduction 73
Structure 73
Recap of Previously Seen Elements 73
Exploring Additional Official Streamlit Elements 76
Formatted Text Elements 76
Data Elements 78
Chart Elements 79
Input Widgets 81
Media Elements 84
Layout Elements 85
Status Elements 93
Conclusion 96
Points to Remember 96

Multiple Choice Questions 97

Answers 98

Questions 99

Key Terms 99

7. Widget Keys and Callbacks 100

Introduction 100

Structure 100

Understanding Widget Keys 100

Statefulness of Widgets 102

Widget Cleanup Process 104

Introduction to Widget Callbacks 104

Implementing Nested Buttons Using Callbacks 106

Callback Caveats 108

Writing to the Application Using a Callback 108

Conclusion 110

Points to Remember 110

Multiple Choice Questions 110

Answers 112

Questions 112

Key Terms 112

8. Introduction to Streamlit Caching and Connections 113

Introduction 113

Structure 113

Introduction to Caching 114

Manually Implementing Simple Caches 114

Caching in Streamlit 117

Caching Data 118

Behavior of `st.cache_data` 118

Difference between `st.cache_data` and `functools.cache` 119

Caching Resources 120

Advanced Caching Options 123

Limiting Cache Size 123

Limiting Cache Duration 123

Clearing the Cache 123

Excluding Input Parameters 124

Using a Custom Hash Function 125

Connecting to External Data 125

Using Usual Python Methods 125

Using Streamlit Connections 128

Conclusion.......130

Points to Remember.......130

Multiple Choice Questions.......130

Answers.......131

Questions.......131

Key Terms.......132

9. Managing Secrets in Streamlit.......133

Introduction.......133

Structure.......133

Introduction to Secrets Management.......133

Common Secrets Management Methods.......134

Managing Streamlit Secrets Locally.......134

Project-Level Secrets.......135

Basic Usage.......135

Organizing Secrets as Sections.......136

Global Secrets.......137

Managing Secrets on Streamlit Community Cloud.......138

Adding Secrets while Deploying Apps.......138

Updating Secrets of Already Deployed Apps.......139

Conclusion.......141

Points to Remember.......141

Multiple Choice Questions.......141

Answers.......143

Questions.......143

Key Terms.......143

10. Advanced App Management Concepts.......144

Introduction.......144

Structure.......144

Installing App Dependencies.......144

Installing Python Dependencies.......145

Installing Non-Python Dependencies.......145

Exploring the Streamlit Workspace.......145

Workspace Menu.......146

Linked Accounts.......147

Limits.......147

Support.......148

My Apps.......149

My Profile.......150

Explore.......151

Create App ... 152
Managing an App from the Community Cloud Workspace ... 153
Managing an App within the Hosted App ... 156
Sharing an App ... 158
Sharing with Developers ... 158
Sharing with Viewers ... 160
The Share Button ... 160
App Resources and Limits ... 162
Conclusion ... 163
Points to Remember ... 163
Multiple Choice Questions ... 164
Answers ... 165
Questions ... 165
Key Terms ... 165
11. App Configuration Options ... 166
Introduction ... 166
Structure ... 166
Overview of Common Configuration Options ... 166
Setting Configuration Options ... 170
Using Configuration Files ... 170
Using Environment Variables ... 170
Using Command Line Arguments ... 170
Using `st.set_option` ... 170
Reading Configuration Options ... 171
Order of Priority ... 172
App Themes ... 172
Conclusion ... 178
Points to Remember ... 178
Multiple Choice Questions ... 179
Answers ... 180
Questions ... 181
Key Terms ... 181
12. Building Multipage Streamlit Apps ... 182
Introduction ... 182
Structure ... 182
Motivation behind Streamlit Pages ... 183
Page Terminology ... 184
Building a Multipage App ... 184
Using the `Pages/`Directory ... 185

Using `st.Page` and `st.navigation`..............187

Creating Pages from Source Files..............187

Creating Pages from Functions..............189

Page Configuration Options..............190

Customizing Navigation..............194

Grouping Pages by Sections..............194

Building Dynamic Navigation Menus..............195

Building a Custom Navigation Menu from Scratch..............198

Programmatically Switching Pages..............203

Widget Behavior in Multipage Apps..............204

Conclusion..............205

Points to Remember..............205

Multiple Choice Questions..............206

Answers..............207

Questions..............207

Key Terms..............207

13. Testing Streamlit Apps..............208

Introduction..............208

Structure..............208

Importance of Testing Streamlit Apps..............209

Introduction to Streamlit's Native Testing Framework..............209

Building and Testing the Login Page..............210

Creating and Using a Dummy User Database..............211

Testing the Login Component..............212

Automating Tests Using pytest..............215

Converting the Login Tests to `pytest` Format..............216

Optimizing the Login Tests Using Parametrization..............218

Adding and Testing a Logout Button..............221

Creating and Testing Role-Based Pages..............223

Manage Users..............223

Bells and Whistles..............224

Adding Role-Based Pages to the App..............227

Testing Role-Based Access Control to Pages..............231

Testing before Pushing to Repo Using Pre-commit Hooks..............231

Continuous Testing Using GitHub Actions..............232

Conclusion..............238

Points to Remember..............239

Multiple Choice Questions..............239

Answers..............240

Questions.....241

Key Terms.....241

14. Building a Data Analysis Streamlit App.....243

Introduction.....243

Structure.....243

Creating the Entrypoint.....244

Providing Sample Datasets.....245

Caching the Datasets for Efficient Performance.....246

Displaying Dataset Information.....248

Adding a Reset Button.....248

Adding Page Navigation Links.....250

Creating the Analyze Page.....250

Preview and Description of the Dataset.....251

Cleaning the Dataset.....252

Handling Missing Values.....252

Handling Outliers.....253

Adding Data Analysis Tools.....255

Generating the Profile Report.....255

Creating Custom Plots.....257

Conclusion.....259

Additional Tasks.....259

Key Terms.....260

15. Building a Machine Learning Streamlit App.....261

Introduction.....261

Structure.....261

Introduction to AutoML.....261

Preparing for Model Training.....262

Customizing AutoGluon Parameters.....263

Resetting AutoGluon Parameters.....265

Training the Models.....267

Exploring Model Details.....268

Making Predictions.....270

Conclusion.....274

Advanced Assignments.....275

Key Terms.....275

16. Building a Chatbot on Streamlit.....276

Introduction.....276

Structure.....276

Brief Exploration of LLM Providers.....277

Gemini API Prerequisites....................277
User Authentication....................278
Chatting with the Chatbot....................279
Selecting a Model....................279
Formatting the Options....................281
Showing Only Relevant Models....................282
Showing Model Description....................283
Creating a Model Selection Dialog....................285
Creating a Chat....................287
Sending and Receiving Messages....................287
Providing Context to the Chatbot....................290
Using the System Prompt....................291
Displaying the Conversation History....................293
Additional Features....................296
Tuning Responses Using the Temperature....................296
Downloading the Conversation....................298
Streaming Responses....................300
Full Code....................301
Conclusion....................304
Points to Remember....................305
Multiple Choice Questions....................305
Answers....................306
Questions....................306
Advanced Assignment....................306
Key Terms....................306
Index....................308

Chapter 1
Introduction to Streamlit

Introduction

This chapter explores the challenges Python practitioners encounter when they need to quickly build interactive web applications for prototyping, without investing significant time and energy in learning non-core web development skills. We will introduce Streamlit as a solution that addresses this challenge through its unique features, such as a simple, Pythonic syntax, hot-reloading for rapid development, and widget-based interactivity.

We will delve into Streamlit's product and corporate history, tracing its evolution from a promising startup to a widely adopted open-source tool. Furthermore, we will illustrate how Streamlit is being used across various industries. Finally, this chapter will compare Streamlit with other solutions in this domain, such as Gradio and Dash, highlighting each framework's unique strengths and ideal use cases.

Structure

In this chapter, we will discuss the following topics:

- The Problem
- The Solution
- Introduction to Streamlit
- History of Streamlit
- Industry Applications
- Exploring Other Tools in the Domain

The Problem

Consider a common scenario for a data scientist: After spending considerable time gathering and cleaning data, a predictive model for house prices is trained and ready. The next significant hurdle is making this model accessible to stakeholders, many of whom may have no experience with Python.

One approach is to upload the model to GitHub and the accompanying Jupyter Notebook to Google Colab. The code can then be updated to use the model from GitHub, and a link to the Colab notebook can be shared with stakeholders. However, this method requires stakeholders to be familiar with the Colab environment. Any accidental changes on their part could render the notebook unusable, and Colab's limited hardware cannot support larger, more complex models.

An alternative is to build a dynamic web application that conceals the back-end code and exposes users to a clean, intuitive interface. The application's URL can then be shared, allowing stakeholders to use the model without any technical setup on their end. While this sounds user-friendly, it requires foundational web development skills, including HTML, JavaScript, and both front-end and back-end development. Additionally, one must find and pay for a platform to host the web app. This seemingly simple task quickly becomes complex. When stakeholder needs evolve, making updates is often slow and complicated due to the various moving parts involved.

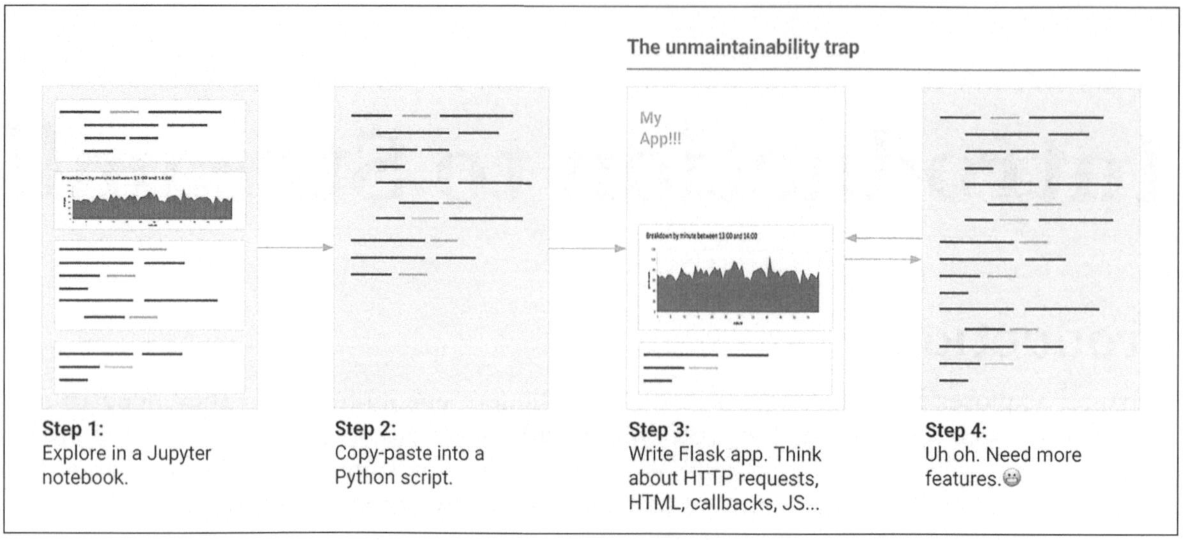

Figure 1.1: *The Machine Learning Engineers' Ad-hoc App-building Flow*[1]

Challenges persist even in a large enterprise with access to dedicated tooling teams. These teams often support multiple other groups and adhere to strict release cycles. This subjects the web application to an external team's schedule, which is not ideal for a data science product that requires frequent and rapid updates.

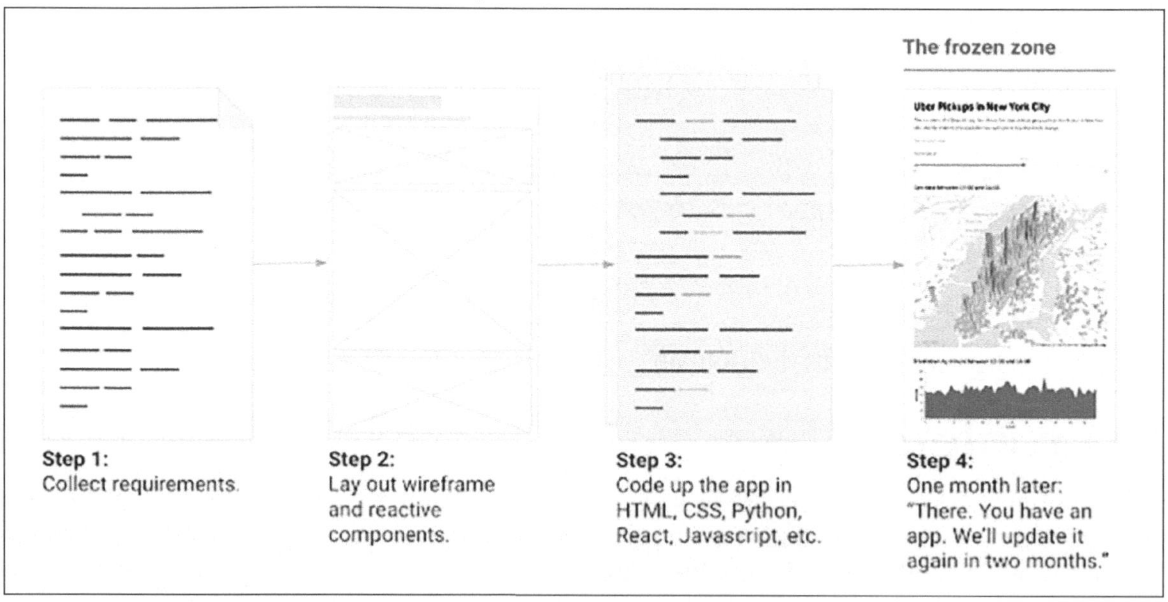

Figure 1.2: *The Tools Team's Clean-slate app-building Flow*[2]

The Solution

Streamlit provides a powerful alternative by enabling the creation of a web application from the same Python script used to train the model and serve predictions. It eliminates the need to delve into the complexities of traditional web development.

[1] *https://towardsdatascience.com/coding-ml-tools-like-you-code-ml-models-ddba3357eace* (Accessed: 25 May 2024)

[2] *https://towardsdatascience.com/coding-ml-tools-like-you-code-ml-models-ddba3357eace* (Accessed: 25 May 2024)

Imagine having access to a free, fully managed platform for hosting your web application, removing concerns about infrastructure and costs. Consider a scenario where updating your app is as simple as modifying the code; the application then updates automatically without navigating complex deployment cycles. This is where Streamlit shines. It elegantly answers the question: *What if building tools could be as easy as writing Python scripts?*

Introducing Streamlit

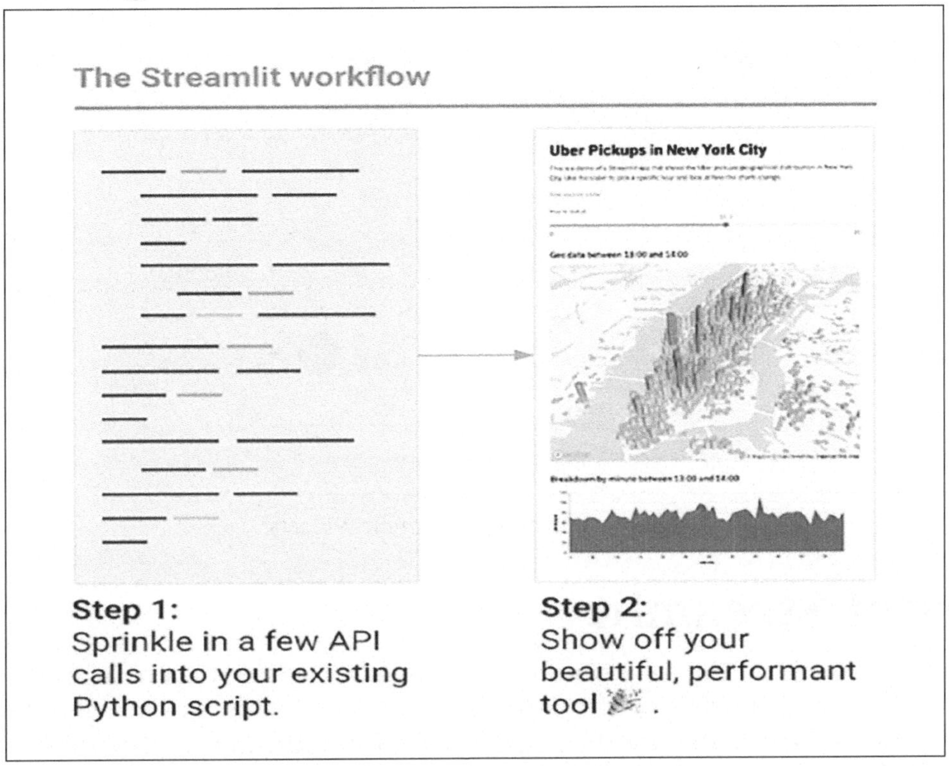

Figure 1.3: *The Streamlit App Building Flow*[3]

Streamlit is an open-source framework that enables you to create dynamic web applications using only a few lines of Python code. It is specifically designed to transform data scripts into interactive web applications. As stated by its founder, Adrien Treuille, Streamlit is a dedicated application framework for Machine Learning Engineers and data scientists.[4]

Streamlit's core appeal is its simplicity; you do not need to be a web development expert to use it. If you are proficient in Python, you are already equipped to create a Streamlit app. Each interactive widget can be crafted with a single line of code that handles rendering, user input, and passing data to the script. The framework is designed to update applications in real-time in response to changes in the source code or user interactions. Furthermore, Streamlit simplifies deployment. You can quickly deploy applications to the Streamlit Community Cloud - a free hosting platform - or other platforms of your choice, such as AWS, Azure, or Heroku.

[3]*https://towardsdatascience.com/coding-ml-tools-like-you-code-ml-models-ddba3357eace* (Accessed: 25 May 2024)

[4]*https://www.youtube.com/watch?v=0It8phQ1gkQ* (Accessed: 25 May 2024)

Figure 1.4: *Example Streamlit Widgets*[5]

History of Streamlit

Streamlit was established in 2018 as a private beta in San Francisco, California, by Adrien Treuille, Amanda Kelly, Nodira Khoussainova, and Thiago Teixeira.[6] The co-founders brought their experience from Google X and the self-driving startup Zoox. In October 2019, Streamlit transitioned to an open-source framework after securing $6 million in seed funding.[7] By the end of that year, it had already amassed 5,000 stars on GitHub.

Progressing to June 2020, Streamlit raised $21 million in a Series A round.[8] By October 2020, it had reached the milestone of 10,000 GitHub stars. In April 2021, the company secured an additional $35 million in a Series B funding round led by Sequoia.[8] A significant development occurred in March 2022 when Snowflake announced its acquisition of Streamlit for $800 million.[9]

This strategic acquisition and continued development have solidified Streamlit's position as a key tool in the data science ecosystem. According to JetBrains's Python Developers Survey 2024, 22% of all data scientists used Streamlit, and it is the most used dashboarding solution in Python.[10] By June 2025, the framework's influence had expanded significantly, boasting over 40,000 GitHub stars and being a critical dependency in nearly one million GitHub repositories and over 2,800 Python packages.[11] This widespread adoption underscores its growing popularity and importance within the developer community.

---

[5] *https://streamlit.io/ (Accessed: 19 May 2024)*
[6] https://www.crunchbase.com/organization/streamlit (Accessed: 25 May 2024)
[7] https://techcrunch.com/2019/10/01/streamlit-launches-open-source-machine-learning-application-development-framework/ (Accessed: 25 May 2024)
[8] https://blog.streamlit.io/our-35-million-series-b/ (Accessed: 25 May 2024)
[9] https://techcrunch.com/2022/03/02/snowflake-acquires-streamlit-for-800m-to-help-customers-build-data-based-apps/ (Accessed: 25 May 2024)
[10] https://lp.jetbrains.com/python-developers-survey-2024/ (Accessed: 16 September 2025)
[11] https://github.com/streamlit/streamlit/network/dependents (Accessed: 13 June 2025)

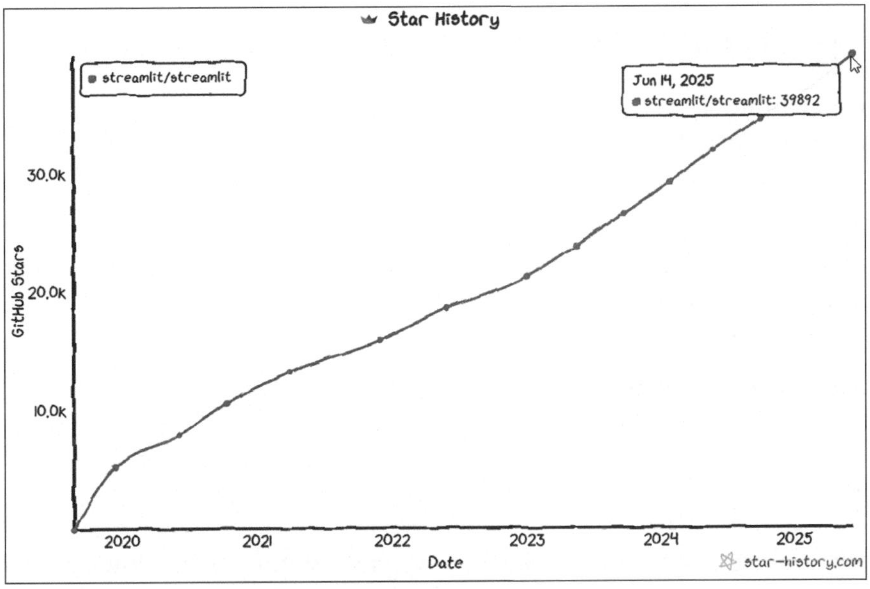

Figure 1.5: *Streamlit GitHub Star History* [12]

Industry Applications

Streamlit has gained widespread acceptance in the industry, with adoption ranging from tech giants like Google to startups such as Uber and Yelp. Even in 2019, when Streamlit had just emerged from its private beta phase, founder Adrien Treuille revealed that they were collaborating with a large company to enable machine learning engineers to build apps that could empower a hundred thousand salespeople to make real-time recommendations.[13]

The most prevalent use case for Streamlit is the development of internal web applications. This is particularly true for smaller data science teams within larger enterprises that need to test their models quickly, demonstrate them to stakeholders, or provide an application for non-technical individuals to utilize their models. Instead of seeking web development expertise, these teams can leverage their existing Python skills and Streamlit's innovative API to transform their data scripts into interactive web applications. This approach saves time and money, and enables rapid feedback collection and iteration. Since Streamlit is open-source, the applications can be deployed on-premises, which is a security requirement for many global enterprises.

Some companies use Streamlit to construct external web applications for their clients. These are primarily smaller AI startups that require a web application to allow their users to access their product without investing in a web development team. This can add friction and costs to their product development and iteration process.

Lastly, individual professionals utilize Streamlit professionally or as a hobby to share their work with a broader audience. They can do this without learning web development skills from scratch or worrying about finding a hosting platform, or managing costs.

Given Streamlit's flexibility and ease of use, it is no surprise that over 80% of Fortune 50 companies are using Streamlit![14]

Tip: *For a deeper understanding of Streamlit's applications, I highly recommend reading some of the case studies on the Streamlit blog here: https://blog.streamlit.io/. These case studies provide in-depth, real-world examples of how Streamlit is used in the industry.*

[12] *https://star-history.com/* (Accessed: 14 June 2025)
[13] *https://youtu.be/0It8phQ1gkQ* (Accessed: 25 May 2024)
[14] *https://streamlit.io/* (Accessed: 19 May 2024)

Exploring Other Tools in the Domain

While discussing Streamlit, it is essential to acknowledge the presence of other tools in this domain. Each tool has its unique strengths and weaknesses. In this section, we will briefly examine some of the key open-source players in this space, highlighting their advantages, disadvantages, and the use cases where they excel.

We will also examine the coding required to create a basic web app that accepts and displays your name using these tools, and what the basic app looks like. This exercise will help us understand the ease of use of these tools and the quality of the result (using app defaults).

Note: *The examples provided in this section are generated using Python 3.10.11 and visualized on Microsoft Edge Version 126.0.2592.13.*

Streamlit

Streamlit turns data scripts into shareable web apps in minutes. It allows developers to create interactive and customizable data applications with minimal effort.

Advantages

- **Simplicity and Pythonic nature:** Streamlit is easy to learn and use, making it a favorite among Python developers.
- **Rapid interactive prototyping:** It enables developers to build data applications swiftly.
- **Free hosting:** Streamlit offers free hosting on its community cloud, reducing the barriers to deployment.

Disadvantages

- **Limited customization options:** While Streamlit is powerful, it is not very customizable in terms of the look and feel of Streamlit apps.
- **Focus on data-centric apps:** Streamlit is primarily suited for data-centric applications, which may not cater to all use cases.

Best Suited for

- **Data visualization dashboards:** Streamlit shines when used to create data visualization dashboards.
- **Prototyping machine learning models:** It is an excellent tool for quickly prototyping and demonstrating machine learning models.
- **Building simple web applications:** Streamlit is ideal for constructing simple, interactive web applications.

Example Code

```
import streamlit as st

if name := st.text_input("Enter your name:"):
    st.write(f"Hello, {name}!")
```

Example App

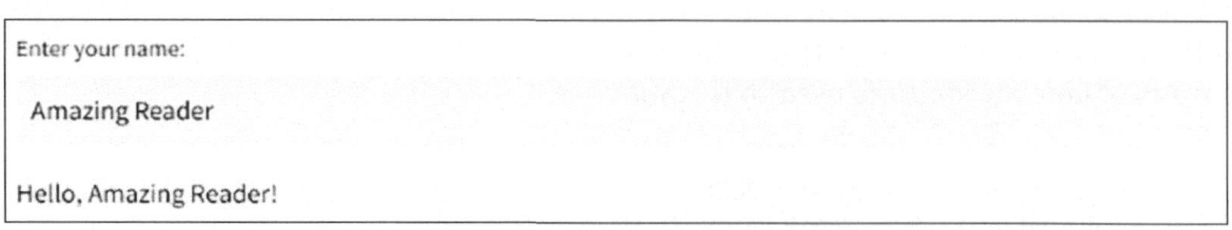

Figure 1.6: *Example Streamlit App*

Note: *The code example and application screenshot are based on Streamlit version 1.35.0.*

Gradio

Gradio is a tool that enables rapid construction of demos or web applications for machine learning models, requiring no prior experience in web development or web hosting.

Advantages

- **Jupyter Notebook Support:** Gradio is one of the few tools in this domain that works natively from inside a Jupyter notebook.
- **Built-in Sharing Features:** It comes with features that facilitate easy sharing of your work.
- **Free Hosting:** Gradio offers free hosting on Hugging Face spaces, making deployment hassle-free.

Disadvantages

- **Limited Scalability:** Gradio may not be the best choice for complex applications due to its scalability limitations.
- **Focused Use Cases:** Its use cases are primarily limited to demonstrations of machine learning models.

Best Suited For

- **Creating Machine Learning Model Demos:** Gradio excels at quickly creating demos for machine learning models.
- **Prototyping and Building Lightweight Web Interfaces:** It is ideal for prototyping and constructing lightweight web interfaces for machine learning applications.

Example Code

```
import gradio as gr

def greet(name):
    return f"Hello, {name}!"

iface = gr.Interface(fn=greet, inputs="text", outputs="text")
iface.launch()
```

Example App

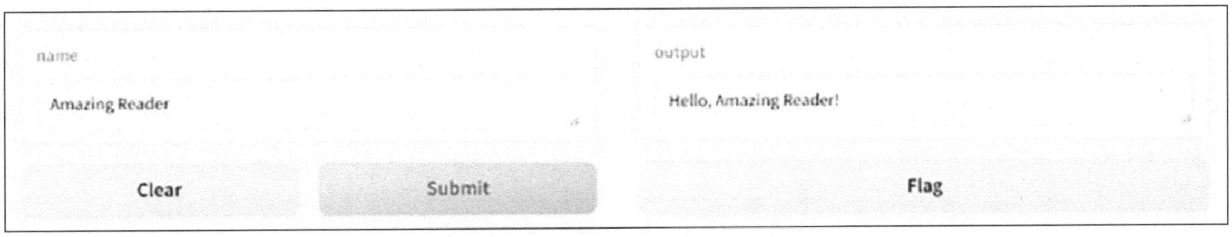

Figure 1.7: *Example Gradio App*

Note: *The code example and application screenshot are based on Gradio version 4.31.5.*

Dash

Dash is a framework that excels in constructing web applications featuring interactive visualizations. It works seamlessly with Plotly, a widely used interactive plotting library for Python, enhancing its data visualization capabilities.

Advantages

- **Scalability:** Dash is scalable and well-suited for handling complex applications.
- **Plotly Integration:** Dash integrates effectively with Plotly, enabling the creation of interactive charts.

Disadvantages

- **Steep Learning Curve:** Dash requires a certain level of knowledge in HTML/CSS, making it a bit challenging for beginners.
- **No Free Hosting:** Dash does not offer free hosting services.

Best Suited for

- **Data-driven web applications:** Dash is ideal for creating data-driven web applications that feature interactive visualizations.

Example Code

```
import dash
from dash import dcc, html
from dash.dependencies import Input, Output

# Create the app
app = dash.Dash(__name__)

# Define the layout
app.layout = html.Div(
    [
        html.P("Enter your name:"),
        dcc.Input(id="name-input", value="", type="text"),
        html.Div(id="output"),
    ]
)


# Define the callback function
@app.callback(Output("output", "children"), [Input("name-input", "value")])
def update_output(name):
    return f"Hello, {name}!"


# Run the app
if __name__ == "__main__":
    app.run_server()
```

Example App

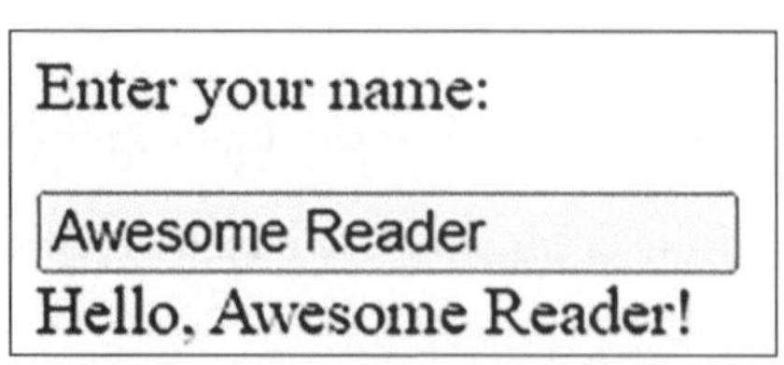

Figure 1.8: *Example Dash App*

Note: *The code example and application screenshot are based on Dash version 2.17.0.*

Flask

Flask is a lightweight Web Server Gateway Interface (WSGI) web application framework designed for Python.

Advantages

- **Quick Prototyping:** Flask is ideal for quick prototyping, thanks to its simplicity and ease of use.
- **Flexibility and Adaptability:** Flask is highly flexible, and can be adapted to a wide range of applications.

Disadvantages

- **Minimal Built-in Features:** Flask comes with minimal built-in features, which means you may need to add more tools and libraries for complex applications.
- **Steep Learning Curve:** Flask requires some knowledge of front-end development, which can be steep for beginners.
- **No Free Hosting:** Flask does not offer free hosting services.

Best Suited for

- Building RESTful APIs, microservices, and lightweight web applications.

Example Code

```
from flask import Flask, request

app = Flask(__name__)


@app.route("/", methods=["GET", "POST"])
def hello():
    form = """
        <form method="POST">
            <label for="name">Enter your name:</label>
            <input type="text" id="name" name="name">
            <input type="submit" value="Submit">
        </form>
    """

    if request.method == "POST":
        name = request.form.get("name")
        if name:
            return f"{form} Hello, {name}!"

    return form


if __name__ == "__main__":
    app.run()
```

Example App

Figure 1.9: *Example Flask App*

Note: *The code example and application screenshot are based on Flask version 3.0.3.*

Django

Django is a high-level Python web framework that excels in building robust, secure, and scalable applications using its comprehensive inbuilt features.

Advantages

- **Comprehensive and Feature-rich:** Django comes packed with a wide array of features, making it a comprehensive tool for web development.
- **Suitable for Large-scale Applications:** Django is designed to handle large-scale applications, making it a go-to choice for complex projects.

Disadvantages

- **Steep Learning Curve:** Django can be challenging to learn, especially for beginners, due to its comprehensive nature.
- **More Opinionated:** Django has a more opinionated approach to web development, which might not suit all use cases.
- **No Free Hosting:** Django does not offer free hosting services.

Best Suited for

- **Complex Web Applications:** Django is ideal for building complex web applications due to its robust and scalable nature.
- **Content Management Systems (CMS):** It is well-suited for creating content management systems.
- **Scalable Projects:** Django is an excellent choice for projects that require scalability.

Example Code

```
from django import forms
from django.conf import settings
from django.http import HttpResponse
from django.urls import path

# Define settings
settings.configure(DEBUG=True, ROOT_URLCONF=__name__, SECRET_KEY="42")


class NameForm(forms.Form):
    name = forms.CharField(label="Enter your name")


def greet(request):
    greeting = ""
    if request.method == "POST":
        form = NameForm(request.POST)
        if form.is_valid():
            name = form.cleaned_data["name"]
            greeting = f"Hello, {name}!"
    else:
        form = NameForm()
    return HttpResponse(f"""
        <form method="POST">
            {form.as_p()}
```

```
            <input type="submit" value="Submit">
        </form>
        <p>{greeting}</p>
    """)


# Define URL patterns
urlpatterns = [
    path("", greet, name="greet"),
]

if __name__ == "__main__":
    from django.core.management import execute_from_command_line

    execute_from_command_line(["django_quickstart.py", "runserver"])
```

Example App

Figure 1.10: *Example Django App*

Note: *The code used and app screenshot are as of Django version 3.0.3.*

FastAPI

FastAPI is a high-performance web framework for building APIs with Python based on standard Python type hints.

Advantages

- **Automatic Documentation Generation:** FastAPI automatically generates interactive API documentation based on Python code and type annotations. This streamlines development, and enhances collaboration.
- **High Performance:** FastAPI is designed for speed, making it an excellent choice for data-intensive applications.
- **Type Validation:** Built-in type validation ensures data consistency and reduces errors.

Disadvantages

- **Steep Learning Curve:** While FastAPI's documentation is excellent, some developers may find the learning curve steep due to its advanced features.
- **No Free Hosting:** FastAPI does not offer free hosting services.

Best Suited for

- **RESTful APIs:** FastAPI excels in creating RESTful APIs with automatic documentation.
- **Microservices:** It is well-suited for building microservices due to its performance and async capabilities.

Example Code

```
from fastapi import FastAPI, Form, Request
from fastapi.responses import HTMLResponse

app = FastAPI()


@app.get("/", response_class=HTMLResponse)
@app.post("/", response_class=HTMLResponse)
async def read_form(request: Request, name: str = Form(None)):
    if request.method == "POST" and name is not None:
        message = f"Hello, {name}!"
    else:
        message = ""
    return f"""
        <form method="post">
            <label for="name">Enter your name:</label>
            <input type="text" name="name" />
            <input type="submit" />
        </form>
        <p>{message}</p>
    """
```

Example App

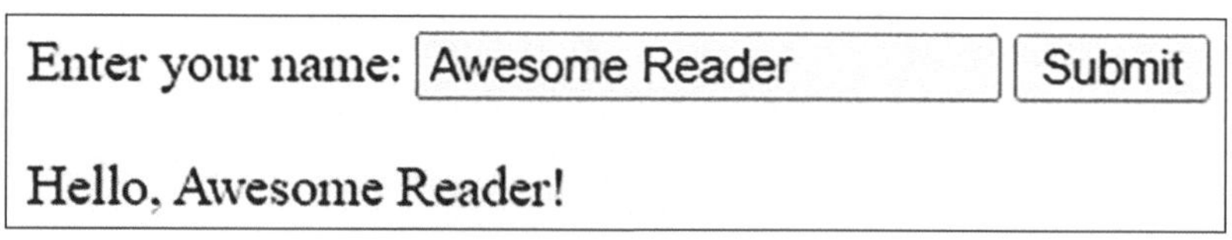

Figure 1.11: *Example FastAPI App*

Summary

	Streamlit	Gradio	Dash	Flask	Django	FastAPI
Easy to use	✓	✓	✗	✗	✗	✗
Rapid prototyping	✓	✓	✓	✓	✗	✗
Free hosting	✓	✓	✗	✗	✗	✗
Highly customizable	✗	✗	✗	✓	✗	✓
Highly scalable	✗	✗	✓	✓	✓	✓
Best suited for	Data and ML apps	ML apps	Data apps	RESTful APIs and lightweight apps	Large and complex applications	RESTful APIs and microservices

Table 1.1: *Comparing Python Web App Frameworks*

Conclusion

We have now understood the challenges that Machine Learning Engineers and data scientists face when prototyping and sharing their models. We have also explored an ideal workflow for these practitioners, and how Streamlit can help alleviate these challenges.

In addition, we have taken a brief tour of some other tools in this domain, delving into their strengths and weaknesses, and assessing the firsthand ease (or complexity) of using these tools.

In the next chapter, we will set up the development environment for coding and deploying Streamlit applications throughout this book.

Points to Remember

- Data scientists and Machine Learning engineers require web development tools to prototype, iterate, and share their work effectively.
- Streamlit is an open-source framework that enables the creation of dynamic web applications using just a few lines of Python code.
- Streamlit is utilized by diverse users, from individuals to startups and large enterprises. It allows the creation of hobby projects and internal as well as external web applications without the need for extensive web development skills or experience.

Objective Questions

1. Streamlit was designed to be:
    a. Easy to use
    b. Highly customizable
    c. Scalable
    d. Secure
2. Where can you host unlimited public Streamlit applications for free?
    a. AWS
    b. Streamlit Community Cloud
    c. Heroku
    d. Snowflake
3. Which company acquired Streamlit in 2022?
    a. Snowflake
    b. Databricks
    c. Microsoft
    d. Salesforce

4. Which of the following tools supports Jupyter Notebooks well?
    a. Streamlit
    b. Gradio
    c. Dash
    d. Django
5. Which of the following tools integrates best with Plotly?
    a. Streamlit
    b. Gradio
    c. Dash
    d. Django

Answers

1. a
2. b
3. a
4. b
5. c

Subjective Questions

1. What are some problems data scientists and MLEs face in prototyping and sharing their models? What solutions can you suggest?
2. What is Streamlit?
3. Why do data science teams use Streamlit to build web applications?
4. How does Streamlit compare with other tools in the same space?
5. Reflect on a past data analysis or machine learning project you have worked on. How could a tool like Streamlit have improved your process for sharing results or gathering stakeholder feedback?

Key Terms

- **Hot Reloading:** Hot reloading is a feature that allows developers to modify code, while an application is running without having to restart it manually.[15]
- **HTML:** HyperText Markup Language (HTML) is the standard markup language for creating web applications.[16]
- **JavaScript:** JavaScript (JS) is a cross-platform, object-oriented scripting language used to make webpages interactive.[17]

[15] *https://hatchjs.com/hot-reload-react-docker/* (Accessed: 27 May 2024)
[16] *https://www.javatpoint.com/what-is-html* (Accessed: 27 May 2024)
[17] *https://developer.mozilla.org/en-US/docs/Web/JavaScript/Guide/Introduction* (Accessed: 27 May 2024)

- **Streamlit:** Streamlit is an open-source framework for creating dynamic web applications with only a few lines of Python code.
- **WSGI:** Web Server Gateway Interface (WSGI) is a standard interface for Python web applications to communicate with web servers.[18]
- **RESTful:** Representational State Transfer (REST) is a web architecture style that provides standards between computer systems on the web, making it easier for systems to communicate with each other. REST-compliant systems are also called RESTful systems.[19]
- **Open-Source:** Open-source software is a software with source code that anyone can inspect, modify, and enhance.[20]

[18] *https://builtin.com/data-science/wsgi* (Accessed: 27 May 2024)
[19] *https://www.codecademy.com/article/what-is-rest* (Accessed: 31 May 2024)
[20] *https://opensource.com/resources/what-open-source* (Accessed: 14 June 2025)

CHAPTER 2
Setting Up the Development Environment

Introduction

This chapter guides you through setting up a development environment to build Streamlit applications. It explores the distinctions between a local and a cloud-based setup, walks through the step-by-step process of creating a local environment, and discusses various options for cloud-based setups.

Note: *While we will describe our preferred setup, feel free to continue using any existing setup you might have, if it works well for you.*

Structure

In this chapter, we will discuss the following topics:

- Local vs. Cloud-Based Development
- Local Setup
    - Installing Visual Studio Code
    - Installing Python
    - Creating a Python Virtual Environment
    - Installing Streamlit
    - Installing Git
    - Creating a GitHub Account and Repository
    - Creating a Streamlit Account
- Cloud-Based Setup
    - GitHub Codespaces
    - Hugging Face Spaces
    - Lightning AI Studio

Local vs. Cloud-Based Development

Although traditional software development predominantly occurs on local machines, the popularity of cloud-based development is skyrocketing, driven by decreasing costs and the improved ease of setting up cloud infrastructure. This section explores the advantages of both approaches, enabling you to make an informed decision for your development environment.

Local Development

Local development involves building, testing, and debugging an application on a personal computer or a local server.

Advantages

Local development offers several benefits that cater to developers who prefer a more hands-on approach to their work environment. Here are some of them:

- **Control:** You have complete control over your development environment, including both hardware and software.
- **Privacy:** Your code and data remain on your local machine, ensuring higher security and privacy.
- **Cost:** No ongoing expenses are associated with using your own machine for development.
- **Offline Access:** You can work on applications without an internet connection.
- **Instant Access:** Hardware resources are available instantly when needed.

Disadvantages

While local development offers numerous benefits, it is not without its challenges. Here are some of the limitations you might encounter:

- **Scalability:** The application's performance is constrained by the resources of your local machine.
- **Collaboration:** Collaborating with others, especially on larger teams, can be more challenging.
- **Setup:** You are responsible for setting up and maintaining the development environment, which can be time-consuming.

Cloud-Based Development

Cloud-based development involves utilizing a cloud service provider's resources to build, test, and debug applications.

Advantages

Cloud-based development offers numerous benefits, offering a range of conveniences and capabilities that can significantly enhance the development process. Here are some of the key advantages:

- **Scalability:** Cloud providers offer virtually unlimited resources, enabling our application to scale as needed.
- **Collaboration:** Cloud-based tools often include features that facilitate collaboration with others.
- **Maintenance:** The cloud provider assumes responsibility for maintaining the development environment, allowing us to focus on coding.
- **Accessibility:** You can access your development environment from anywhere with an internet connection.

Disadvantages

However, there are also some considerations when opting for cloud-based development. The following are some of the potential drawbacks:

- **Cost:** While cloud providers offer free tiers, expenses can escalate as we consume more resources.

- **Privacy:** Your code and data reside on the cloud provider's servers, which may concern some users.
- **Dependency:** You rely on the cloud provider for your development environment, which could pose challenges during outages or service disruptions.

Both local and cloud-based approaches have their merits and drawbacks, and the choice between them depends on our specific requirements and limitations.

Note: We *will be using a local setup, but feel free to use a cloud-based setup, if you prefer.*

Local Setup

Setting up a local development environment requires more configuration, as you must handle the setup yourself. If you already use your computer for programming, you likely have a working setup that includes Python, a virtual environment, and a code editor. However, this section begins with the fundamentals for those new to this process.

Installing Visual Studio Code

Visual Studio Code (VS Code), an open-source code editor developed by Microsoft, is available for Windows, Linux, macOS, and web browsers. While other Python code editors like PyCharm, Jupyter, and Notepad++ exist, VS Code is popular and feature-rich. We will use VS Code in this book, but feel free to choose another code editor. Keep in mind that setup steps may vary based on your preferred editor.

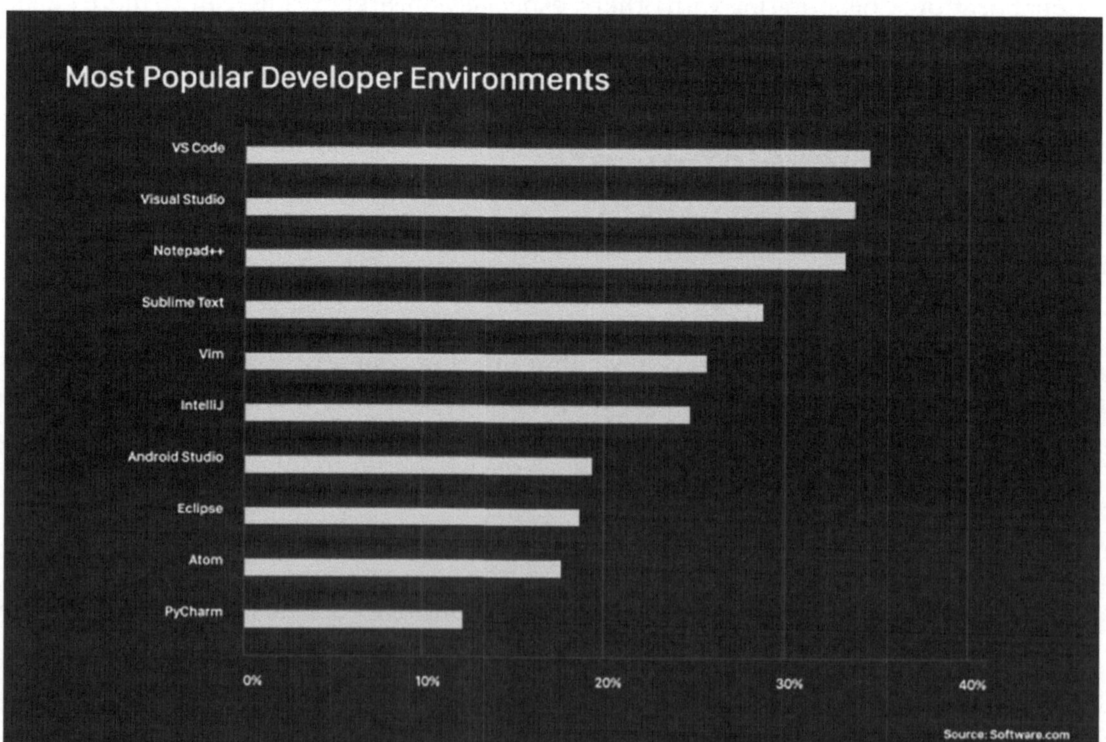

Figure 2.1: Most Popular Code Editors[1]

[1] *https://www.software.com/src/ranking-the-top-5-code-editors-2019* (Accessed: 2 June 2024)

1. Download VS Code from **`https://code.visualstudio.com/download`**. Remember to choose the correct version for your Operating System (OS) and chipset architecture.

   Note: *The screenshots and instructions reflect that the Windows installer since Windows 11 is used here. If you are on Linux or macOS, there might be slight differences.*

2. Open the downloaded file, and follow the installation instructions.
3. During installation, in the **`Select Additional Tasks`** step, check all the **`Other`** checkboxes.

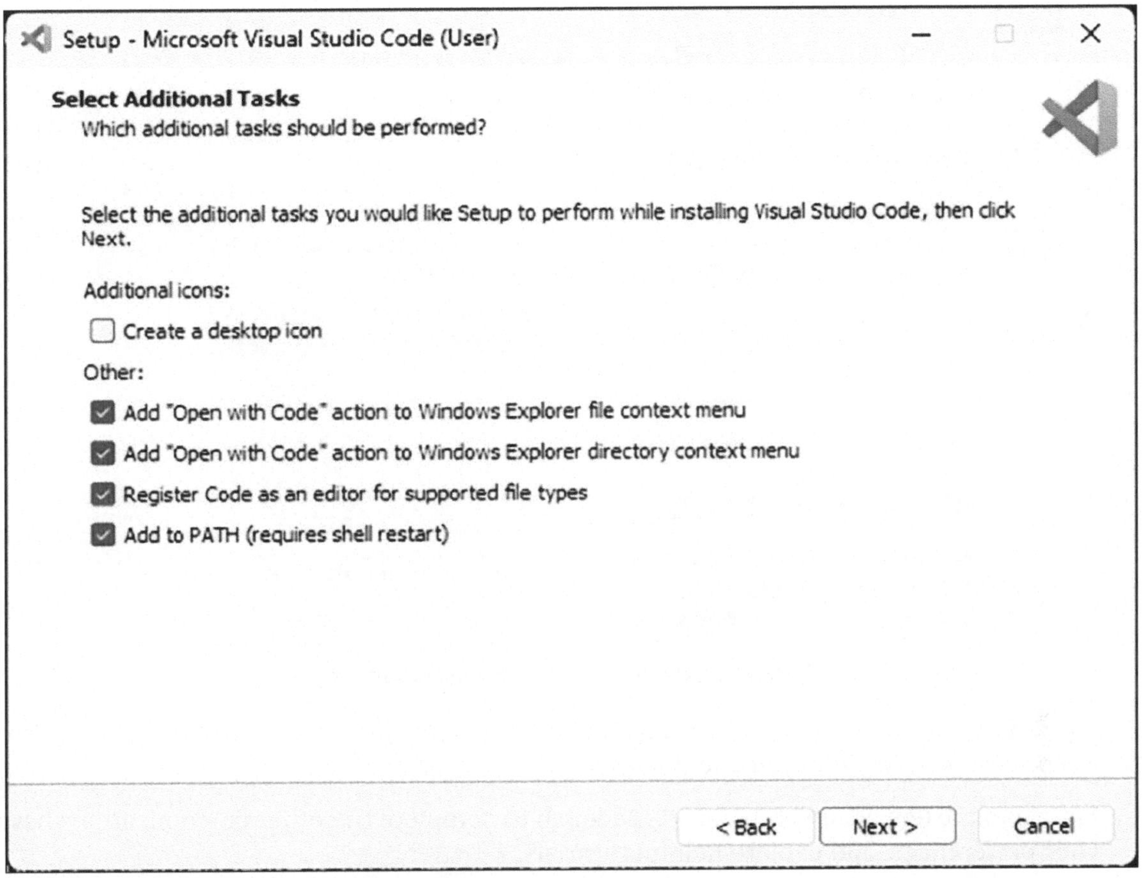

Figure 2.2: *VS Code Setup Additional Tasks*

4. Once the installation is complete, launch VS Code.
5. In the **`Get Started with VS Code`** screen, click **`Browse Language Extensions`**, and install the **`Python`** extension.

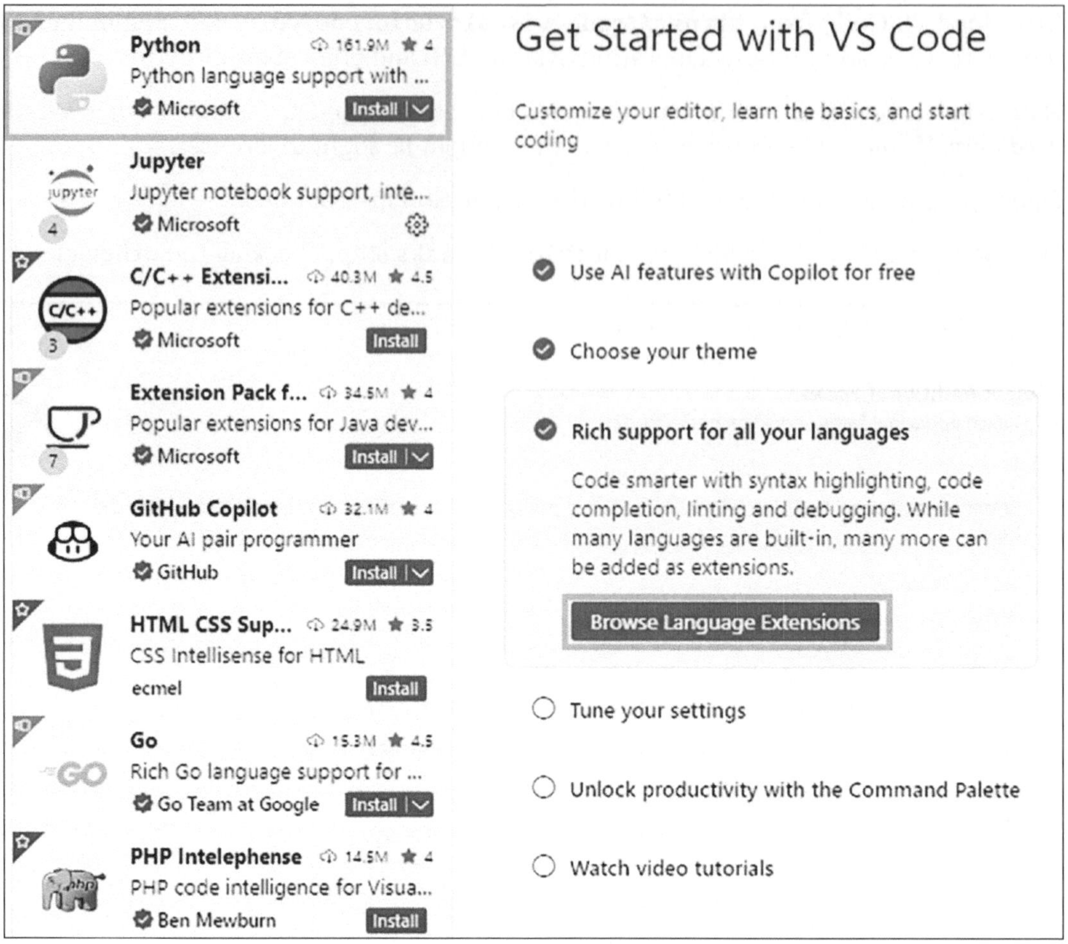

Figure 2.3: *Install Python Language Support*

6. A **`Get Started with Python Development`** tab will open after installing the Python extension. Keep this open; we will return to it later.
7. Return to the **`Get Started with VS Code`** tab to complete the other customizations based on your preferences, and explore helpful tutorials.
8. Finally, when you are done, close VS Code.

   Tip: *While this basic installation is enough to follow everything in the book, I highly recommend going through VS Code's documentation at https://code.visualstudio.com/docs to customize the settings and user interface according to your needs, learn tips and tricks to make you a faster and better coder, and explore the extensions that make VS Code one of the most popular code editors.*

   Note: *My local installation of VS Code is heavily customized. Although I have tried to recreate a new setup from scratch, some elements in the screenshots might not be exactly the same as what you see in yours. However, if you have followed the steps mentioned, you should not have any issues.*

Installing Python

Installing Python varies depending on your Operating System (OS). If you are using a Linux distribution, Python may already be installed by default.

To check if Python is already installed, open the VS Code terminal by pressing **`Ctrl+``** and run the following command:

```
python --version
```

If Python is installed, you will see the installed version of Python as the output.

If not, or if you need a different Python version, follow these steps:

1. Download the required version of Python from **https://www.python.org/downloads/**

   Note: *I am using Python 3.10, but would recommend using the latest version. Do note that some things might be slightly different across Python versions.*

2. Open the downloaded file
3. If you are on Windows,
   a. Check **`Use admin privileges when installing py.exe`**.
   b. Select **`Add python.exe to PATH`**.
   c. Adapt these steps as needed if you are using a different OS.

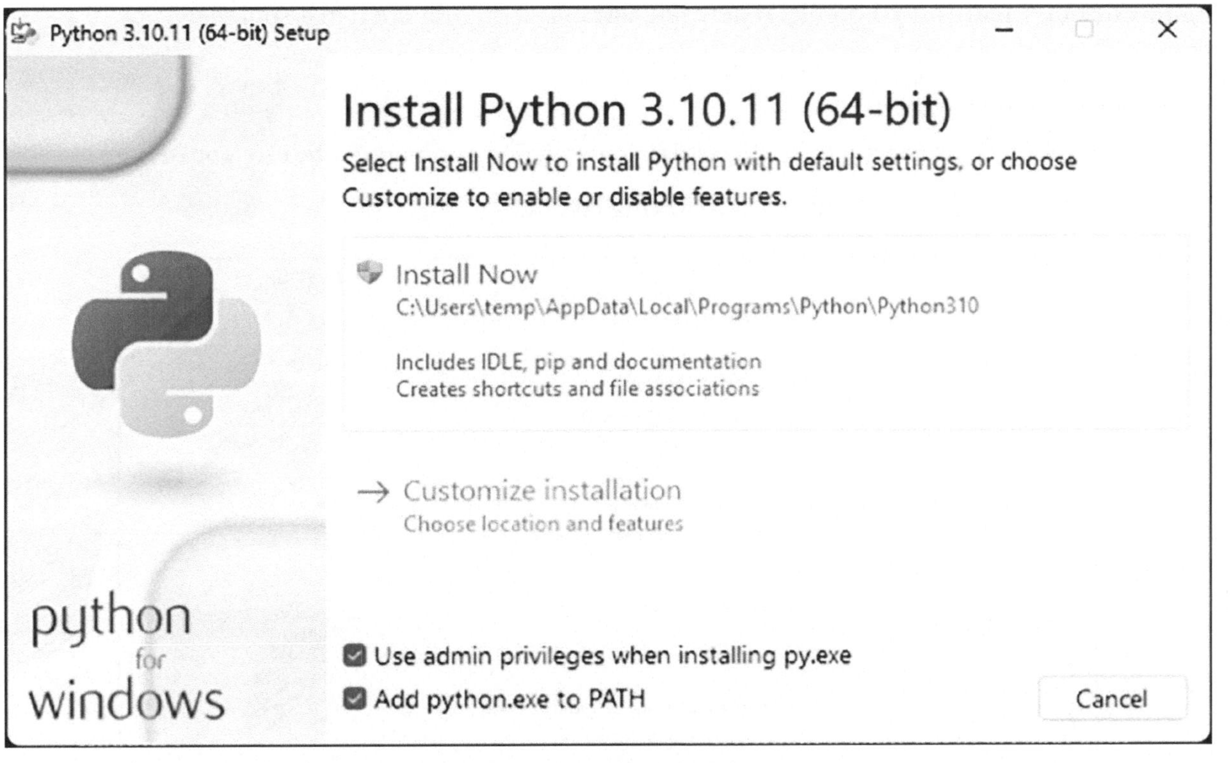

***Figure 2.4:** Install Python*

1. Click **`Install Now.`**
2. If you receive a pop-up asking, **`Do you want to allow this app to make changes on your device?`** Click **`Yes.`**
3. Close the installer once the installation is complete.
4. To verify installation, restart VS Code and run **`python --version`** again in your terminal. You should now see the Python version installed in the output.

Note: *This book expects readers to have basic Python knowledge. However, do not worry if you are new to Python. It is very easy to learn, and although many good resources are available online for free, I would always recommend starting with the official Python docs at https://docs.python.org/3/tutorial/introduction.html.*

Creating a Python Virtual Environment

Python is notorious for dependency incompatibilities, so using separate virtual environments for different projects is advisable. Isolating dependencies within each environment helps prevent version conflicts, especially when working on multiple projects.

Follow these steps to set up a virtual environment:

1. Open VS Code. If the **`Get Started with Python Development`** tab does not reopen automatically, open it manually.
2. Open or create the folder where you will create your Python files. For example, I am using a folder named **`Chapter 2`** in the following screenshot.
3. If prompted with **`Do you trust the authors of the files in this folder?`**, click **`Yes, I trust the authors.`**
4. Click on Create a Python file. A new tab, **`Untitled-1,`** will open in a split view.
5. Type the following Python code in the new tab.
   `print("Hello World!")`
6. Save the file by pressing **`Ctrl+S (Cmd+S on`** macOS) and name it **`hello_world.py`**.
7. Your screen should resemble the following layout.

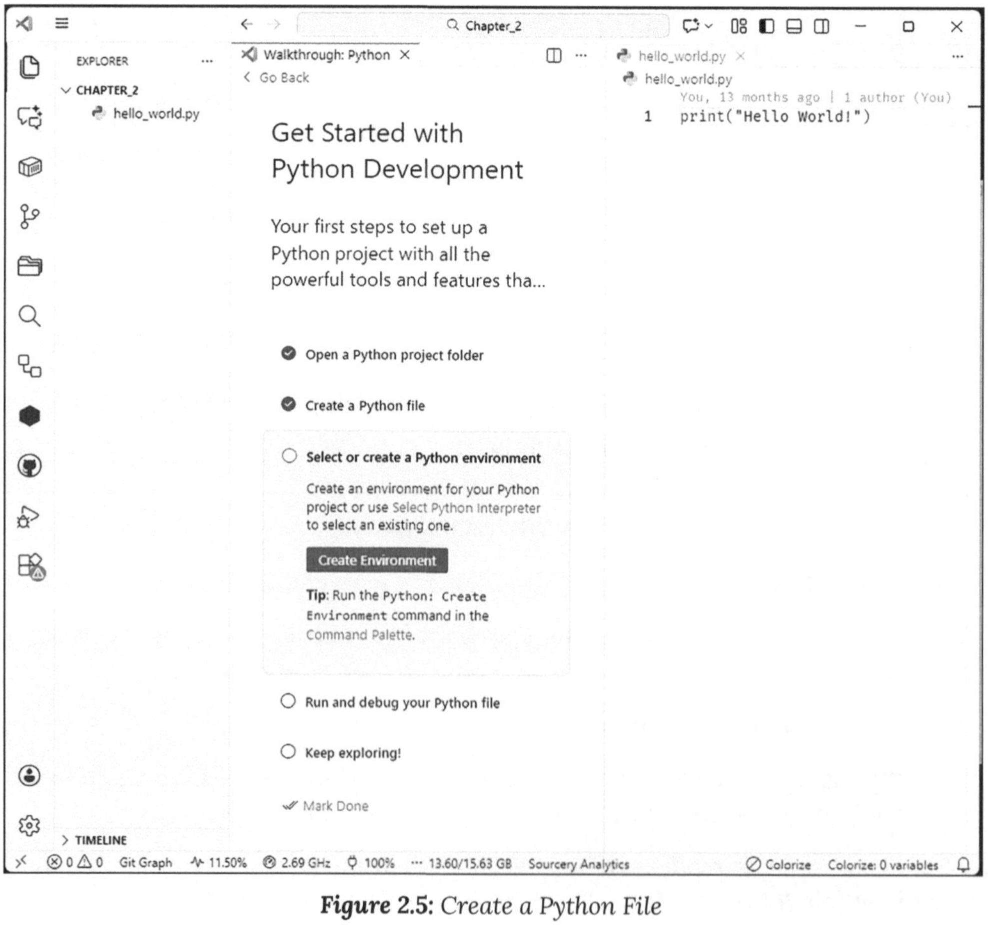

Figure 2.5: *Create a Python File*

8. Back in the Welcome tab, click **`Select or create a Python environment`**, and then choose **`Create Environment`**.
9. Select **`Venv`** as the environment type.

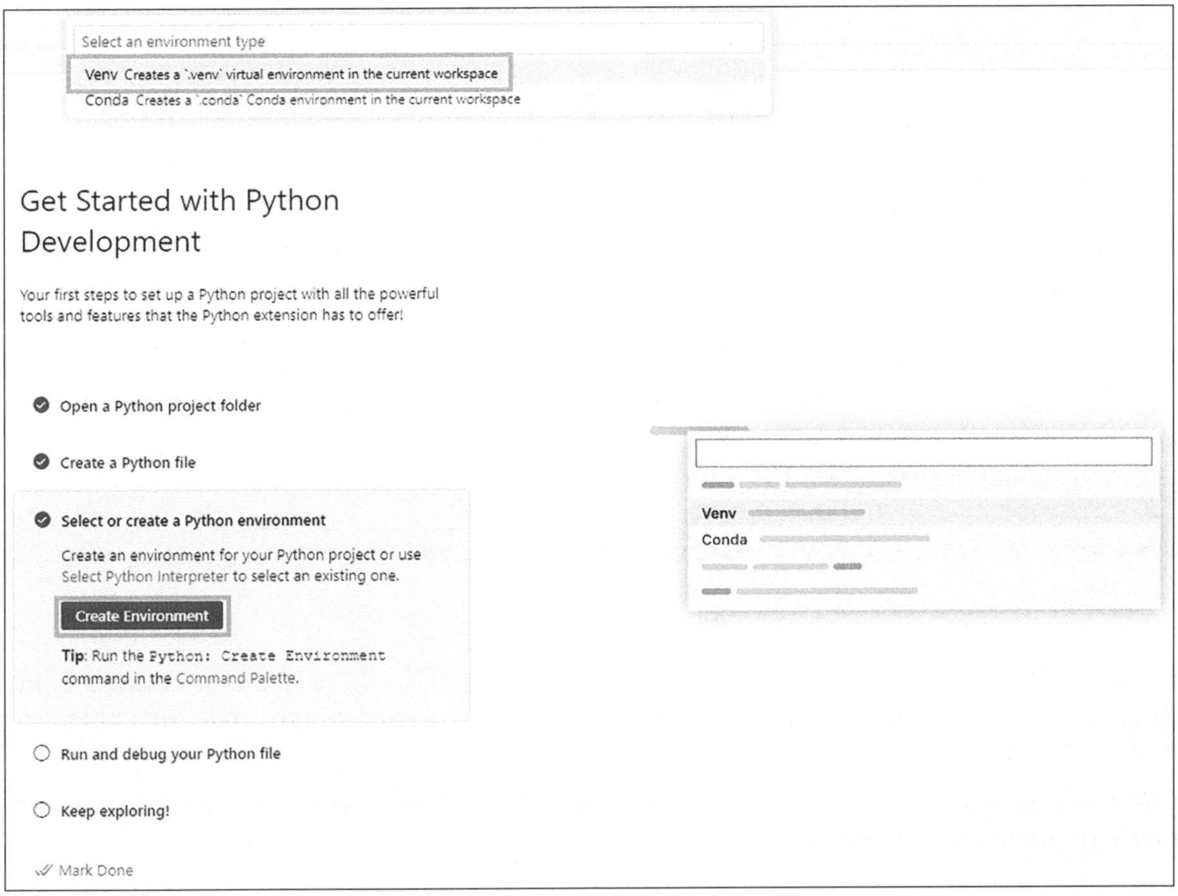

Figure 2.6: *Create a Python Environment*

10. The Python version you installed should be visible in the dropdown. If you have multiple Python versions installed, select the one you want to use for creating the virtual environment.

Figure 2.7: *Select the Python Version*

11. Once the virtual environment is created, you will see a **`.venv`** folder in the Explorer on the left. This folder contains the virtual environment, its dependencies, and configurations.
12. Open the VS Code terminal by pressing **`Ctrl+``** (**`Cmd+``** on macOS) and enter one of the following commands based on your OS and terminal:
    - Windows command prompt
      `.venv\Scripts\activate.bat`
    - Windows PowerShell
      `.venv\Scripts\Activate.ps1`
    - Linux and macOS
      `source .venv/bin/activate`
13. The name of the virtual environment will appear on the terminal, once it is activated.

```
● PS C:\Users\siddh\OneDrive\Desktop\Book\Code\Chapter 2> .venv\Scripts\Activate.ps1
○ (.venv) PS C:\Users\siddh\OneDrive\Desktop\Book\Code\Chapter 2> []
```

Figure 2.8: Activated Virtual Environment on Windows PowerShell

Note: *On Windows, if you get an error saying* **`running scripts is disabled on this system`**, *open Windows search and search for* **`Allow local PowerShell scripts to run without being signed`**. *Open the settings and turn on* **`Change execution policy to allow local PowerShell scripts to run without signing`**.

Rerun the previous command once done, and the virtual environment should now be activated.

14. To run the **`hello_world.py`** file, enter the following command in the terminal,

    `py hello_world.py.`

15. You should see **`Hello World!`** printed on the screen.

```
● (.venv) PS C:\Users\siddh\OneDrive\Desktop\Book\Code\Chapter 2> py hello_world.py
  Hello World!
```

Figure 2.9: Hello World!

Note: *Remember how to activate the virtual environment. You must do so before installing any Python package or running any code to ensure that the packages are installed and the code runs in the correct virtual environment.*

Tip: *To learn more about Python virtual environments, I recommend https://realpython.com/python-virtual-environments-a-primer/.*

Installing Streamlit

1. Download Xcode command line tools using the instructions provided at https://mac.install.guide/commandlinetools/4.html (only required for macOS).

2. In the VS Code terminal, with the virtual environment activated, run the following command.

   `pip install streamlit`

   Note: *I will be using Streamlit 1.50.0. If you want to install this specific version, run the following command:*

   `pip install streamlit==1.50.0`

   To install the latest version of Streamlit available (recommended), run the following command:

   `pip install -U streamlit`

3. Once Streamlit is installed, test the installation by running

   `streamlit hello.`

4. If Streamlit was installed correctly and this was the first installation on your computer, a welcome message asking for an email will appear. You can either enter your email or leave it blank, and press *Enter*.

5. If a popup asks **`Do you want to allow public and private networks to access this app?`**, click **`Allow.`**

6. The Streamlit **`Hello app`** should open in your web browser.

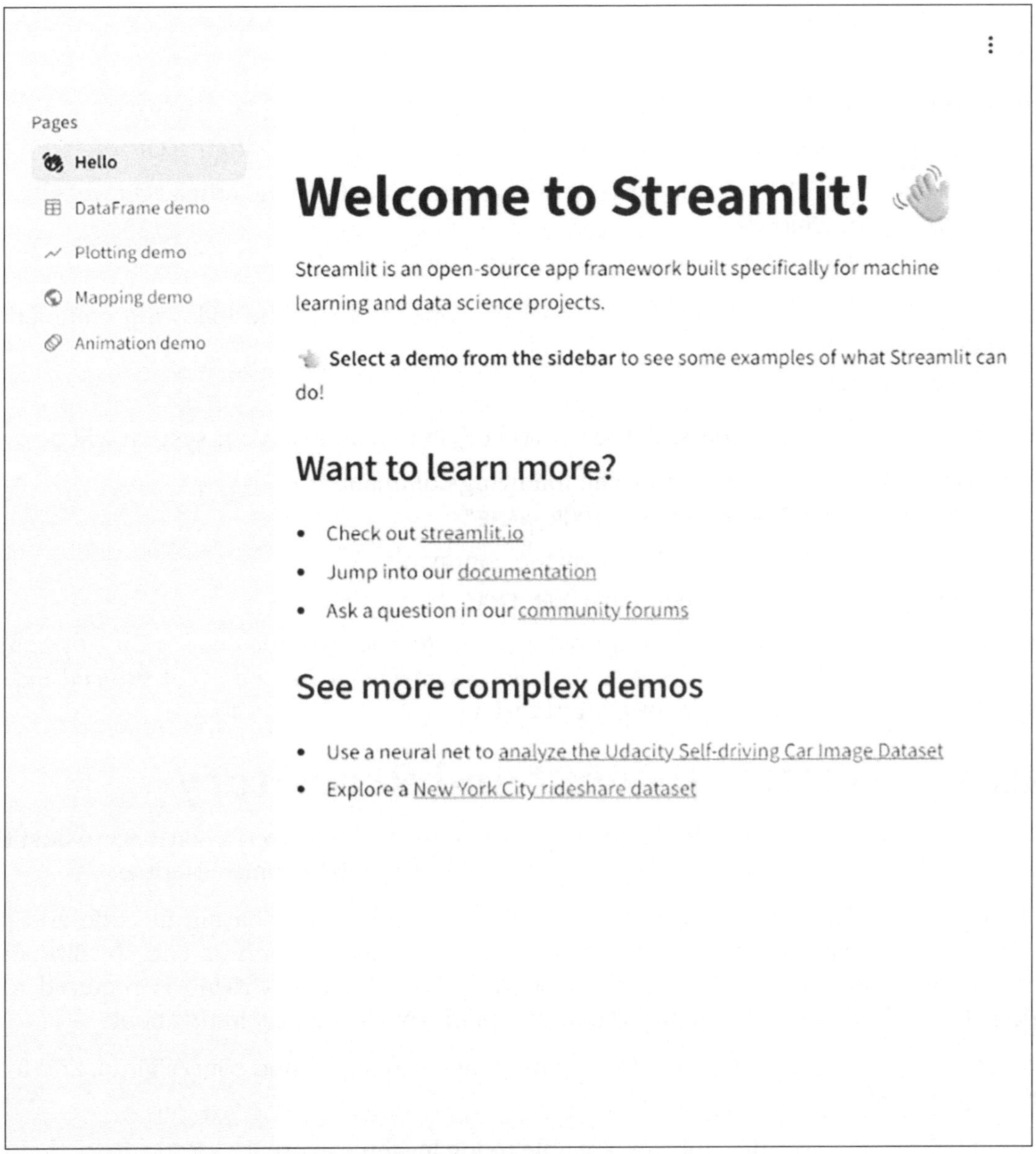

Figure 2.10: *Streamlit Hello App*

7. Spend some time exploring the app.
8. To close the app, close the terminal where it was run or press **`Ctrl+C`** (**`Cmd+C`** on macOS).
9. Congratulations! You have successfully installed Streamlit, and have already run your first application!

Installing Git

Writing code requires implementing a robust code versioning system, which allows you to revert to a previous version, if necessary. Git, the most widely used version control system for software development, enables you to manage different versions of code within a repository (commonly referred to as a *repo*).

Most modern operating systems come with Git pre-installed. To verify, if Git is installed on your system, follow these steps:

1. Open your VS Code terminal.

2. Run the following command:
```
git version
```
3. If Git is installed, the version of Git installed on your system will be displayed.

If Git is not installed on your system, follow these steps to install and configure Git:

1. Download the installer suitable for your operating system from the official Git website: https://git-scm.com/downloads.
2. Execute the installer using the default options.
3. After the installation is complete, restart VS Code, and run the following command in the terminal:
```
git version
```
4. If the installation was successful, the version of Git installed on your system will be displayed.
5. Set your Git username by running the following command:
```
git config --global user.name "YOUR_NAME"
```
6. Set your Git email by running the following command:
```
git config --global user.email "YOUR_EMAIL"
```

Tip: *While only basic knowledge of Git is required to follow this book, proficiency in Git can significantly enhance your coding skills. To improve your Git skills, consider following a Git tutorial like the one available at https://www.geeksforgeeks.org/git-tutorial/.*

Creating a GitHub Account and Repository

While Git enables you to version code locally on your system, you will need a platform to host the code if you collaborate with others. This is where platforms like GitHub become essential.

GitHub is a platform for developers that facilitates the storage and sharing of code and provides version control using Git. Although other platforms are available, such as GitLab, BitBucket, and AWS CodeCommit, GitHub remains the most popular. Furthermore, GitHub is required to deploy applications to the Streamlit Community Cloud, the platform we will use in this book.

To create a GitHub account, visit the GitHub signup page https://github.com/signup, and follow the instructions provided.

Once your email has been verified and you are able to log in, you can create a Repository that will host the apps you will develop as a part of this book.

Enter the name of the repository, and choose whether the repository should be `Public` or `Private`.

Note: *Streamlit Community Cloud lets you host any number of public apps but only one private app at a time. You can choose to have your repository as Private now, but you will need to update this to Public later, if you wish to deploy more apps to the Streamlit Community Cloud. Do not worry, this can easily be updated later.*

Click on `Create a new repository` once done.

Tip: *This book will teach you everything you need to know about GitHub for creating and deploying Streamlit apps. However, if you wish to enhance your GitHub skills further, it is recommended that you visit the GitHub documentation at https://docs.github.com/en/get-started.*

Creating a Streamlit Account

A Streamlit account is needed to deploy applications to the Streamlit Community Cloud. Follow the following steps to create one:

1. Head to https://share.streamlit.io/signup, and click on `Continue to sign in`.

2. Click on **`Continue with GitHub.`**
3. Follow the instructions to create your account.
4. Once done, you will be **`taken to your Streamlit Hub workspace.`**

Congratulations! You are now all set to start building and deploying your Streamlit apps!

Cloud-Based Setup

When exploring cloud setups for Streamlit development, you have several options, each with its own setup process. This section will highlight three straightforward options, provide some features and free-usage limits, and demonstrate how Streamlit looks in each environment. Additionally, we will provide links to detailed setup instructions.

Note: *The Streamlit app used in the following examples is hosted at https://pdfworkdesk.streamlit.app/, and the code is available at https://github.com/SiddhantSadangi/pdf-workdesk.*

GitHub Codespaces

GitHub Codespaces provides fully configured, secure development environments directly within GitHub, with up to 120 core-hours and 15GB of monthly storage.[2] It integrates seamlessly with GitHub, so we do not have to wait to clone repositories and install dependencies in our local environment.

Streamlit offers a one-click setup of a GitHub Codespaces environment for forked apps. The experience is focused on development, and is the same as that of VS Code, with the code and app visible side-by-side if the Codespace is created by forking an existing Streamlit app.

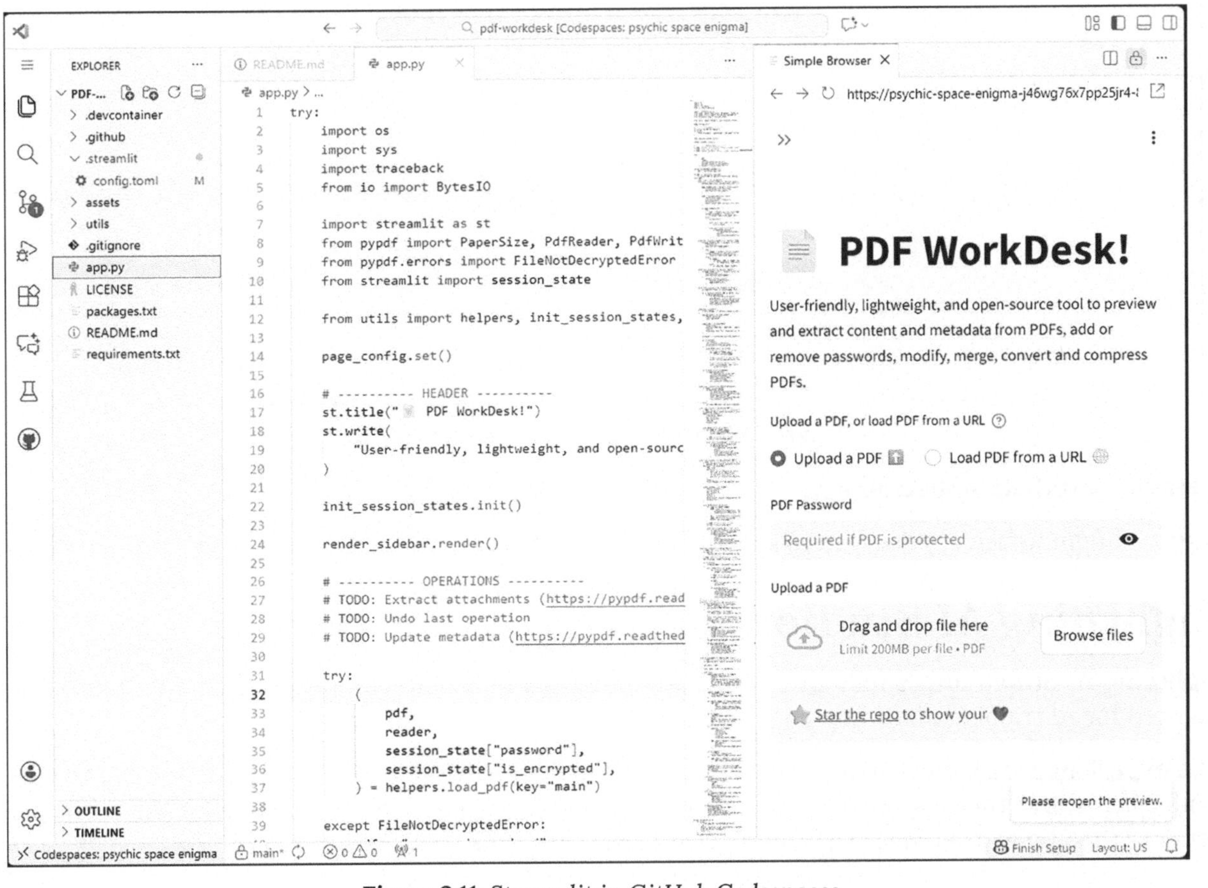

Figure 2.11: *Streamlit in GitHub Codespaces*

[2] *https://github.com/features/codespaces* (Accessed: 3 June 2024)

Detailed installation instructions

https://docs.streamlit.io/get-started/installation/community-cloud

Hugging Face Spaces

Hugging Face Spaces is a platform designed to create and deploy ML-powered demos. It offers free access to 16GB RAM, 2 CPU cores, and 50GB of disk space (not persistent). It also seamlessly links with Datasets and Models hosted on Hugging Face Hub.[3]

The experience is more focused on sharing, resembling that of GitHub for code version control. Deployed Streamlit apps can be accessed through the **App** tab, and easily embedded on other web pages.

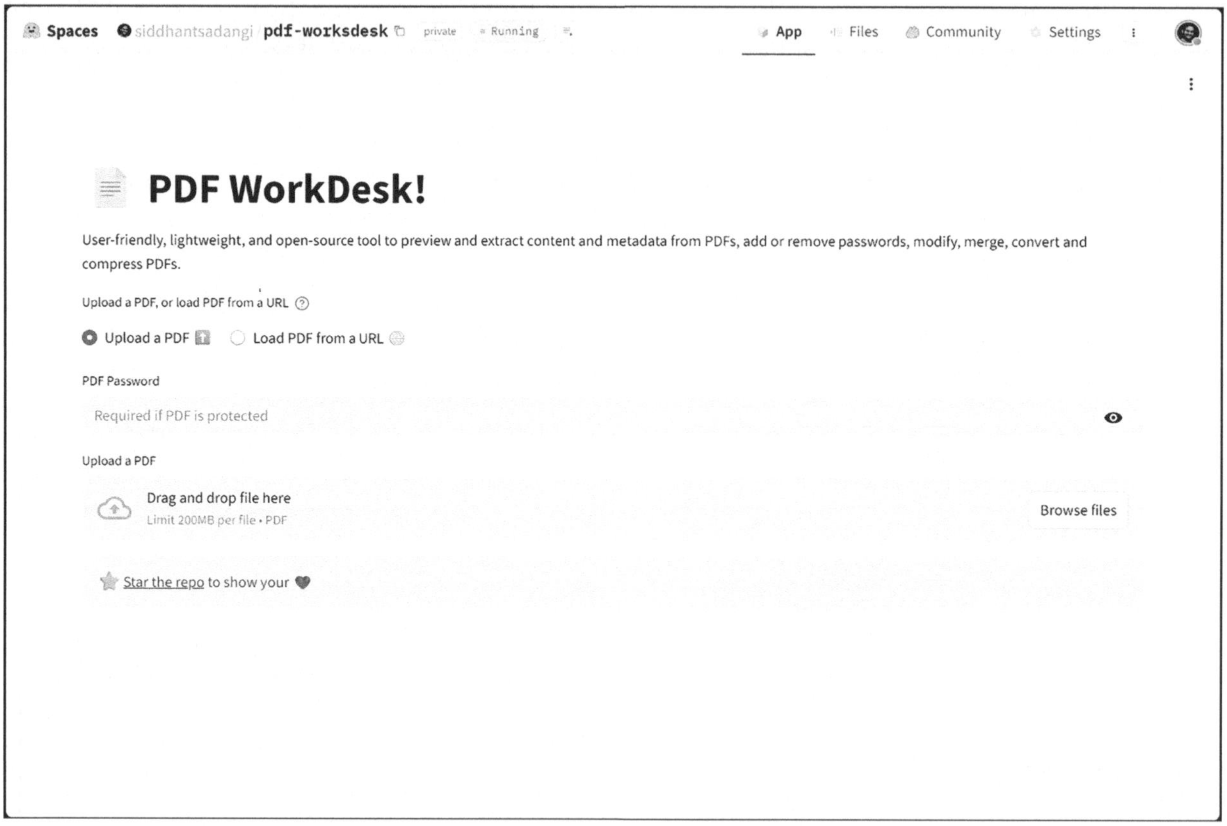

Figure 2.12: *Streamlit in Hugging Face Spaces*

Detailed installation instructions

https://huggingface.co/docs/hub/spaces-sdks-streamlit

Lightning AI Studio

Lightning AI Studio offers fully pre-configured and customizable cloud development environments tailored for AI training and web apps with 22 GPU hours monthly for free.[4]

The experience is a hybrid of development and sharing. The IDE resembles VS Code, similar to GitHub Codespaces, but there is no side-by-side view of the code and the app. Instead, a Streamlit plugin renders the app in a separate view, and provides a public link to share your app.

[3] *https://huggingface.co/docs/hub/spaces-overview* (Accessed: 3 June 2024)
[4] *https://lightning.ai/pricing* (Accessed: 3 June 2024)

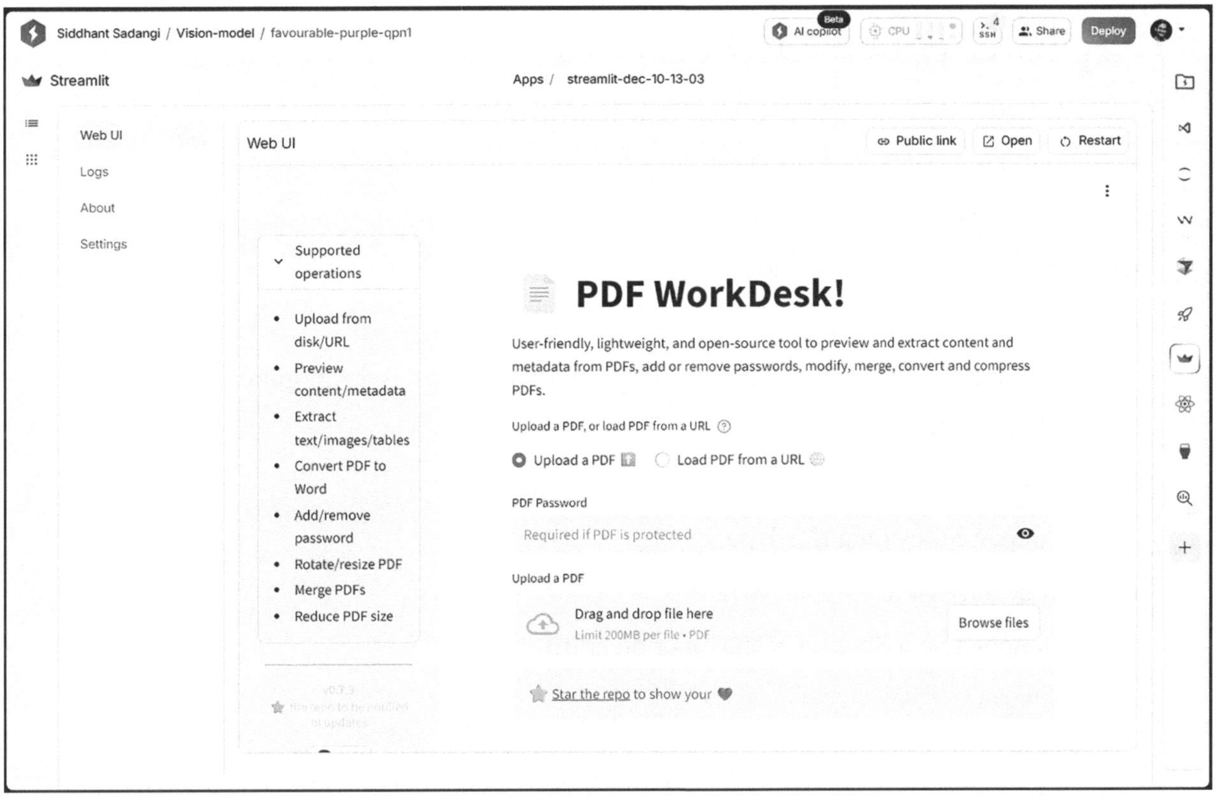

Figure 2.13: *Streamlit in Lightning AI Studio*

Detailed installation instructions

https://lightning.ai/docs/overview/deploy-ai-web-apps/streamlit-apps

Conclusion

In this chapter, we have explored the advantages and disadvantages of local versus cloud-based development environments. We have also created a local development environment from scratch for Streamlit apps, including installing VS Code, Python, Streamlit, and Git, as well as creating a Python virtual environment and a GitHub account. Finally, we have delved into different cloud-based development options.

In the next chapter, we will create a simple Streamlit app, run it locally, and deploy it on Streamlit Community Cloud.

Points to Remember

- Local development refers to building, testing, and debugging an application on a personal computer or a local server. It is generally cost-effective but lacks scalability.
- Cloud-based development involves using a cloud service provider's resources to build, test, and debug applications. It offers scalability and a quick setup, but may incur additional costs.
- A Python virtual environment provides an isolated workspace for each Python project, ensuring dependency management and version control.
- To be able to deploy an application to Streamlit Community Cloud, the application code has to be pushed to a GitHub Repository.

Multiple Choice Questions

1. Which among the following is an advantage of a local development environment?
   a. Unlimited resources for scaling
   b. It can be accessed from anywhere
   c. Control over hardware and software
   d. Easier collaboration
2. Which among the following is an advantage of a cloud-based development environment?
   a. Higher level of security and privacy
   b. No usage costs
   c. No dependency on a third-party
   d. Can be accessed from anywhere
3. Which among the following is NOT a code editor?
   a. PyCharm
   b. Jupyter
   c. MS Word
   d. Notepad++
4. Which among the following is NOT a cloud-based development environment?
   a. PyCharm
   b. GitHub Codespaces
   c. Hugging Face Spaces
   d. Lightning AI Studio
5. Which of the following do you need to be able to deploy apps to Streamlit Community Cloud?
   a. GitLab
   b. AWS CodeCommit
   c. BitBucket
   d. GitHub

Answers

1. c
2. d
3. c
4. a
5. d

Questions

1. What are some advantages and disadvantages of local development?
2. What are some advantages and disadvantages of cloud-based development?
3. What is a Python virtual environment? Why is it needed?
4. Name a few code editors. Which one do you prefer and why?
5. What is the difference between Git and GitHub?
6. Name a few cloud-based development environments. Which one do you prefer and why?

Key Terms

- **Code Editor:** A software application for writing and editing code.
- **IDE (Integrated Development Environment):** An IDE is a software that combines commonly used developer tools into a compact GUI (Graphical User Interface) application. It combines tools like a code editor, compiler, and debugger with an integrated terminal.[5]
- **Code Versioning:** Code versioning, also known as version control or source control, is the practice of tracking and managing changes to software code.[6]
- **Git:** A version control system for software development that enables you to manage different versions of code within a repository.
- **GitHub:** A developer platform owned by Microsoft that lets developers store, manage, and share their codes. It uses Git for version control.
- **PATH Environment Variable:** PATH is a global operating system variable that contains the set of directories where executable programs are located.
- **`pip`:** The Package Installer for Python (`pip`) is a tool for installing packages from the Python Package Index (PyPI) and other indexes. It is generally bundled with Python and does not need to be downloaded and installed separately.
- **Python Dependencies:** A dependency is a software component required for your program to run.
- **Python Environment Manager:** A tool for creating and managing Python virtual environments. Examples include `venv`, `pyenv`, `conda`, `poetry`, and so on.
- **Python Virtual Environment:** An isolated workspace for managing Python dependencies.

[5] *https://www.geeksforgeeks.org/what-is-ide/* (Accessed: 14 June 2024)
[6] *https://www.atlassian.com/git/tutorials/what-is-version-control* (Accessed: 7 June 2024)

CHAPTER 3

Creating and Deploying Your First Streamlit App

Introduction

This chapter provides a step-by-step guide on how to build and deploy a basic Streamlit application, both locally and on the cloud. The process begins with the construction of a straightforward data analysis script. Following this, we will be demonstrating the simplicity of incorporating Streamlit into pre-existing Python data scripts by integrating Streamlit into it.

Subsequently, we will execute the application locally. This will allow us to observe its functionality in real time, while we progressively enhance our script. The final step involves deploying the application on the Streamlit Community Cloud. This deployment will make our application accessible to anyone with an internet connection, enabling them to appreciate the fruits of our labor.

Structure

In this chapter, we will discuss the following topics:

- Writing a Simple Data Analysis Script
- Incorporating Streamlit into the Script
- Executing the Streamlit Application Locally
- Enhancing the Script with Additional Streamlit Widgets
- Deploying the Application to Streamlit Community Cloud

Writing a Simple Data Analysis Script

In this section, we will construct a basic script designed to analyze the Iris dataset.

Setup

1. Begin by opening VS Code. Then, navigate to the **`Explorer`** tab on the left side of the interface. Right-click within this tab to create a New File.
2. Name this file as **`iris_analysis.py`**.
3. Verify that the Python Interpreter being used is the one from the virtual environment we established in the preceding chapter. This can be confirmed by checking the bottom right corner of the VS Code interface. If the correct interpreter is not displayed, you can select the **`Python Interpreter`** option, and choose the appropriate one from the dropdown menu at the top. Refer to following *Figure* 3.1 for guidance on selecting the **`Python Interpreter`**:

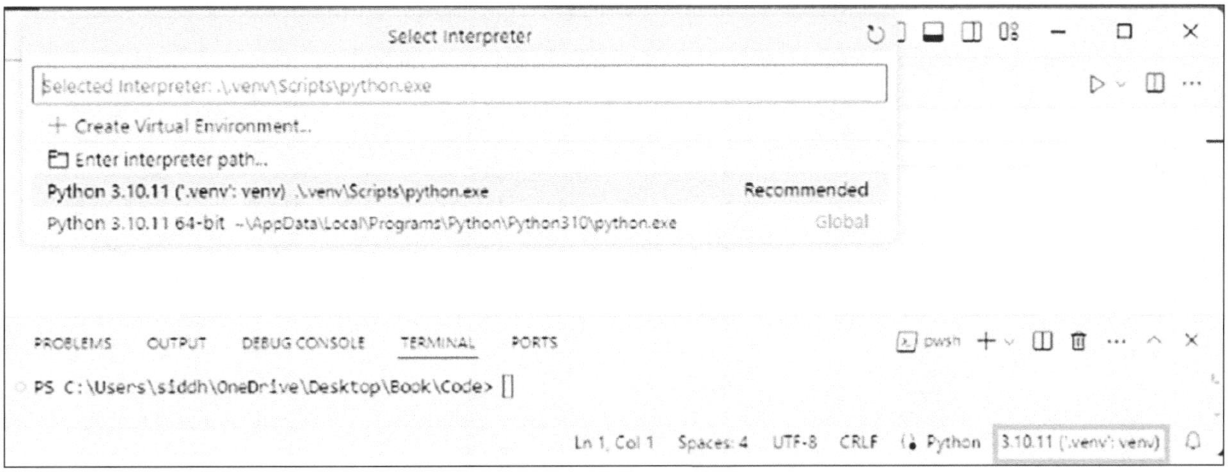

Figure 3.1: *Selecting the Python Interpreter*

4. You will also need to activate the virtual environment in your terminal, as detailed in the previous chapter.
5. Finally, install Seaborn, a Python package designed for data visualization. This can be done by executing the following command in your terminal:

   `pip install seaborn`

Basic Script

In this section, we will create a script designed for rudimentary data analysis.

1. To begin, we need to import the necessary Python packages into our script. Enter the following commands into the **`iris_analysis.py`** file:

```
import matplotlib.pyplot as plt
import seaborn as sns
```

2. Next, load the Iris dataset from **seaborn** with the following command:

```
iris_df = sns.load_dataset("iris")
```

3. To view the dataset, print it using the following commands:

```
print("Dataset")
print(iris_df)
```

4. For a more detailed view of the dataset, use the following **`describe()`** method:

```
print("Dataset description")
print(iris_df.describe())
```

5. To execute the script, click on the **`Run Python File`** button located at the top right of the code editor. Refer to *Figure* 3.2 for guidance.

Figure 3.2: *Run Python File*

6. The output will be displayed in the terminal, as shown in *Figure* 3.3.

```
Dataset
     sepal_length  sepal_width  petal_length  petal_width    species
0             5.1          3.5           1.4          0.2     setosa
1             4.9          3.0           1.4          0.2     setosa
2             4.7          3.2           1.3          0.2     setosa
3             4.6          3.1           1.5          0.2     setosa
4             5.0          3.6           1.4          0.2     setosa
..            ...          ...           ...          ...        ...
145           6.7          3.0           5.2          2.3  virginica
146           6.3          2.5           5.0          1.9  virginica
147           6.5          3.0           5.2          2.0  virginica
148           6.2          3.4           5.4          2.3  virginica
149           5.9          3.0           5.1          1.8  virginica

[150 rows x 5 columns]
Dataset description
       sepal_length  sepal_width  petal_length  petal_width
count    150.000000   150.000000    150.000000   150.000000
mean       5.843333     3.057333      3.758000     1.199333
std        0.828066     0.435866      1.765298     0.762238
min        4.300000     2.000000      1.000000     0.100000
25%        5.100000     2.800000      1.600000     0.300000
50%        5.800000     3.000000      4.350000     1.300000
75%        6.400000     3.300000      5.100000     1.800000
max        7.900000     4.400000      6.900000     2.500000
```

Figure 3.3: *Dataset Details*

7. Now, let us create some plots to visualize our data. We will start by examining the relationship between the sepal length and width for each species using Seaborn's **`scatterplot()`** method. Add the following lines to your script and execute it:

```
sns.scatterplot(
    x="sepal_length",
    y="sepal_width",
    data=iris_df,
    hue="species",
)
plt.show()
```

8. A plot will open in a new window, as shown in the following *Figure* 3.4.

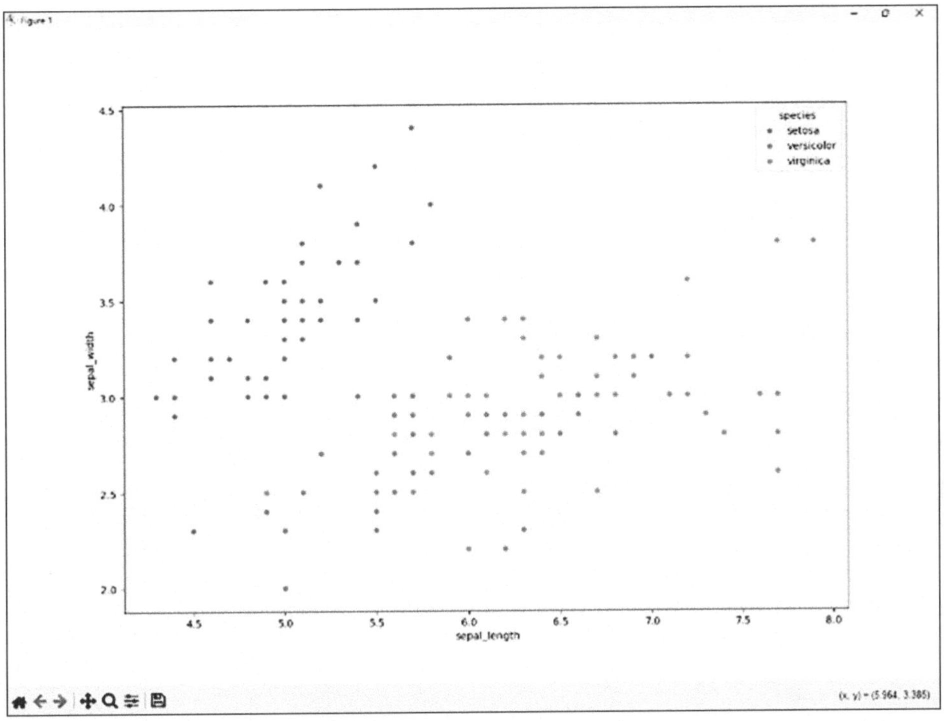

Figure 3.4: *Seaborn Scatterplot*

> **Tip:** *To learn more about Seaborn and the types of plots it can generate, you can visit its documentation here: https://seaborn.pydata.org/tutorial.html.*

9. To make this script interactive, add a section that prompts the users to specify the columns they want to visualize using the scatterplot. Add the following lines above your scatterplot call:

```
x = input("Enter x-axis column: ")
y = input("Enter y-axis column: ")
```

10. Then, update your scatterplot call as shown:

```
sns.scatterplot(x=x, y=y, data=iris_df, hue="species")
```

11. At this point, your script should look like this:

```
import matplotlib.pyplot as plt
import seaborn as sns

iris_df = sns.load_dataset("iris")
print("Dataset")
print(iris_df)

print("Dataset description")
print(iris_df.describe())

x = input("Enter x-axis column: ")
y = input("Enter y-axis column: ")
sns.scatterplot(x=x, y=y, data=iris_df, hue="species")
plt.show()
```

12. Run this script. You will be prompted to enter the **`x-axis`** and **`y-axis`** columns. This time, let us visualize the relationship between the petal length and petal width:

```
Enter x-axis column: petal_length
Enter y-axis column: petal_width
```

13. A plot similar to the one shown in the following *Figure* 3.5 will open in a new window.

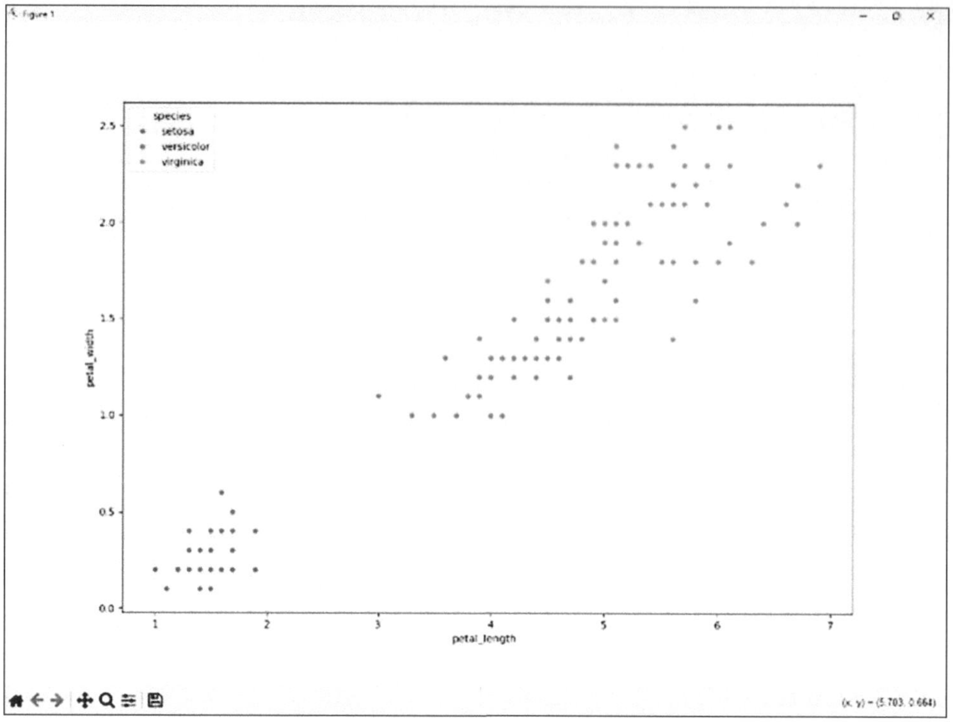

Figure 3.5: *Petal Length vs. Petal Width*

Incorporating Streamlit into the Script

We will now turn our script into an app by integrating Streamlit into it.

1. As with any Python library, we must first import Streamlit into our script. The standard convention is to import Streamlit as **st**. Add the following line to the imports section of your script at the top:

   ```
   import streamlit as st
   ```

2. Since we aim to display the output and plots within the application and not the console, we should replace all **`print()`** statements with **`st.write()`**. This can be easily achieved using the replace-all function of your IDE. In VS Code, this function can be activated by pressing *Ctrl/Cmd*+H. In the pop-up that appears, find **`print(`** and replace it with **`st.write(`**, then click on **`Replace All`**. Refer to the following *Figure* 3.6 for guidance.

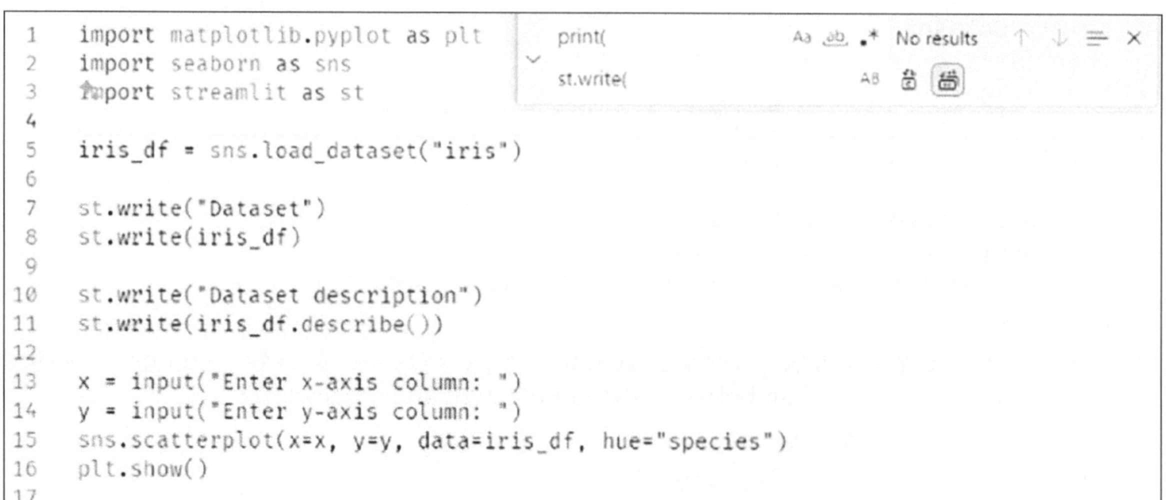

Figure 3.6: *Replacing **`print()`** with **`st.write()`***

3. Similar to console output, we want the plot to be displayed within the application, not in a separate window. Since **`st.write()`** requires us to pass the matplotlib **`Figure`** object explicitly, we must first create an instance of it. Add the following line just above **`sns.scatterplot()`**:

   ```
   fig = plt.figure()
   ```

4. Then, we can replace **`plt.show()`** with **`st.write(fig)`**.
5. Finally, we want the viewer to enter the input via the application, not the console. This can be achieved by using **`st.text_input()`**. Replace both occurrences of **`input(`** with **`st.text_input(`** as shown in the following *Figure* 3.7.)

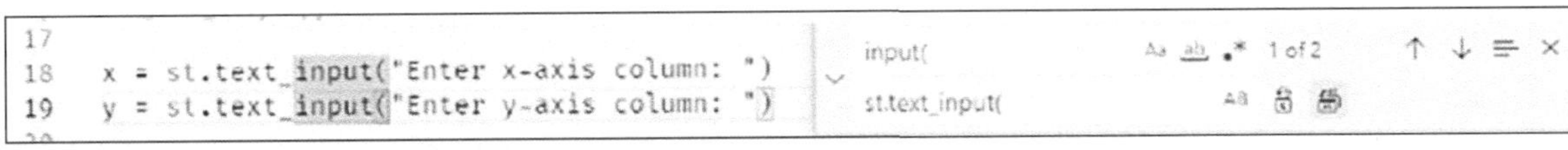

Figure* 3.7:** *Replaced* ***`input()` *with* ***`st.text_input()`***

6. At this point, your script should look like this:

```
import matplotlib.pyplot as plt
import seaborn as sns
import streamlit as st

iris_df = sns.load_dataset("iris")

st.write("Dataset")
st.write(iris_df)

st.write("Dataset description")
st.write(iris_df.describe())

x = st.text_input("Enter x-axis column: ")
y = st.text_input("Enter y-axis column: ")

fig = plt.figure()
sns.scatterplot(x=x, y=y, data=iris_df, hue="species")
st.write(fig)
```

Executing the Streamlit Application Locally

With the Streamlit script now prepared, it can be executed by entering the following command into your terminal:

```
streamlit run iris_analysis.py
```

The console output will display the application's **`Local URL and Network URL`**. If the app does not automatically open in a browser tab, you can manually access it by navigating to the **`Local URL`**.

Upon opening the application, it should resemble the interface shown in *Figure* 3.8.

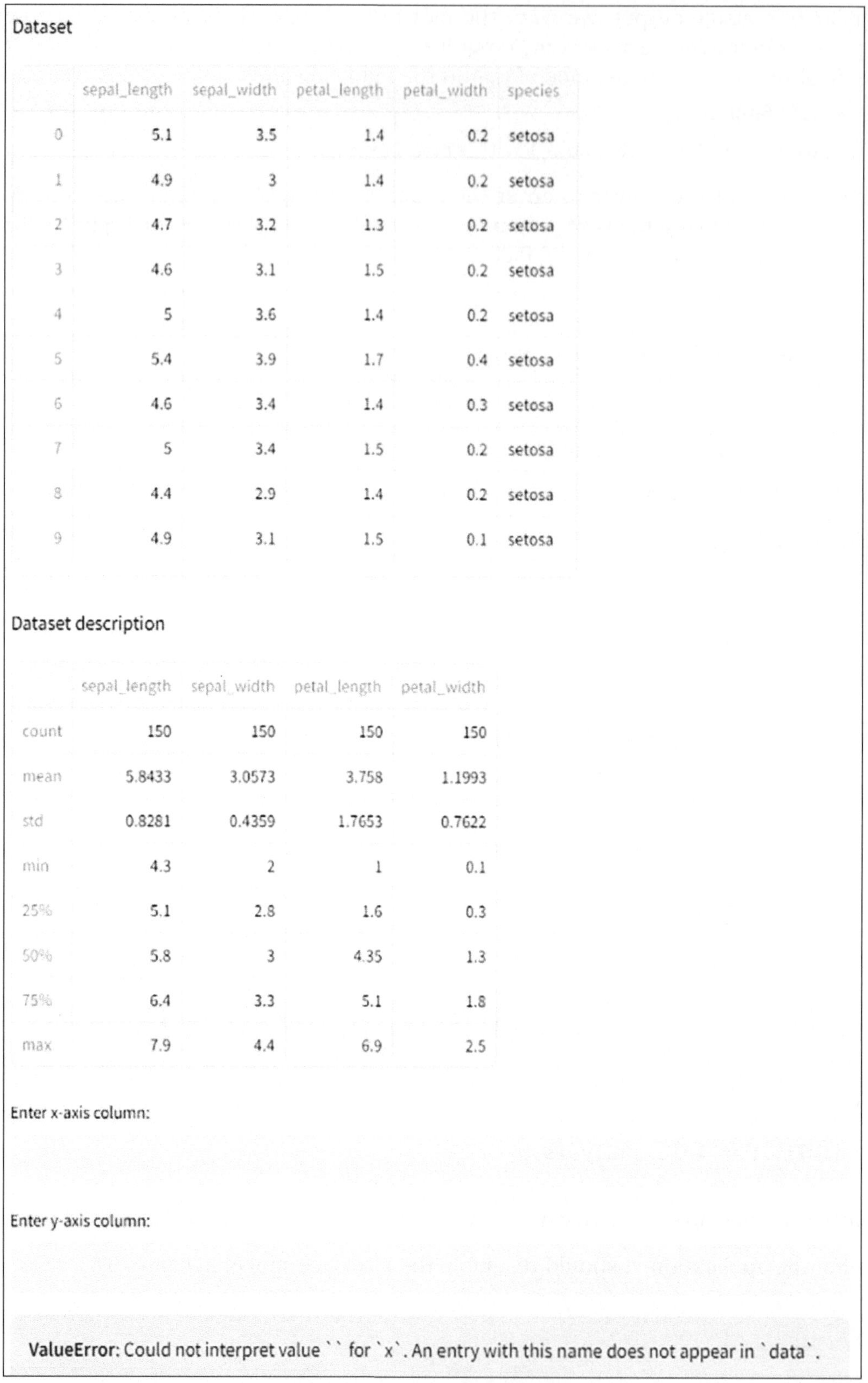

Dataset

	sepal_length	sepal_width	petal_length	petal_width	species
0	5.1	3.5	1.4	0.2	setosa
1	4.9	3	1.4	0.2	setosa
2	4.7	3.2	1.3	0.2	setosa
3	4.6	3.1	1.5	0.2	setosa
4	5	3.6	1.4	0.2	setosa
5	5.4	3.9	1.7	0.4	setosa
6	4.6	3.4	1.4	0.3	setosa
7	5	3.4	1.5	0.2	setosa
8	4.4	2.9	1.4	0.2	setosa
9	4.9	3.1	1.5	0.1	setosa

Dataset description

	sepal_length	sepal_width	petal_length	petal_width
count	150	150	150	150
mean	5.8433	3.0573	3.758	1.1993
std	0.8281	0.4359	1.7653	0.7622
min	4.3	2	1	0.1
25%	5.1	2.8	1.6	0.3
50%	5.8	3	4.35	1.3
75%	6.4	3.3	5.1	1.8
max	7.9	4.4	6.9	2.5

Figure 3.8: *Iris Analysis Basic App*

One of the first things, you may notice is the interactivity of the tables. Hovering over the column names allows for resizing columns or sorting the table based on column values. Additionally, hovering over the table reveals a tooltip in the top right corner, providing options to download the table as a CSV file, search for a specific value, or view the table in full screen.

Another noticeable feature is the error displayed in place of the scatterplot at the bottom. This occurs because the scatterplot requires the names of the x and y-axis columns. When running the script as a Python file, execution halts at the **`input()`** command, awaiting the entry of column names before proceeding to display the scatterplot based on the entered columns. However, Streamlit executes the entire script from top to bottom, without pausing for input, hence the error. We will delve into this behavior in more detail in the next chapter, and discuss best practices for circumventing this issue.

For the time being, we can enter the required columns, and the scatterplot will be displayed as shown in *Figure* 3.9.

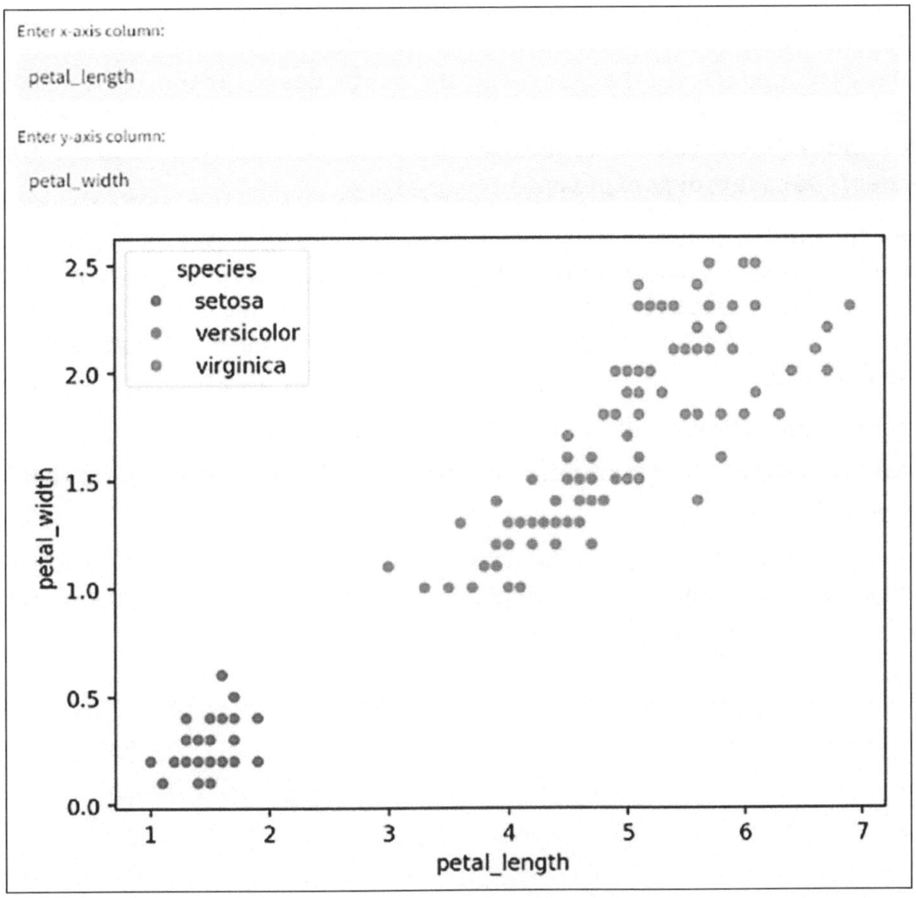

Figure 3.9: *Basic Scatterplot in Streamlit*

A final, less obvious observation is that although we have used the same Streamlit display method **`write()`**, the display format varies depending on the data type passed to the method. For instance, strings such as **`Dataset`** and **`Dataset description`** are displayed as standard text, dataframes as tables, and Matplotlib plots as figures.

Tip: *To learn more about* **`st.write()`** *and the different data types it supports, refer to its documentation at the official Streamlit website here: https://docs.streamlit.io/develop/api-reference/write-magic/st.write.*

Enhancing the Script with Additional Streamlit Widgets

While our application is already more user-friendly and interactive than a standard Python script, it can be further enhanced.

1. Every application should have a title. We can add a title to our application using **`st.title()`**. Insert the following line into your script immediately after the imports:

   ```
   st.title("Iris Analysis App")
   ```

   Upon saving your script, you will notice a small **i** icon at the top right of the application. Hovering over it reveals that Streamlit has detected a change in the source file, and offers the option to rerun the application based on the updated source file. You can also select: "**Always rerun**" to ensure that the application automatically updates, whenever a change is detected.

   Let us choose "**Always rerun**". You can now see the app's title at the top!

   Note: *Automatic rerun is a powerful Streamlit feature that helps you quickly iterate and improve apps by updating the source code, without rerunning them manually.*

2. Next, we can enhance the **Dataset** and **Dataset description** sections by emphasizing the section headings using **`st.header()`**. Replace the **`st.write("Dataset")`** and **`st.write("Dataset description")`** lines with **`st.header("Dataset")`** and **`st.header("Dataset description")`** respectively.

3. We then turn our attention to the scatterplot. The current plot is static, meaning it is not interactive. You cannot pan around the chart or obtain more information about a data point by hovering over it. **`st.scatter_chart()`** provides all these features in just one line of code! To add an interactive scatterplot, replace the code block from **`fig = plt.figure()`** to **`st.write(fig)`** with the following line:

   ```
   st.scatter_chart(x=x, y=y, data=iris_df, color="species")
   ```

   Since **`matplotlib`** is no longer required in this script, you can remove the **`import matplotlib.pyplot as plt`** line.

   After making these changes, we should see a different scatterplot, as shown in *Figure* 3.10. This scatterplot is interactive: We can pan around the plot, and hovering above the individual points gives us additional details about those points.

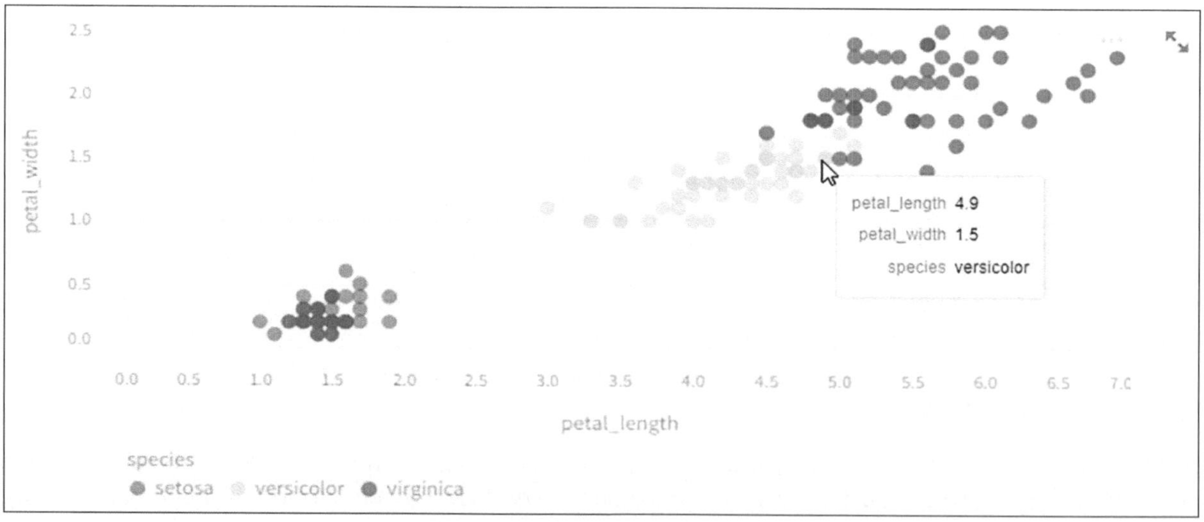

Figure 3.10: *Interactive Scatterplot in Streamlit*

We can also view the plot on the full screen, and download it using the options at the top right of the chart, when hovering above it.

Tip: *Streamlit's interactive charts are powered by* **Vega-Altair** *– a powerful and popular visualization library for Python. You can read more about it here: https://altair-viz.github.io/index.html.*

4. As we are already enhancing the plot, let us also improve the input method. Currently, we pass the column names as free text, which is prone to errors. If the input does not exactly match the column names, the application will display an error. Since we know in advance that the input can only be from among the columns of the **`iris_df`** dataframe, we can present the users with options and allow them to choose instead of typing. This can be achieved using **`st.selectbox()`**. Replace the two **`st.text_input()`** lines with the following:

```
x = st.selectbox(
    "Enter x-axis column: ",
    options=iris_df.columns,
)
y = st.selectbox(
    "Enter y-axis column: ",
    options=iris_df.columns,
)
```

Head back to the app, and you will be able to see the text box replaced by a dropdown that lets the viewer select the required column, as shown in *Figure* 3.11.

Figure 3.11: *Replacing* **st.text_input()** *with* **st.selectbox()**

This is more user-friendly than the text box, as the viewer does not have to type out the full column name. It also eliminates the scope for error, as there can be no typos. Since **`st.selectbox()`** selects the first option by default, it is never blank, and we will not see the initial error we saw about the x and y columns, not being present when refreshing the app. *Try it yourself!*

At this point, our script should look like this:

```
import seaborn as sns
import streamlit as st

st.title("Iris Analysis App")

iris_df = sns.load_dataset("iris")

st.header("Dataset")
st.write(iris_df)

st.header("Dataset description")
st.write(iris_df.describe())
```

```
    x = st.selectbox(
        "Enter x-axis column: ",
        options=iris_df.columns,
    )
    y = st.selectbox(
        "Enter y-axis column: ",
        options=iris_df.columns,
    )

    st.scatter_chart(x=x, y=y, data=iris_df, color="species")
```

Our application should now resemble the interface shown in *Figure 3.12*.

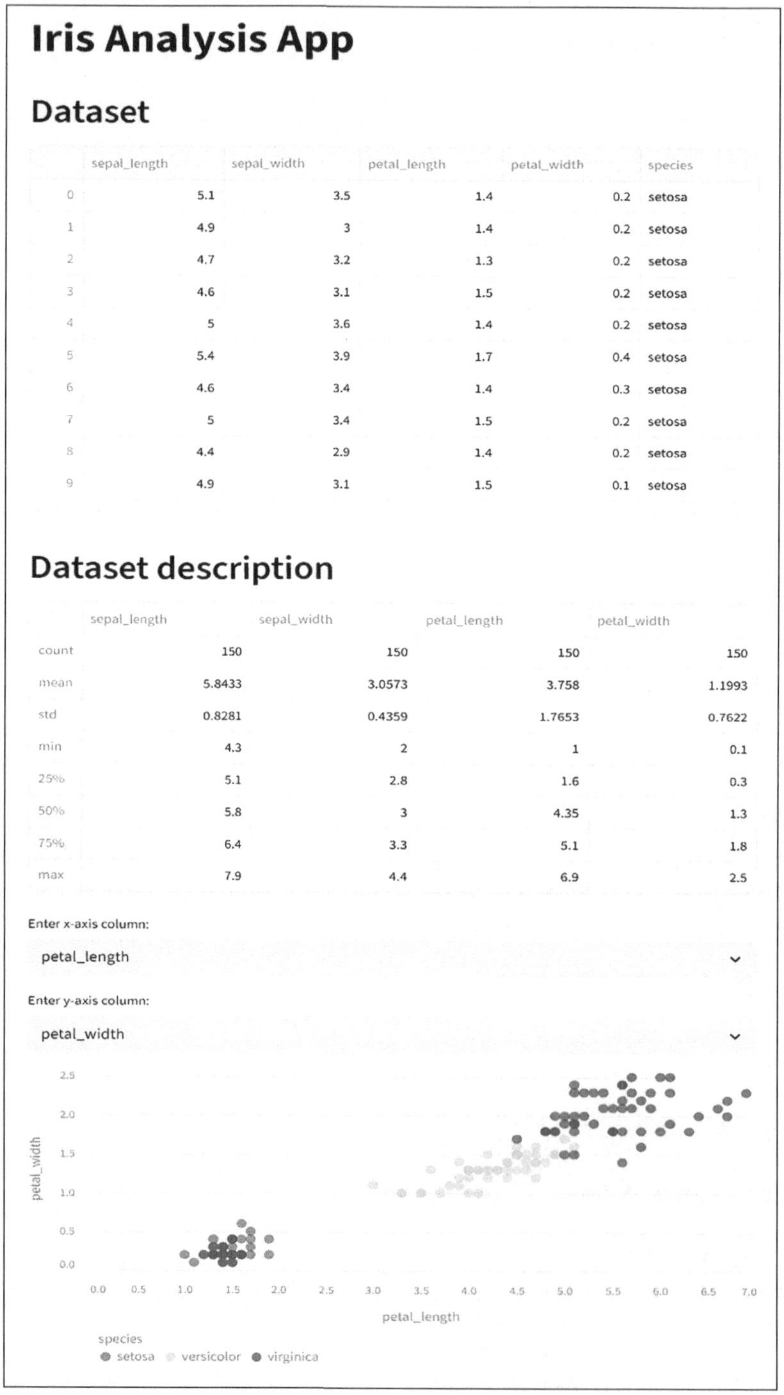

	sepal_length	sepal_width	petal_length	petal_width	species
0	5.1	3.5	1.4	0.2	setosa
1	4.9	3	1.4	0.2	setosa
2	4.7	3.2	1.3	0.2	setosa
3	4.6	3.1	1.5	0.2	setosa
4	5	3.6	1.4	0.2	setosa
5	5.4	3.9	1.7	0.4	setosa
6	4.6	3.4	1.4	0.3	setosa
7	5	3.4	1.5	0.2	setosa
8	4.4	2.9	1.4	0.2	setosa
9	4.9	3.1	1.5	0.1	setosa

	sepal_length	sepal_width	petal_length	petal_width
count	150	150	150	150
mean	5.8433	3.0573	3.758	1.1993
std	0.8281	0.4359	1.7653	0.7622
min	4.3	2	1	0.1
25%	5.1	2.8	1.6	0.3
50%	5.8	3	4.35	1.3
75%	6.4	3.3	5.1	1.8
max	7.9	4.4	6.9	2.5

Figure 3.12: *Iris Analysis App*

Task: **`st.write()`** *calls* **`st.dataframe()`** *to display dataframes as interactive tables. You can use* **`st.dataframe()`** *directly for showing* **`Dataset`** *and* **`Dataset description`**. *This also allows you to customize the display further and adds additional features. As homework, check out the* API guide for **`st.dataframe()`** *at https://docs.streamlit.io/develop/api-reference/data/st.dataframe and replace* **`st.write()`** *with* **`st.dataframe()`** *for displaying the tables.*

Deploying the Application to Streamlit Community Cloud

The moment has arrived to deploy our application and share it with the world! The first step involves pushing our application code to the GitHub Repository that we created in the previous chapter. We will then use that repository to deploy the application on Streamlit Community Cloud.

Pushing the Code to GitHub

1. Begin by initializing a new git repository locally. This can be done by running the following command in your terminal:

   ```
   git init
   You should see the following output:
   Initialized empty Git repository in path/to/the/folder/.git/
   ```

2. Next, associate your local repository with the one you created on GitHub in the previous chapter. This can be achieved by running the following command in your terminal:

   ```
   git remote add origin https://github.com/[Username]/[Repo].git
   ```

   Remember to replace **`[Username]`** and **`[Repo]`** with your GitHub username, and the name of your GitHub repository.

3. Stage, commit, and push the **`iris_analysis.py`** file to GitHub by running the following commands:

   ```
   git add iris_analysis.py
           git commit -m "Added iris analysis"
                   git push -u origin main
   ```

4. Open your GitHub repository in your browser. You can do this by typing the following URL into your browser's address bar, replacing **`[Username]`** and **`[Repo]`** with your GitHub username, and the name of your repository:

   `https://github.com/[Username]/[Repo]`

5. You should now be able to see the **`iris_analysis.py`** file in your repository.

Deploying the Application

1. Return to the application, and select **`Deploy`** located at the top-right corner.
2. In the **`Deploy this app`** popup, click on **`Deploy now`** under **`Streamlit Community Cloud.`**
3. If you have not already signed into Streamlit Hub, follow these steps:
   a. Select **`Continue to sign-in`** in the Streamlit Hub page that opens.
   b. Choose **`Continue with GitHub.`**
   c. If necessary, sign into GitHub, and select **`Authorize Streamlit.`**
   d. Enter the verification code that you received in your email.

4. The details should be prefilled in the **`Deploy an app`** page. Verify the details, and make any necessary changes.
5. In the **`Advanced settings…`** section, select the version of Python, you are using and click on **`Save!`**
6. Click on **`Deploy!`**
7. **`Your app is in the oven page`** will open, while the app is being loaded.
8. If you have followed all the steps mentioned here, you should get a **`ModuleNotFoundError`**. Do not worry; this is part of the learning process!
9. Click on **`Manage app`** at the bottom right.
10. You should see the following error message at the bottom:

    `ModuleNotFoundError: No module named 'seaborn'`

    Why does this occur?

    Remember that we had earlier installed Seaborn? Although it is installed in our environment, it still needs to be installed in the environment where the Streamlit app is being deployed. We will discuss this nuance in detail in a later chapter, but for now, we need to instruct Streamlit to install Seaborn in the environment where the app will be hosted. This can be done using a **`requirements.txt`** *file.*
11. Create a **`requirements.txt`** file in the same folder as the **`iris_analysis.py`** file.
12. Type **`seaborn`** in the file, and save it.

    Tip: *The requirements.txt file is integral to managing dependencies in Python. If you have not already done so, you should acquaint yourself with this file. Here is a good tutorial: https://datagy.io/python-requirements-txt/.*
13. Push the **`requirements.txt`** file to GitHub by running the following commands in your terminal.

    ```
    git add requirements.txt
    git commit -m "Added requirements"
    git push
    ```
14. Return to the deployed app. Since Streamlit monitors your GitHub repository for changes, it will automatically detect the new **`requirements.txt`** file, and install Seaborn. Your app should now be running fine!

Congratulations! You have just deployed your first Streamlit application!

If your GitHub repository is public, anyone can access your application by visiting its URL.

Tip: *The Streamlit Community Cloud is a great way to deploy and share public apps worldwide. However, being a free public service, it has some resource and privacy restrictions. The good news is that there are other platforms where you can deploy Streamlit. If you have special needs, you can choose among one of the many different platforms documented by Streamlit here: https://discuss.streamlit.io/t/streamlit-deployment-guide-wiki/5099.*

Conclusion

In this chapter, we have gained insights into how to incorporate Streamlit widgets into a Python script, execute a Streamlit application locally, upload the application's code to GitHub, and navigate some intricacies associated with deploying the application to Streamlit Community Cloud.

In the forthcoming chapter, we will delve into some fundamentals of Streamlit's architecture, encompassing aspects of development, data handling, and execution flow. Additionally, we will learn more about its Client-Server architecture.

Points to Remember

- Ensure that you are installing packages in and running code from your Python virtual environment.
- When importing Streamlit, **st** is the commonly used alias.
- The terminal command **streamlit run** is used to run a Streamlit application.
- Streamlit executes the entire script from top to bottom, without pausing for any user input.

  Any additional Python dependencies must be added to a **`requirements.txt`** file, and uploaded to the repository.

Multiple Choice Questions

1. What is the most conventional alias used while importing Streamlit?
   a. `sns`
   b. `str`
   c. `st`
   d. `sl`
2. Which output method can display the most data types?
   a. `st.title()`
   b. `st.table()`
   c. `st.scatter_chart()`
   d. `st.write()`
3. Which command can you run a Streamlit script named **`app.py`**?
   a. `app run app.py`
   b. `streamlit run app.py`
   c. `python app.py`
   d. `streamlit app.py`
4. Which Python library powers Streamlit's interactive charts?
   a. Altair
   b. Matplotlib
   c. Plotly
   d. Bokeh

5. What is the default value of `st.selectbox()`:
    a. Blank
    b. The first option
    c. The last option
    d. The most recent option chosen by the viewer

Answers

1. c
2. d
3. b
4. a
5. b

Questions

1. List all the Streamlit input and output methods mentioned in this chapter. What is each used for?
2. Based on what you have learned in this chapter, how can you further improve the user-friendliness and interactivity of the Iris Analysis App?
3. Why is a `requirements.txt` file needed while deploying a Streamlit app to Streamlit Community Cloud?

Key Terms

- **App Chrome:** Streamlit calls the app/kebab menu *app chrome*. It is located at the top right of a Streamlit app, and is represented by three vertical dots (⁝). Clicking on it opens a dropdown menu for app developers and viewers.
- **Iris Dataset:** A classic machine learning dataset commonly used for classification tasks. It consists of 50 sepal and petal lengths and widths for each of three types of irises - Setosa, Versicolor, and Virginica - for a total dataset size of 150 rows and five columns - four features and one target.
- **`ModuleNotFoundError`:** An error in Python that is raised when an imported module cannot be found.
- **Scatterplot:** A scatterplot, also known as a scatter chart, scatter graph, or scatter diagram, is a type of data display that shows the relationship between two numerical variables.
- **Streamlit Community Cloud:** A platform provided by Streamlit to deploy and share public Streamlit applications worldwide.
- **requirements.txt:** A text file that lists all the Python package dependencies for a project. It is commonly used in Python projects to help manage dependencies.

Chapter 4
Exploring Streamlit's Flow and Architecture

Introduction

This chapter delves into the fundamentals of Streamlit, focusing on aspects related to development, data flow, execution flow, and client-server architecture.

We will revisit the automatic reloading feature of Streamlit applications when there are updates in the source code. This section will also explain the reloading process when users interact with a Streamlit widget. We will delve into some of the less intuitive issues that arise from this behavior.

In the latter part of the chapter, we will dissect Streamlit's client-server architecture. We will discuss its impact on deployed applications, especially when the client and the server reside on different machines. We will also provide insights on designing applications with this architecture in mind.

Note: *From this chapter onwards, our discussions and examples will be based on Streamlit version 1.50.0.*

Structure

In this chapter, we will discuss the following topics:

- Automatic Application Reloads Triggered by Source Code Updates
- Application Reloads Prompted by Widget State Updates
- Unforeseen Consequences of Application Reloads
- Understanding Streamlit's Client-Server Architecture
- Influence of the Client-Server Architecture on Application Design

Automatic Application Reloads Triggered by Source Code Updates

Do you recall from the previous chapter when the Streamlit application detected an update in the source code and prompted us to rerun the application? Upon rerunning, the changes made in the source code were instantly reflected in the application. You might wonder how Streamlit knew what changes were made to the script or which widget was added and where.

The answer is more straightforward than it appears. Streamlit reruns the entire script from start to finish! When we select the **`Always rerun`** option, Streamlit reruns the script, and reloads the application whenever the source code is updated. What might seem like a magical update of the script is, in fact, a straightforward rerun!

This behavior of Streamlit makes it incredibly efficient for prototyping. You run the script, load the application, modify the script, and the application reloads automatically!

Tip: *If your screen is large enough, we recommend arranging your code editor and application browser windows side-by-side. This setup allows you to observe changes in your application in real time without switching between windows.*

Application Reloads Prompted by Widget State Updates

In the previous chapter, we observed how the scatterplot updated based on the columns selected using the text box or select box. You might wonder how Streamlit managed to update the plot. One might assume that Streamlit reruns the script from the point of the widget change, updating every subsequent widget. However, those familiar with Python scripts would know that, unlike a Jupyter Notebook, it is not possible to execute only parts of a Python script.

So, how does Streamlit update the downstream widgets when an upstream widget changes? Again, Streamlit reruns the entire script!

Let us see this with a live example. Create a simple Python script with the following content:

```
import streamlit as st

print("Starting script")

if st.button("Click me!"):
    print("Button was clicked")
```

In this script, we use the standard **`print()`** function to output to the terminal, not a Streamlit method to print within the app. The script prints **`Starting script`** whenever it starts, and **`Button was clicked`** whenever the Streamlit button is pressed.

Intuitively, if we click the button twice, we might expect to see **`Starting script`** printed once and **`Button was clicked`** printed twice in the terminal. However, when we run the script using streamlit run, and click the button twice, the terminal output is as follows:

```
Starting script
Starting script
Button was clicked
Starting script
Button was clicked
```

This is not what we expected. We anticipated **`Button was clicked`** to be printed twice, not **`Starting script`**. So, why does this happen?

1. When the app first runs, only **`Starting script`** is printed as the button has not yet been clicked.
2. Clicking the button changes its state, which prompts Streamlit to rerun the entire script from top to bottom.
3. As a result, **`Starting script`** is printed again when the script reruns, and since Streamlit buttons return **`True`** when the script reruns due to their activation, **`Button was clicked`** is also printed.
4. Therefore, each time you click the button, both the **`Starting script`** and the **`Button was clicked`** will be printed.

This behavior can be summarized as shown in *Figure 4.1*.

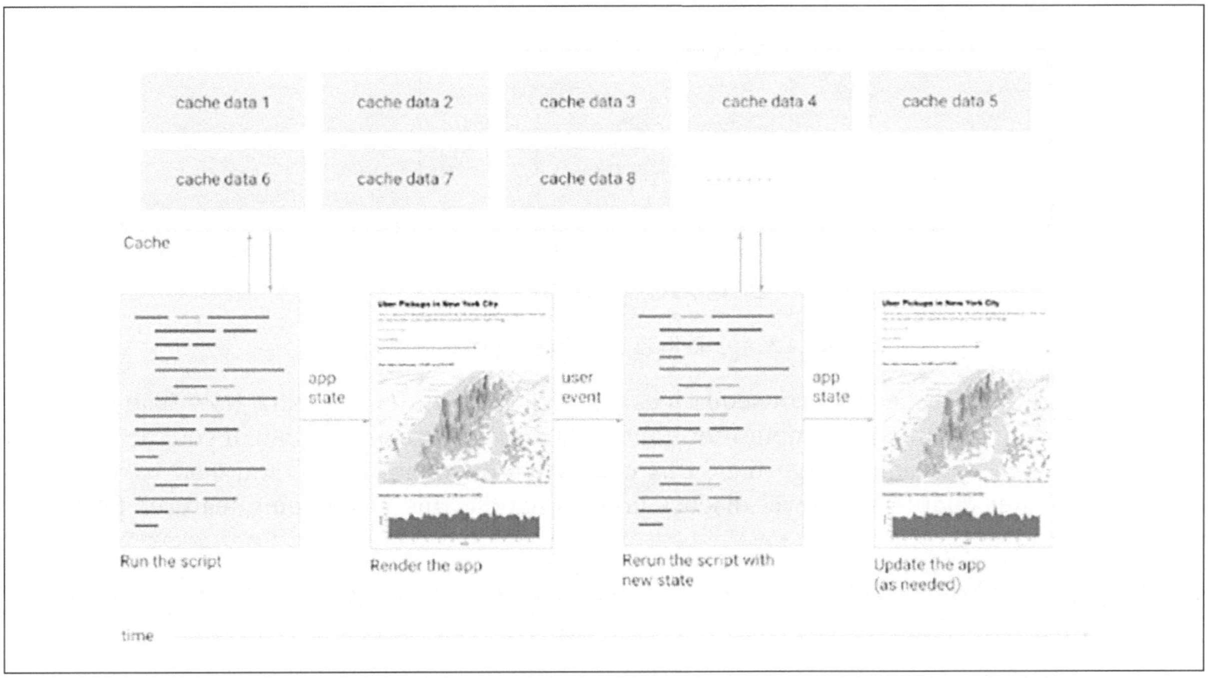

Figure 4.1: *Streamlit's App Flow*[1]

We will cover **cache data** in a later chapter. For now, remember that any change in the source code or user interaction with the app that updates any widget's state will cause Streamlit to rerun the entire source script from top to bottom, and reload the app.

Note: *While it is important to understand that Streamlit reruns the entire script, it also provides functionality to control this behavior by altering the execution flow. We will discuss these features in later chapters. You can also read more about these in the Streamlit documentation here: https://docs.streamlit.io/develop/api-reference/execution-flow.*

Unforeseen Consequences of Application Reloads

Streamlit's behavior of reloading the app can lead to some unexpected outcomes. Although this might seem counterintuitive and confusing, it makes sense in practical applications where we ideally display output within the app, not in the terminal. For instance, when running the app, we would want the message **`Starting script`** to appear every time the app runs, regardless of whether the button is clicked. Streamlit's full rerun behavior allows us to achieve this.

To illustrate this, let us replace **`print()`** in the previous script with **`st.write()`**. Now, when we run the script, we initially see **`Starting script`** displayed as expected, and **`Button was clicked`** only appears when the button is clicked. Unlike the terminal output, clicking the button multiple times does not duplicate the output. So, even if we click the button twice, we see the **`Starting script`** and **`Button was clicked`** displayed only once, as shown in *Figure* 4.2. Thus, the multiple outputs occur only in the terminal, not the actual app.

[1] *https://docs.streamlit.io/get-started/fundamentals/summary* (Accessed: 20 June 2024)

Figure 4.2: *App Reload on Change in Widget State*

However, other, more noticeable consequences can disrupt the development flow. The first is that every time the script reruns, all computations and calls must be executed again. If your script involves large computations or loading large files, this can slow down the reload, and lead to a poor user experience. In later chapters, we will discuss how to handle this using some features provided by Streamlit.

Secondly, since Python objects and variables persist only within the script's scope, they are all destroyed when the script reruns.

Tip: *Here, we assume the variables have a global scope, i.e., they are accessible anywhere within the Python script. However, variables can also have a local scope. You can learn more about the scope of Python variables here: https://www.w3schools.com/PYTHON/python_scope.asp.*

Finally, because Streamlit buttons created with **`st.button`** do not retain their state, nesting content inside code blocks controlled by the button's state does not work as expected.

Let us explore the last two effects with examples in the following sections.

Understanding the Reset of Variables in Streamlit

To observe how variables reset to their initial values when the script reruns, let us modify our previous script as follows:

```
import streamlit as st

st.write("Starting script")

count = 0

if st.button("Click me!"):
    count += 1
    st.write(f"Button was clicked {count} times")
```

In this script, we have added a variable count to track the number of times the button is clicked, incrementing its value by one each time.

When you run this script using **`streamlit run`**, and click the button multiple times, you will notice that no matter how many times you click the button, it always indicates that you clicked it once (as shown in *Figure* 4.3).

Figure 4.3: *Variable Being Reset on App Rerun*

Why does this happen?

Since Python variables persist only within their scope, and are destroyed once the script finishes executing, the **`count`** variable is destroyed and recreated with a value of ***`0`*** each time the script reruns. Every time we click the button, Streamlit sets its state to **`True,`** and reruns the script. This creates a new **`count`** variable with a value of ***`0`***. Since the button state is now **`True`**, the condition is satisfied, and the value of **`count`** is increased to ***`1`***. This process repeats each time you click the button, with the value of **`count`** constantly resetting to ***`0`*** at the start of the script, and increasing to ***`1`***. This process is visualized in the flowchart, as shown in *Figure* 4.4.

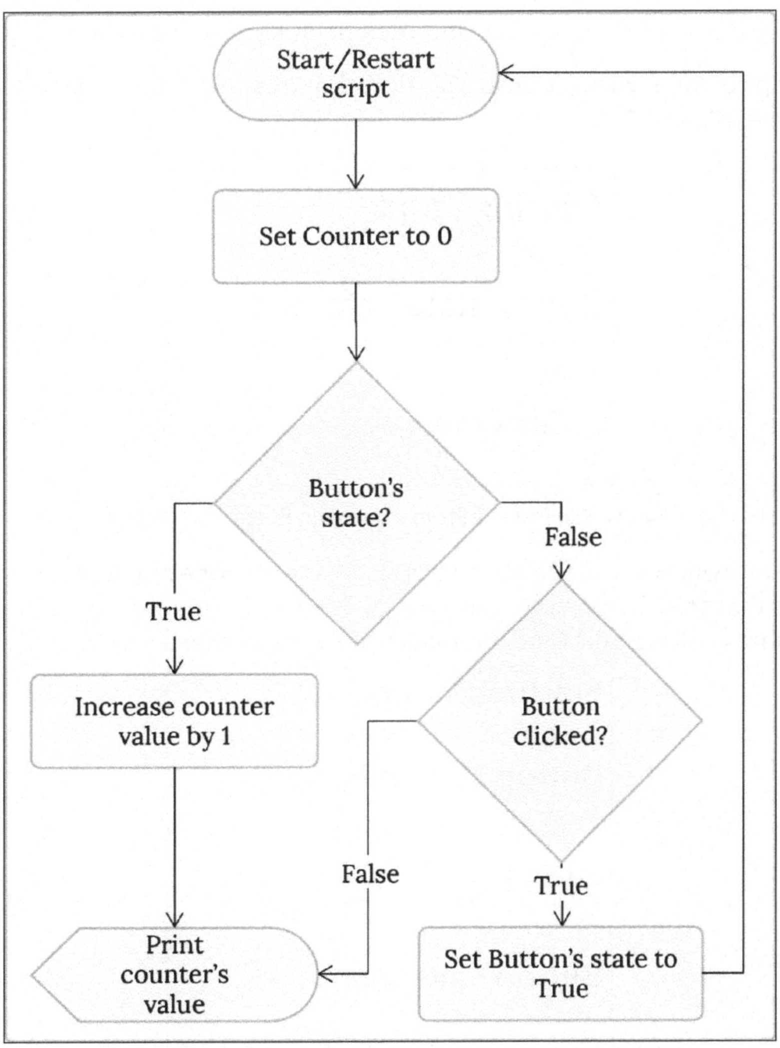

Figure 4.4: *Visualizing Variable State on Script Rerun*

This flowchart shows that since the script reruns every time the button is clicked, **count** is always set to **0** at the beginning of the script, and can never exceed **1**.

Note: *This reload is for any widget state change, not just a button.*

Streamlit also provides **session_state** functionality to monitor a widget's state in real-time. We will cover **session_state** in detail in the next chapter. For now, know that you can retrieve any widget's state by providing its key to **session_state**.

To illustrate this, update your script as follows:

```
import streamlit as st

st.write("Starting script")

count = 0

st.write("Button state before:", st.session_state.get("button"))

if st.button("Click me!", key="button"):
    st.write("Button state after:", st.session_state.button)
    count += 1
    st.write(f"Button was clicked {count} times")
```

Here, we assign a key **button** to the button, and then print its state both before and after it is clicked.

Now, rerun the script using **streamlit run**. The first time the app runs, you will see that the **Button state before** is **None** (*Figure* 4.5).

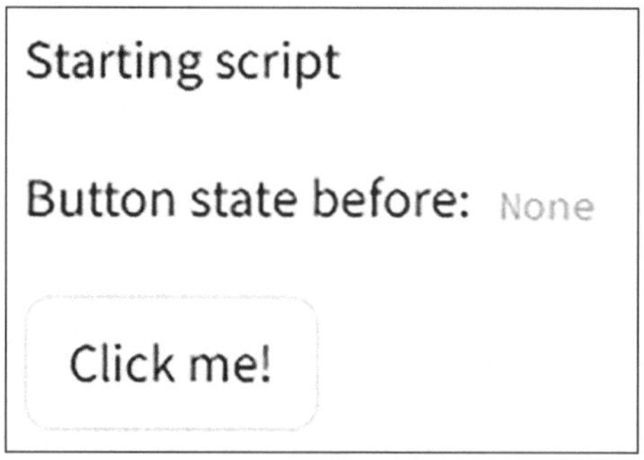

***Figure* 4.5:** *Button State before the Button is Clicked*

When you click the button, you will see both **Button state before** and **Button state after** change to **True**, confirming that the button state changes to **True**, if the app reloads due to a button click. In this example, the states will remain **True**, no matter how many times you click the button.

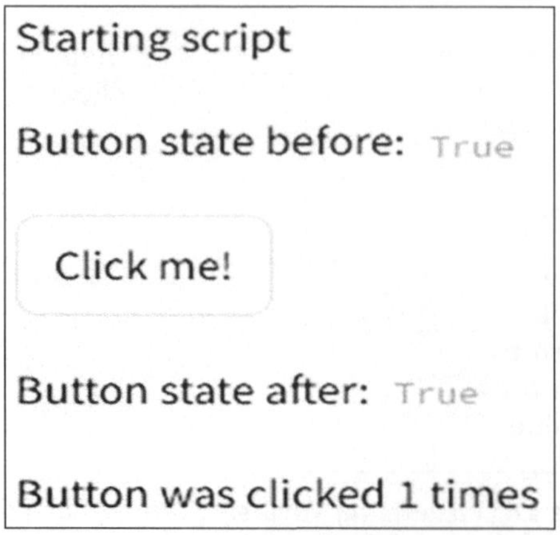

***Figure* 4.6:** *Button State after the Button is Clicked*

Understanding the Behavior of Nested Streamlit Buttons

The fact that Streamlit buttons return **True**, if the app reruns following a button click, but immediately return to **False**, leads to some unexpected behavior. Let us explore this by updating our previous script to nest another button within the existing one:

```
import streamlit as st

st.write("Starting script")

st.write("Button1 state before:", st.session_state.get("button1"))
st.write("Button2 state before:", st.session_state.get("button2"))

if st.button("Click me!", key="button1"):
    st.write("Button1 was clicked")
    st.write("Button1 state after:", st.session_state.button1)

    if st.button("Click me too!", key="button2"):
        st.write("Button2 was clicked")
        st.write("Button2 state after:", st.session_state.button2)
```

In this script, we have renamed the original button to **Button1**, and added a nested button, **Button2**, under it.

Before running the script, consider what you expect to happen when you click both buttons. We assume that when the app starts, we will see **Starting script** and **None** printed for both **Button1** and **Button2**.

What would happen if you clicked just **Button1**? Based on our previous discussion, we expect the app to reload, the state for **Button1** to change to **True** both, before and after. **Button1 was clicked** to be displayed, and **Button2** to become visible.

And what if you clicked **Button2**? Similar to **Button1**, we expect all the states to now be **True**, and **Button2 was clicked** to be displayed.

Let us see if this is what actually happens. Run the script using **streamlit run**, and click on the first button. This behaves as expected, as shown in *Figure 4.7*.

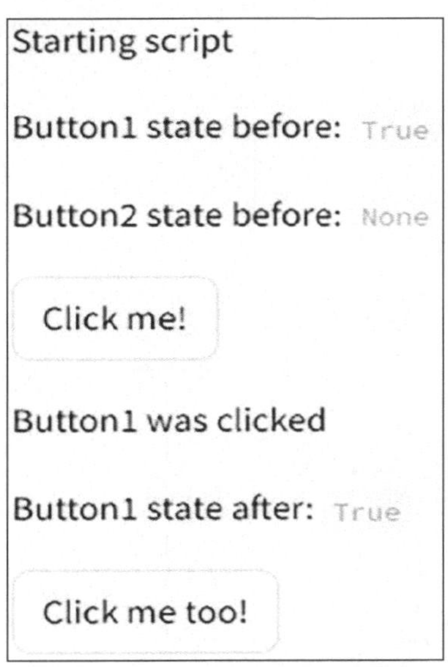

Figure 4.7: *On Clicking Button1*

Now click on the second button, **`Click me too!`** What do you see? Instead of **`Button2 was clicked`** being printed, we see that the state for **`Button1`** turns to **`False`**, while that for **`Button2`** is **`True`**, and **`Button2`** is no longer displayed, as shown in *Figure* 4.8. This is not an error. Click on the two buttons a few more times to confirm. Every time, you click the second button, the app will show this.

***Figure* 4.8:** *On Clicking Button2*

Why does this happen?

Remember that when a button is clicked, its state in the following app rerun is **`True`**, but immediately changes to **`False`** later. When the app reruns the second time, and we click on **`Button2`**, the state for **`Button1`** in the following rerun remains **`False`** as **`Button1`** was not clicked, but that for **`Button2`** changes to **`True`** as **`Button2`** was clicked. And since **`Button1`** is now **`False`**, the condition is not satisfied, and **`Button2`** is not displayed. Clicking on **`Button1`** now will take you back to the state shown in *Figure* 4.7. Following this logic, both **`Button1`** and **`Button2`** can never be **`True`** together, and the code nested under **`Button2`** will never be executed!

This can be visualized in the flowchart shown in *Figure* 4.9.

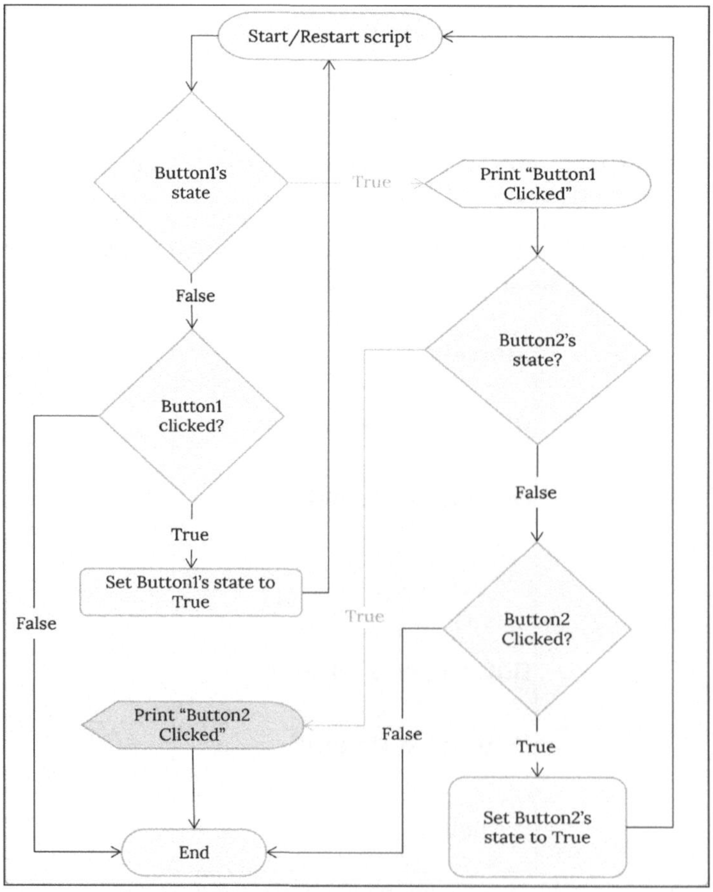

***Figure* 4.9:** *Flow When Using Nested Buttons*

As we can see, to print **`Button2 clicked`**, the states of both **`Button1`** and **`Button2`** need to be **`True`**. As seen previously, this can never happen, so **`Button2 clicked`** will never be printed.

We will discuss how to handle this behavior in a later chapter.

Understanding Streamlit's Client-Server Architecture

Let us revisit an issue we encountered earlier. Do you recall seeing the **`ModuleNotFoundError`** when we first deployed our Iris Analysis app? At that time, we explained that this error occurred because **seaborn** was installed in our local environment, but not in the environment where the Streamlit app was deployed.

The environment where the app is deployed is known as the Streamlit server. Streamlit apps operate on a client-server architecture. The Python source script that powers the app acts as the server, while the front end, which a user views through a browser, serves as the client.

When we execute **streamlit run**, the system where it is run creates a Streamlit server using Python. This system is also referred to as a host. When different users access the app's front end from their browsers, the client sends requests to the server. The server is responsible for performing all the computations requested by all the clients.

This architecture is illustrated in *Figure 4.10*.

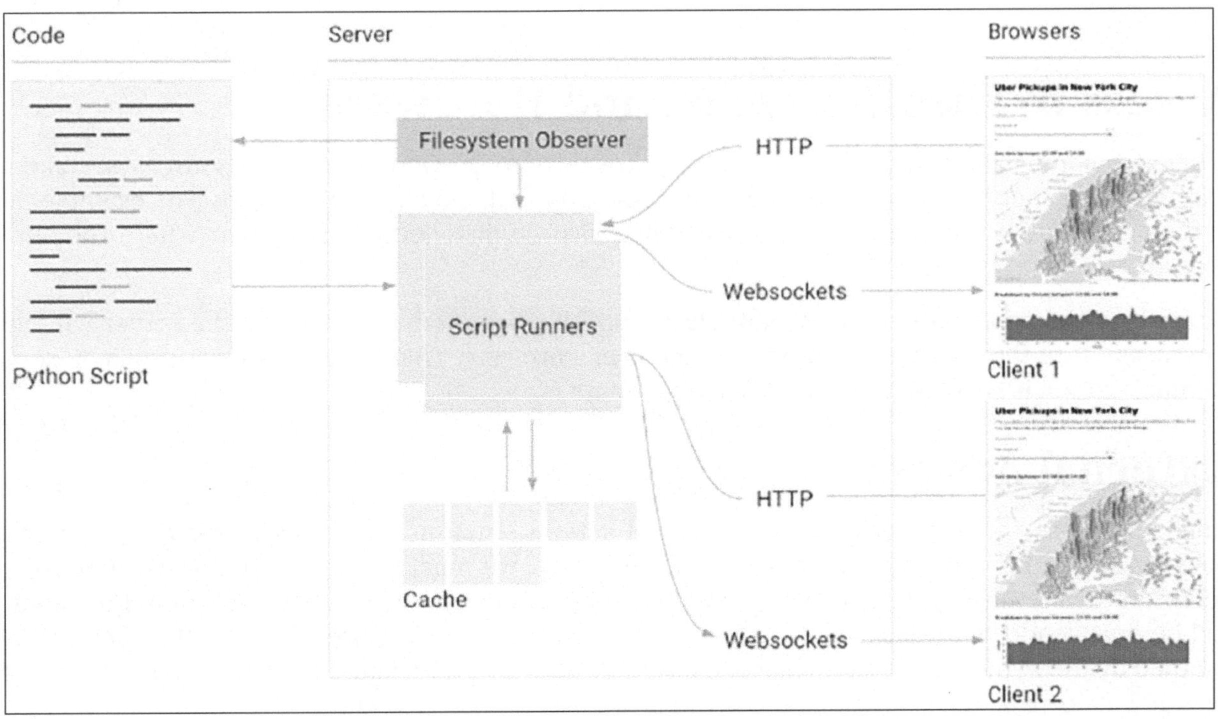

Figure 4.10: *Streamlit's Client-Server Architecture*[2]

When developing and running Streamlit apps locally, both the server and client operate on our local system. However, when we deploy Streamlit to a network, the server and clients run on separate machines.

[2] *https://towardsdatascience.com/coding-ml-tools-like-you-code-ml-models-ddba3357eace* (Accessed: 24 June 2024)

Influence of the Client-Server Architecture on Application Design

During the local development and running of Streamlit apps, both the **streamlit run** command and the browser operate on our local system. In this scenario, our local system serves as both the client and the server.

However, when we deploy Streamlit to a network, the **`streamlit run`** command operates only on the host system, while users access the app through browsers on their local systems. In this case, the server (host system) and clients (user systems) operate on different machines.

This architectural shift can lead to specific challenges, which we will discuss briefly in this section.

Server Capacity

The server must have sufficient computing power and storage resources to run the app and manage the resources for all users. For instance, if our app allows users to upload files, the server should have enough RAM to store all the files uploaded by users simultaneously.

Note: *Files uploaded to Streamlit apps are stored in the RAM, and not on the disk, and are accessible only while the user session is active.*[3] *Therefore, the server needs only enough RAM to store all uploads from simultaneous users.*

Access to Files, Software, and Hardware

When developing and running the app locally, it is easy to overlook that the resources we take for granted might not be available to users when the app is deployed to a network. For example, any Python packages or software the app uses must also be installed on the server where the app is hosted.

Similarly, if the app needs to use specific hardware (like speakers or cameras), the server will need to access those through the client, that is, the user's browser. Thankfully, most of this client-server communication is handled by Streamlit's components for us.

External Actions

Finally, suppose the app performs any external actions, such as running an external program or downloading a file from an external server; in that case, we must remember that these actions will occur on the server, not the user's client. For example, if our app downloads a file from the cloud, it will be downloaded on the server, and not directly accessible to the user through the client, unless handled by the Python script running on the server. Similarly, if the app opens a web browser for the user, it will do so on the server, and the browser will not be visible to the user.

Conclusion

In this chapter, we delved into the intricacies of Streamlit's flow, and its client-server architecture.

Through practical examples, we gained insights into the circumstances and mechanisms that trigger the reloading of Streamlit apps. We also examined the implications of such reloads on the development process, and the execution flow.

---

[3] *https://docs.streamlit.io/knowledge-base/using-streamlit/where-file-uploader-store-when-deleted* (Accessed: 23 June 2024)

Furthermore, we discussed the influence of Streamlit's client-server architecture on the design considerations necessary when deploying apps on networks.

The next chapter will focus on the strategies for preserving app data and state across app reloads. This knowledge will enable us to create a more seamless development flow, and enhance the user experience by increasing the speed of interaction.

Points to Remember

- Streamlit apps are Python scripts that execute from top to bottom[4].
- Whenever the script changes, Streamlit automatically reruns the script from top to bottom, and reloads the app.
- Each time a user alters the state of a widget, the script reruns, and the app reloads.
- Variables reset when a Streamlit app reloads.
- Buttons created using **`st.button`** do not retain their state. They return **`True`**, if the script reruns due to the user clicking on the button but immediately return to **`False`**[5].
- Nesting Streamlit buttons can make the code under the nested button unreachable.
- Streamlit operates on a client-server architecture.
- The server is the Python source script of the application.
- The client is the web browser that accesses the frontend of the Streamlit app.
- The server must have sufficient capacity to handle the computational and storage needs of all the users.
- Any Python packages or software used by the app must also be installed on the server where the app is hosted.
- If the app performs any external actions, like running an external program or downloading a file from an external server, these actions will occur on the server, not on the user's client.

Multiple Choice Questions

1. How does an app recognize changes to its source script when adding a new Streamlit widget?
   a. It does not. It simply reruns the entire script from top to bottom.
   b. It does not. We have to reload the app to reflect the new changes manually.
   c. It does not. We have to rerun the script from the terminal.
   d. It monitors the script's contents, and only reruns the following code with the changes made.
2. If the following script is run and the button is clicked twice, how many times would "**`Hello`**" be printed on the terminal?

```
import streamlit as st

print("Hello")

if st.button("Click me!"):
    print("Welcome")
```

[4] *https://docs.streamlit.io/get-started/fundamentals/summary* (Accessed: 20 June 2024)
[5] *https://docs.streamlit.io/develop/concepts/design/buttons* (Accessed: 23 June 2024)

   a. Once

   b. Twice

   c. Three times

   d. Four times

3. If the following script is run, and the button is clicked twice, how many times would "**Hello**" be printed in the app?

```
import streamlit as st

st.write("Hello")

if st.button("Click me!"):
    st.write("Welcome")
```

   a. Once

   b. Twice

   c. Three times

   d. Four times

4. What happens to a Python variable, once the Python script has finished execution?

   a. It is reset to its initial value.

   b. It is saved to the disk, and can be used later.

   c. It is saved to RAM, and can be used later.

   d. It is destroyed.

5. What is the state of a Streamlit button when the app is rerun after clicking on it?

   a. None

   b. True

   c. False

   d. Undefined

6. Where must any required packages be installed when a Streamlit app is hosted on a network?

   a. Client only

   b. Server only

   c. Both client and server

   d. None of the above

Answers

1. a
2. c
3. a
4. d

5. b
6. b

Questions

1. What output would you see printed on the terminal, if you ran the following app, and clicked the button once? Please explain the results.

```
import streamlit as st

print("Starting script")

if st.button("Click me!"):
    print("Button was clicked")
```

2. Could you briefly describe some consequences of reloading a Streamlit app when the source code or a widget state has been updated?
3. If the following script is run, and **`Button2`** is clicked twice, what will be the values of **`count1`** and **`count2`**? Please explain your answer.

```
import streamlit as st

count1 = count2 = 0

if st.button("Button1"):
    count1 += 1

    if st.button("Button2"):
        count2 += 1
```

4. Could you briefly describe some of the considerations to keep in mind regarding Streamlit's client-server architecture when hosting an app on a network?

Key Terms

- **Scope of a Python variable:** In Python, the scope of a variable refers to the context or region in which that variable is visible or accessible.
- **Client-Server Architecture:** In web development, the client-server architecture is a model that partitions tasks between providers of a resource or service, known as servers, and the service requesters, known as clients.[6]
- **Client:** A client is a computer (or a web browser) that sends a request for data or a service from the server.[6]
- **Server:** A server is a remote computer that provides the requested information or service to the client.[6]
- **Widget State:** In Streamlit, the state of a widget refers to its current condition or value, which can change based on user interaction.

[6] *https://www.geeksforgeeks.org/client-server-model/* (Accessed: 23 June 2024)

CHAPTER 5
Persisting Data and State Across App Reruns

Introduction

This chapter builds upon the previous one, addressing how to overcome script and app rerun challenges. We will explore a powerful feature provided by Streamlit: *Session State*.

In the previous chapter, we briefly introduced *Session State*. This chapter will delve deeper into its functionality, and learn how to utilize it effectively. We will apply *Session State* to implement the counter app discussed earlier successfully. Doing so will give you practical experience in solving real-world problems using *Session State*, enhancing the learning process.

Lastly, we will discuss some of *Session State*'s limitations and potential pitfalls.

Structure

In this chapter, we will discuss the following topics:

- Introduction to Session State
- Using Session State
- Using Session State to Fix the Button-Click Counter App
- Caveats and Limitations of Session State

Introduction to Session State

Before delving into the specifics of *Session State*, let us briefly define what a *session* entails. In the context of Streamlit, a *session* corresponds to a user's interaction with a Streamlit app within a browser tab. A fresh session is created each time a user opens the app in a new tab. This session persists as long as the tab remains open, and the app's frontend communicates with the backend.

The *session state* represents the *session* itself, capturing all widgets' values and associated parameters. Like the *session*, the *session state* remains persistent as long as the tab remains open and the app's frontend and backend stay connected. This means that the *session state* can store information across app reruns as long as the tab is not closed or refreshed. However, refreshing the tab resets the *session state*, causing all stored data to be lost.

Streamlit's *Session State* provides a convenient dictionary-like interface. You can save and modify information between script runs using this interface. For example, in a previous chapter, we accessed the button's value from the session state using **`st.session_state.button`** and **`st.session_state["button"]`**.

Using Session State

As previously mentioned, Session State in Streamlit behaves like a Python dictionary. So, you can add, update, and delete keys from it as you would with a Python dictionary. However, there are a few caveats that we will discuss now.

Adding and Deleting Keys

As previously mentioned, *Session State* in Streamlit behaves like a Python dictionary. This means that we can store values in *Session State* by assigning them to keys. Here are the two ways to do it:

- **Using dictionary-like key-value syntax: `st.session_state["key"] = "value"`**
- **Using attribute-based syntax: `st.session_state.key = "value"`**

Once a value is stored in **Session State**, you can retrieve it using the same key-based or attribute-based syntax, as follows:

```
st.write(st.session_state["key"])
```

or

```
st.write(st.session_state.key)
```

To explore this interactively, let us create a new Python script, and add the following lines:

```
import streamlit as st

st.session_state["key1"] = "This works!"
st.session_state.key2 = "This also works!"

st.write(st.session_state["key1"])
st.write(st.session_state.key2)
```

Save and run this script using **`streamlit run`**. The app will open in a new browser window, showing the messages:

```
This works!
This also works!
```

Since **Session State** is essentially a dictionary, you can also inspect all the key-value pairs stored in it. Add the following line to the end of the script, and check the app once it reloads:

```
st.write(st.session_state)
```

The app should now display the stored values, as shown in *Figure* 5.1, allowing you to explore and manage your **Session State** effectively.

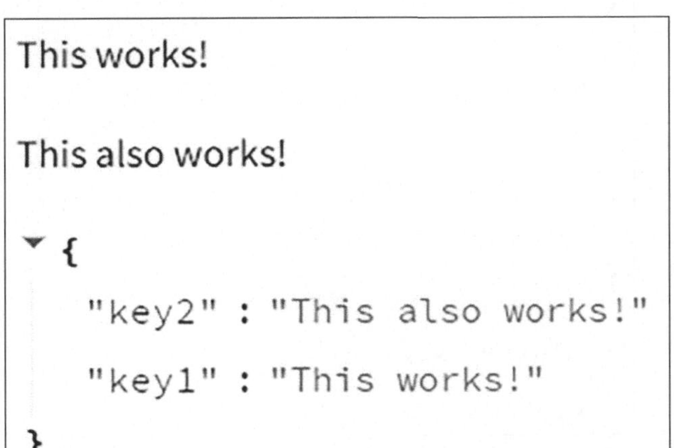

Figure 5.1: *Writing to and Reading from Session State*

Deleting key-value pairs in **Session State** works similarly to how it works with a Python dictionary. To remove a specific key from **Session State**, use **`del st.session_state.key`** or **`del st.session_state["key"]`**. If you want to delete all the keys, iterate over them and delete each one, as follows by adding the following lines to our script, and rerunning the app:

```
# Adding a new key-value pair
st.write("Adding `key3`")
st.session_state.key3 = "value"
st.write(st.session_state)

# Deleting `key3`

st.write("Deleting `key3`")
del st.session_state.key3
st.write(st.session_state)

# Deleting all keys

st.write("Deleting all keys")
for key in st.session_state.keys():
    del st.session_state[key]
st.write(st.session_state)
```

The app should now look as shown in *Figure* 5.2.

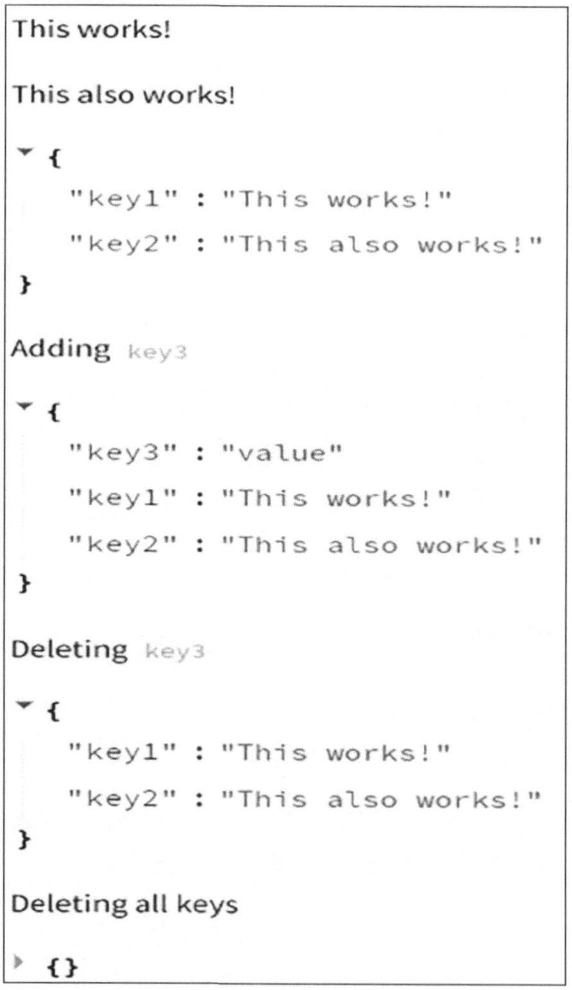

Figure 5.2: *Deleting Keys from Session State*

Automatic Key Creation

In the previous chapter, we explored how Session State allows us to retrieve the state of widgets. You might observe that we did not explicitly assign the button's value to **Session State**. This is because Streamlit automatically adds any widget with a key to the **Session State.**

Let us see this in action. Create a new script with the following snippet:

```
import streamlit as st

st.write(st.session_state)

st.text_input("Enter your name", key="name")
st.write(st.session_state)
```

Now, run this script using **streamlit run**. The resultant app should look as shown in *Figure* 5.3.

***Figure* 5.3:** *Automatic Creation of a Session State Key*

You will notice that the name, '**key**' does not appear when the **Session State** is printed before the text box, but only after it. This is because once a widget with a key is encountered, Streamlit automatically creates a key-value pair for it in **Session State.**

Once you enter your name in the text box, the app will update, and the **Session State** will now include the name key with its corresponding value. It should now look like as shown *in Figure* 5.4.

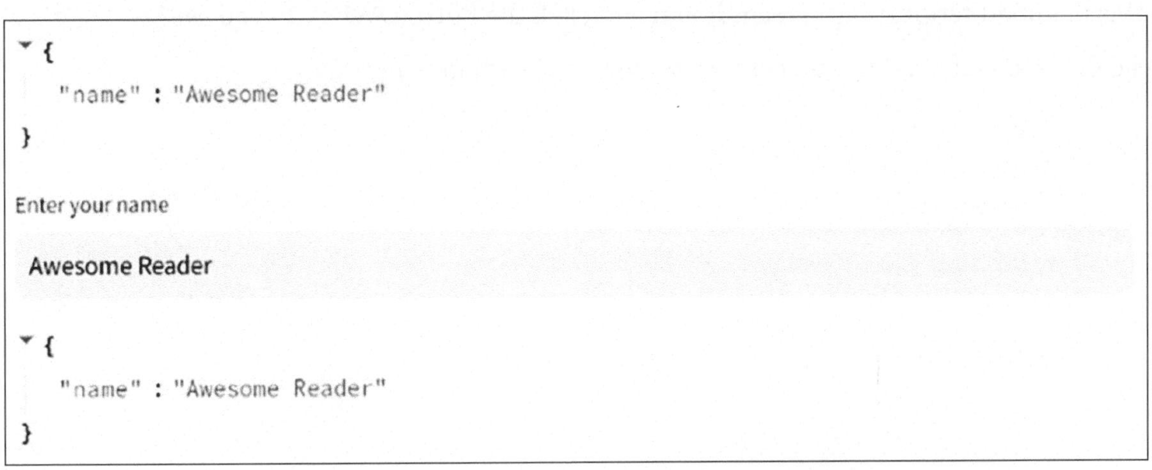

***Figure* 5.4:** *Session State after the Name is Entered*

The name key and its value are available before the text box, because the **Session State** persists after the app is rerun. Since the automatic app rerun was triggered by our entering a value in the text box with the key **name**, the **Session State** in the next run has this value.

Using Session State to Fix the Button-Click Counter App

In *Chapter 4*, *Exploring Streamlit's Flow and Architecture*, we encountered an issue with the **count** variable in our button-click counter app. Specifically, the count was reset to zero whenever the app was rerun by clicking the button. Here is the original script for reference:

```
import streamlit as st

st.write("Starting script")

count = 0

if st.button("Click me!"):
    count += 1
    st.write(f"Button was clicked {count} times")
```

Now that we understand how **Session State** can persist data across reruns, let us use it to fix the counter. Instead of relying on the **count** variable, we will create a new **Session State** key to hold the counts: **st.session_state["count"]**.

To achieve this, follow the following steps:

1. Remove the **count = 0** line as we do not want to reset the count to zero, every time the app reruns.
2. Replace all other instances of the **count** variable with **st.session_state.count**.

The updated script should now look like this:

```
import streamlit as st

st.write("Starting script")

if st.button("Click me!"):
    st.session_state["count"] += 1
    st.write(f"Button was clicked {st.session_state.count} times")
```

Run this modified script using **streamlit run** and click the button. What do you see?

Instead of the counter value, you get a **KeyError**, as shown in *Figure* 5.5.

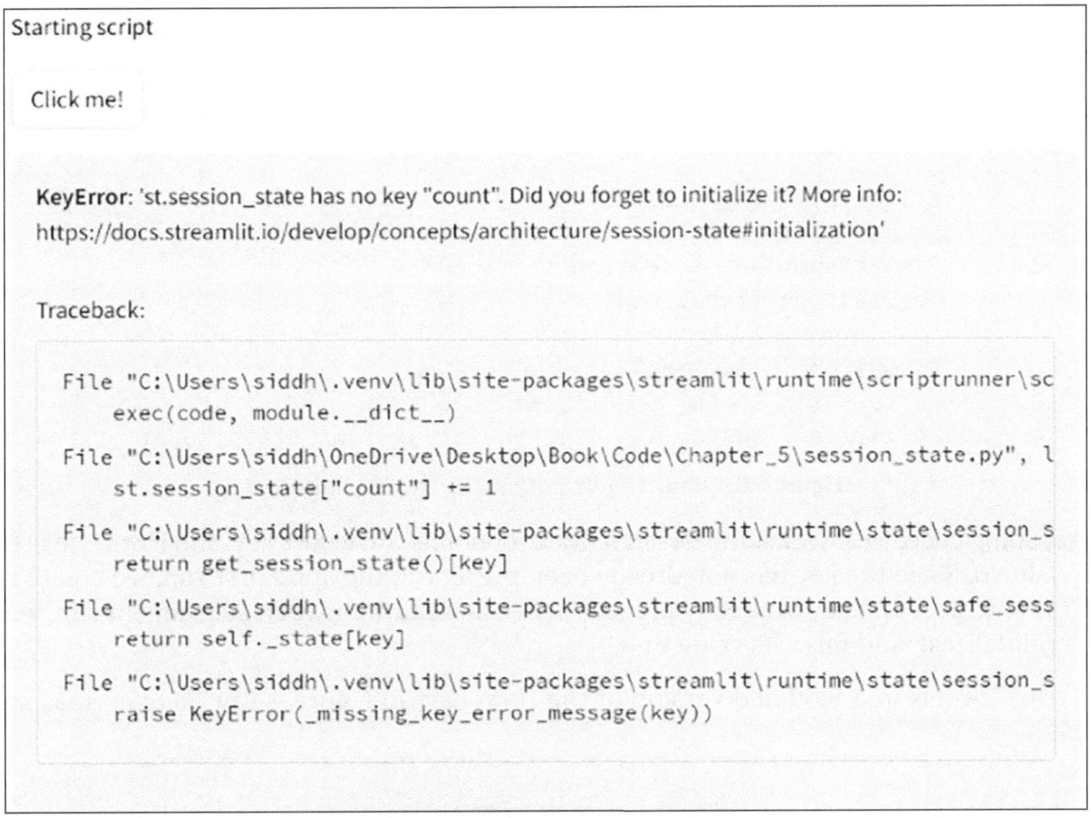

Figure 5.5: *KeyError on Clicking the Button*

Why is this the case?

The line **`st.session_state["count"] += 1`** takes the existing value of **`count`** and increments it by one (it is the same as **`st.session_state["count"] = st.session_state["count"] + 1`**). However, we have not explicitly initialized the **`count`** key anywhere in the code. As a result, Streamlit throws a **`KeyError`** because it cannot find an existing value for the **`count`** key in **Session State**.

How do we fix this?

Similar to how we initialized the **`count`** variable to 0 in the previous chapter, we can do the same for the **count** key in **Session State**. To do this, add the **`st.session_state.count = 0`** line in the code, just above the `Click Me!` button as shown:

```
import streamlit as st

st.write("Starting script")

st.session_state.count = 0

if st.button("Click me!"):
    st.session_state["count"] += 1
    st.write(f"Button was clicked {st.session_state.count} times")
```

Once the app automatically reruns following the change in the source code, click on the button a few times. Instead of the error, you will see that the counter again maxes out at 1, like it was in the previous chapter.

This is because, although we added **`st.session_state.count = 0`** to initialize the **`count`** key, the first time the app is run, this line will be run every time the script reloads, and the **`count`** value will reset to 0. This is similar to our issue with the **`count`** variable in Chapter 4, *Exploring Streamlit's Flow and Architecture*.

To fix this, we have to initialize the **count** key only if it does not already exist in **Session State**. We can do this by adding a condition before initializing the key, as shown in *Figure 5.6*.

```
import streamlit as st

st.write("Starting script")

if "count" not in st.session_state:
    st.session_state.count = 0

if st.button("Click me!"):
    st.session_state["count"] += 1
    st.write(f"Button was clicked {st.session_state.count} times")
```

Figure 5.6: *Conditionally Initializing Session State Key*

In the preceding code, we check if the **Session State** contains the **count** key, and if not, we create one with the value 0. Since the key has not already been present in the app's first run, we create it with a value of 0. Now, since the key is already present in **Session State** for each subsequent run, we do not need to reinitialize it, and reset its value to 0.

We can visualize this in a modified version of the flowchart in *Figure 4.4* in *Chapter 4*, as shown in *Figure 5.7*.

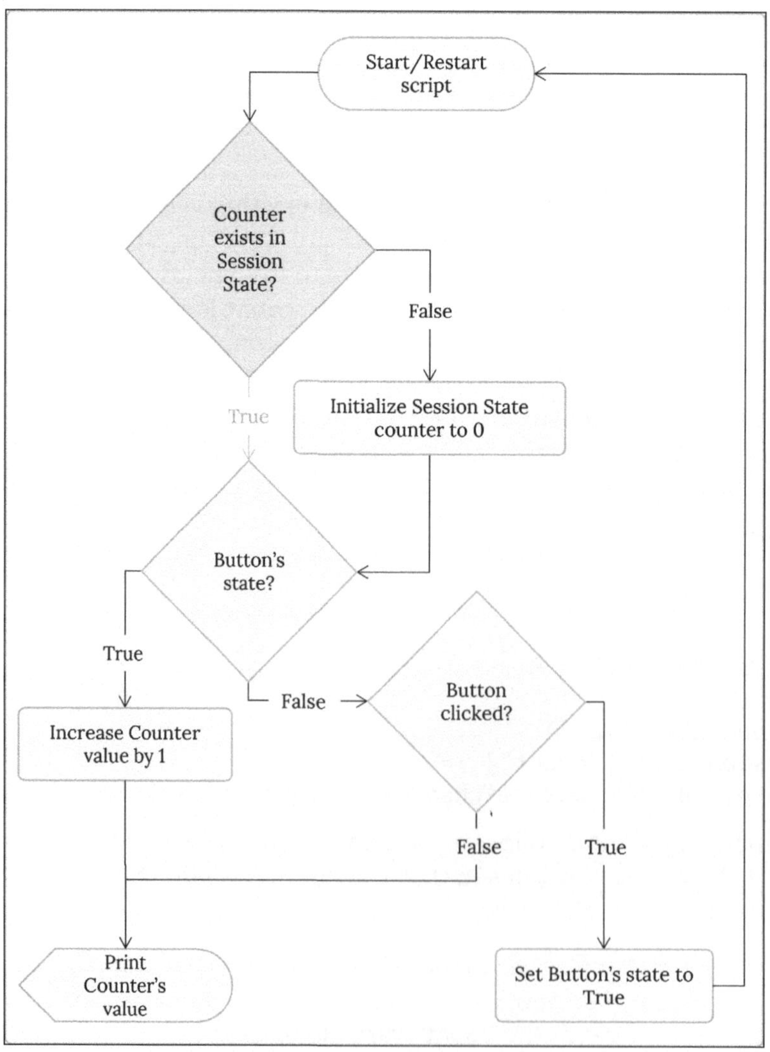

Figure 5.7: *Counter Logic Using Session State*

The only difference is that now we can skip initializing the counter to 0 for each rerun, enabling an accurate count, instead of maxing out at 1.

When rerunning the app, the count is displayed correctly when the button is clicked multiple times, as shown in *Figure* 5.8.

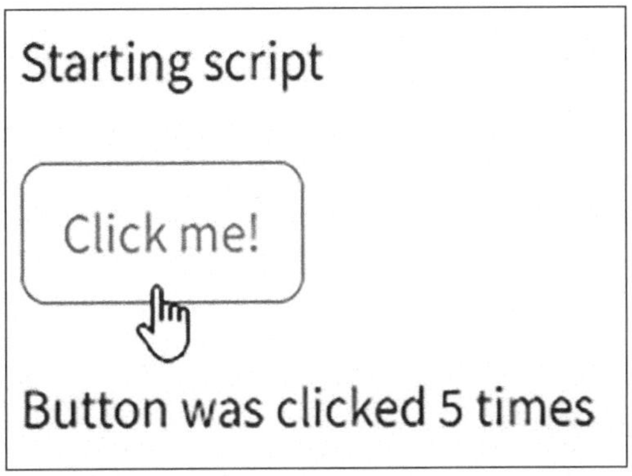

***Figure* 5.8:** *Counter Working Correctly*

Caveats and Limitations of Session State

While Session State is a powerful tool for managing the state of Streamlit widgets and apps, it does have some limitations. Let us discuss a few of them.

Updating the Value of a Widget

Session State cannot be used to update the value of a widget after it has been created.

For reference, let us revisit the example shown in *Figure* 5.3, where we used **Session State** to display the value of a widget. The script is provided again as follows:

```
import streamlit as st

st.write(st.session_state)

st.text_input("Enter your name", key="name")
st.write(st.session_state)
```

Now, we know that **Session State** is just a dictionary, so we can update the values of its keys as well. Let us try doing this in the preceding script by adding a key-value pair for the name key in Session State, and updating it before and after the widget. The updated script is shown as follows:

```
import streamlit as st

st.write("Initial `name`: ", st.session_state.get("name"))

if "name" not in st.session_state:
    st.session_state.name = "Awesome Reader"

st.write("`name` after adding key:", st.session_state.name)

st.session_state.name = "Another Awesome Reader"
st.write("`name` after updating before widget: ", st.session_state.name)

st.text_input("Enter your name", key="name")
st.write("`name` after widget: ", st.session_state.name)
```

```
st.session_state.name = "Still Another Awesome Reader"
st.write("`name` after updating after widget: ", st.session_state.name)
```

Before running this, let us predict the output for each **st.write** statement. Take a minute to go through the code, and write down your answers. Do they look like the ones shown as follows?

```
Initial name: None
name after adding key: Awesome Reader
name after updating before widget: Another Awesome Reader
name after widget: Another Awesome Reader
name after updating after widget: Still Another Awesome Reader
```

Run the script using **streamlit run** to see if your predictions are correct. The app should resemble the one shown in *Figure 5.9*.

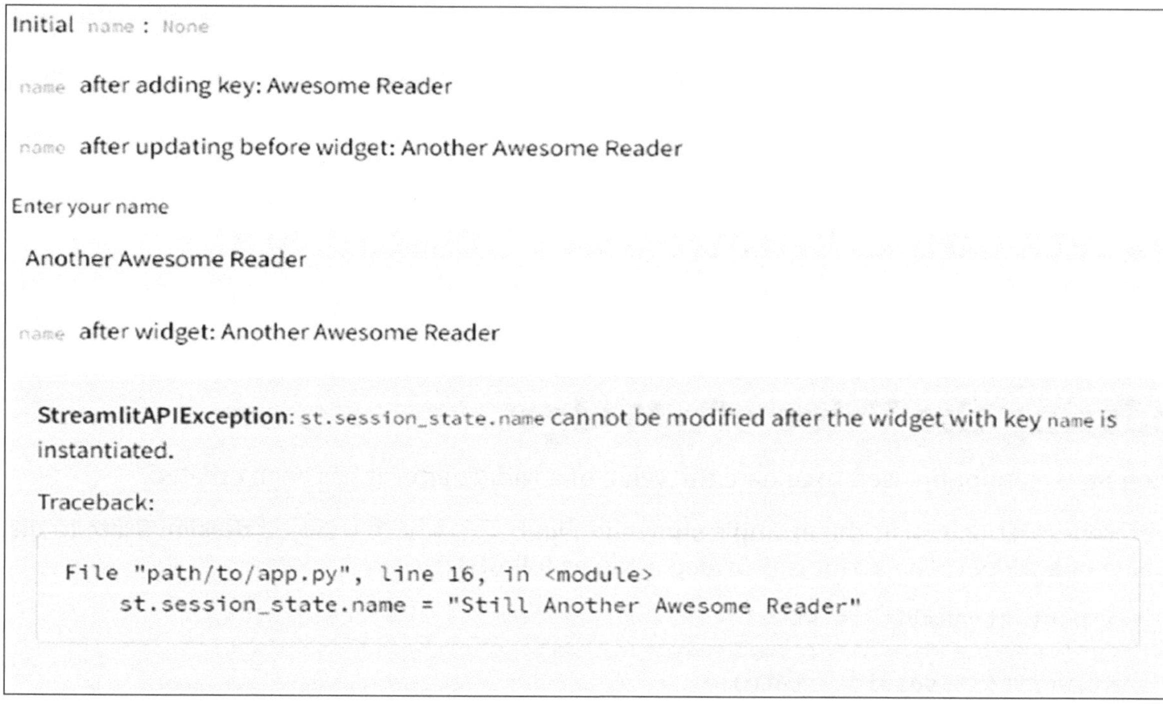

Figure 5.9: *Updating the Value of a Widget Using Session State*

Do not worry if you got the last one wrong. This is not you, but a limitation of Streamlit's **Session State**. As demonstrated in the code, you can update the value of a **Session State** key multiple times – but only if a widget with the same key has not been created yet. Once such a widget exists, attempting to update the key using Session State will result in a **StreamlitAPIException**.

Session State and Default Widget Values

In the previous code, what would happen if we passed a default value to the **text_input** using the **value** parameter, as shown in the following code?

```
import streamlit as st

st.write("Initial `name`: ", st.session_state.get("name"))

if "name" not in st.session_state:
    st.session_state.name = "Awesome Reader"

st.write("`name` after adding key:", st.session_state.name)
```

```
st.session_state.name = "Another Awesome Reader"
st.write("`name` after updating before widget: ", st.session_state.name)

st.text_input("Enter your name", key="name", value="John Doe")
st.write("`name` after widget: ", st.session_state.name)

st.session_state.name = "Still Another Awesome Reader"
st.write("`name` after updating after widget: ", st.session_state.name)
```

Unless the user changes it, we would assume that the text input now shows this default value, `John Doe`.

However, when you restart the app (by shutting down the previous execution by pressing *Ctrl/Cmd* + C in the terminal where it was run, and rerunning **streamlit run**), you will notice a yellow warning, as shown in *Figure* 5.10.

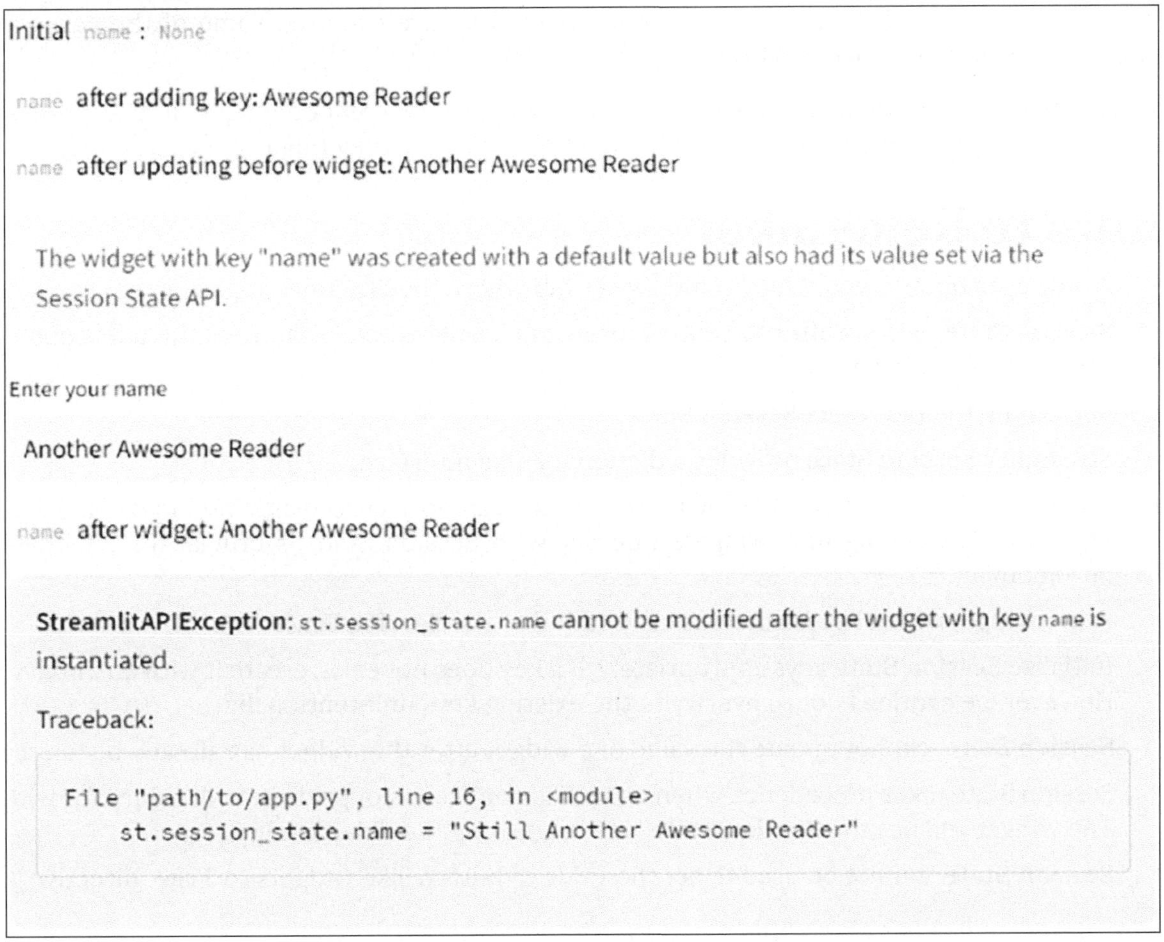

Figure 5.10: *Over Session State Overriding Widget's Default Value*

The warning indicates that the widget with the key `name` was created with a default value, but also has its value set via Session State. You can also notice that the text box takes the value set via **Session State**, `Another Awesome Reader`, not its default value, `John Doe`.

Whenever you set a widget's value using **Session State** and default, Streamlit will display the warning, but only on the first run (you can verify this by rerunning the app–the warning will disappear), and ignore the default value in favor of the one set by **Session State**.

Session State and Button-Like Widgets

Session State cannot be used to set the value of widgets like `st.button`, `st.download_button`, and `st.file_uploader` to `True` directly. These widgets are inherently Boolean (by default, they start as `False`), and their `True` states are ephemeral, lasting only for one single app run.[1] Attempting to set their value to `True` using **Session State** will result in a `StreamlitAPIException`.

This limitation means that **Session State** alone cannot address the issue with nested buttons we discussed in Chapter 4, *Exploring Streamlit's Flow and Architecture*. In a later chapter, we will explore advanced features for more complex scenarios involving button interactions.

Conclusion

In this chapter, we have delved into **Session State**, learned how to use it effectively, and applied it to enhance our button-click counter app. Additionally, we have explored some of the caveats and limitations associated with **Session State**.

In the next chapter, we will dive into more Streamlit widgets and components, including third-party widgets developed by the Streamlit community, and observe how they function in a live app.

Points to Remember

- A new `session` is created for each browser tab where the Streamlit app is open.
- **Session State** persists after the app is rerun, and remains valid as long as the tab is open, and the app's frontend and backend are connected.
- Refreshing the tab resets **Session State**.
- Streamlit's **Session State** provides a dictionary-like interface.
- Widgets in Streamlit have their own state, which can be accessed and modified using **Session State**. Understanding how widgets interact with Session State is crucial for effective app development.
- Every widget with a key is automatically added to the **Session State**.
- Initialize **Session State** keys appropriately. If a key does not exist, create it with an initial value. However, be cautious not to overwrite the existing keys unintentionally.
- **Session State** cannot update the value of a widget after the widget has already been created.
- Session State takes precedence when using Session State alongside default values for widgets. The widget will use the **Session State** value, ignoring the default value.
- **Session State** cannot be used to set the value of button-like widgets to **True** directly.

Multiple Choice Questions

1. If two users open a Streamlit App in three tabs each, how many **sessions** have been created for the app?
   a. One
   b. Two
   c. Three
   d. Six

[1] *https://docs.streamlit.io/develop/api-reference/caching-and-state/st.session_state#caveats-and-limitations* (Accessed: 30 June 2024)

2. What Python datatype does Session State's structure look like?
    a. Set
    b. List
    c. Dictionary
    d. Dataframe
3. How can you reset the Session State? Choose all the correct options.
    a. Rerunning the app
    b. Refreshing the tab
    c. Clearing the cache
    d. Using **del** to delete the **Session State** keys
4. Which of the following is **True** about **Session State**:
    a. A **Session State key** can be updated anywhere in the code, as long as it is not the **key** of a widget.
    b. A **Session State key,** which is also the **key** of a widget, can only be updated once the widget has been created.
    c. **Session State** cannot be used to set the value of a Streamlit button to **False.**
    d. Using both **Session State** and **default** value to set the value of a widget leads to an error.
5. What will be the output of the following code?

```
import streamlit as st

st.session_state.number = 12

number = st.number_input("Enter a number", key="number", value=42)

st.write(st.session_state.number)
```

    a. StreamlitAPIException
    b. 12
    c. 42
    d. Depends on the user input

Answers

1. d
2. c
3. a, b, c
4. a
5. b

Questions

1. What is a **session**, and what is a **Session State**? How can you reset **Session State**?
2. How can you read, write, delete, and update **Session State** key-value pairs?

Key Terms

- **Session:** A single instance of viewing an app. Each tab with the app open has its own **session.**
- **Session State:** A **Session State** is a representation of the session. All the values of widgets and parameters of a **session** are captured in its state.

Chapter 6
Exploring Streamlit's Page Elements

Introduction

Page elements, such as widgets and components, form the foundation of a Streamlit app. In this chapter, we explore some of the most frequently used elements provided by Streamlit.

While this list is not exhaustive, it covers the essential widgets and their parameters. Due to the sheer number of elements and their various usage methods, a comprehensive discussion would require an entire book.

We will focus on the most commonly used widgets and demonstrate how to use them in basic examples based on Streamlit version 1.36.0.

For the most up-to-date information, including function signatures, parameters, and advanced usage examples, please consult the official Streamlit documentation at *https://docs.streamlit.io/develop/api-reference*.

Structure

In this chapter, we will discuss the following topics:

- Recap of Previously Seen Elements
- Exploring Additional Official Streamlit Elements
    - Formatted Text Elements
    - Data Elements
    - Chart Elements
    - Input Widgets
    - Media Elements
    - Layout Elements
    - Status Elements

Recap of Previously Seen Elements

Before we delve into new elements, let us review the ones we have encountered in previous chapters.

- `header`: Displays text in header formatting.
- `text_input`: Presents a single-line text-input widget.
- `number_input`: Shows a numeric input widget.
- `selectbox`: Provides a dropdown list for selecting an option.

- **write**: The write element dynamically generates output widgets based on the input data type. It can also accept multiple input arguments, and display them.
- **button**: Renders a button.
- **scatter_chart**: Displays an interactive scatter plot chart.

To see all the elements in action, create a script as follows. When you run it using **streamlit run**, you will see an app similar to *Figure 6.1*.

```
import numpy as np
import pandas as pd
import streamlit as st

st.title("Quick Widget Recap")

st.header("Inputs", divider=True)

name = st.text_input(
    "Enter your name",
    placeholder="Type here...",
)

number = st.number_input(
    "Enter a number",
    min_value=20,
    max_value=60,
)

animal = st.selectbox(
    "Pick an animal",
    options=["🐶 Dog", "🐱 Cat", "🐰 Rabbit"],
)

show_chart = st.button("Show chart")

st.header("Outputs", divider=True)

st.write(f"Hello, _{name}_ :wave:")
st.write(f"Showing __{number}__ points")

if show_chart:
    chart_data = pd.DataFrame(
        np.random.randn(number, 4),
        columns=["a", "b", "c", "d"],
    )

    st.scatter_chart(chart_data)
```

The script elements correspond to specific app elements for easy reference.

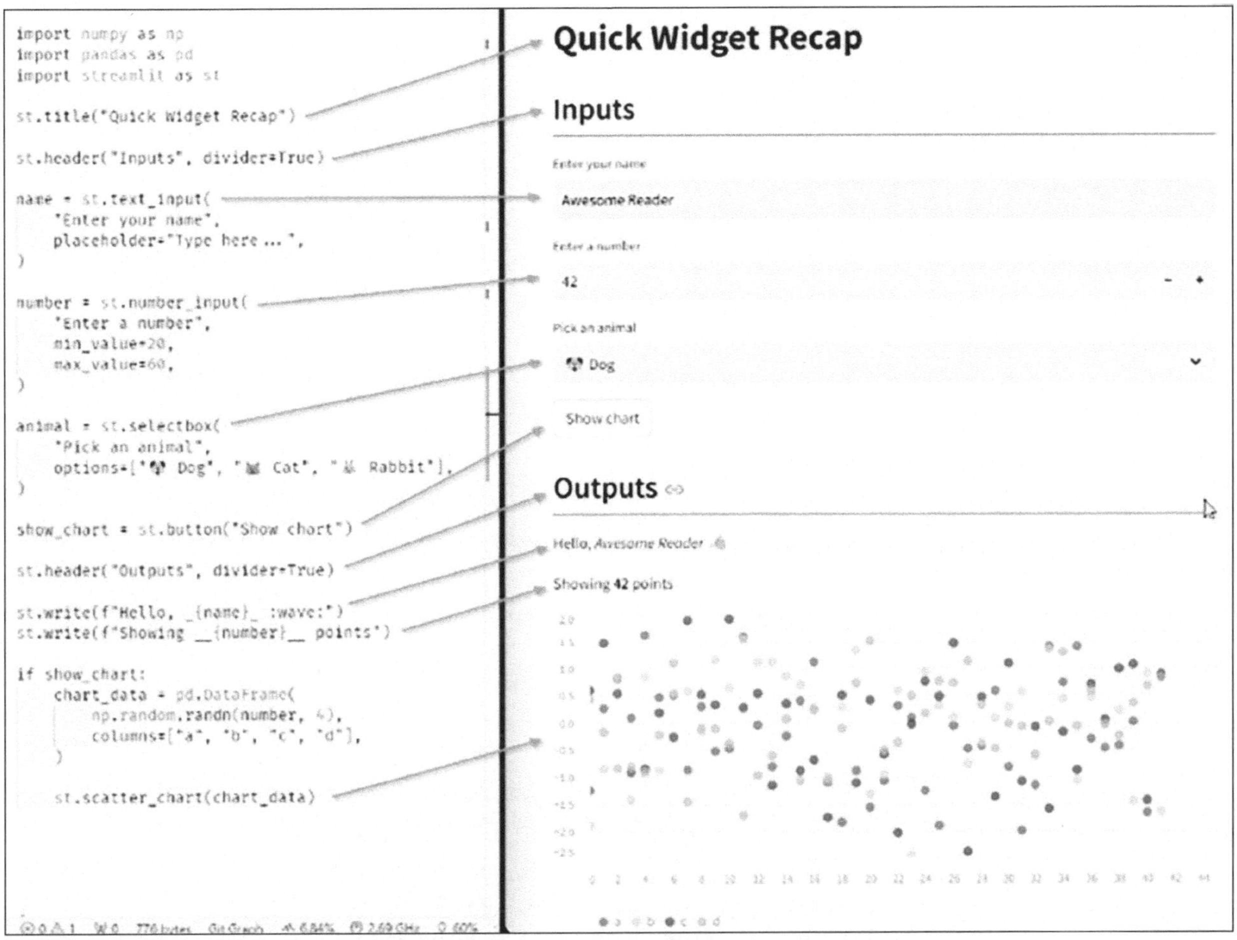

***Figure 6.1:** Recap of Previously Seen Widgets*

Click on the **`Show Chart`** button, and then update the value of any widget. Notice that the scatter plot disappears. Why? When the app reruns, the button's state resets to **`False`**. Since the condition is not satisfied, the chart is not displayed.

- **`session_state`**: It is used to persist data, and the state across app reruns as well as can address the issue of the chart disappearing when an input is changed.

Follow these steps:

1. Initialize a **`button_clicked`** session state variable.
2. Set **`button_clicked`** to **`True`** when the **`Show Chart`** button is clicked.
3. Check the value of **`button_clicked`** to show the chart.

The modified script is shown in *Figure 6.2*.

```python
import numpy as np
import pandas as pd
import streamlit as st

st.title("Quick Widget Recap")

if "button_clicked" not in st.session_state:
    st.session_state.button_clicked = False

st.header("Inputs", divider=True)

name = st.text_input(
    "Enter your name",
    placeholder="Type here ... ",
)

number = st.number_input(
    "Enter a number",
    min_value=20,
    max_value=60,
)

animal = st.selectbox(
    "Pick an animal",
    options=["🐶 Dog", "🐱 Cat", "🐰 Rabbit"],
)

if st.button("Show chart"):
    st.session_state.button_clicked = True

st.header("Outputs", divider=True)

st.write(f"Hello, _{name}_ :wave:")
st.write(f"Showing __{number}__ points")

if st.session_state.button_clicked:
    chart_data = pd.DataFrame(
        np.random.randn(number, 4),
        columns=["a", "b", "c", "d"],
    )

    st.scatter_chart(chart_data)
```

Figure 6.2: *Adding Session State*

By using **session_state.button_clicked**, we ensure that the chart remains displayed even after input changes. The condition remains satisfied because the value of **button_clicked** persists across app reruns.

Exploring Additional Official Streamlit Elements

Now that we are more familiar with the elements we have already covered in this book, let us delve into some additional official Streamlit components, we can use in our apps.

Formatted Text Elements

Like the **title** and **header** elements discussed earlier, Streamlit provides dedicated components for displaying text in various formats, including **subheaders**, **captions**, **code snippets**, **Markdown**, **LaTeX**, and **plaintext**. The following *Figure 6.3* showcases these text elements.

- **echo:** This unique element prints code to the app, and executes it! We will use **echo** frequently in this book to demonstrate code snippets, and their corresponding output.

- **`chat_message`:** This widget displays a text output widget in chat format. It is handy for chatbot apps, where user input and bot responses are presented in a conversational style.

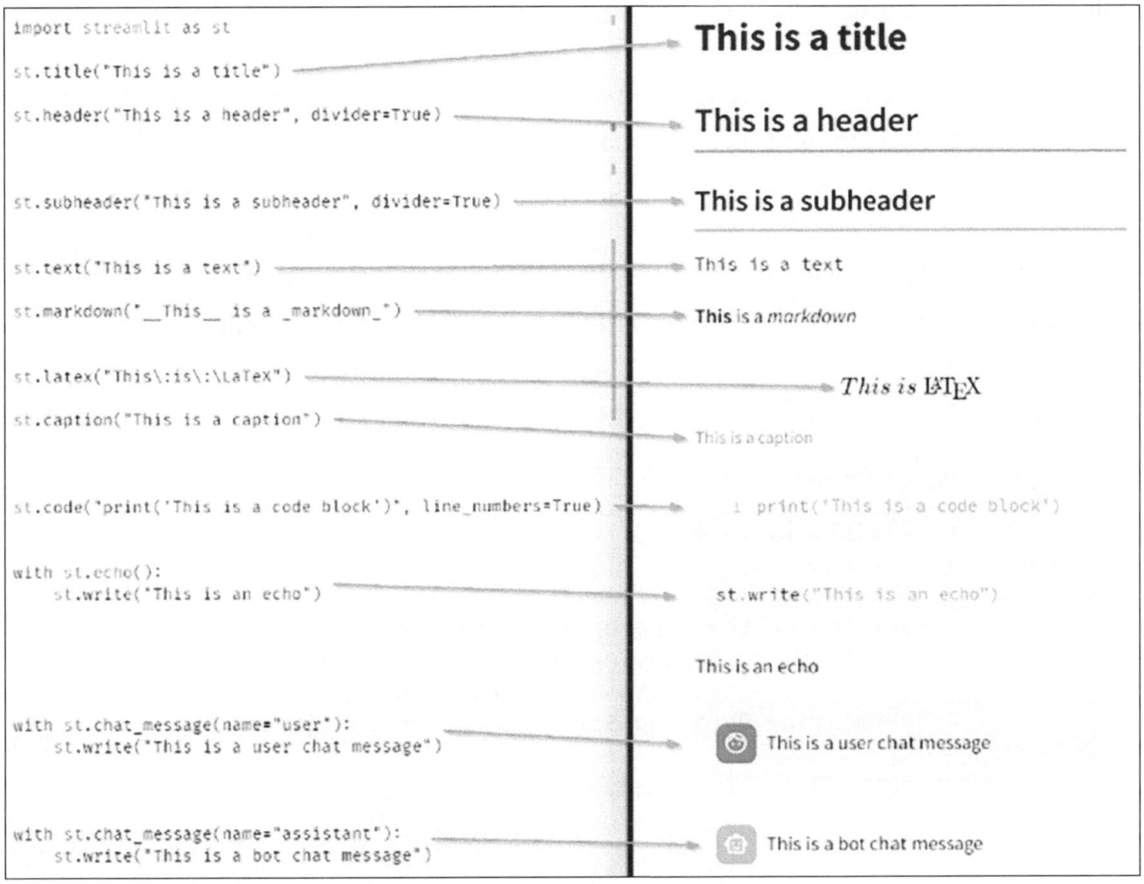

Figure 6.3: *Formatted Text Elements*

- **`write_stream`**: It allows us to stream output to the app from a generator, iterable, or stream-like sequence.[1] It is commonly used with **`chat_message`** in chat apps, where streaming output (such as from OpenAI or LangChain Streams) can create a typewriter effect.

  To witness this in action, run the following script as a Streamlit app:

```
from time import sleep

import streamlit as st


def number_stream():
    for i in range(10):
        yield i
        sleep(0.5)

def text_stream():
    for i in range(10):
        yield str(i) + " "
        sleep(0.5)


st.write_stream(number_stream)
st.write_stream(text_stream)
```

[1] *https://docs.streamlit.io/develop/api-reference/write-magic/st.write_stream* (Accessed: 7 July 2024)

Data Elements

Streamlit provides various data elements to visualize data in different formats. In this section, we will cover some of these elements.

- **metric**: Displays a value in a large, bold font, optionally indicating how it has changed.[2]
- **table**: Renders a dataframe as a static table.
- **dataframe**: Presents a dataframe as an interactive table, similar to the **iris_df** table we encountered in *Chapter 3, Creating and Deploying Your First Streamlit App*.
- **data_editor**: Behaves as both an input and output widget, displaying an editable table.

To observe these elements' behavior, run the following script as a Streamlit app.

```
import pandas as pd
import streamlit as st

df = pd.DataFrame(
    {
        "Ch. #": [1, 2, 3, 4, 5],
        "Title": [
            "Introduction to Streamlit",
            "Setting up the Development Environment",
            "Creating and Deploying Your First Streamlit App",
            "Exploring Streamlit's Flow and Architecture",
            "Persisting Data and State Using Session State",
        ],
        "Rating": [3, 3, 3, 3, 3],
    },
)

st.write("This is a static table")
st.table(df)

st.write("This is an interactive table")
st.dataframe(df)

st.write("This is an editable table")
edited_df = st.data_editor(df)

st.write(
    f"Highest rated chapter: __{edited_df['Title'][edited_df['Rating'].
idxmax()]}__"
)

st.metric(
    "__Average Rating__",
    edited_df["Rating"].mean(),
    edited_df["Rating"].mean() - df["Rating"].mean(),
)
```

The resulting app is shown in the following *Figure* 6.4:

[2] *https://docs.streamlit.io/develop/api-reference/data/st.metric* (Accessed: 7 July 2024)

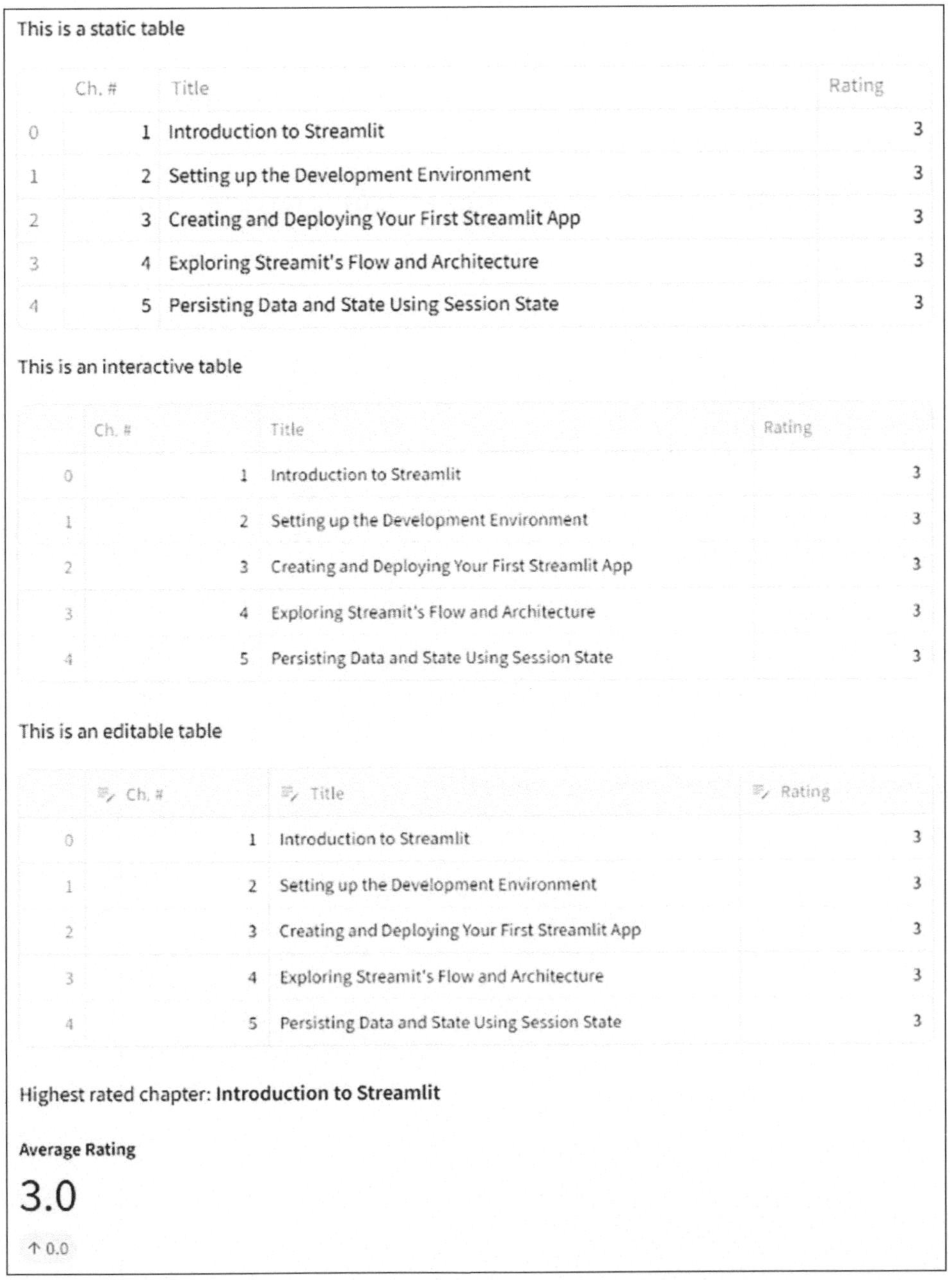

Figure 6.4: *Data Elements*

Try changing a chapter's rating in the resulting app, and observe how the `Highest rated chapter` and `Average Rating` values adjust. Note that any changes to the editable table do not affect the original dataframe or other tables.

Chart Elements

In addition to the `scatter_chart` element we have already encountered, Streamlit provides several other charting elements. These elements allow you to render simple charts directly. Here are some of them:

- `area_chart`: Displays an area chart.
- `bar_chart`: Renders a bar chart.
- `line_chart`: Shows a line chart.
- `map`: Displays a map.

To observe these elements in action, run the following script using **streamlit run**.

```
import numpy as np
import pandas as pd
import streamlit as st

chart_data = pd.DataFrame(np.random.randn(50, 2), columns=["LAT", "LON"])

lcol, rcol = st.columns(2)

lcol.write("Scatter plot")
lcol.scatter_chart(chart_data)

rcol.write("Area chart")
rcol.area_chart(chart_data)

lcol.write("Bar chart")
lcol.bar_chart(chart_data)

rcol.write("Map")
rcol.map(chart_data + [22, 79])
```

Note: *The* **`columns`** *layout element (used here) will be covered later in this chapter. It is included to fit all the charts on the same page.*

The resulting app is shown in the following *Figure* 6.5.

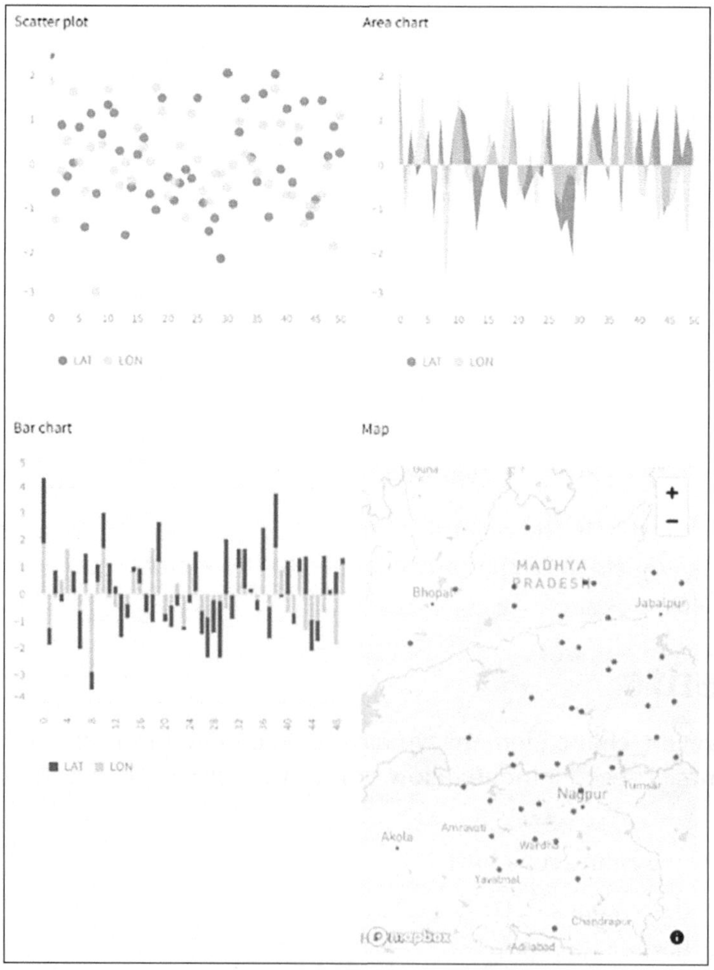

Figure 6.5: *Chart Elements*

Streamlit supports libraries like **matplotlib**, **Altair**, **Vega-Lite**, **Plotly**, **Bokeh**, **PyDeck**, and ***GraphViz*** for more advanced charting. These elements take plot objects from their respective libraries, and render them in the Streamlit app. For usage guides and examples, refer to the official Streamlit documentation at *https://docs.streamlit.io/develop/api-reference/charts*.

Input Widgets

Streamlit provides a variety of input widgets that allow users to interact with your app using just one line of code. These widgets make prototyping fast and straightforward. Let us discuss some of the input widgets available in Streamlit:

- **checkbox/toggle**: Displays a checkbox or a toggle widget. Both widgets serve similar purposes but differ in appearance.
- **color_picker**: Shows a color picker widget.
- **multiselect:** Similar to a **selectbox**, but it allows users to choose multiple options from the dropdown.
- **radio**: Displays a radio button widget, behaving like a **selectbox** but with a different appearance.
- **slider**: Allows users to select a number, date, or time. By default, it behaves like a **selectbox** for single-item selection within the specified range. However, if you pass a list or tuple of two values as the value, users can select a range instead.
- **select_slider**: Similar to the **slider**, but users choose items from a list.
- **date_input/time_input**: Display date or time input widgets, respectively.
- **text_area**: Similar to **text_input**, but it displays a multi-line input widget.
- **chat_input**: Similar to **text_input**, but clears the input text from the widget, once submitted. Useful for collecting user input in chatbot apps.

The following is a sample script that demonstrates all these input widgets.

```
import streamlit as st

lcol, rcol = st.columns(2)

checkbox = lcol.checkbox("This is a checkbox")
lcol.write(f"Value of checkbox: {checkbox}")

toggle = rcol.toggle("This is a toggle")
rcol.write(f"Value of toggle: {toggle}")

color = lcol.color_picker("This is a color picker")
lcol.write(f"Value of color picker: {color}")

multiselect = rcol.multiselect(
    "This is a multiselect", ["Option 1", "Option 2", "Option 3"]
)
rcol.write(f"Value of multiselect: {multiselect}")

radio = lcol.radio(
    "This is a radio",
    ["Option 1", "Option 2", "Option 3"],
    horizontal=True,
)
lcol.write(f"Value of radio: {radio}")
```

```
select_slider = rcol.slider(
    "This is a slider",
    value=(0, 10),
)
rcol.write(f"Value of slider: {select_slider}")

select_slider = lcol.select_slider(
    "This is a select slider",
    ["Option 1", "Option 2", "Option 3", "Option 4", "Option 5"],
    value=["Option 1", "Option 3"],
)
lcol.write(f"Value of select slider: {select_slider}")

date = rcol.date_input("This is a date input")
rcol.write(f"Value of date input: {date}")

time = lcol.time_input("This is a time input")
lcol.write(f"Value of time input: {time}")

text_area = rcol.text_area("This is a text area")
rcol.write(f"Value of text area: {text_area}")

chat_input = lcol.chat_input()
lcol.write(f"Value of chat input: {chat_input}")
```

The following *Figure* 6.6 shows how the example app would look:

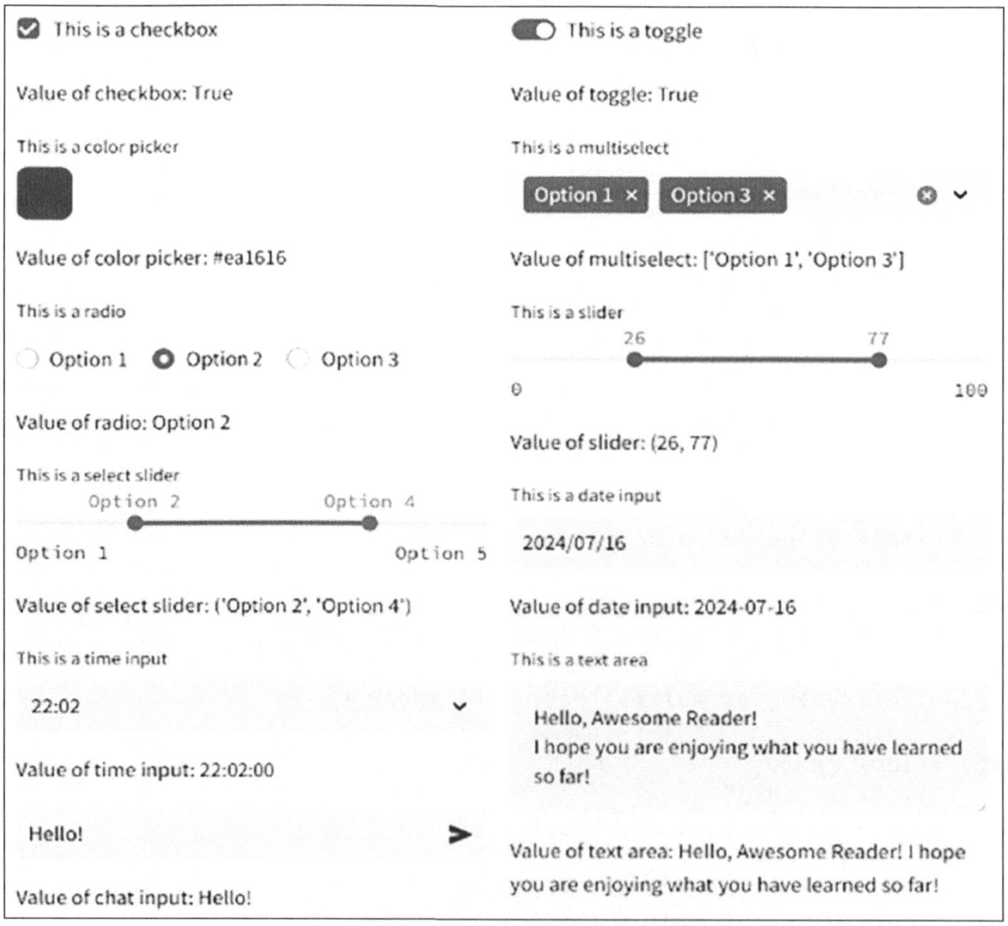

Figure 6.6: *Input Widgets*

- **`download_button`**: It displays a button that allows users to download files directly from your Streamlit app. You can provide a title for the button, and when clicked, it triggers the download of the specified file.

  Run the script as shown in *Figure* 6.7 as a Streamlit app, and click the download buttons. You should be able to download an Excel and a text file.

```
import numpy as np
import pandas as pd
import streamlit as st

df = pd.DataFrame({"A": np.random.randn(100), "B": np.random.rand(100)})

df.to_csv("data.csv", index=False)

st.download_button(
    "Download CSV",
    data=df.to_csv(index=False).encode("utf-8"),
    file_name="dataframe.csv",
    mime="text/csv",
)

st.download_button(
    "Download text",
    data="Hello, world!",
)
```

Figure 6.7: *Download Button*

  Streamlit's download button also supports other data types, such as images, media, binary, and so on. It determines the type of file using **`data`** or **`MIME`**.

  Tip: *You can learn more about different* **`MIME`** *types from Mozilla's documentation here: https://developer.mozilla.org/enUS/docs/Web/HTTP/Basics_of_HTTP/MIME_types*

  Note: *The data to be downloaded is stored in-memory, while the user is connected. So, it is best to keep file sizes reasonable to conserve memory.*[3]

- **`camera_input:`** This widget allows users to take photos using their webcam. It returns the captured image as a **`BytesIO`** object. The following *Figure* 6.8 shows an example of how to use it.

[3] *https://docs.streamlit.io/develop/api-reference/widgets/st.download_button* (Accessed:19 July 2024)

Figure 6.8: *Camera Input*

- **`file_uploader:`** This widget lets users upload files directly into your Streamlit app. It accepts various file types, and returns a **`BytesIO`** object (or a list of them, if multiple files are accepted).

```
import streamlit as st

if uploaded_file := st.file_uploader("Upload a CSV file", type="csv"):
    # Process the uploaded file (e.g., read data or perform analysis)
    ...
```

You can customize the accepted file types, and handle the uploaded files accordingly.

Media Elements

Streamlit provides convenient widgets for rendering audio, video, and images within your Streamlit apps. These widgets accept various inputs, including files, bytes, arrays, or URLs. Additionally, you can enable users to download the rendered media objects directly from the app.

The following *Figure* 6.9 shows some examples of Streamlit media elements.

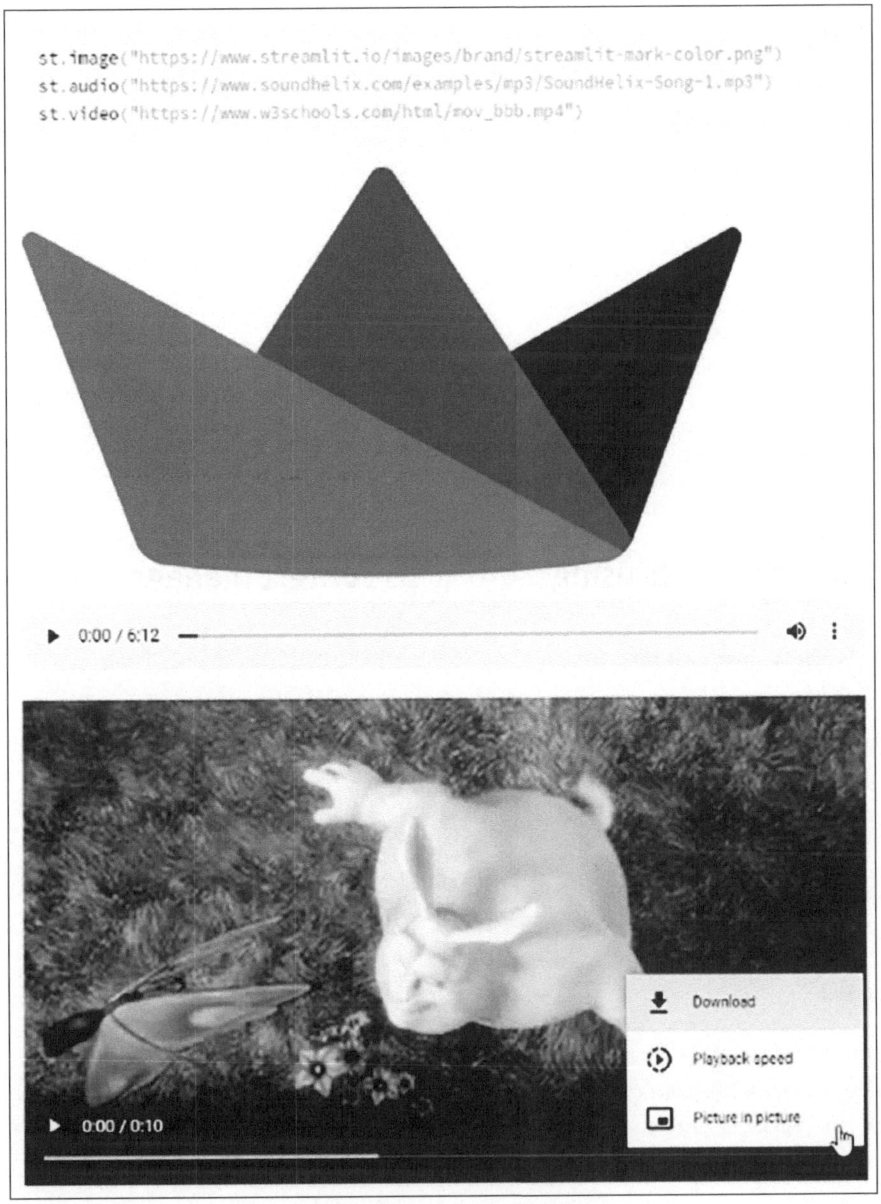

***Figure* 6.9:** *Media Elements*

Layout Elements

In Streamlit, layout elements allow you to customize how your app's components are arranged. Let us explore some of these layout options:

- **`columns`:** The **`columns`** element creates a container to arrange elements side by side. You can use it in two ways:
    - By creating a widget using the **`column`** object (as seen in some previous examples).
    - By using the **`column`** as a context manager.

The following *Figure* 6.10 illustrates both methods:

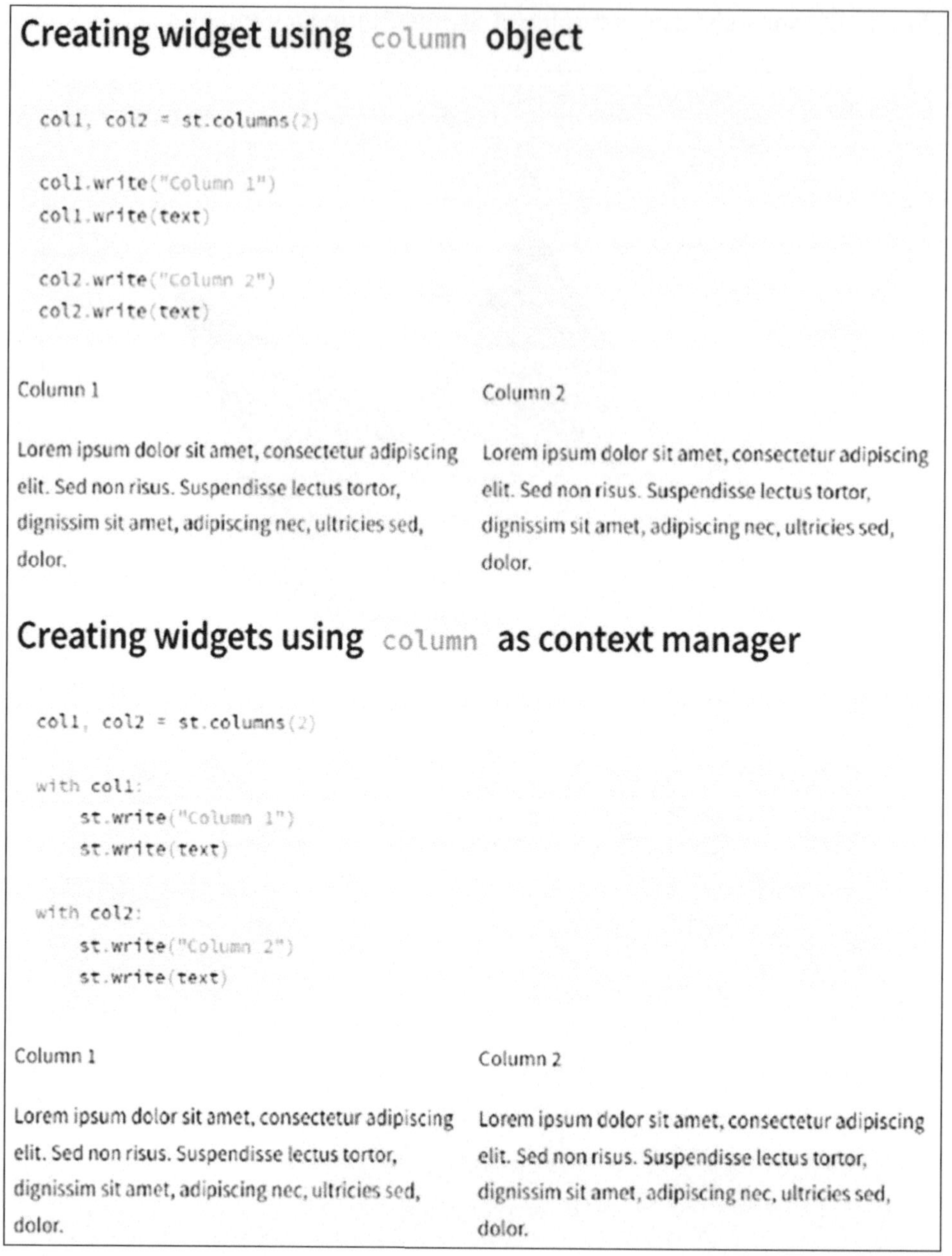

Figure 6.10: *Different Ways of Using Columns*

Regardless of the approach, the result remains consistent. You can also adjust the relative width of columns by passing an iterable of numbers. The columns will be sized proportionally based on these values. Additionally, columns can be nested, allowing a column to contain others.

The following *Figure* 6.11 demonstrates custom column widths and nested columns.

```
col1, col2, col3 = st.columns([1, 3, 2])

with col1:
    st.write("__Column 1__")
    st.write("This column is `1/(1+3+2)` = 1/6th of the total width")

with col2:
    st.write("__Column 2__")
    st.write(
        "This column is `3/(1+3+2)` = 1/2 of the total width, thrice the width of
    )

    col2_1, col2_2 = st.columns([2, 1])

    with col2_1:
        st.write("__Column 2.1__")
        st.write("This nested column is double the width of column 2.2")

    col2_2.write("__Column 2.2__")

with col3:
    st.write("__Column 3__")
    st.write(
        "This column is `2/(1+3+2)` = 1/3rd of the total width, twice the width of
    )
```

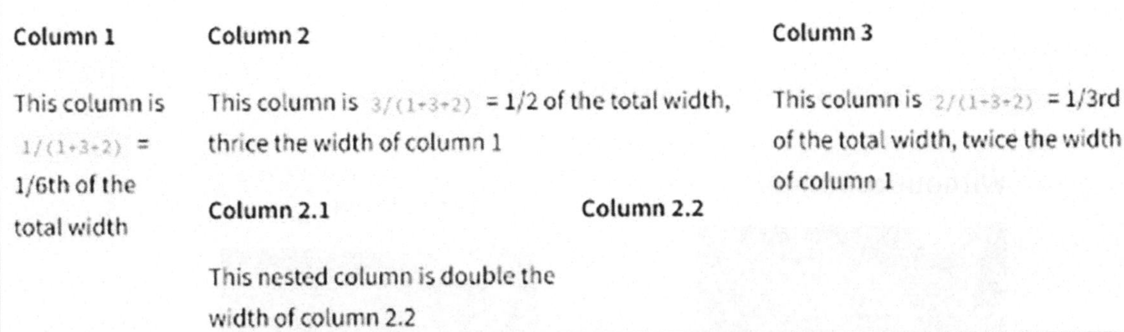

***Figure 6.11:** Adjusting Column Width and Nested Columns*

- **`container`:** The **`container`** element allows you to display elements out of the order in which they appear in your script. When scripts are executed sequentially, the corresponding app elements follow the same order. However, you can change this order using a **`container`**.

  For example, in the usage shown in *Figure* 6.12, if we did not use a **`container`**, the sequence of elements in the app would be the same as in the script—**`Line 1`**, **`Line 2`**, **`Line 3`**.

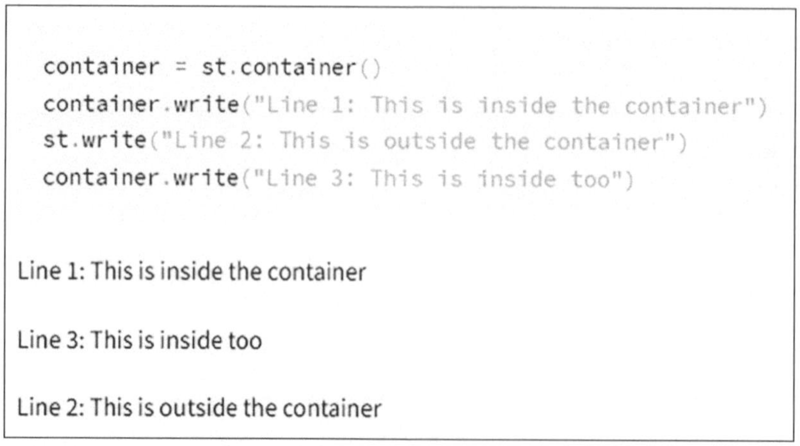

Figure 6.12: *Using a Container to Show Elements Out of Order*

Other uses of **`container`** include adding borders around multiple elements or specifying a container height to save space. Scroll bars can be added to navigate horizontally and vertically within the **`container`**. For instance, **`columns`**, **`container`** can also be used as a context manager, and can be nested. These uses are shown in *Figure* 6.13.

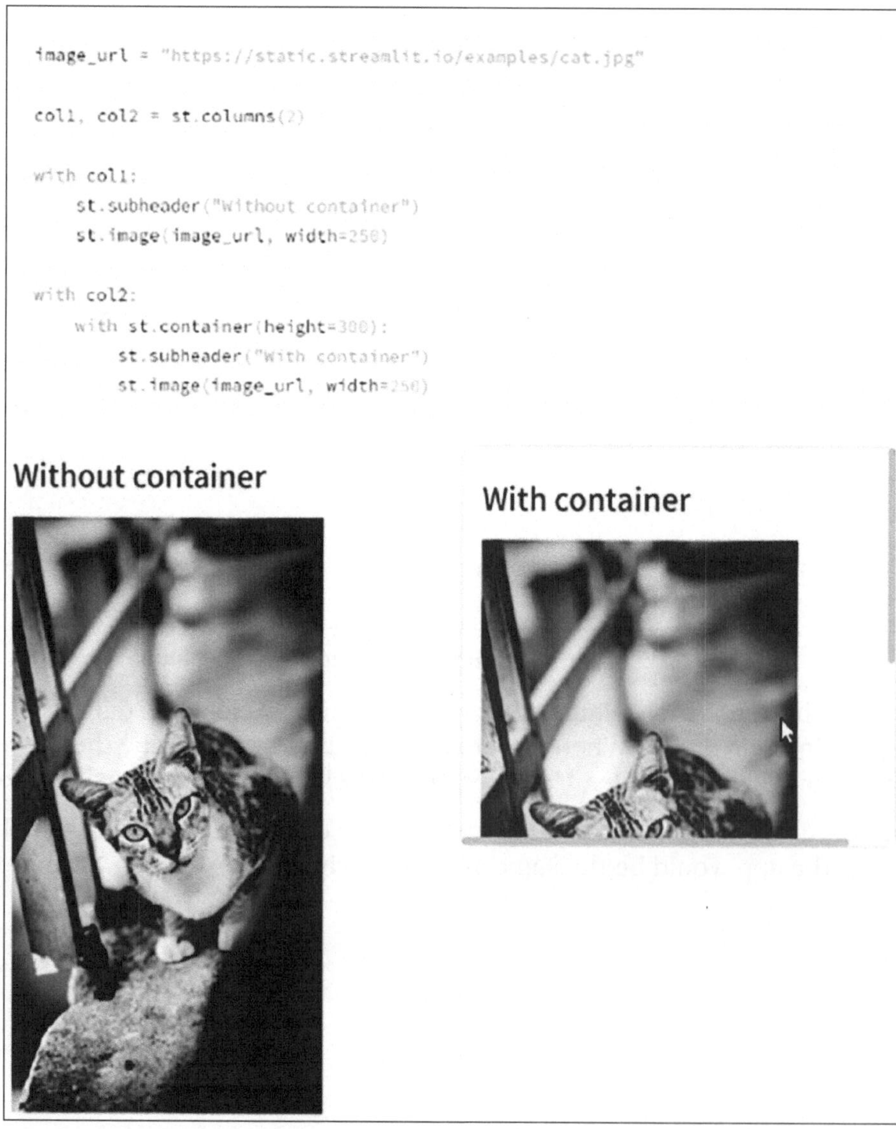

Figure 6.13: *Using a Container to Add a Border and Save Space*

Containers can also be used to control the horizontal and vertical alignment of their elements using the **horizontal_alignment** and **vertical_alignment** parameters.

- **empty:** The **empty** element behaves like a **container** but with two key differences:
  - It can hold only a single element.
  - It can be emptied (that is, its element can be removed).

You can use **empty** to replace an existing element with another.

In the following *Figure* 6.14, clicking "**Replace Widget**" replaces the **Default Widget** text with **Widget Replace**, and clicking "**Clear Widget**" removes the **Default Widget** element altogether.

Figure 6.14: *Using Empty to Replace or Remove a Widget*

- **expander:** An **expander** is a **container** that allows its contents to be expanded or collapsed. By default, an **expander** is collapsed, showing only its label. Clicking on it expands to reveal its elements. To show an expanded expander by default, set its **expanded** parameter to **True**. Like a **container**, an **expander** can also be nested.

The following *Figure* 6.15 shows an **expander** in its collapsed and expanded states.

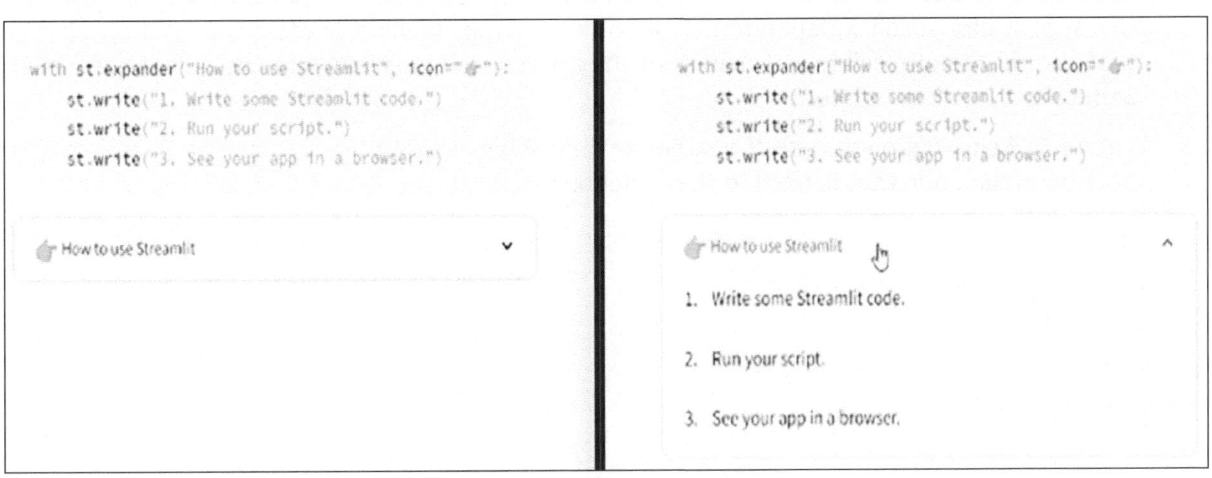

Figure 6.15: *Using an Expander*

- **`form`:** Forms provide a way to batch elements together. Unlike other containers, updating elements inside a form does not immediately rerun the app. Instead, it triggers a rerun only when the **`form_submit_button`** is clicked. Forms can also reset all widgets to their default values by setting the **`clear_on_submit`** flag to **`True`**. Unlike containers, forms cannot contain **`buttons or download buttons`**, and cannot be nested.

The following *Figure* 6.16 shows how to use **`form`** and **`form_submit_button`**.

```
with st.form("my_form"):
    fname = st.text_input("First Name")
    lname = st.text_input("Last Name")
    submit = st.form_submit_button("Submit")
if submit:
    st.write(f"Welcome, {fname} {lname}")
```

Figure 6.16: *Form and form_submit_button*

Tip: *You can learn more about forms in Streamlit's detailed guide on forms available here: https://docs.streamlit.io/develop/concepts/architecture/forms.*

- **`sidebar`:** The **`sidebar`** is a resizable and collapsible container located in the left portion of the app. It can scroll independently of the main app, making it ideal for holding elements that should remain visible, regardless of the app's scroll position, such as navigation options. **`Sidebars`** cannot be nested.

  Figure 6.17 shows how to use the **`sidebar`**, and what it looks like in an app. The highlighted portion is the code that is used in the **`sidebar`**.

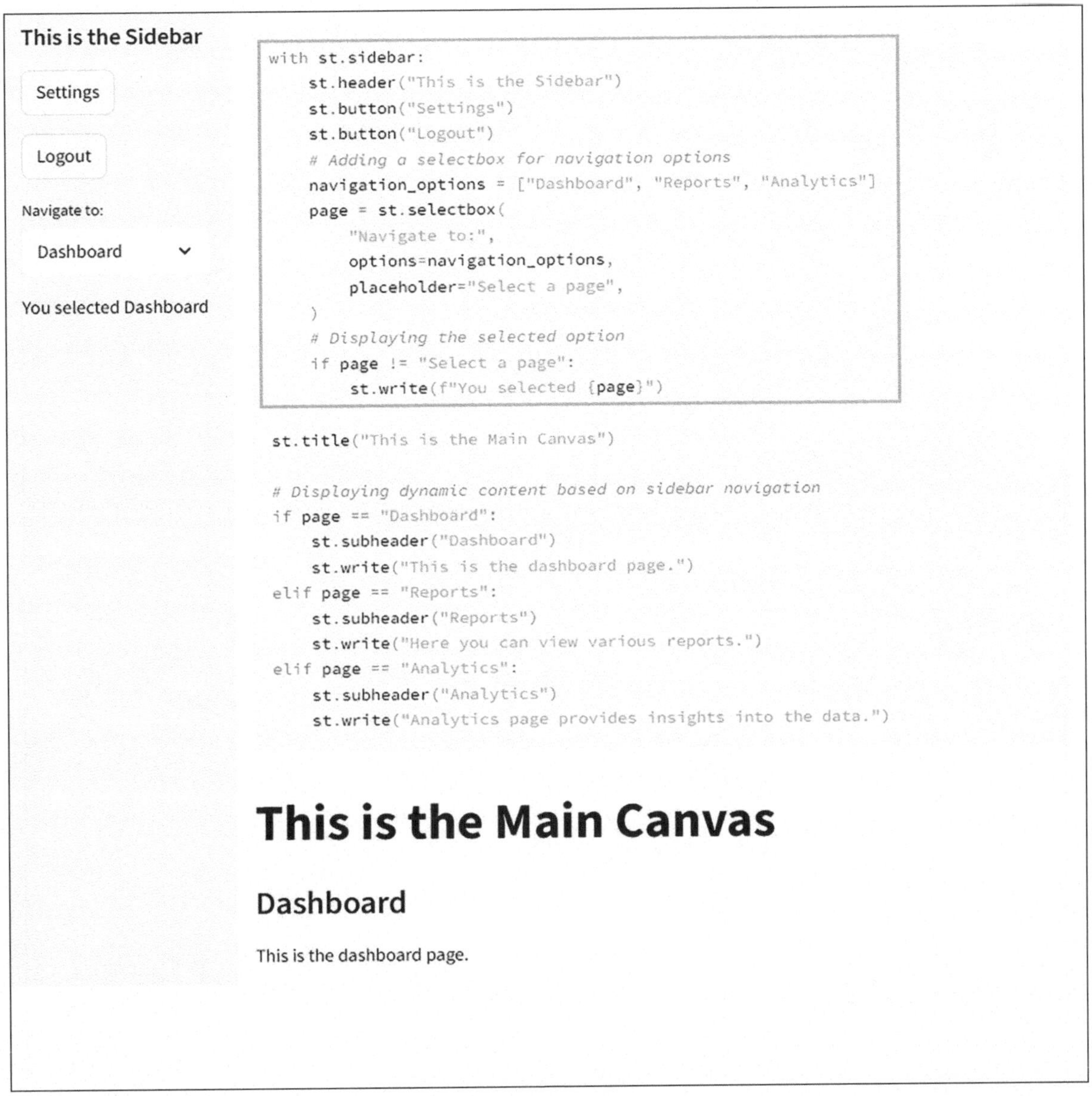

***Figure 6.17:** Sidebar*

- **`tabs`:** Tabs allow you to insert multiple containers arranged as tabs. You can switch between different tabs to see different content. Tabs can also be nested.

The following *Figure* 6.18 shows how to use **`tabs`**, and how they look.

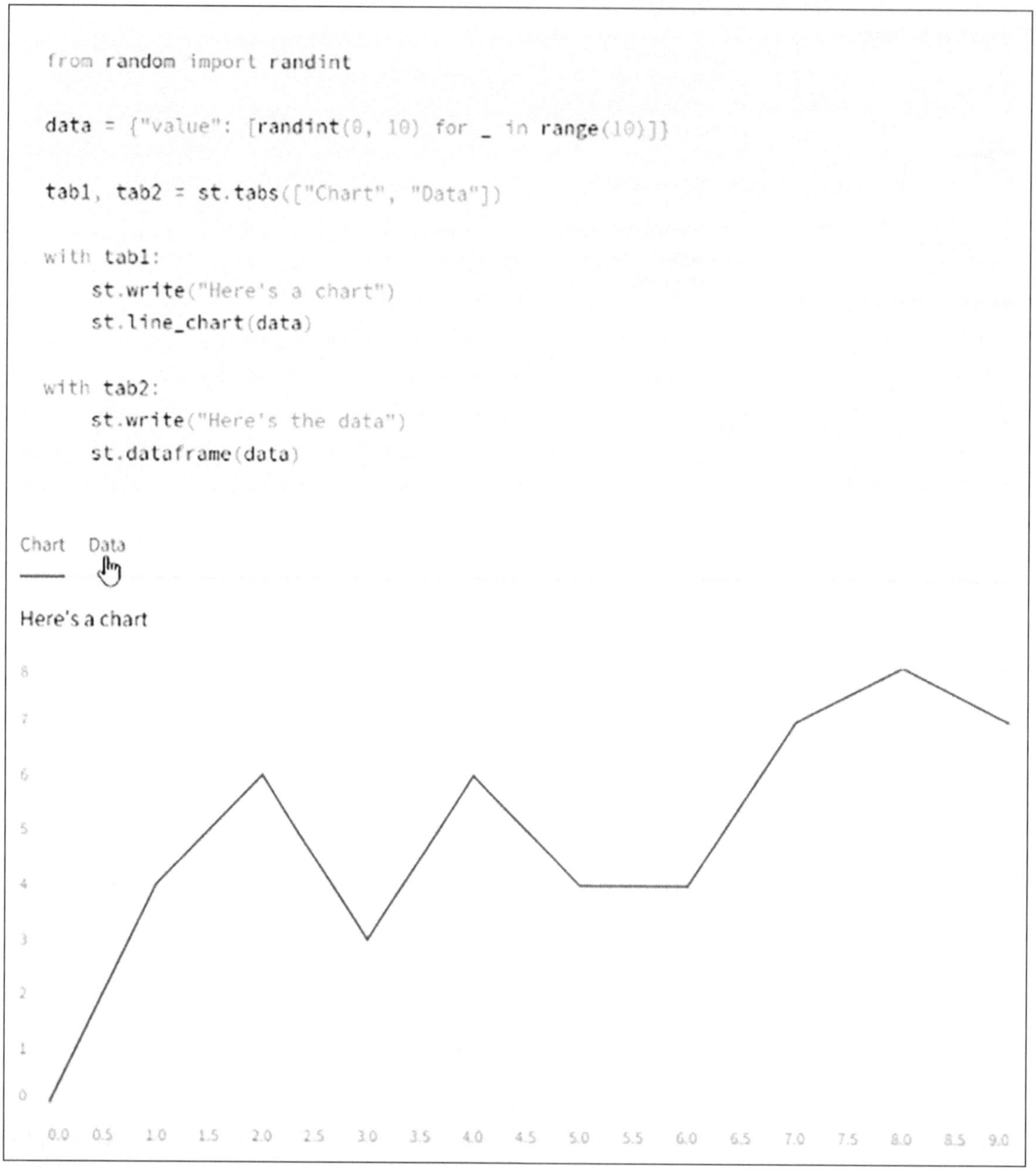

Figure 6.18: Tabs

In the example shown in *Figure* 6.18, you can switch between the **`Chart`** and **`Data`** tabs to see the chart and the constituent data.

Note that even if a tab is not currently visible, its elements still hold their values and are rendered in the same sequence as defined in the script. For example, in *Figure* 6.19, even though **`Tab1`** is visible, any value entered in **`Tab2`** is still available. This is demonstrated by the variables **`tab1_text`** and **`tab2_text`**. Be cautious, when using the same variable to store inputs from multiple tabs, as its value will be that of the last-defined element in the script. This can be seen from the value of the **`number`** variable, which is **`10.0`**, even though the value supplied in **`Tab1`** is **`5.00`**

```
tab1, tab2 = st.tabs(["Tab1", "Tab2"])

with tab1:
    tab1_text = st.text_input("Enter some text")
    number = st.number_input("Enter a number")

with tab2:
    tab2_text = st.text_input("Enter some different text")
    number = st.number_input("Enter a different number")

st.write(f"{tab1_text=}")
st.write(f"{tab2_text=}")
st.write(f"{number=}")
```

Figure 6.19: *All Elements of a Tab are Always Rendered and Hold Their Value*

Status Elements

Streamlit provides various status elements to enhance user experience in data applications by providing visual feedback on the app's state or progress. Let us explore some of these elements:

- **Callouts:** Callouts include **`success`**, **`info`**, **`error`**, and **`exception`** messages. The following *Figure* 6.20 illustrates how these look.

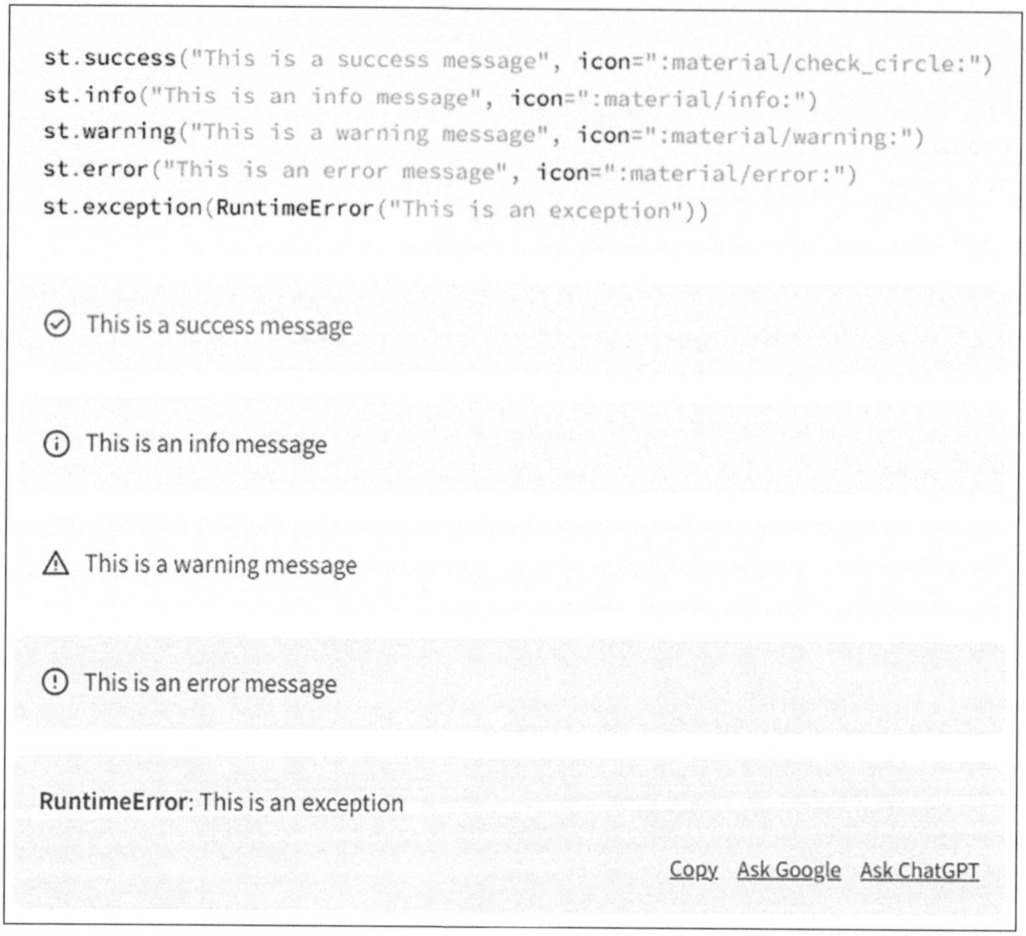

Figure 6.20: *Callouts*

- **`progress`:** The **`progress`** element displays an animated progress bar with customizable text and steps. The following *Figure 6.21* shows an example of a complete progress bar.

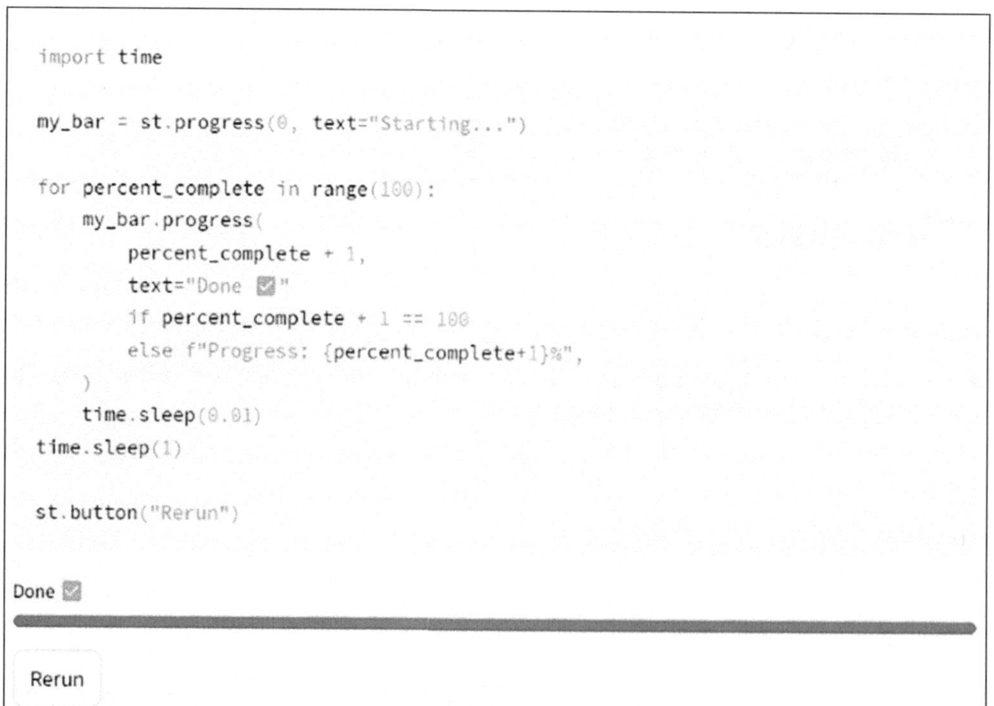

Figure 6.21: *Progress*

Tip: Although **progress** *is an official Streamlit component, we recommend a third-party component,* **stqdm**, *to show progress bars in Streamlit. It is a wrapper around the popular* **tqdm** *library. You can find more details about* **stqdm** *in its GitHub repository: https://github.com/Wirg/stqdm.*

- **spinner:** The **spinner** displays a loading spinner with accompanying text, while executing a code block. The spinner disappears once the block is completed.

To see it in action, run the following snippet as a Streamlit application:

```
import time
import streamlit as st

with st.spinner('Doing something...'):
    time.sleep(5)
st.success('Done!')
```

- **status:** The **status** element combines an **expander** with a **spinner**. When expanded, it shows the detailed output for long-running tasks, and collapses to display only the task's status. *Figure* 6.22 demonstrates this.

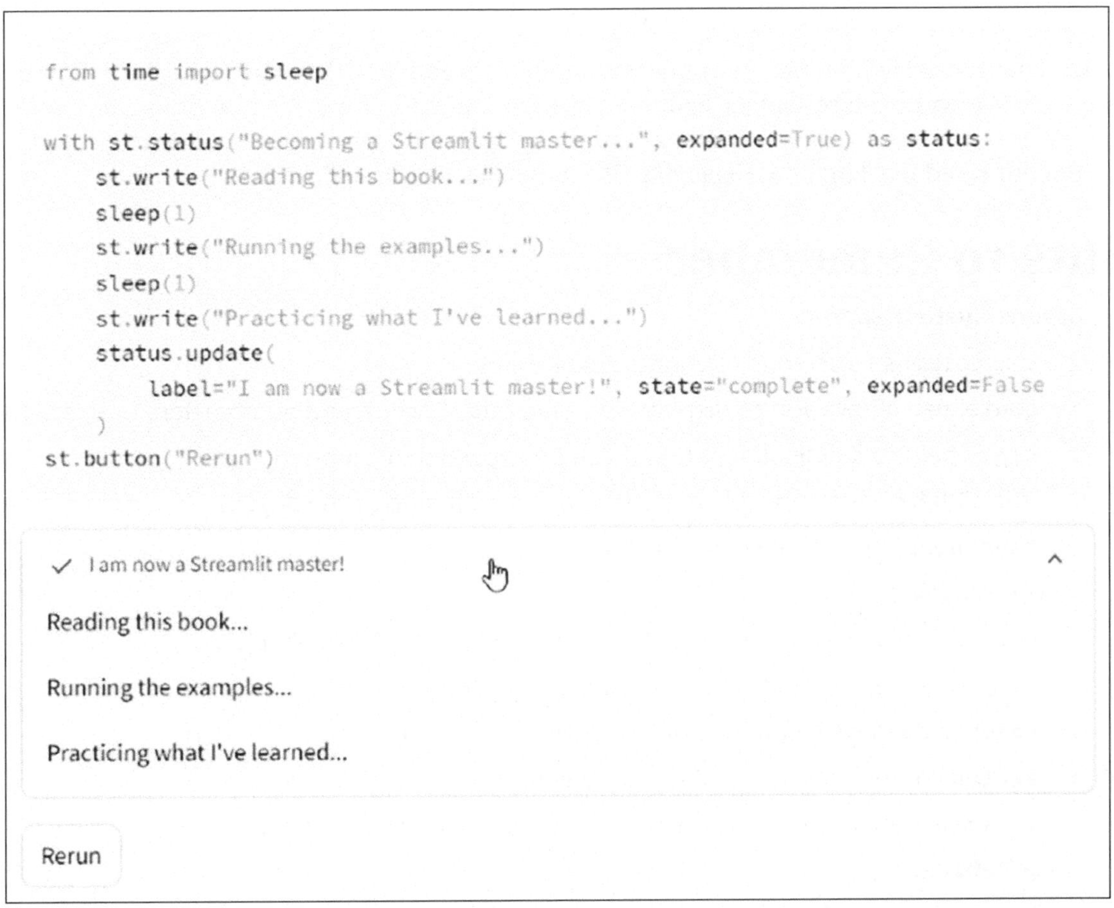

Figure 6.22: *Status*

In the example shown in *Figure* 6.22, we use the **update()** method to update the **label** and the **state** of the status container, and automatically collapse it by passing **expanded=False**.

- **toast:** The **toast** displays a notification pop-up on the right side of the app. By default, unless hovered over, the notification automatically disappears after four seconds, although this can be increased to 10 seconds or infinite using the **duration** parameter. The following *Figure* 6.23 shows an example.

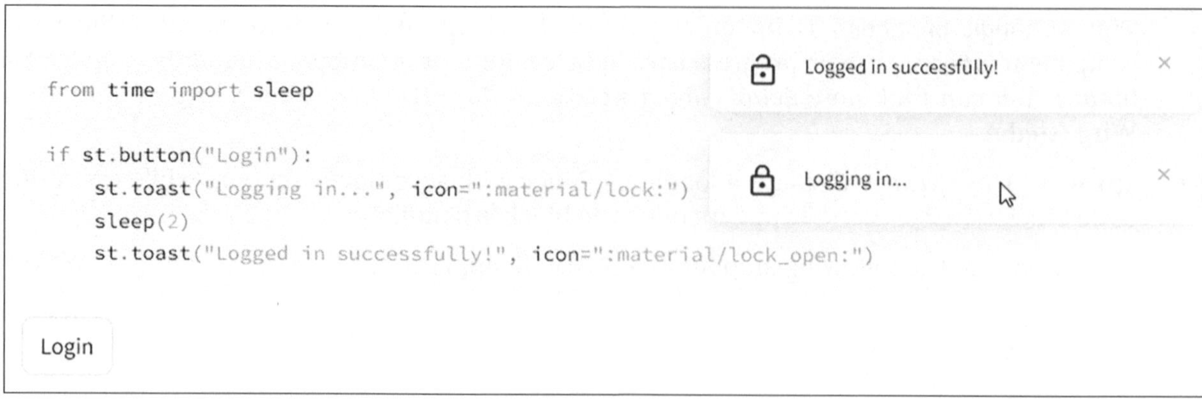

Figure 6.23: *Toast*

Conclusion

In this chapter, we reviewed familiar Streamlit elements from the previous chapters, and explored additional text, data, chart, input, media, layout, and status elements. By now, we have covered most of the essential components needed to build a functional Streamlit app.

In the next chapter, we will deepen our understanding of Streamlit widgets by diving into their behavior and lifecycle. We will explore widget callbacks, which allow us to perform actions after interacting with a widget but before the app reruns. Additionally, we will address the issue with nested buttons that we encountered in *Chapter 4, Exploring Streamlit's Flow and Architecture*.

Points to Remember

- **Layout Customization:**
  - Use **`columns`** to arrange elements side by side.
  - **`container`** allows you to display elements out of order, and add borders or scroll bars.
  - **`empty`** holds a single element, and can be replaced or emptied.
  - The **`sidebar`** is a resizable container on the left side of the app.
  - **`tabs`** organize multiple containers as tabs.
- **Status Feedback:**
  - Use callouts (success, info, error, exception) to provide feedback.
  - The **`progress`** element shows an animated progress bar.
  - **`spinner`** displays loading feedback during execution.
  - **`status`** combines an **`expander`** with a spinner.
  - **`toast`** provides notifications that disappear after a few seconds.
- **Form Behavior:**
  - Forms allow batching of elements and rerun control.
  - Use **`form_submit_button`** to trigger reruns.
  - Set **`clear_on_submit`** to reset widgets to default values.

Multiple Choice Questions

1. Which element can be used to print a code snippet, and then execute it?
    a. `code`
    b. `text`
    c. `echo`
    d. `write_stream`
2. Which element writes string output in a typewriter effect?
    a. `write_stream`
    b. `text`
    c. `echo`
    d. `markdown`
3. Which element can be used to both display and edit a table?
    a. `write`
    b. `table`
    c. `dataframe`
    d. `data_editor`
4. Which element allows text to be entered across multiple lines?
    a. `text_input`
    b. `text_area`
    c. `chat_input`
    d. `input`
5. If three columns are defined as `col1, col2, col3 = st.columns([1,1,3])`, how wide is `col3` compared to `col1`?
    a. Same width
    b. Two times
    c. Three times
    d. 1.67 times
6. Which element can be used to batch elements together by sending all of their updated values to the back-end at the same time?
    a. container
    b. form
    c. sidebar
    d. tabs

7. Which among the following containers cannot be nested? Choose all the correct options.
   a. columns
   b. expander
   c. sidebar
   d. tabs
8. Which element combines a **`spinner`** and an **`expander`**?
   a. progress
   b. status
   c. toast
   d. form
9. What is the purpose of the `form` element in Streamlit?
   a. To create a resizable container
   b. To batch elements together and control reruns
   c. To display a loading spinner
   d. To organize elements as tabs
10. Which Streamlit element allows you to display a notification pop-up that disappears after a few seconds?
    a. callout
    b. spinner
    c. toast
    d. status

Answers

1. c
2. a
3. d
4. b
5. c
6. b
7. c
8. b
9. b
10. c

Questions

1. Using the components discussed in this chapter, create a simple Streamlit app that writes a user-defined range of numbers using a typewriter effect at a speed chosen by the user.
2. Create a chatbot app that repeats a user's message back to the user. Users can input text, and the chatbot responds with the same text.
3. Create an app to upload a CSV file with name and age columns. The app should display the uploaded data, and create a bar chart with names on the x-axis and ages on the y-axis.

Key Terms

- **BytesIO:** A BytesIO object in Python is data stored in an in-memory buffer as bytes.[4] It allows you to read or write binary data as if it were a file.
- **Context Manager**: A context manager is an object that defines a runtime context for executing code within the `with` statement.[5] It provides setup and teardown actions, such as opening and closing files, managing resources, or acquiring and releasing locks.
- **Iterable**: An iterable is a Python object that can be looped through to return its values one at a time. These values are already loaded into the memory, and can be accessed together. For example, a list `[1,2,3,4,5]` is an iterable, as we can loop through its values individually, and see them collectively.
- **Generator:** In Python, a generator is an iterable whose values are generated at runtime. Unlike lists or other iterables, generators do not simultaneously store all values in memory. Instead, they produce values on the fly as needed. For example, **range(10)** is a generator because we can loop through its values individually, but cannot access them since they are generated dynamically.
- **MIME (Multipurpose Internet Mail Extensions):** MIME types indicate the nature and format of a file.[6] They define the type of data contained in a file (for example, text, image, audio, video, and so on) and are necessary for software applications to handle and interpret files properly.

[4] *https://www.digitalocean.com/community/tutorials/python-io-bytesio-stringio#python-bytesio* (Accessed: 12 July 2024)
[5] *https://www.pythontutorial.net/advanced-python/python-context-managers/* (Accessed: 13 July 2024)
[6] *https://developer.mozilla.org/en-US/docs/Web/HTTP/Basics_of_HTTP/MIME_types* (Accessed: 9 July 2024)

CHAPTER 7
Widget Keys and Callbacks

Introduction

This chapter will deepen our understanding of Streamlit widgets by examining the details of widget keys, particularly the internals of how and why Streamlit assigns keys to widgets that do not have one explicitly assigned. Considering these considerations, we will explore some nuances of this behavior and best practices for designing our applications.

We will also introduce callbacks, a handy feature Streamlit provides that performs an action between changing the state of a widget and rerunning the application. We will demonstrate how to use callbacks to implement nested buttons, a problem we explored in *Chapter 4, Exploring Streamlit's Flow and Architecture*.

Finally, we will familiarize ourselves with some caveats of using callbacks, we should remember while designing our applications.

Structure

In this chapter, we will discuss the following topics:

- Understanding Widget Keys
  - Statefulness of Widgets
  - Widget Cleanup Process
- Introduction to Widget Callbacks
  - Implementing Nested Buttons Using Callbacks
  - Callback Caveats
    - Writing an Application Using a Callback
    - Transient Nature of Widgets Created by Callbacks

Understanding Widget Keys

We already know that Streamlit assigns a key to each widget, and the values of these keys are saved in **`Session State`**. In this section, we will learn how these keys are created, and under what circumstances we would want, as well as sometimes need to manually assign keys to widgets.

But first, why do we, or Streamlit, even need widget keys?

Widget keys serve two primary purposes in Streamlit: User-facing and internal. We have already seen the user-facing purpose of widget keys – accessing and updating a widget's value using **`Session State`**.

Internally, Streamlit also uses widget keys to distinguish between identical widgets. This is important because Streamlit updates widgets incrementally on the frontend, instead of rebuilding them with each run whenever possible.[1] When not explicitly provided, Streamlit assigns an ID to each widget based on the arguments passed to the widget – such as label, min, max or default value, placeholder, help text, and so on, as well as the page where the widget appears.[2] These auto-assigned keys are internal only, and cannot be accessed using **Session State**.

Note: *Internal widget keys can be accessed using* **streamlit.runtime.scriptrunner.get_script_run_ctx().session_state**. *While this is not always needed, it might be helpful for debugging purposes. Also note that this API is not public, and can change without notice in a future release.*

This means if similar widgets are on the same page, Streamlit cannot differentiate between them, and throws a **StreamlitDuplicateElementId** error.

To see how this works, consider the following script:

```
import streamlit as st

st.button("Click here")
st.write(st.runtime.scriptrunner.get_script_run_ctx().session_state)

st.button("Click here")
st.write(st.runtime.scriptrunner.get_script_run_ctx().session_state)
```

When you run this script using **streamlit run**, you will get an error, as shown in *Figure 7.1*.

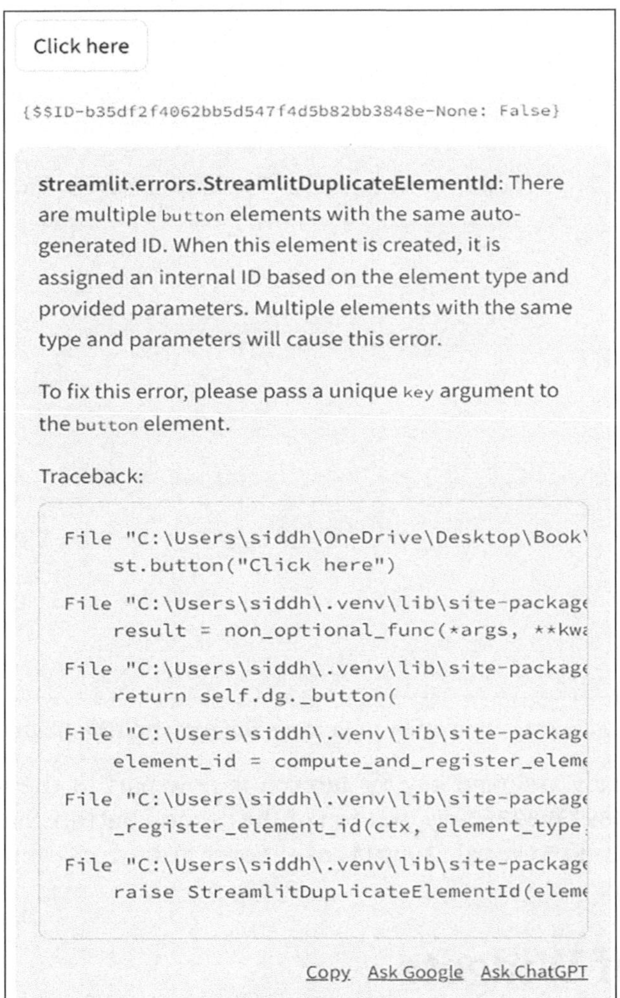

Figure 7.1: *StreamlitDuplicateElementId Error*

[1] *https://docs.streamlit.io/develop/concepts/architecture/widget-behavior* (Accessed: 29 July 2024)
[2] *https://docs.streamlit.io/develop/concepts/architecture/widget-behavior* (Accessed: 29 July 2024)

A couple of things to note here:

First, **`$$ID-b35df2f4062bb5d547f4d5b82bb3848e-None`** is the internal element ID created by Streamlit for the first button. The `None` part indicates that no key has been explicitly assigned to it. If the button is not clicked, its value will be **`False`**; otherwise, it will be **`True`**. This is how Streamlit keeps track of widgets and their state, if a key is not explicitly assigned.

Second, when Streamlit reaches the second button declaration, it tries to create another ID for it. However, since this button is the same as the previous button, and is on the same page, the generated ID is also the same, causing Streamlit to throw a **`StreamlitDuplicateElementId`** error.

Note: *We will learn about multipage Streamlit apps in a later chapter.*

To ensure that a unique ID is generated for the second button, we can either manually assign it a **`key`** or update any of its input parameters so that it differs from the first button.

To see this in action, add the **`key my_button`** to the second button as shown in the following:

```
st.button("Click here", key="my_button")
```

Upon rerunning the application, it should look as shown in *Figure* 7.2.

Figure 7.2: *Manually Assigning a Key to Remove the StreamlitDuplicateElementId Error*

As you can see, the manually assigned key **`my_button`** is now part of the internal element ID **`$$ID-f697746901a4503d2196d83923b890f0-my_button`** of the second button. Since the IDs of both widgets are now different, there is no **`StreamlitDuplicateElementId`** error, even though both the buttons appear identical in the app.

Statefulness of Widgets

Since Streamlit identifies widgets using their internal ID, and these internal IDs are created based on parameters passed to the widget, updating a parameter of the widget can cause Streamlit to treat it as a new widget altogether, and reset its values.

To see this in practice, spin up a Streamlit app using the code shown in *Figure* 7.3, and follow these steps:

1. Increase the slider to a random value. Note the **ID** corresponding to the new value. This is the **ID** of this slider. This value is highlighted in *Figure* 7.3, but it can be different for you.

Figure 7.3: *Initial Element ID*

2. Change the minimum value to something else. What do you observe? This state is shown in *Figure* 7.4. Note that the IDs can be different for you.
   a. The slider resets to the minimum value.
   b. A new **ID** with the latest value of the slider appears (highlighted in green).
   c. The original ID with the old value of the slider is still available (highlighted in red).

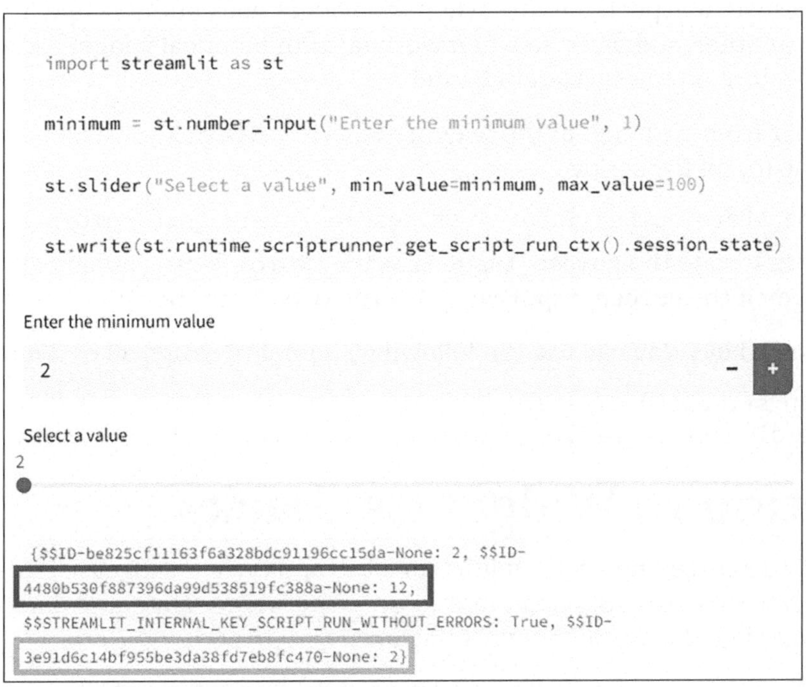

Figure 7.4: *Updated Element ID*

3. Select any other random value in the slider. You will notice that the original `ID` is no longer displayed.

Now, let us understand what is happening here.

In step 2, since we have updated the parameters of the slider, Streamlit treats this as an entirely new slider, and resets its value. This is why we see a new `ID` altogether. The disappearance of the original **`ID`** in step 3 results from Streamlit's widget cleanup process, which is the id discussed in the next section.

Widget Cleanup Process

When Streamlit reaches the end of a script run, it deletes any data for widgets not rendered on the screen, including any key-value pairs in **`Session State`** associated with the widget.[3]

To see how this works, create a simple app using the following script:

```
import streamlit as st

st.number_input("Enter a number", key="number_input")
st.write(st.session_state.number_input)
```

When you run this app, enter a number. You will see that written using the **`number_input`** widget's **`Session State`** key-value pair.

Now, delete the line containing the number input from the script. You can still see the widget's last value when the app reruns due to the code change. However, on rerunning the app again (you can do this by pressing `R` on the keyboard with the app in focus), you will get the following error:

```
AttributeError: st.session_state has no attribute "number_input". Did you for-
get to initialize it?
```

This is because when the script was rerun following the code change, Streamlit removed the **`number_input`** widget's data and associated **`Session State`** key-value pairs from memory when it reached the end of the script. When we triggered the manual rerun again, the **`number_input`** key did not exist anymore in the **`Session State`**, and hence, the error.

This behavior can cause unexpected issues when the widget goes out of scope in one execution, but is back in scope in another, and more so when working with identical widgets across different pages of a multipage app (more on this in a later chapter).

To prevent Streamlit from cleaning up the widget's **`Session State`** key-value pairs, you can add the following line to the top of the script:

```
st.session_state.number_input = st.session_state.get("number_input")
```

Streamlit will now associate the **`number_input`** **`Session State`** key as a manually assigned key, and will not delete it even if the **`number_input`** widget is removed from the app.

If you have many such keys, you can use the following snippet to assign all of them manually:

```
for key in st.session_state:
    st.session_state[key] = st.session_state[key]
```

Introduction to Widget Callbacks

We have repeatedly discussed how Streamlit reruns the app once a widget's state has been updated. This behavior necessitates using Session State to preserve widget state and data across app reruns, and introduces issues like the inability to nest buttons.

[3] *https://docs.streamlit.io/develop/concepts/architecture/widget-behavior#widget-clean-up-process* (Accessed: 4 August 2024)

However, Streamlit does provide a way to perform a task after a widget has been interacted with, and before the app is rerun. This is achieved through the use of **`callbacks`**.

In general terms, a **`callback`** function is a function passed as an argument to another function, which is then called inside the outer function to perform some task.[4] In Streamlit, a **`callback`** is called when an input widget changes.[5] Most input widgets let you pass a callback using the **`on_change`** or **`on_click`** parameter. Like other Python functions, callbacks can accept parameters passed using the input widget's **`args`** or **`kwargs`** parameters.

Let us see a basic usage of callbacks using the `Counter` app we built in *Chapter 5, Persisting Data and State Using Session State.*

For reference, here is the script we used to build this app:

```
import streamlit as st

st.write("Starting script")

if "count" not in st.session_state:
    st.session_state.count = 0

if st.button("Click me!"):
    st.session_state["count"] += 1

st.write(f"Button was clicked {st.session_state.count} times")
```

You will notice that we increment **`session_state.count`** once the button is clicked. This is a perfect example where we can use a **`callback`** instead.

Since we need a function to pass to the button as a callback, let us create a simple function that will increment **`session_state.count`** and pass that function to the button as an **`on_click`** callback. With the increment removed from below the button, we no longer need it to be a conditional.

The following *Figure* 7.5 shows the updated script, and the resultant app.

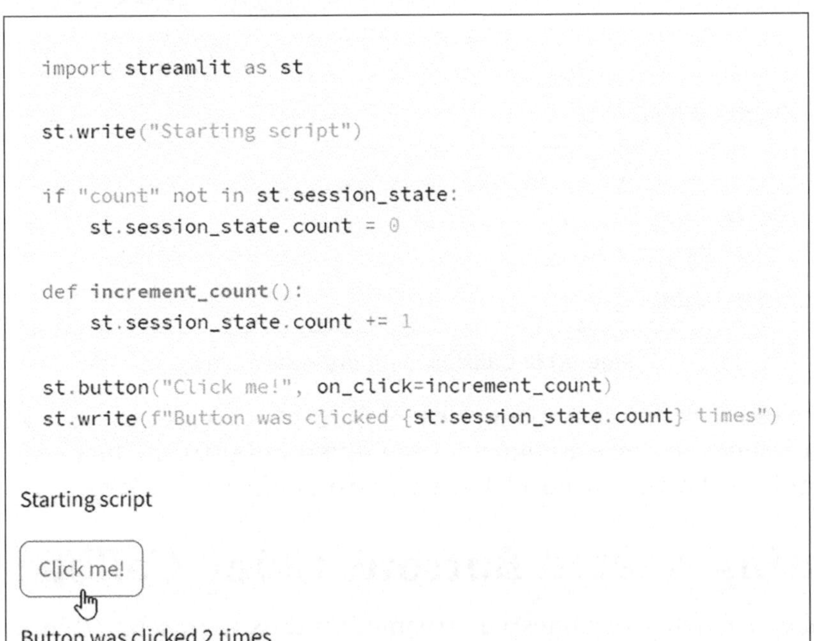

***Figure* 7.5:** *Counter with Callback*

[4] *https://developer.mozilla.org/en-US/docs/Glossary/Callback_function* (Accessed: 24 February 2025)
[5] *https://docs.streamlit.io/develop/concepts/architecture/session-state#example-2-session-state-and-callbacks* (Accessed: 31 July 2024)

We can use the button's **args** and **kwargs** parameters to pass positional and keyword arguments to the callback function. Consider the following example shown in *Figure* 7.6.

```
import streamlit as st

if "count" not in st.session_state:
    st.session_state.count = 0

def change_count(kind, change_by):
    if kind == "increase":
        st.session_state.count += change_by
    elif kind == "decrease":
        st.session_state.count -= change_by

st.button(
    "Increase by 5",
    on_click=change_count,
    args=("increase", 5),
)
st.button(
    "Decrease by 2",
    on_click=change_count,
    kwargs=dict(kind="decrease", change_by=2),
)

st.write("Counter value: ", st.session_state.count)
```

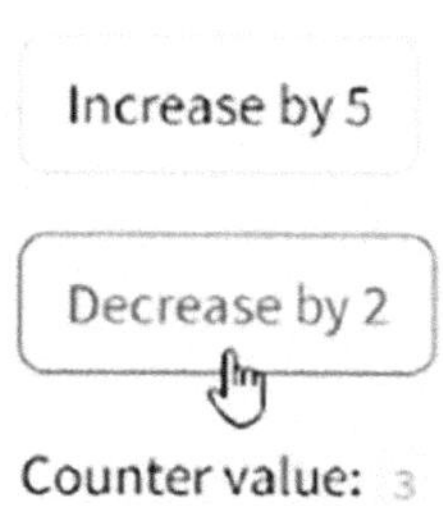

Figure 7.6: *Callback with args and kwargs*

In this example, the callback function, **change_count**, accepts two arguments – kind and **change_by**. By passing different values to these arguments from different buttons – Increase by 5 and Decrease by 2, we can change how the same callback behaves across different widgets.

Implementing Nested Buttons Using Callbacks

You might remember the behavior of nested Streamlit buttons we discussed in *Chapter 4, Exploring Streamlit's Flow and Architecture*. As shown in the flowchart in Figure 4.9, to access the code block under a nested Streamlit button, the state of both the parent and child buttons must be True. However, this is not possible under normal circumstances because the app immediately reruns when the nested button is clicked, reverting the state of the parent button to False.

This issue can be resolved using a *combination of callbacks and Session State*. Specifically, we use a callback to set a Session State key when a button is clicked, and then we use the value of the key instead of the button's state to guard the condition. Since, unlike the button's state, the Session State key does not revert to False when the other button is clicked, the code block under the nested button is accessible.

The following *Figure* 7.7 shows what the implementation and the resulting app look like.

```
import streamlit as st

st.write("Button1 clicked:", st.session_state.get("button_1"))
st.write("Button2 clicked:", st.session_state.get("button_2"))

def update_status(button, state):
    st.session_state[button] = state

st.button("Click me!", on_click=update_status, args=("button_1", True))

if st.session_state.get("button_1"):
    st.write("Button1 was clicked")

    st.button(
        "Click me too!",
        on_click=update_status,
        args=("button_2", True),
    )

    if st.session_state.get("button_2"):
        st.write("Button2 was clicked")
```

***Figure** 7.7: Nested Buttons with Callbacks and Session State*

As you can see, in this case, both **Button1** and **Button2** can be clicked, and any code nested under Button2 is reachable.

Let us dissect the code. First, we have created a callback function – **update_state** – that will update the relevant key (button in this case) with its state. This function is called with the relevant **args** whenever the parent (**Click me!**) or child (**Click me too!**) buttons are clicked.

When the parent button is clicked, the callback sets the state of **button_1** to True, and the app reruns. Since the **button_1 Session State** is **True**, the child button is displayed. Similarly, when clicking the child button, the callback sets the state of **button_2** to True, and the app reruns. Now, since **button_1** and **button_2** are our custom keys, and not the actual widget keys of the buttons, they retain their True value, unlike button states that are True only transiently. So, after the second rerun, since both the conditions are satisfied, the code nested under the child button is reached, and Button2 that was clicked is displayed.

Callback Caveats

Since callbacks run only between widget interaction and the script rerun, there are some caveats to remember, while using them, especially when writing anything to the app using a callback.

Writing to the Application Using a Callback

Anything written to the app using a callback will be rendered at the top of the app, irrespective of the location of the callback function or the widget within the callback function.

For example, consider the following script:

```
import streamlit as st

st.header("Callback Caveats")


def write_something():
    st.write("Hello, Awesome Reader!")


st.button("Click to start", on_click=write_something)
```

When clicking the button, you might assume that the app would look as shown in *Figure 7.8*.

Figure 7.8: *Assumed Callback Behavior*

However, if you run this app, and click the button, what you see instead is shown in *Figure 7.9*.

Figure 7.9: *Actual Callback Behavior*

Even though the title Callback Caveats is at the top of the script, the output of **st.write()** is shown above the title before both the callback function, and the write statement. This is because a callback function is not the last thing to run after widget interaction, and before the script rerun; it is, in fact, the first thing to run after the script rerun.[6] As such, when the script reruns, the callback function is first executed, and its output is displayed on the screen, followed by any other widgets in the script.

Transient Nature of Widgets Created by Callbacks

Now that we have seen that callback functions are run as a prefix to the script rerunning, it introduces us to another issue with using callbacks to create widgets.

Consider the following script, a modified version of the previous script, where we show a nested button, once the first button has been clicked.

```
import streamlit as st

st.header("Callback Caveats")

def write_something():
    st.write("Hello, Awesome Reader!")
    st.session_state.clicked = True

st.button("Click to start", on_click=write_something)

if st.session_state.get("clicked"):
    if st.button("Click again"):
        st.write("Second click")
```

What will happen if you click the second button labeled Click again? You might expect Second Click to be printed in the app.

However, you will see something shown in the following *Figure* 7.10, when you try it out yourself.

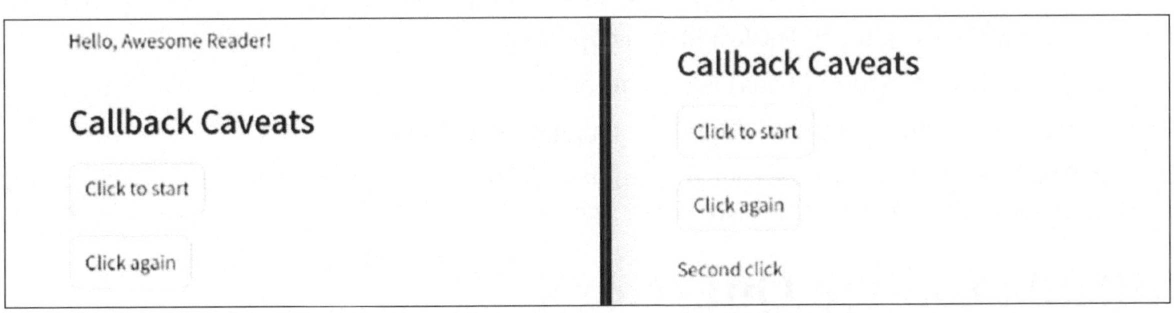

Figure 7.10: *Transient Nature of Callback Widgets*

The greeting and second button are shown as expected, when clicking the first button. The second click message is also shown as expected, when clicking the second button. However, the greeting displayed by the callback disappears. Why is that?

Since the first button was not clicked again when the script was rerun, its callback is not executed when the script reruns after clicking the second button. Hence, all the output shown in the callback disappears.

[6] *https://docs.streamlit.io/develop/concepts/architecture/widget-behavior#order-of-operations* (Accessed: 4 August 2024)

This means that anything written to the script using a callback function will disappear as soon as another widget is interacted with. This is why creating elements within a callback function is generally not recommended, unless this behavior is accounted for.[7]

Conclusion

In this chapter, we explored the details of widget keys, why they are needed, and how Streamlit assigns IDs to widgets for identification. Considering these considerations, we examined some nuances of this behavior and best practices for designing our applications.

We were also introduced to callbacks, and learned how to use them to solve issues encountered in the previous chapters. Finally, we discussed some caveats of using callbacks that we should remember, while designing our applications.

In the next chapter, we will learn how to use caching within our apps to dramatically improve performance, and how to connect our Streamlit apps to external data sources manually, using Streamlit's connectors.

Points to Remember

- Streamlit assigns an internal ID to each widget based on its arguments, key, and the page it appears on.
- Element IDs are unique. If two widgets share the same ID, Streamlit throws a **`StreamlitDuplicateElementId`** error.
- To remove the **`StreamlitDuplicateElementId`** error, update the arguments of the widgets so that they are different or, preferably, assign a unique key to the widget.
- When Streamlit reaches the end of a script run, it will delete any data for widgets not rendered on the screen, including any key-value pairs in Session State associated with the widget.[8]
- When a user interacts with a widget, the order of logic is:[9]
    - The widget's value in Session State is updated.
    - Its callback function (if any) is executed.
    - The app reruns with the widget returning its new value.
- Anything written by a callback will be rendered at the top of the application, and will disappear upon subsequent interaction with other widgets.

Multiple Choice Questions

1. How can you access a widget's ID?
    a. `streamlit.session_state`
    b. `streamlit.runtime.scriptrunner.get_script_run_ctx().session_state`
    c. Both of the above
    d. None of the above

[7] *https://docs.streamlit.io/develop/concepts/architecture/widget-behavior#order-of-operations* (Accessed: 4 August 2024)
[8] *https://docs.streamlit.io/develop/concepts/architecture/widget-behavior#widget-clean-up-process* (Accessed: 4 August 2024)
[9] *https://docs.streamlit.io/develop/concepts/architecture/widget-behavior#order-of-operations* (Accessed: 4 August 2024)

2. What is the primary purpose of manually assigning keys to widgets in Streamlit?
    a. To change the widget's appearance
    b. To ensure unique identification of widgets
    c. To improve the app's performance
    d. To enable widget animations
3. Which of the following plays no role in generating the element ID of a widget?
    a. Widget parameters
    b. Widget value
    c. Widget key
    d. Page in which the widget appears
4. What is true about Streamlit's widget cleanup process?
    a. It deletes data for widgets not rendered on the screen.
    b. It retains all widget data indefinitely.
    c. It only deletes data for widgets with no assigned key.
    d. It never deletes any widget data.
5. What happens if two similar widgets are on the same page of a Streamlit app without any key assigned?
    a. Nothing happens.
    b. The first widget is overwritten by the second.
    c. The second widget is ignored.
    d. Streamlit throws an error.
6. How can you prevent Streamlit from cleaning up a widget's Session State key-value pairs?
    a. By assigning a unique key to the widget
    b. By manually reassigning the Session State key at the top of the script
    c. By updating the widget's parameters
    d. By using a different widget type
7. What happens when a callback function is executed in Streamlit?
    a. It runs after the script rerun.
    b. It runs simultaneously with the script rerun.
    c. It does not affect the script rerun.
    d. It runs before the script rerun.
8. Where is the output from a callback printed in the app?
    a. Top of the app
    b. Bottom of the app

   c. Depends on the location of the callback function in the script
   d. Depends on the location of the widget in the script

9. Why is it generally not recommended to create widgets within a callback function in Streamlit?
   a. It can cause the app to crash.
   b. The widgets will not be displayed.
   c. The widgets will disappear after another widget interaction.
   d. It slows down the app's performance.

Answers

1. b
2. b
3. b
4. a
5. d
6. b
7. d
8. a
9. c

Questions

1. Describe a scenario where manually assigning a key to a widget is necessary. What issues might arise if this is not done?
2. What must you do to ensure that the value of a widget with the key, `my_key` is always available in Session State, even when the widget is removed?
3. Using the concepts learned so far, create a Streamlit app that allows users to either increase or decrease a counter by a value of their choice. Use sliders or number inputs to select the value and buttons to increase or decrease the counter.
4. Discuss the implications of Streamlit's widget cleanup process. How can developers ensure that the essential data is not lost during this process?

Key Terms

- **Element ID:** A unique identifier assigned to each widget by Streamlit based on its arguments, key, and the page it appears on.
- **Args and kwargs:** In Python, `args` and `kwargs` refer to positional and keyword-only arguments passed to a function, respectively.
- **Callback:** A callback is a Python function called when an input widget changes.[10]

[10] *https://docs.streamlit.io/develop/concepts/architecture/session-state#example-2-session-state-and-callbacks* (Accessed: 31 July 2024)

CHAPTER 8
Introduction to Streamlit Caching and Connections

Introduction

Streamlit was built to create web apps for data analysis scripts quickly. Therefore, it is essential to efficiently connect our Streamlit apps to various data sources to provide a good uscr experience.

This chapter will first explore how to cache data and resources in Streamlit to prevent data from being reloaded or recomputed whenever the app reruns. We will learn how caching works in Streamlit, the different caching methods available, and some best practices and caveats related to caching.

We will also learn how to connect our Streamlit apps to external data sources by implementing robust caching mechanisms.

Finally, we will learn how to use Streamlit Connections, a native Streamlit method with built-in caching and secrets management, to connect to external data sources efficiently.

This chapter will also touch upon secrets management in Streamlit, which will be discussed in detail in the next chapter.

Structure

In this chapter, we will discuss the following topics:

- Introduction to Caching
- Manually Implementing Simple Caches
- Caching in Streamlit
  - Caching Data
    - Behavior of **`st.cache_data`**
    - Difference between **`st.cache_data`** and **`functools.cache`**
  - Caching Resources
  - Advanced Caching Options
    - Limiting Cache Size
    - Limiting Cache Duration
    - Clearing the Cache
    - Excluding Input Parameters
    - Using a Custom Hash Function
- Connecting to External Data
  - Using Usual Python Methods
  - Using Streamlit Connections

Introduction to Caching

Caching is a process by which frequently accessed data is stored in a location from where it can be easily and quickly accessed.[1] This location is called a *cache*.

For example, consider a file you refer to frequently on the internet. If the file does not change over time, you can download it once and refer to the downloaded file whenever required instead of downloading it every time you want to refer to it. This is because the former is much faster than the latter. This is exactly what caching is. We fetch or compute a value once, then store it in a place where we can easily access it for future use.

In addition to being faster, caching can also improve the stability of an app as the data is available locally, and does not have to be fetched from the internet, thus avoiding network issues. Some APIs also have rate limits. Frequently making API calls can breach those limits, leading to problems with fetching data. Caching helps avoid this by reducing API calls.

This behavior can also reduce the operating costs of an app by reducing the number of API calls made if you are using a commercial API and paying per call or by the amount of data transferred. If the data is computed locally, caching can help prevent recomputation, reducing hardware and, by extension, power use.

Manually Implementing Simple Caches

Let us implement caching ourselves to better understand how it works, and demonstrate its benefits.

First, let us see how caching improves speed, and reduces API calls if data needs to be accessed over the internet.

The following is an example without caching:

```
from timeit import timeit

import pandas as pd

counter = 0
url = "https://raw.githubusercontent.com/mwaskom/seaborn-data/master/iris.csv"


def read_data():
    global counter
    counter += 1
    df = pd.read_csv(url)

    return df


print(f"Average time taken to read data: {timeit(read_data, number=100)}s")
print(f"Number of API calls: {counter}")
```

In this example, we use the **read_data** function to read the Iris dataset online. We use the **timeit** function to get the time taken to access the data 100 times, and a **counter** variable to count the number of times we had to read the data from the internet. On running this script, the following output is obtained:

```
Average time taken to read data: 5.136666599999444s
Number of API calls: 100
```

[1] *https://docs.streamlit.io/develop/concepts/architecture/caching#minimal-example* (Accessed: 11 August 2024)

The time taken can vary depending on your internet speed, but the number of API calls will remain 100.

Now, let us add caching to this script as follows:

```
from timeit import timeit

import pandas as pd

counter = 0
df_cache = None
url = "https://raw.githubusercontent.com/mwaskom/seaborn-data/master/iris.csv"


def read_data():
    global counter, df_cache

    if df_cache is None:
        counter += 1
        df_cache = pd.read_csv(url)

    return df_cache


print(f"Average time taken to read data: {timeit(read_data, number=100)}")
print(f"Number of API calls: {counter}")
```

We have added a **df_cache** variable to act as a cache for the data being read online. Whenever we run **read_data**, we first check if the data exists in the cache. If it does, we get it from the cache. If not, we add it to the cache by reading it from the internet and increase the **counter**.

Upon running this, I got the following results:

```
Average time taken to read data: 0.07319640000059735s
Number of API calls: 1
```

As you can see, reading data from the cache was approximately 70 times faster than downloading it every time from the internet, and we reduced the number of API calls to just 1. This was the initial call to load the cache; we never had to download it from the internet after that.

Another example of how caching speeds up computation times would be the classic implementation of the Fibonacci sequence using recursion. An implementation is shown as follows:

```
from timeit import timeit

counter = 0


def fibonacci(n):
    global counter
    counter += 1

    if n <= 0:
        return 0
    elif n == 1:
        return 1
    else:
        return fibonacci(n - 1) + fibonacci(n - 2)
```

```
print(f"Time taken: {timeit(lambda: fibonacci(35), number=1)}s")
print(f"Number of function calls: {counter}")
```

Upon running this script, my output was as follows:

```
Time taken: 2.6278540000021167s
Number of function calls: 29860703
```

This means that it took us 2.63 seconds and almost 60 million calls to the **fibonacci** function to get the 35th element of the Fibonacci sequence.

Now, let us add caching to this script as follows:

```
from timeit import timeit

counter = 0
cache = {}

def fibonacci(n):
    if n in cache:
        return cache[n]

    global counter
    counter += 1

    if n <= 0:
        result = 0
    elif n == 1:
        result = 1
    else:
        result = fibonacci(n - 1) + fibonacci(n - 2)

    cache[n] = result
    return result

print(f"Time taken: {timeit(lambda: fibonacci(35), number=1)}s")
print(f"Number of function calls: {counter}")
```

In this case, we use a dictionary cache to store the position **n** and the Fibonacci number corresponding to that position.

Upon running this script, my output was as follows:

```
Time taken: 1.9899998733308166e-05s
Number of function calls: 36
```

This time, it only took me 0.00002 seconds and 69 function calls to get the same result!

Whenever the function is called, we store the argument **n** and the **result** in the cache. The next time the function is called with the same arguments, we can fetch it from the cache instead of recomputing the results. This is how caching works in general.

Python provides caching functionality through the **functools** library. We can use **functools.cache** as a decorator instead of having to implement caching from scratch, as follows:

```
from functools import cache
from timeit import timeit

counter = 0

@cache
def fibonacci(n):
```

```
        global counter
        counter += 1

        if n <= 0:
            return 0
        elif n == 1:
            return 1
        else:
            return fibonacci(n - 1) + fibonacci(n - 2)

print(f"Time taken: {timeit(lambda: fibonacci(35), number=1)}s")
print(f"Number of function calls: {counter}")
```

The code is now shorter and simpler, and the results are still the same:

```
Time taken: 2.049999966402538e-05s

Number of function calls: 36
```

Tip: *You can read more about* **`functools.cache`** *in the official Python documentation here: https://docs.python.org/3/library/functools.html#functools.cache.*

Caching in Streamlit

Caching is especially important in Streamlit due to the nature of the execution of Streamlit apps. Since the app reruns on each interaction, if long-running processes were executed or API calls were made each time it reruns, it would seriously degrade the user experience.

Thankfully, like **`functools.cache`**, Streamlit also provides functions that can be used as decorators to cache a function easily. These functions allow us to save the output of a function in a cache so that the next time the function is called with the same arguments; we can fetch the results from the cache instead of running the function.

Streamlit provides two functions, **`cache_data`**, and **`cache_resource`**, to cache serializable data and non-serializable resources. Let us explore each of them.

Figure 8.1: *st.cache_data and st.cache_resource*[2]

[2] *https://docs.streamlit.io/develop/concepts/architecture/caching#minimal-example* (Accessed: 11 August 2024)

Caching Data

`cache_data` is recommended when we want to cache functions that return serializable data.[3]

For example, consider a simple app that loads the Iris dataset. Implementations of this with and without caching are shown in *Figure 8.2*.

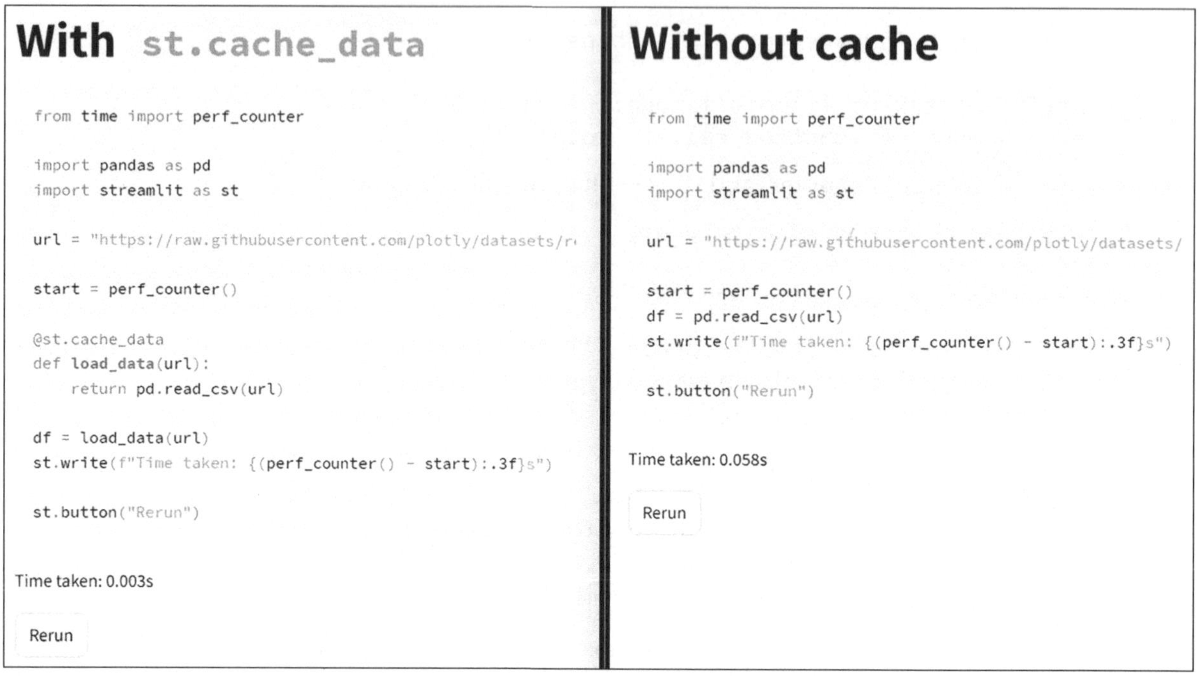

Figure 8.2: *Loading Data without and with Cache*

Note: *When running for the first time, the time taken with and without the cache will be the same. However, when we rerun the apps, the time taken without cache will remain the same as before, while the time taken with cache will be drastically lower.*

Behavior of `st.cache_data`

Why does the first run with `cache_data` take longer? Let us see how Streamlit works in the background when `cache_data` is used.[4]

1. When running for the first time, Streamlit does not find any entry in the cache for the **`load_data`** function with the passed URL. So, the function is run, and the file is downloaded.

2. Before exiting the context of the function, Streamlit creates an entry in the cache with the parameters (the URL) and the serialized return value (the DataFrame).

3. When the script is rerun, Streamlit checks if there is an entry in the cache for the **`load_data`** function with the same parameters. Since the parameters (URL) have not changed, it can find the cache entry. This object is then deserialized and returned. There is no need to download the file again.

4. If the URL has changed, Streamlit would not find an entry in the cache, and would proceed with Steps 1 and 2 to build an entry for the new URL.

---

[3] *https://docs.streamlit.io/get-started/fundamentals/advanced-concepts#caching* (Accessed: 11 August 2024)
[4] *https://docs.streamlit.io/develop/concepts/architecture/caching#behavior* (Accessed: 12 August 2024)

Difference between `st.cache_data` and `functools.cache`

`st.cache_data` may seem like a drop-in replacement for **`functools.cache`**, but there are essential differences in how they work, especially in the context of a Streamlit app.

The example in *Figure* 8.3 shows the difference in their behavior when run in the context of a Streamlit app.

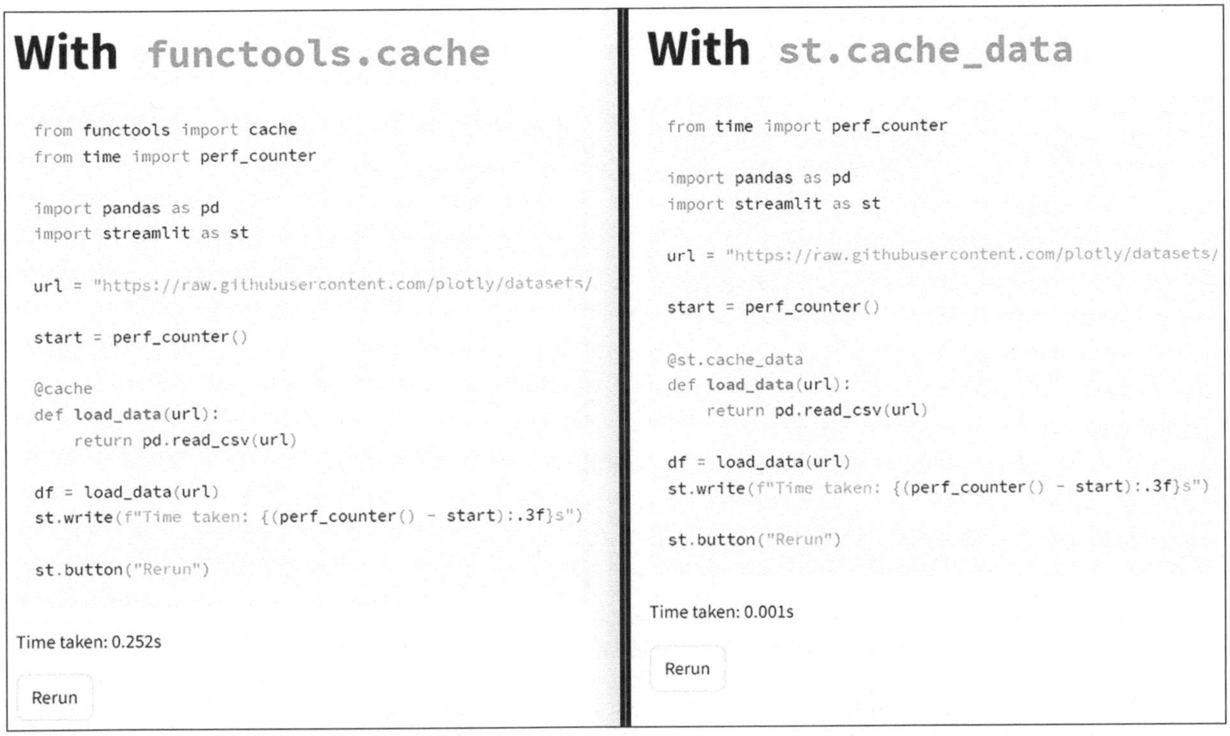

Figure 8.3: *functools.cache and st.cache_data*

Again, when running the app for the first time, the time taken for both **`functools.cache`** and **`st.cache_data`** would be almost the same. However, on rerunning the app, the time taken with **`st.cache_data`** drastically decreases (as expected), but that with **`functools.cache`** remains the same. Why is this?

This is because **`functools.cache`** works only in the context of script execution. When the script is rerun, the cache must be rebuilt. This is not very useful in Streamlit apps where the script has to be rerun on any user interaction. Unlike **`functools.cache`**, **`st.cache_data`** works in the context of the app server. So, as long as the server is up, the cache persists across script reruns, sessions, and even users on the same server. This means that once a cache entry has been created, it is available to all the users on the server. For example, another user trying to load the same Uber Rides data on the same Streamlit app will not have to wait for the data to be read from the URL, as a cache entry is already present.

Streamlit cache persisting across users is also why, unlike **`functools.cache`**, **`st.cache_data`** returns a copy of the cached object, instead of the original. The original object is the serialized object, while what is returned is a deserialized copy of the original. This protects the original object from corruption that can be caused if the object is modified later in the code and concurrency issues that can arise when multiple users are using the same app.

Let us see the former using the example shown in *Figure* 8.4.

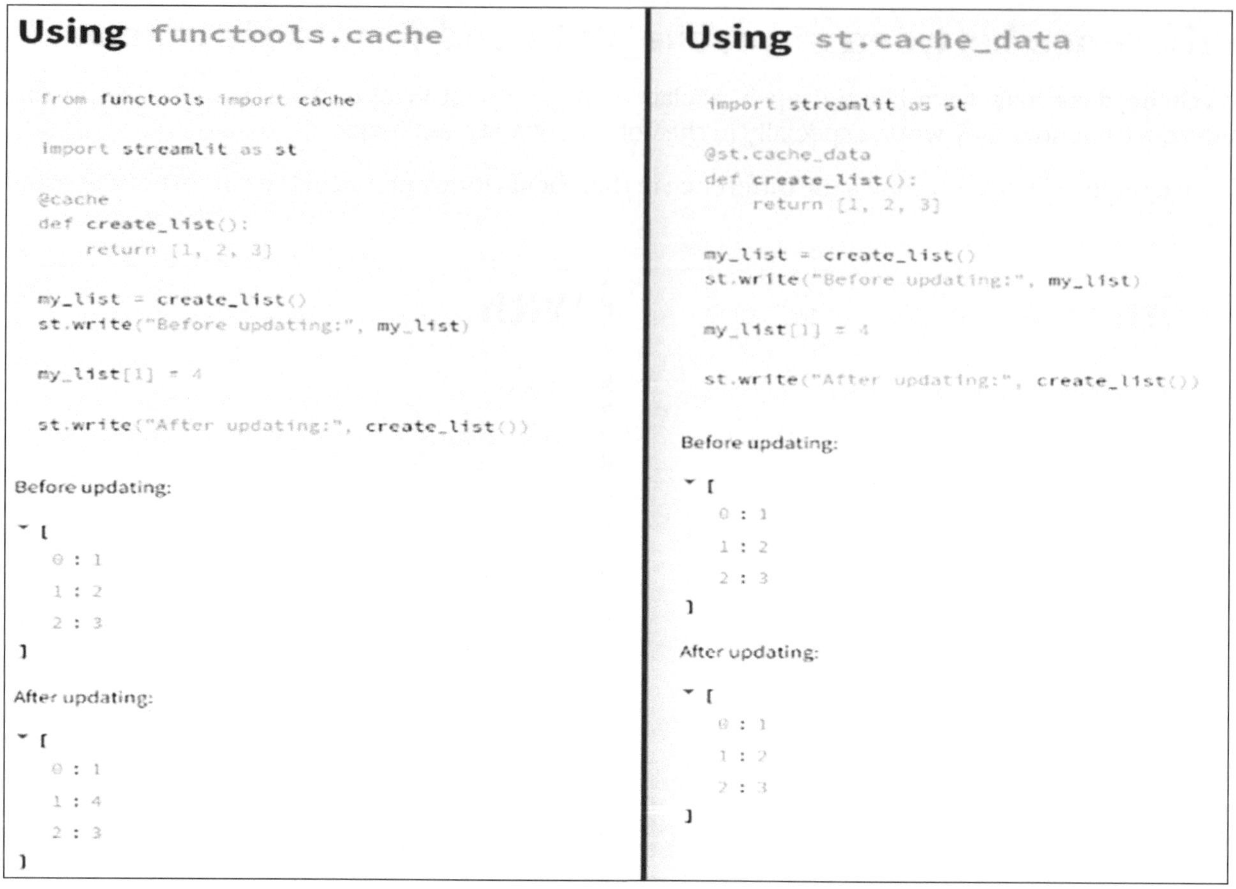

Figure 8.4: *Updating Returned Value after Calling the Function*

In the example shown in *Figure* 8.4, we have cached a function **`create_list`** that returns a list when called. We then update the list, and see how **`functools.cache`** and **`st.cache_data`** handle this update.

As you can see with **`functools.cache`**, when we call the function again, we get the updated list. Meanwhile, with **`st.cache_data`**, we get the original list. This is because, since **`functools.cache`** returns the original object from the cache, any modification to the object modifies the object stored in the cache itself. This can cause data corruption.

In contrast, **`st.cache_data`** returns a copy of the object. So, any change to the object affects only the copy, and the original object in the cache remains unaffected. This is why we get the original list when calling the function again.

Similarly, if multiple app users accessing the app concurrently change the object, they only affect their copy of the cache's results and not anyone else's.

Caching Resources

`cache_resource` is recommended to cache unserializable data, such as machine learning models or database connections. Since **`cache_data`** needs the return value of a function to be serializable, it cannot be used if a function returns an unserializable data type, like database connections, some machine learning models, file handles, and so on.[5] In such cases, we can use **`cache_resource`**.

[5] *https://docs.streamlit.io/develop/concepts/architecture/caching#minimal-example* (Accessed: 12 August 2024)

Let us see how cache_resource works using an example as follows:

```
from time import perf_counter, sleep

import pandas as pd
import streamlit as st
from sklearn.datasets import load_iris
from sklearn.ensemble import RandomForestClassifier

def load_model():
    iris = load_iris()
    X, y = iris.data, iris.target_names[iris.target]
    model = RandomForestClassifier()
    model.fit(X, y)
    sleep(5)  # Simulating a long loading time
    return model

st.title("Cache Resource Example")

sepal_length = st.slider("Sepal Length", 4.0, 8.0)
sepal_width = st.slider("Sepal Width", 2.0, 4.5)
petal_length = st.slider("Petal Length", 1.0, 7.0)
petal_width = st.slider("Petal Width", 0.1, 2.5)

input_data = pd.DataFrame(
    [[sepal_length, sepal_width, petal_length, petal_width]],
    columns=["sepal_length", "sepal_width", "petal_length", "petal_width"],
)

start = perf_counter()
model = load_model()
st.write(f"Time taken to load the model: {(perf_counter() - start):.3f}s")

prediction = model.predict(input_data)
prediction_proba = model.predict_proba(input_data)

st.write(f"Prediction: {prediction[0]}")
st.write(f"Prediction Probability: {max(prediction_proba[0])}")
```

Note: *You will need to have scikit-learn installed to run this example. You can install it using pip install scikit-learn.*

Running this script using streamlit run opens an app like the one shown in *Figure* 8.5.

Figure 8.5: *cache_resource Example*

In the preceding example, the **`load_model`** function loads the Iris dataset, and then trains a Random Forest Classifier model. We then use the sliders to simulate different inputs to the model, and get a prediction for those inputs. We also note the time taken to load the model. Since this is a small model, we artificially simulate a long loading time using sleep so that the **`cache_resource`** behavior is more apparent.

Play around with the sliders for a while, and note the time it takes for each prediction. Because the script is rerun on every slider change, the entire model must be loaded every time you change.

Now, add **`@st.cache_resource`** just above the **`load_model`** definition as follows:

```
@st.cache_resource
def load_model():
    ...
```

Update the sliders again. Do you notice any change? From almost 5 seconds per change earlier, the model loads almost instantaneously. This is because once the model has been cached by **`cache_resource`**, the next time **`load_model`** is called, Streamlit returns the cached model without training it from scratch.

Note: *In this example, you can use* **`cache_data`** *instead of* **`cache_resource`** *as almost all scikit-learn models are serializable. But in general, you will want to use* **`cache_resource`** *whenever you wish to cache machine learning models.*

`cache_resource`'s behavior is similar to **`cache_data`** but with one crucial difference. Unlike **`cache_data`**, which returns a copy of the cached object, **`cache_resource`** returns the object itself. While this helps reduce memory consumption because there is no need to create copies of the object, it can lead to data corruption if the returned object is modified, as any modification will update the original object.[6]

However, this behavior can be beneficial if we deal with large data. Since `cache_data` serializes the data on the first run and then deserializes it on every subsequent run, this operation can take time if the data is extensive. In such cases, we can use `cache_resource` as it does not serialize and deserialize data, which makes it much faster.

Note: *Performance benchmarks for* ***cache_data*** *and* ***cache_resources*** *are available at https://docs.streamlit.io/develop/concepts/architecture/caching#dealing-with-large-data.*

Advanced Caching Options

Now that we know why, how, and when to use `cache_data` and `cache_resource`, let us dive deeper into a few advanced options that help us fine-tune how the cache is used.

Limiting Cache Size

Since cache entries are stored in memory, there is a chance that we might run out of memory if the cache becomes too large. We can use the `max_entries` parameter of `cache_data` and `cache_resource` to specify the maximum number of entries in the cache, thus preventing out-of-memory errors.

When `max_entries` is used, the oldest entry from the cache is removed, once the maximum size is reached.[7] This maintains a good balance between cache size and frequently accessed retrieved cache items, similar to `functools.lru_cache`.[8]

Limiting Cache Duration

We know that caching in Streamlit works by checking if a cache entry is present for a given set of function parameters. If it is, the entry is returned from the cache without executing the function.

But what happens if the function reads data from an external source that can change? For example, it is possible that a database can return different results for the same query if the database has been updated. In this case, caching the returned value indefinitely might return incorrect results if the database is updated after the entry is cached.

This can be handled by using the time-to-live (`ttl`) parameter. This parameter lets us specify how long an entry should live in the cache. Any cache entries older than `ttl` will be dropped from the cache. This helps us get more accurate results by removing older cache entries, and prevents the cache from growing too large.

Clearing the Cache

We can also clear the cache manually. The easiest way of doing this is by clicking on "`Clear cache`" from the Kebab menu (⋮) at the top-right of the app (also known as the app chrome) or pressing C when the app is in focus. This will fully clear both the data and resource caches.

---

[6] *https://docs.streamlit.io/develop/concepts/architecture/caching#behavior-1* (Accessed: 13 August 2024)

[7] *https://docs.streamlit.io/develop/concepts/architecture/caching#controlling-cache-size-and-duration* (Accessed: 15 August 2024)

[8] *https://docs.python.org/3/library/functools.html#functools.lru_cache* (Accessed: 15 August 2024)

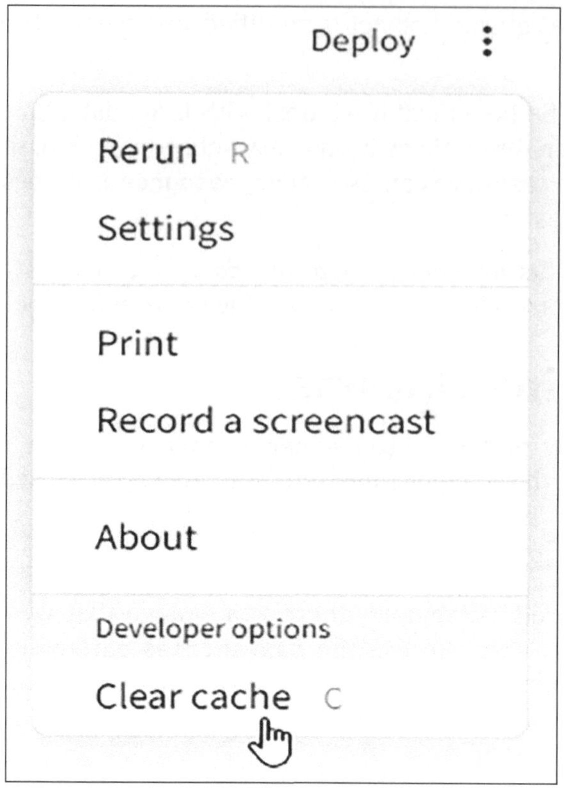

Figure 8.6: *Clearing the Cache from the App Chrome*

If you want to clear only the data cache or the resource cache, you can use **`cache_data.clear()`** or **`cache_resource.clear()`** respectively.

For more granular control, you can use the clear method of the cached function. It only clears the cache of that function, leaving others intact. For even more granularity, you can pass the arguments for which you want to clear the cache entry.[9]

For example, if a function, **`foo`** is defined as follows:

```
@st.cache_data
def foo(bar):
    ...
```

Calling **`foo.clear()`** will clear the entire cache for **`foo`**, while calling **`foo.clear(42)`** will only clear the cache entry corresponding to **`bar`**=42.

Excluding Input Parameters

We know that Streamlit caching functions work by checking, if a record exists in the cache for the given set of input parameters to a function. For this to work, all the input parameters must be hashable. The most commonly used data types are hashable, like strings, integers, dataframes, and so on. However, sometimes you might want to pass unhashable parameters like database connections, machine learning models, and so on. If you try to cache such a function, Streamlit will raise an **`UnhashableParamError`**.

For example, consider a function foo defined as **`foo(arg1, arg2, arg3)`**. If arg1 is not hashable, using **`cache_data`** or **`cache_resource`** on **`foo`** will lead to a **`UnhashableParamError`**.

[9] *https://docs.streamlit.io/develop/api-reference/caching-and-state/st.cache_data#cachedfuncclear* (Accessed: 15 August 2024)

To work around this issue, we can prepend the parameter name with an underscore (_), and Streamlit will not use the parameter for caching. So, in the foo example, we can define the function as **foo(_arg1, arg2, arg3).** Now, Streamlit will ignore **_arg1** when caching the function, and only use arg2 and arg3. Consequently, for a given set of input parameters, the results returned by the cache will be the same as long as arg2 and **arg3** are the same. For example, passing **foo(0, 2, 3)** will give the same results as **foo(1, 2, 3)**. Keep this in mind when excluding a parameter from caching.

Using a Custom Hash Function

Sometimes, you do not want to exclude a parameter from caching, even though Streamlit cannot hash it. Or more advanced users might want to override Streamlit's caching mechanism for a parameter. This is where you can use the **hash_funcs** parameter.

hash_funcs takes a dictionary of the parameter to be hashed and the custom hashing function. For the preceding example, the implementation would look as follows:

```
@st.cache_data(hash_funcs={arg1 : my_hash_func})
def foo(arg1, arg2, arg3):
    ...
```

In this case, we apply a custom hash function – **my_hash_func** – to **arg1**, while **arg2** and **arg3** are hashed using Streamlit's default hashing mechanism. Since we no longer exclude **arg1** from the cache, we do not need to prefix it with an underscore.

Note: *Using* **hash_funcs** *and custom hash functions is an advanced topic beyond the scope of this book. To learn more about it, refer to the official Streamlit documentation: https://docs.streamlit.io/develop/concepts/architecture/caching#the-hash_funcs-parameter.*

Connecting to External Data

As mentioned at the beginning of this chapter, since Streamlit is intended to build web apps for data analysis scripts quickly, we must be able to efficiently connect our Streamlit apps to different data sources to provide a good user experience.

We have seen how caching helps in enhancing the app user experience by drastically speeding up data retrieval. In this section, we will learn how to connect our Streamlit apps to external data sources using the usual methods we use in Python outside Streamlit and then use Streamlit Connectors, the Streamlit's way of securely and efficiently connecting to data.

Using Usual Python Methods

Generally, any method you use to connect to or read data in standard Python scripts will also work in Streamlit.

For example, consider the following Python script, which can connect to a MySQL database.

Note: *The following scripts are just for reference, and running them is optional.*

To run them, you will need to have MySQL installed and running at localhost:3306, a user's table populated, and the **mysql-connector-python** *package installed. Read the MySQL documentation for details: https://dev.mysql.com/doc/refman/8.4/en/.*

```
import mysql.connector

# Connect to the MySQL database
connection = mysql.connector.connect(
    host="localhost",
```

```
    database="example_db",
    port=3306,
    user="root",
    password="password",
)

print("Connected to MySQL database")

# Create a cursor object
with connection.cursor() as cursor:

# Query data from the table
cursor.execute("SELECT * FROM users")
rows = cursor.fetchall()

# Print the queried data
for row in rows:
    print(row)

# Close the connection
connection.close()
print("MySQL connection is closed")
```

We can easily make it work in Streamlit by adding a few Streamlit elements and widgets.

```
import mysql.connector
import streamlit as st

# Connect to the MySQL database
host = st.text_input("Enter DB host:")
port = st.number_input("Enter DB port:", value=None)
database = st.text_input("Enter DB name:")
username = st.text_input("Enter DB username:")
password = st.text_input("Enter password", type="password")

if st.button("Connect"):
    connection = mysql.connector.connect(
        host="localhost",
        port=port,
        database=database,
        user=username,
        password=password,
    )

st.success("Connected to MySQL database")

# Create a cursor object
with connection.cursor() as cursor:

# Query data from the table
query = st.text_area("Enter SQL query:", value="SELECT * FROM users;")

if st.button("Run Query"):
    cursor.execute(query)
    rows = cursor.fetchall()

    # Print the queried data
    for row in rows:
```

```
            st.write(row)

        # Close the connection
        if st.button("Close Connection"):
            connection.close()
            st.info("MySQL connection is closed")
```

However, there are a couple of issues:

- **Secrets Management:** We will have to enter the database credentials every time the application is run. We could hardcode them into the code, but this is a bad practice as it exposes credentials to anyone who can see the code (especially, when using Streamlit Community Cloud, as the code will be open-source in that case). We will have to make a code change whenever we want to update the credentials. We could also store credentials in the environment variables or a configuration file. However, the former is not an option for applications deployed to Streamlit Community Cloud as we cannot add environment variables there, and the latter will also expose credentials to anyone who has access to the codebase. To solve this problem, Streamlit provides a native file-based secrets management system to quickly and securely store and access your secrets in your Streamlit app.[10] We will discuss this in more detail in the next chapter.
- **App Performance:** As we know, the application will be rerun for every interaction, every time a user interacts with the application, the connection and cursor will have to be recreated, and the data will have to be queried again. This adds unnecessary latency to the application and results in a poor user experience. Also, since there will be multiple reruns of the script with some of them not reaching **`connection.close()`**, we will end up with orphaned connections that have not been closed. But as we have discussed already, we can use **`cache_resource`** to cache the connection so that we keep reusing the same connection whenever the application reruns, without having to create new ones, ending up with orphaned connections, and **`cache_data`** to cache the queried results. We do not have to query the database again.

These recommendations for improving secrets management and performance have been incorporated into the following script.

Note: *The following script is just for reference, as it uses Secrets, which have not yet been covered in detail.*

```
import mysql.connector
import streamlit as st

@st.cache_resource
def connect_to_db(host: str, port: int, database: str, user: str, password:
str):
    connection = mysql.connector.connect(
        host=host,
        port=port,
        database=database,
        user=user,
        password=password,
    )
    return connection

@st.cache_data
def query_data(connection (no_), query: str)
    with connection.cursor() as cursor:
        cursor.execute(query)
        rows = cursor.fetchall()
```

[10] *https://docs.streamlit.io/develop/concepts/connections/secrets-management* (Accessed: 17 August 2024)

```
        return rows

    # Connect to the MySQL database
    host = st.text_input("Enter DB host:")
    port = st.number_input("Enter DB port:", value=None)
    database = st.text_input("Enter DB name:")

    if st.button("Connect"):
        connection = connect_to_db(
            host=host,
            port=port,
            database=database,
            user=st.secrets["DB_USERNAME"],
            password=st.secrets["DB_PASSWORD"],
        )

    st.success("Connected to MySQL database")

    # Query data from the table
    query = st.text_area("Enter SQL query:", value="SELECT * FROM users;")
    if st.button("Run Query"):
        rows = query_data(connection, query)

        # Print the queried data
        for row in rows:
            st.write(row)

    # Close the connection
    if st.button("Close Connection"):
        connection.close()
        st.info("MySQL connection is closed")
```

Although this approach solves the issues with secrets management by using Streamlit Secrets and performance by caching the connection and data, we are still using standard Python methods for connecting to the database, which requires us to take care of the above optimizations from our end.

Using Streamlit Connections

Streamlit Connections is a convenient way of handling all the nuances of caching and managing secrets so that we can focus more on building our apps.

Streamlit connections can be accessed using the **`st.connection`** method. Creating a connection using **`st.connection`** is easy, as shown in the following code:

```
connection = st.connection("connection_name", type="connection_type")
```

This one line of code creates and caches the connection, so we do not have to make a wrapper function and cache it ourselves.

Using this connection object, we can query the database as follows:

```
    rows = connection.query("SELECT * FROM users")
```

The query method of the connection has a data cache built in, so reruns of the application will be faster, and fewer API calls will be needed to query the same data repeatedly. Since we are querying a database that can be updated, it is recommended to set an expiry duration for the cached items so that we do not fetch old values from the cache, instead of fetching the latest results from the database. This can be done using the **ttl** parameter as follows:

```
rows = connection.query("SELECT * FROM users", ttl=600)
```

This query will retain results for 600 seconds in the cache. If the item is older than 600 seconds, it will be discarded from the cache, the database will be queried for the latest results, and these results will be cached.

You might be wondering how credentials are passed to the connection. We can do this by creating a **.streamlit/secrets.toml** file in the application's working directory. A basic example is as follows:

```
# .streamlit/secrets.toml
[connections.connection_name]
DB_USERNAME = "root"
DB_PASSWORD = "password"
```

You will need to create this file and populate it with the required credentials. Streamlit Connections will read the necessary secrets automatically from this file.

Note: *We will learn about Secret Management in Streamlit in detail in the next chapter.*

Using what we have learned so far about Streamlit Connections, our MySQL connection script can be simplified a lot, as follows:

```
import streamlit as st

if st.button("Connect"):
    connection = st.connection("mysql", type="sql")

    st.success("Connected to MySQL database")

    # Query data from the table
    query = st.text_area("Enter SQL query:", value="SELECT * FROM users;")
    if st.button("Run Query"):
        rows = connection.query(query, ttl=600)

        # Print the queried data
        for row in rows:
            st.write(row)

    # Close the connection
    if st.button("Close Connection"):
        connection.close()
        st.info("MySQL connection is closed")
```

The **secrets.toml** file needed will look as follows:

```
[connections.mysql]
url = "mysql+pymysql://root:password@localhost:3306/example_db"
```

We can see that this code is much shorter than the previous examples, but at the same time, more secure due to secrets being stored in an external file, and as performant as before due to caching being built-in.

Note: *Remember to add the* **secrets.toml** *file to* **.gitignore**, *as we do not want to upload this file to the repository.*

Streamlit has connections to the most popular data sources. A complete list is available in the Streamlit docs here: *https://docs.streamlit.io/develop/tutorials/databases*. Some of these are community-built connections, for example, the Streamlit Supabase Connector built by the author which can be used to connect Streamlit to Supabase Database, Storage, and Auth. It is available here: *https://github.com/SiddhantSadangi/st_supabase_connection.*

An end-to-end working tutorial of the MySQL connection is available here: *https://docs.streamlit.io/develop/tutorials/databases/mysql.* If you prefer not to set up MySQL, you can use SQLite by following the tutorial: *https://docs.streamlit.io/develop/concepts/connections/connecting-to-data.*

Conclusion

In this chapter, we have covered the basics of caching - why it is needed, how to implement it, and how it works, both within and outside the context of a Streamlit app. We have also learned about the difference between cache_data and cache_resource in Streamlit, when to use them, some of their nuances, and some advanced options that let us control the cache behavior.

Further in the chapter, we learned how to connect to the external data in Streamlit using the usual Python methods and Streamlit Connections. We learned about the advantages of Streamlit Connections, especially regarding secrets management and code simplicity.

Finally, we were introduced to Secrets Management in Streamlit. The next chapter will be dedicated to this topic.

Points to Remember

- Caching makes apps faster, more stable, and cheaper by removing redundant computations and API calls.
- **`cache_data`** should be used when the return value of a function can be serialized.
- **`cache_resource`** should be used when the return value of a function cannot be serialized.
- The maximum number of entries in the cache can be set using **`max_entries`**.
- The maximum time an entry should be kept in the cache can be set using **`ttl`**.
- Function parameters can be excluded from caching by prefixing them with an underscore (_).
- Usual Python methods of connecting to data also work in Streamlit, but there are issues with secrets management and performance, if they are not handled explicitly.
- Streamlit Connections (**`st.connection`**) implicitly handle secrets management and caching.

Multiple Choice Questions

1. Which of the following is true about **`cache_data`**?
    a. It persists across both sessions and users.
    b. It persists only across sessions.
    c. It persists only across users.
    d. It does not persist either across sessions or users.
2. Which caching method would you use to cache a function that returns a DataFrame with 100 million rows?
    a. `st.cache_data`
    b. `st.cache_resource`
    c. `functools.cache`
    d. `functools.lru_cache`

3. Which of the following cache parameters can you use to cache a function parameter that cannot be hashed by Streamlit's default hashing mechanism?
    a. `ttl`
    b. `max_entries`
    c. `hash_funcs`
    d. None of the above
4. What are the main challenges with using the standard Python methods to connect to the external data from a Streamlit app?
    a. Code complexity
    b. Latency
    c. Secrets management
    d. All of the above
5. What is the advantage of using **`st.connection`** for connecting to the external data sources in Streamlit?
    a. It simplifies the connection process.
    b. It handles secrets management.
    c. It has built-in caching.
    d. All of the above.

Answers

1. a
2. b
3. c
4. d
5. d

Questions

1. What is caching? Why is it important?
2. What are some significant differences between **`functools.cache`** and **`st.cache_data`**? Why are these differences important in the context of a Streamlit app?
3. What are some of the differences between **`cache_data`** and **`cache_resource`**?
4. What can be the adverse effects of not limiting the size and age of cache entries?
5. Under what circumstances would you want to exclude an input parameter to a function from the cache? What are some consequences of excluding a parameter from the cache?
6. What is the use of the **`hash_funcs`** parameter? Why is this needed?
7. What are the advantages of using Streamlit Connections over usual Python methods to connect to external data sources?

Key Terms

- **Caching:** This is a process by which frequently accessed data is stored in a location from where it can be easily and quickly accessed.[11] Such a location is called a cache.
- **Decorator:** A decorator, in Python, is a function that extends the behavior of another function without explicitly modifying it.[12]
- **Fibonacci Series:** The Fibonacci series is a sequence of numbers where each is the sum of the previous two numbers.[13]
- **`.gitignore`:** It is a file that specifies which files to exclude from Git tracking, and consequently, not upload to the repository.
- **Hashing:** In programming, hashing refers to taking an object and returning an integer, which represents the hash value of that object. This is generally used internally by dictionaries and sets to find keys or check for their existence quickly. Python has a built-in hash() function to return the hash value of an object if it has one.[14]
- **Recursion:** It is a programming concept where a function calls itself. Such a **function is called a recursive function.**[15]
- **Secrets:** In programming, secrets refer to digital credentials like passwords, API tokens, SSH keys, and so on, used to gain access to protected databases or APIs.[16]
- **Serialization:** This is also known as pickling, and is the process of converting a Python object (or hierarchy of objects) into a form, most often a byte stream, that can be shared and preserved in its format when used later. The process of recovering the original object or objects from a serialized object is called deserialization or unpickling.[17]

[11] *https://www.geeksforgeeks.org/caching-system-design-concept-for-beginners/* (Accessed: 10 August 2024)
[12] *https://realpython.com/primer-on-python-decorators/* (Accessed: 10 August 2024)
[13] *https://www.britannica.com/science/Fibonacci-number* (Accessed: 10 August 2024)
[14] *https://www.geeksforgeeks.org/python-hash-method/* (Accessed: 17 August 2024)
[15] *https://www.geeksforgeeks.org/what-is-recursion/* (Accessed: 10 August 2024)
[16] *https://www.ekransystem.com/en/blog/secrets-management* (Accessed: 17 August 2024)
[17] *https://docs.python.org/3/library/pickle.html* (Accessed: 11 August 2024)

CHAPTER 9

Managing Secrets in Streamlit

Introduction

In the previous chapter, we discussed secrets management in Streamlit. In this chapter, we will explore this topic in greater detail. First, we will provide an overview of secrets management and examine some common methods for managing secrets. Next, we will delve into Streamlit's native secrets management method, and demonstrate how to use it when developing applications locally. This includes managing secrets at the project level for individual applications and globally for all Streamlit applications on the system. Finally, we will cover how to manage secrets for applications deployed on the Streamlit Community Cloud.

Structure

In this chapter, we will discuss the following topics:

- Introduction to Secrets Management
- Common Secrets Management Methods
- Managing Streamlit Secrets Locally
    - Project-Level Secrets
        - Basic Usage
        - Organizing Secrets as Sections
    - Global Secrets
- Managing Secrets on Streamlit Community Cloud
    - Adding Secrets while Deploying Apps
    - Updating Secrets of Already Deployed Apps

Introduction to Secrets Management

Secrets management in programming involves securely storing, managing, and accessing sensitive information, such as passwords, API keys, SSH keys, and certificates. This information, often called secrets, is essential for accessing protected resources and services in applications, scripts, and automated processes.

Due to the sensitive nature of these secrets, it is crucial to implement practices and techniques that prevent unauthorized access, whether deliberate or accidental, without hindering end-users.

Common Secrets Management Methods

Some common methods of managing secrets, along with their advantages and disadvantages, are:

- **Environment Variables:** Storing secrets as environment variables is the simplest and most common method. It keeps secrets out of the source code, and allows for easy configuration changes without updating the code. This method makes secrets easily accessible and adaptable for authorized users. However, it is limited in scope as it can only be used by applications running on the system where the environment variable has been defined. In Python, environment variables can be accessed using the **`os.getenv()`** method. They can also be set dynamically during code execution using the syntax **`os.environ["ENV_VARIABLE_NAME"] = value`**. Note that updating an environment variable this way is only effective while the app is running. The environment variable reverts to its previous value once the app has been terminated.
- **Configuration Files**: Secrets can be stored in configuration files kept separate from the source code. Common formats for these files include **`.env`**, **`.json`**, **`.yaml`**, and **`.toml`**. This method is straightforward, does not require additional infrastructure or tools, and allows for easy sharing of secrets with authorized users. However, the ease of sharing can also be a security risk if these files are not encrypted and access-controlled. Sensitive information can be exposed, especially if accidentally included in a version control system like **`Git`**. Therefore, these files should be added to **`.gitignore`** *to prevent them from being committed to the repository. Streamlit's native secrets management uses configuration files in the form of a* **`secrets.toml`** *file.*
- **Secrets Management Tools**: Dedicated tools like HashiCorp Vault, AWS Secrets Manager, Azure Key Vault, and Google Cloud Secret Manager provide robust solutions for storing, managing, and accessing secrets. These tools offer features like secret rotation, access control, and auditing. While such tools generally provide greater protection than configuration files or environment variables by completely decoupling secrets from the code's environment and requiring separate access to secrets, they come with a financial cost.
- **Hardware Security Modules (HSMs)**: HSMs are physical devices that provide secure generation, storage, and management of cryptographic keys. They are used in high-security environments where hardware-based security is required. These devices generally come as a plug-in card or an external device that attaches directly to a system to authenticate the device holder. HSMs provide enhanced security as they are isolated from the software system they protect. However, they are generally expensive to purchase and maintain, and are susceptible to physical theft and tampering.

Tip: *We highly recommend Open Worldwide Application Security Project's (OWASP) secrets management cheat sheet if you are interested in learning more about secrets management in general. You can find it here: https://cheatsheetseries.owasp.org/cheatsheets/Secrets_Management_Cheat_Sheet.html.*

All of these methods can be used with Python and, consequently, with Streamlit, as long as Streamlit's Client-Server architecture is taken into account (as discussed in *Chapter 4, Exploring Streamlit's Flow and Architecture*).

Managing Streamlit Secrets Locally

Streamlit's native secrets management offers an easy-to-use and intuitive method for securely managing secrets in Streamlit applications. It utilizes configuration files in the form of a **`secrets.toml`** file. Depending on the placement of this file, secrets can be made available for a specific project or shared globally across all local applications during development.

Tip: *In the following sections, we will cover the basics of using TOML files for Streamlit Secret Management. For an in-depth tutorial on working with TOML files in Python, we recommend https://www.pythonforbeginners.com/basics/working-with-toml-files-in-python.*

Project-Level Secrets

If the **`secrets.toml`** file is located at **`$CWD/.streamlit/secrets.toml`**, where **`$CWD`** is the folder, you are running Streamlit from, the secrets will be available only to the apps running from that directory. These are known as project-level secrets or local secrets.

Note: *Since these secrets are stored in the same folder as the source code, they should be added to* **`.gitignore`** to prevent them from being automatically committed to the Git repository, and exposed to unauthorized users.

Basic Usage

Let us create a **`secrets.toml`** file, and see how we can use it in an app.

Assuming that you are working inside a folder titled **`Chapter_9`**, create a **`.streamlit`** folder and a **`secrets.toml`** file with a username and a password inside the **`.streamlit`** folder, as shown in *Figure 9.1*.

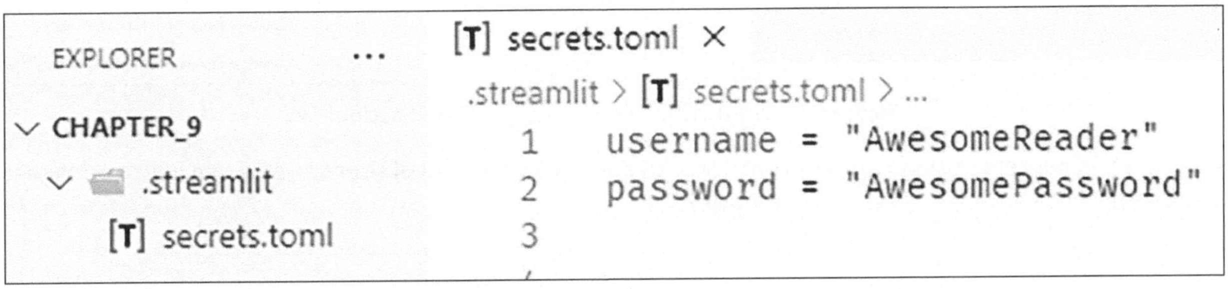

Figure 9.1: *Local Secrets File*

These secrets can be accessed in a Streamlit app using the syntax **`st.secrets["<KEY_NAME>"]`**.

Create a new Streamlit app in the same folder (**`Chapter_9`** in this case) to read the username and password from the secrets. A simple example, including the folder structure, secrets file, app code, and output, is shown in the following *Figure* 9.2.

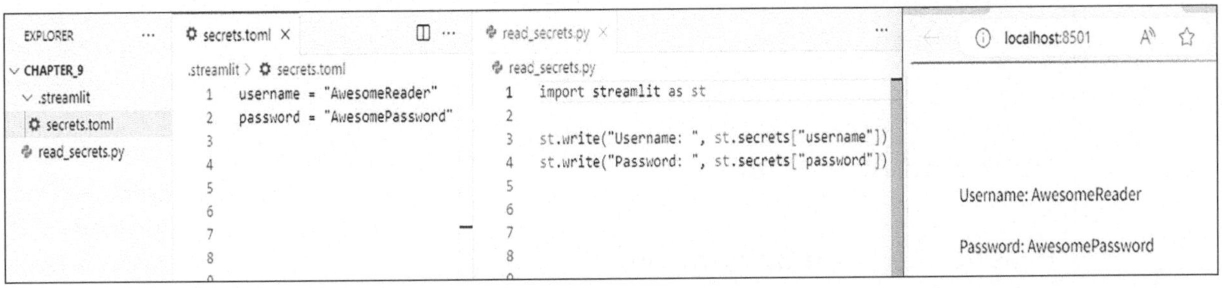

Figure 9.2: *Reading from secrets.toml*

One useful feature of using Streamlit's native secrets management is that, like source code, the app reruns automatically whenever the secrets or **`secrets.toml`** file are changed. You can test this by updating the **`username`** or **`password`** in the **`secrets.toml`** file. If an external secrets management solution were used, you would have to rerun the app manually for it to pick up the new secrets.

Note: *Automatic reload of the app only works if the* **`secrets.toml`** *file already exists when the app is run for the first time. If the file is created while the app is running, the app must be reloaded manually to start reading from the* **`secrets.toml`** *file.*

Organizing Secrets as Sections

TOML files can have multiple sections to organize attributes. You can use these sections to organize secrets, and read them as nested key-value pairs.

For example, you can create a new section for a different database, **`database_1`**, and access those values, as shown in the following *Figure* 9.3.

Figure 9.3: *Organizing Secrets Using TOML Sections*

The top-level secrets outside any section are also known as root-level secrets, and can also be accessed as environment variables, as shown in *Figure* 9.4.

Figure 9.4: *Accessing Root-level Secrets as Environment Variables*

Finally, since secrets are just key-value pairs in a dictionary format, they can also be passed to relevant functions more compactly, as packed iterables, as shown in the following *Figure* 9.5.

***Figure 9.5**: Packing Secrets*

Global Secrets

Local secrets work well if you only have a few apps with their unique secrets. However, managing local secrets can be challenging when sharing secrets across multiple applications, as you would need to update each **`secrets.toml`** file whenever a secret changes.

To address this, Streamlit offers global secrets. The process remains the same, but the location of the global secrets file changes to your home directory: **`~/.streamlit/secrets.toml`** for macOS/Linux or **`%userprofile%/.streamlit/secrets.toml`** for Windows. All secrets in this **`secrets.toml`** file will be available to all local applications.

If both global and local secrets are found, the local secrets take precedence.

To illustrate this, refer to the following *Figure* 9.6. The global secrets file is shown on the left, the project-level secrets in the center, and the app on the right.

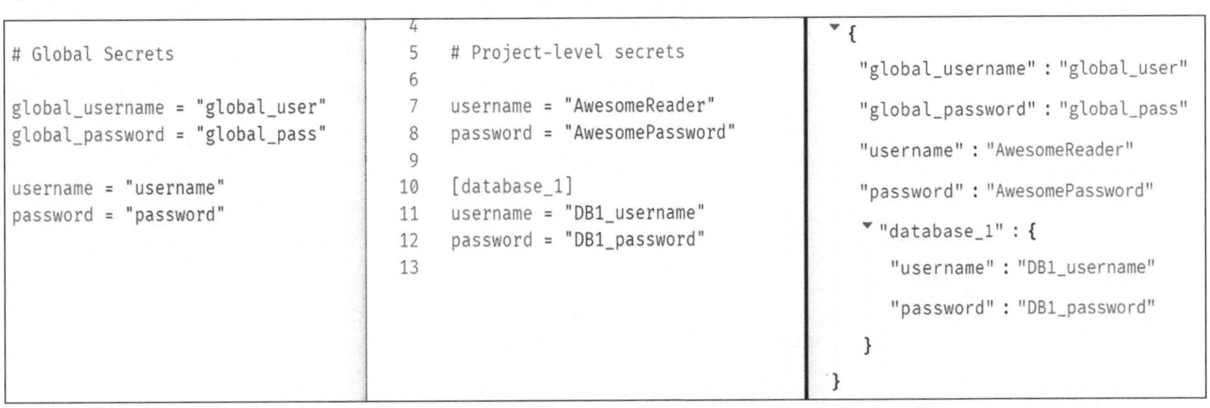

***Figure 9.6**: Using Global and Local Secrets Together*

As you can see, the values of the **username** and **password** secrets are taken from the local secrets, even though they also exist in the global secrets. Since the **global_username** and **global_password** secrets exist only in the global secrets, they are read from the global secrets file, and are available to the app.

Managing Secrets on Streamlit Community Cloud

When using Streamlit Secrets, no code changes are needed to deploy the app to Streamlit Community Cloud. However, since the **secrets.toml** file is not committed to GitHub, another method is required to make secrets securely available to the apps running on Streamlit Community Cloud. This is achieved through the Community Cloud Secrets Management console.

Adding Secrets while Deploying Apps

While deploying new apps, this console is available under Advanced settings, as shown in *Figure 9.7*. Deployment steps were discussed in detail in *Chapter 3, Creating and Deploying Your First Streamlit App*.

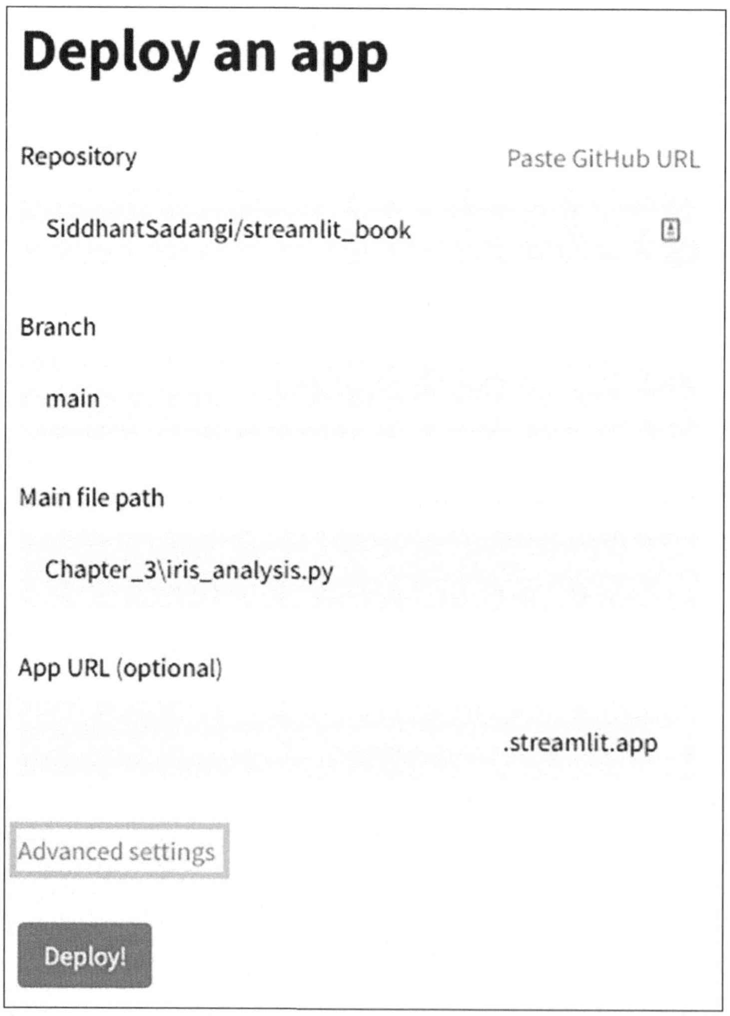

Figure 9.7: *Advanced Deployment Settings*

Clicking Advanced settings opens a modal that lets you select the Python version for hosting your app and a text-area input box for your secrets, as shown in *Figure 9.8*.

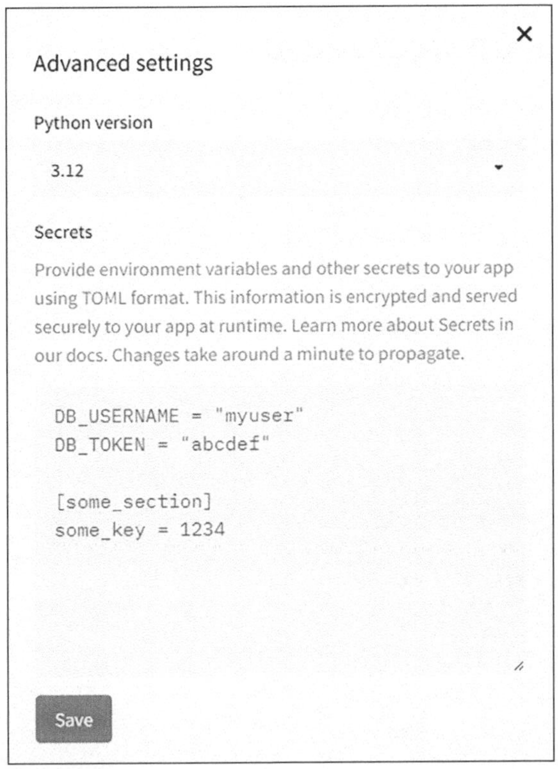

Figure 9.8: *The Community Cloud Secrets Management Console*

You can paste all the required secrets from both the local and global **`secrets.toml`** files here. Remember to paste section headers along with the key-value pairs if you are using sections. Once done, **Save** the changes, and deploy your app.

Updating Secrets of Already Deployed Apps

Secrets can be added or edited for an app that has already been deployed from the app's settings.

The settings can be accessed either through the overflow menu icon (⋮) next to the app when you sign in to https://share.streamlit.io/, as shown in *Figure* 9.9, or by expanding the Manage app section at the bottom right of the deployed app in the Community Cloud and clicking the menu icon (⋮), as shown in the following *Figure* 9.10.

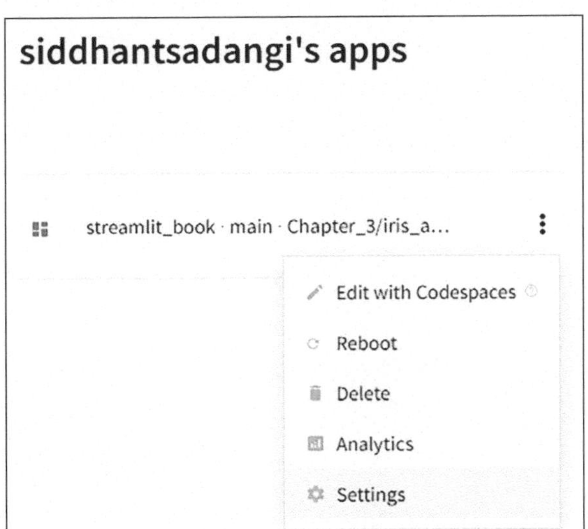

Figure 9.9: *Accessing Settings from the Apps List*

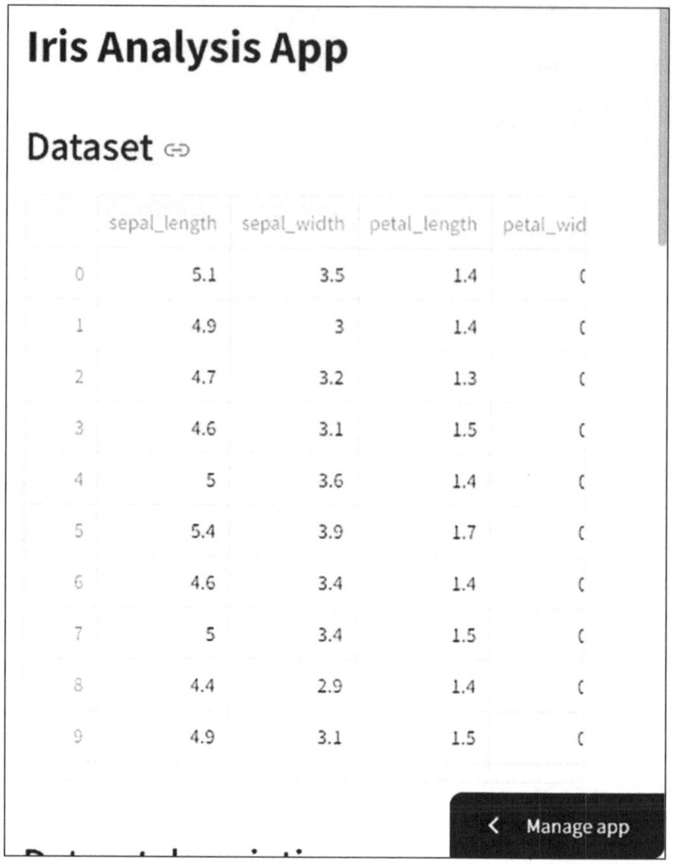

Figure 9.10: *Accessing Settings from the Deployed App*

Inside **`Settings`**, the Secrets Management console is available in the **`Secrets`** tab, as shown in the following *Figure* 9.11.

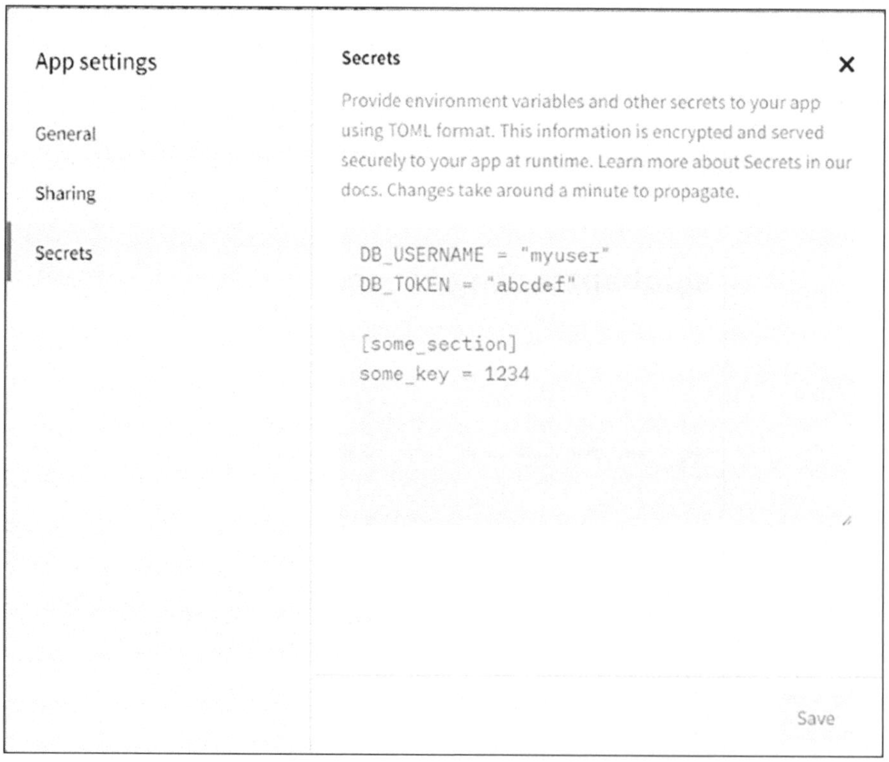

Figure 9.11: *Community Secrets Management Console for Already Deployed Apps*

Conclusion

In this chapter, we explored various methods of managing secrets and their advantages and disadvantages. We also delved into secrets management in Streamlit applications, examining how to use Streamlit's native secrets management for local development at both the project and global levels. Finally, we discussed managing secrets for applications deployed to Streamlit Community Cloud using the Community Cloud Secrets Management Console. In the next chapter, we will expand our knowledge on deploying applications to Streamlit Community Cloud. and managing deployed applications by exploring advanced deployment concepts.

Points to Remember

- Any secrets management method that works with regular Python scripts will also work with Streamlit.
- Streamlit's native secrets management uses configuration files in the form of a **`secrets.toml`** file.
- Streamlit apps automatically reload when the **`secrets.toml`** file is updated, provided the file existed when the app was first run.
- Streamlit allows two levels of secrets using the **`secrets.toml`** file: global or local.
- Local or project-level secrets are available only to apps in the same directory.
- Global secrets are available to all of the user's apps in the system.
- Local secrets take precedence over global secrets, if both are present.
- Streamlit Secrets follow a key-value syntax, and can be accessed using **`st.secrets`**.
- When using sections in the **`secrets.toml`** file, include the section headers and key-value pairs to maintain organization.
- Always remember to add sensitive files, like **`secrets.toml`**, to **`.gitignore`** to prevent accidental leakage of secrets and credentials.
- The Community Cloud Secrets Management Console can be used to manage secrets for apps deployed to the Streamlit Community Cloud.

Multiple Choice Questions

1. Which secrets management methods can be used with Streamlit?
    a. Environment variables
    b. Configuration files
    c. AWS Secrets Manager
    d. All of the above
2. Which of the following is a disadvantage of using configuration files for secrets management?
    a. They are difficult to share with authorized users.
    b. They require additional infrastructure.
    c. They can expose sensitive information, if not properly secured.
    d. They cannot be used with Streamlit.

3. What is the primary advantage of using Streamlit's native secrets management?
    a. It requires no additional infrastructure or tools.
    b. It automatically encrypts all secrets.
    c. It integrates with all cloud providers.
    d. It provides hardware-based security.
4. How can you access secrets in a Streamlit app?
    a. Using **os.getenv()**
    b. Using **st.secrets["<KEY_NAME>"]**
    c. Using **configparser**
    d. Using **json.load()**
5. Which secrets in the **secrets.toml** file can be accessed as environment variables?
    a. Root-level secrets
    b. Secrets under any section
    c. Secrets under the **[environment]** section
    d. All of the above
6. Under which conditions will a Streamlit app automatically rerun?
    a. New **secrets.toml** file created. while the app is running.
    b. Existing **secrets.toml** file updated, while the app is running.
    c. Both of the above
    d. None of the above
7. Where should the **secrets.toml** file be placed to make secrets available globally?
    a. In the project directory
    b. In the home directory
    c. In the system root directory
    d. In the Streamlit installation directory
8. If a secret exists in both local and global secrets, what happens when you try to access the secret in a Streamlit app?
    a. **DuplicateSecretError**
    b. Value read from local secrets
    c. Value read from global secrets
    d. Values read from both local and global secrets

Answers

1. d
2. c
3. a
4. b
5. a
6. b
7. b
8. b

Questions

1. What are some common secrets management methods? List their advantages and disadvantages.
2. Create a sample **`secrets.toml`** file having a root-level **`username`** and **`password`**, as well as a separate **`username`** and **`password`** for a MySQL and an SQLite database. Write a simple Streamlit script to read and display all these secrets.
3. What are the differences between local and global **`secrets.toml`** files in Streamlit?

Key Terms

- **Environment Variables:** A variable whose value is set outside the program, typically through functionality built into the operating system or microservice.[1]
- **TOML File:** TOML (Tom's Obvious, Minimal Language) is a configuration file format designed to be both human and machine-readable.
- **`secrets.toml`:** The configuration file used by Streamlit to manage secrets.
- **Community Cloud Secrets Management Console:** This console manages secrets for apps deployed on the Streamlit Community Cloud.

[1] *https://medium.com/chingu/an-introduction-to-environment-variables-and-how-to-use-them-f602f66d15fa* (Accessed: 21 August 2024)

Chapter 10
Advanced App Management Concepts

Introduction

Now that we have learned about handling secrets locally and for deployed Streamlit apps, this is an excellent time to learn about more advanced app deployment and management concepts. We will begin by revisiting the topic of app dependencies. In addition to Python dependencies, we will also cover how to install other software on the Streamlit Community Cloud server instance hosting our app. Next, we will explore the Streamlit workspace and its components in detail. Following this, we will learn how to manage our app, both from our workspace, and directly from within the app itself. This will be followed by a brief overview of the options and resources available for sharing our apps with developers and viewers. Finally, we will discuss the computing resources available for our app in Streamlit Community Cloud and their associated limits.

Structure

In this chapter, we will discuss the following topics:

- Installing App Dependencies
    - Installing Python Dependencies
    - Installing Non-Python Dependencies
- Exploring the Streamlit Workspace
- Managing an App
    - From the Community Cloud Workspace
    - From within the Hosted App
- Sharing an App
    - With Developers
    - With Viewers
        - The Share Button
- App Resources and Limits

Installing App Dependencies

As discussed in *Chapter 3, Creating and Deploying Your First Streamlit App*, the Streamlit Community Cloud server hosting our app starts with a clean environment. Therefore, we must specify which packages our app requires. The environment includes Python by default, so we do not need to specify it unless we want to use a specific version of Python. This can be controlled via deployment options, which will be discussed in the next section.

App dependencies can be divided into two categories: Python dependencies and non-Python dependencies.

Installing Python Dependencies

Installing Python dependencies on the Community Cloud mostly follows the same process as installing them locally, using popular Python package managers such as **pip**, **conda**, **poetry**, or **pipenv**.

We need to inform Streamlit Community Cloud which packages to install. This is done using any dependency file recognized by the Streamlit Community Cloud. As of the time of writing, the Community Cloud recognizes the following files and their corresponding Python package managers:

File	Python Package Manager
uv.lock	Uv
Pipfile	pipenv
environment.yml	conda
requirements.txt	pip
pyproject.toml	poetry

Table 10.1: *Python Package Managers Supported by Streamlit Community Cloud*[1]

The Community Cloud comes with the latest version of Streamlit preinstalled, so unless we want to use an older version, we do not need to mention it in the dependencies file. Also, although we do not need to mention any built-in Python libraries such as **math** or **random**, or Streamlit dependencies such as **pandas** and **numpy**, as these are installed with Python and Streamlit, respectively. It is a good practice to include all direct dependencies in the dependency file (pinned to the version number) as otherwise any breaking change in a future version of a dependency can break the app.

Note: *The list of all built-in Python packages is available at https://docs.python.org/3/py-modindex.html.*

Streamlit searches for a matching dependencies file first in the directory of the Streamlit app, and then in the repository's root. It will only use the first file if multiple dependency files are found.[2]

Installing Non-Python Dependencies

If our Streamlit app also has non-Python dependencies, these must be mentioned in a **packages.txt** file in your repository's root, with one package name per line. Streamlit Community Cloud will install the dependencies listed in this file using **apt-get**. For example, the following packages.txt file will install **libjpeg-dev**, **zlib1g-dev**, and **libpng-dev**:

```
libjpeg-dev
zlib1g-dev
libpng-dev
```

Exploring the Streamlit Workspace

The Streamlit Community Cloud is organized into workspaces, which group apps by the corresponding GitHub repository owner. Every user with an app deployed to the Community Cloud has at least

[1] *https://docs.streamlit.io/deploy/streamlit-community-cloud/deploy-your-app/app-dependencies#other-python-package-managers* (Accessed: 28 October 2025)
[2] *https://docs.streamlit.io/deploy/streamlit-community-cloud/deploy-your-app/app-dependencies#other-python-package-managers* (Accessed: 31 August 2024)

one workspace that matches their GitHub username and any additional workspaces for GitHub organizations or users who have granted them access.[3]

The workspace is divided into different tabs: `My apps`, `My profile`, and `Explore`. A workspace dropdown menu at the top-left shows the currently active workspace and a `Create app` button at the top-right.

Let us explore the different components of the workspace, starting from the workspace menu dropdown at the top left.

Note: *The content in this section reflects the state of the workspace as of October 2025.*

Workspace Menu

The workspace menu dropdown is shown in the following *Figure 10.1*.

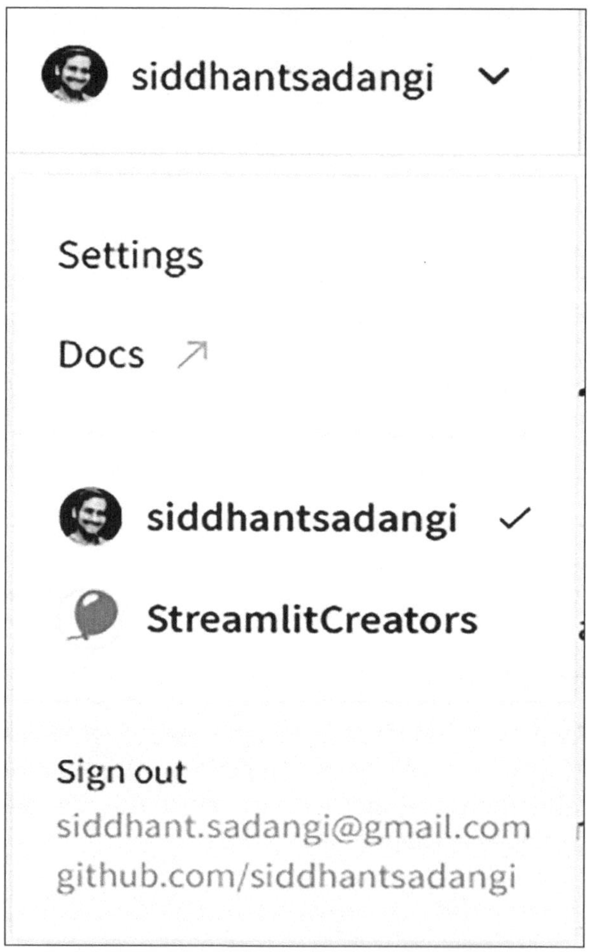

Figure 10.1: *Workspace Settings and Switcher*

This dropdown contains the workspace settings, a link to the Streamlit documentation, a list of all workspaces you are a part of (with the current workspace marked with a ✔), and the option to sign out from the current workspace.

Starting with the workspace settings, it has three sections:

[3] *https://docs.streamlit.io/deploy/streamlit-community-cloud/manage-your-app#manage-your-app-from-your-workspace* (Accessed: 1 September 2024)

Linked Accounts

This section contains the email and GitHub accounts linked to the selected workspace and the **`Delete account`** button.

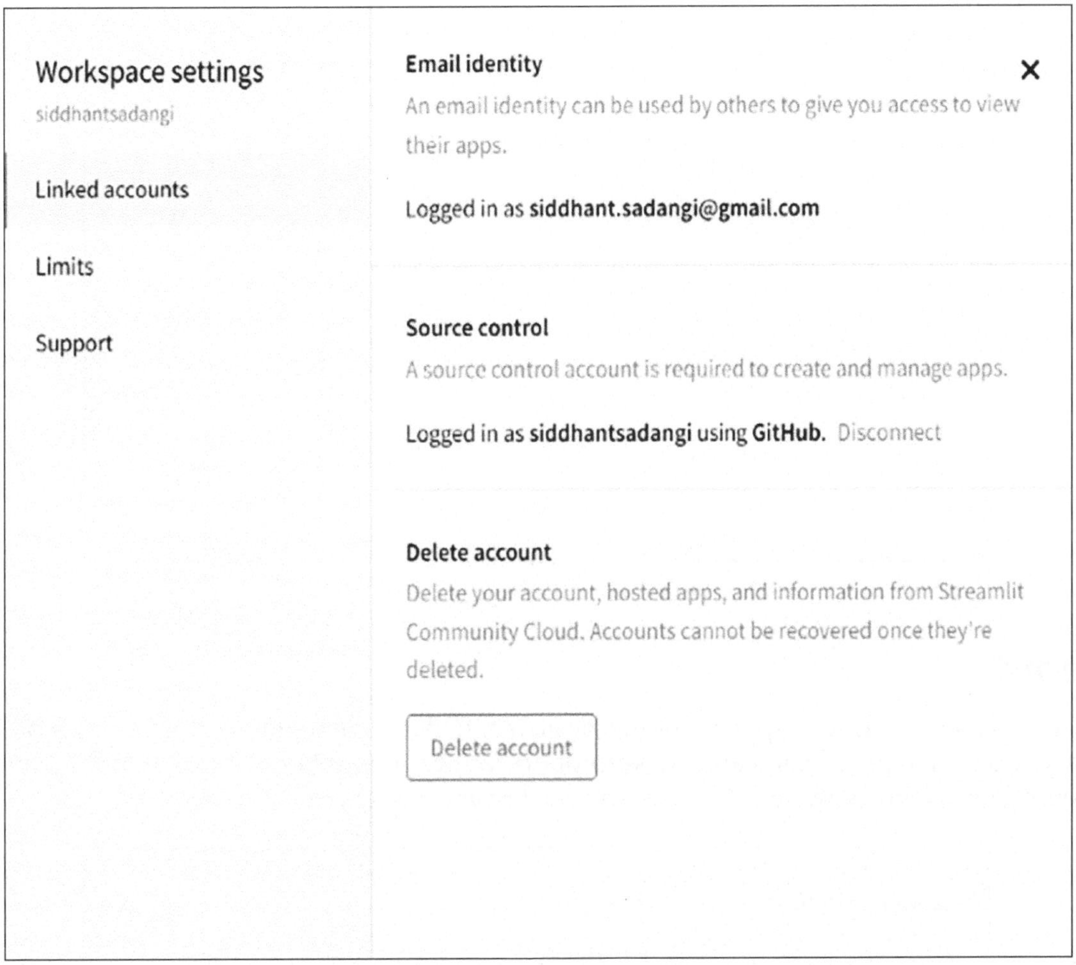

Figure 10.2: *Linked Accounts*

This section contains the email and GitHub accounts linked to the selected workspace and the **`Delete account`** button.

Limits

This section lists the limits in place in the workspace, such as the storage space available for each app, and the number of private and public apps allowed. We will discuss these limits in more detail later in this chapter.

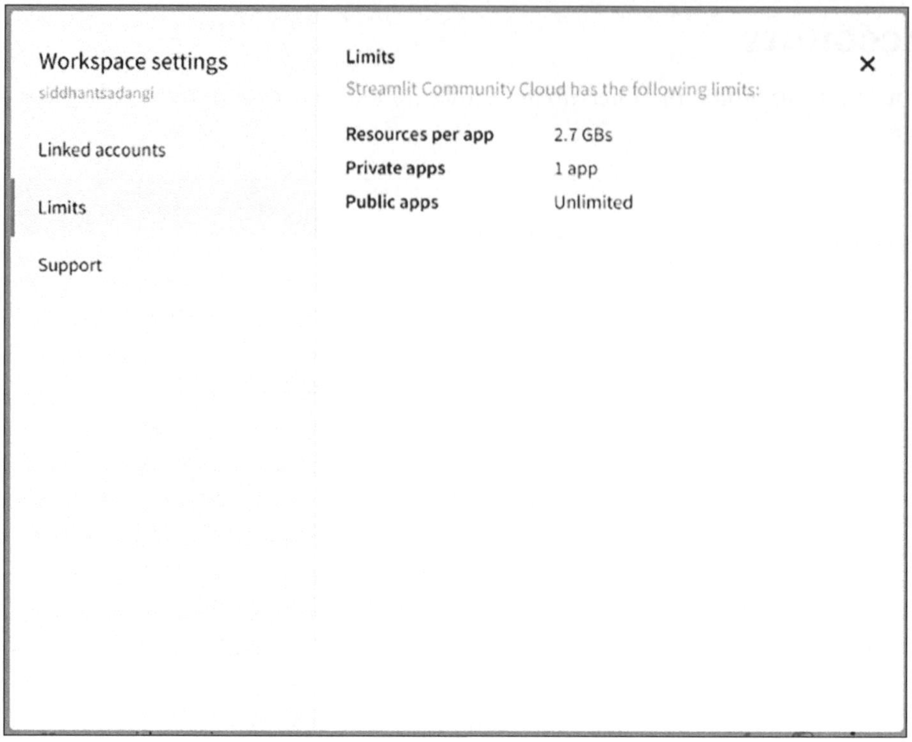

Figure 10.3: *Workspace Limits*

Support

This section lists the various support options available, including documentation, discussion forums, and instructions on how to reach Snowflake support for account-related issues. It also includes legal documents such as the `Terms of Service` and the `Privacy Notice`.

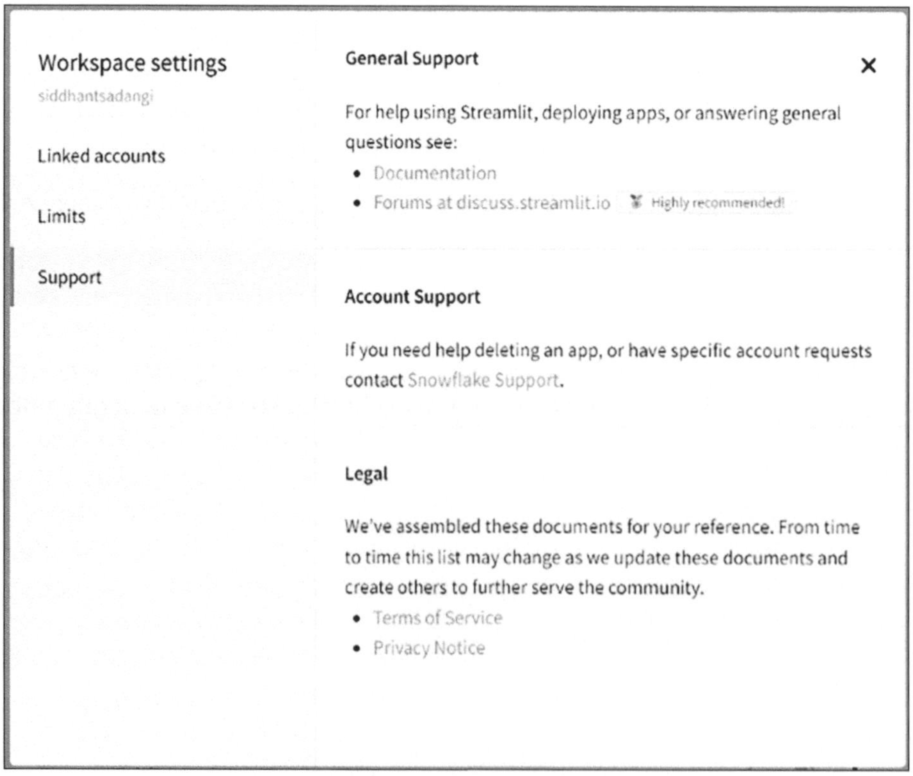

Figure 10.4: *Support*

The workspace menu is also where you can switch between different workspaces. Switching to a different workspace will show you the apps present in that workspace in the **My apps** tab.

My Apps

This tab lists all the apps available in the current workspace, a few templates to help you get started, and a link to view all the available templates.

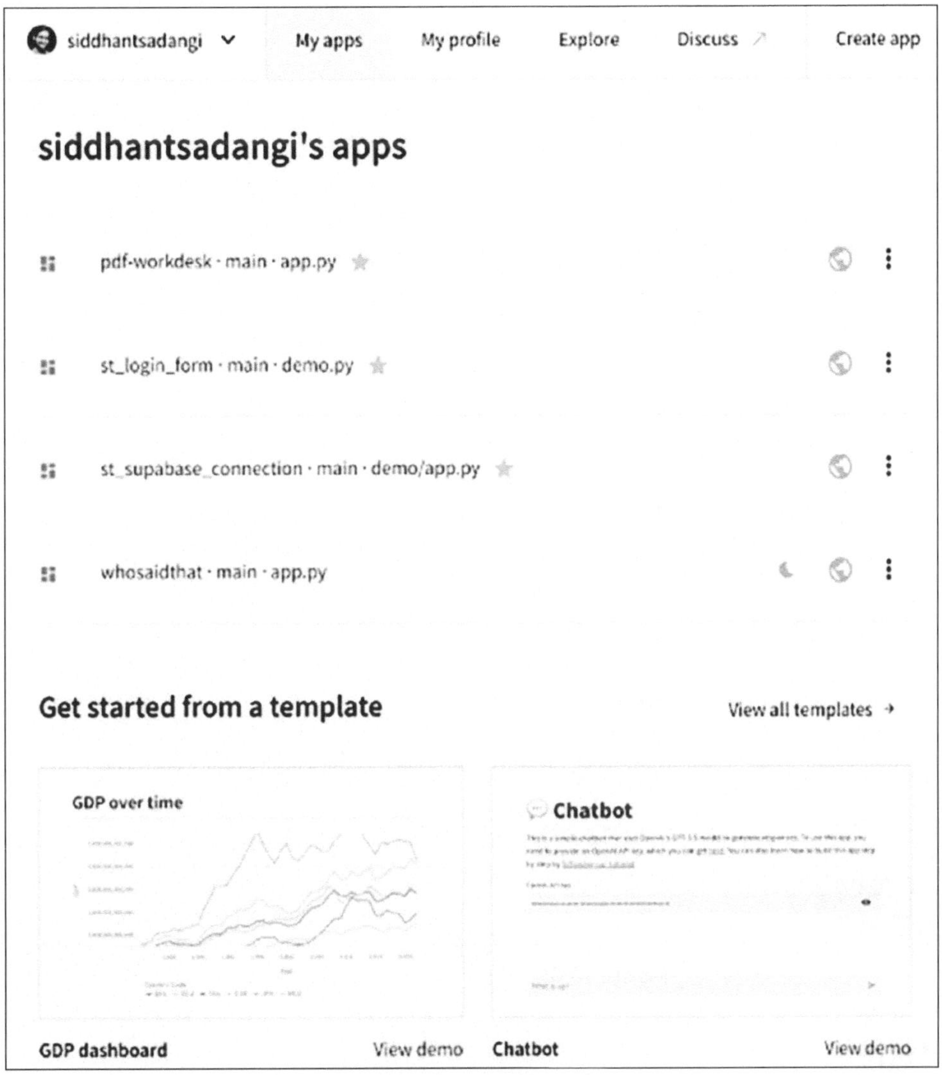

Figure 10.5: *My Apps Tab*

The apps have a few indicators:

- **Star (★)** indicates if the app has been marked as a favorite.
- **Cresent moon** (☾) indicates if the app is in sleep mode. We will discuss this in a more detailed manner later in this chapter.
- **Globe** (🌐) indicates if the app is public.

Finally, the app overflow menu (⋮) to the right lets you manage the app. We will discuss this in more detail later in this chapter.

At the bottom of the apps list are a few templates for creating a new app. Clicking on any of these templates opens the **Deploy from a template** page (as shown in *Figure 10.6*), which lets you choose a template, clone it to GitHub Codespaces, and deploy it directly from the browser.

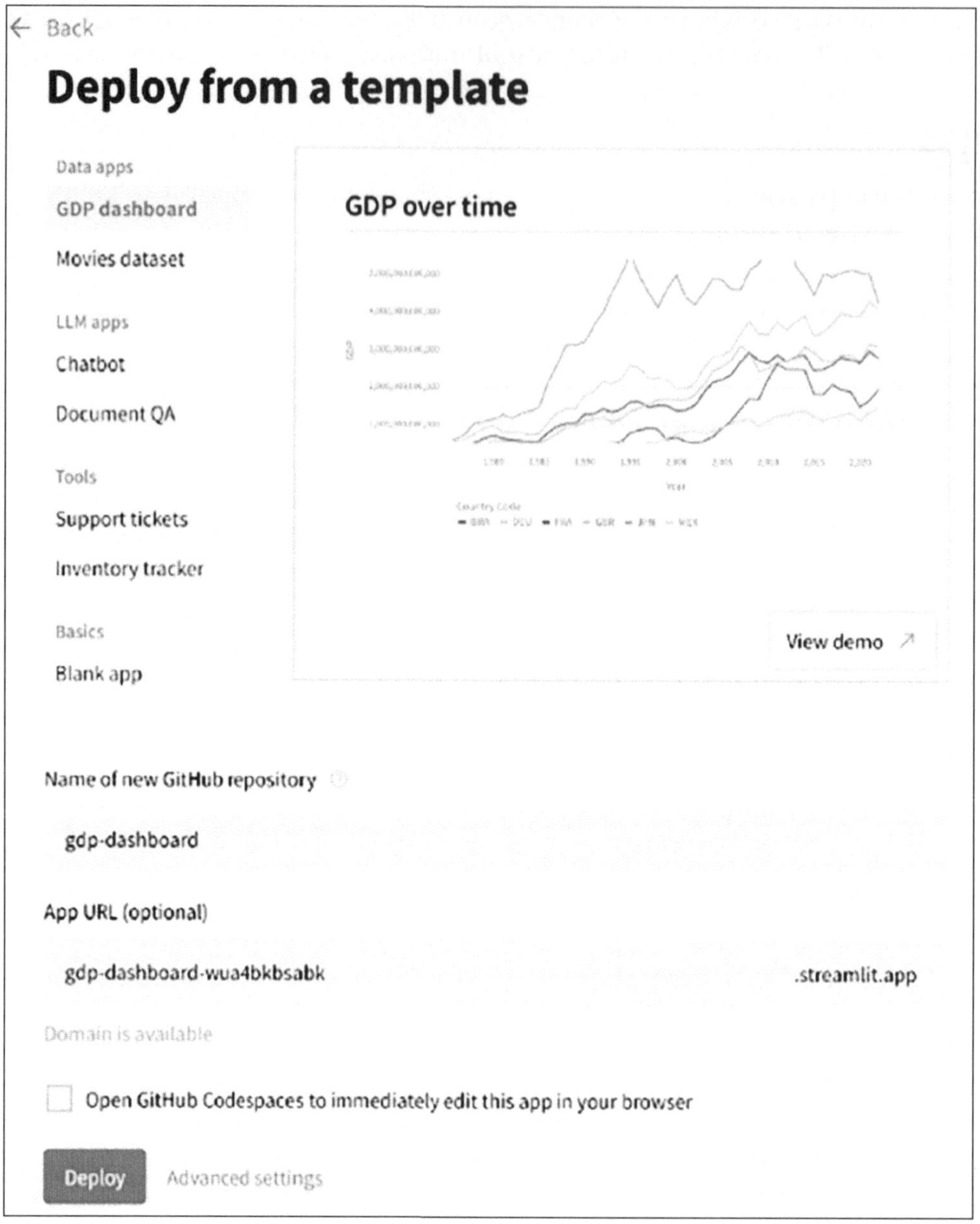

Figure 10.6: *Deploy from a Template*

My Profile

This tab is your public Streamlit profile, and contains information such as location, social links, description, and your public apps. All of these details are optional.

It also shows how many times each app was viewed. You can copy a link to the app or hide it from your profile using the overflow menu (⁝) next to it.

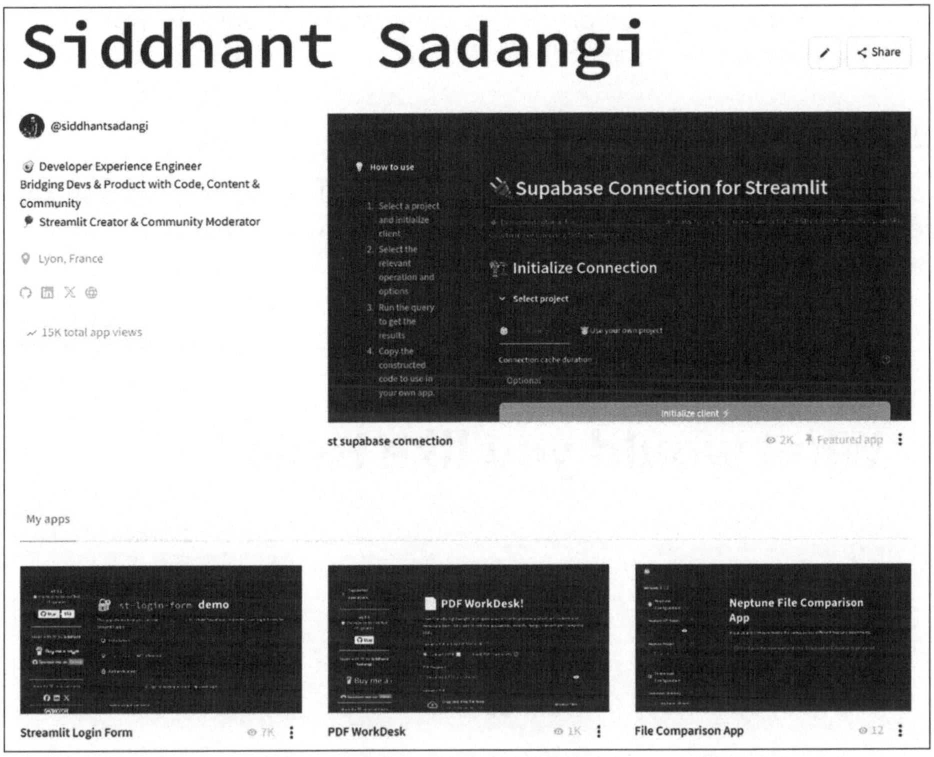

Figure 10.7: *My Profile*

Explore

This tab lets you search for or explore public Streamlit apps. The apps are grouped into categories, and can be sorted by a number of views, relevancy, or recency.

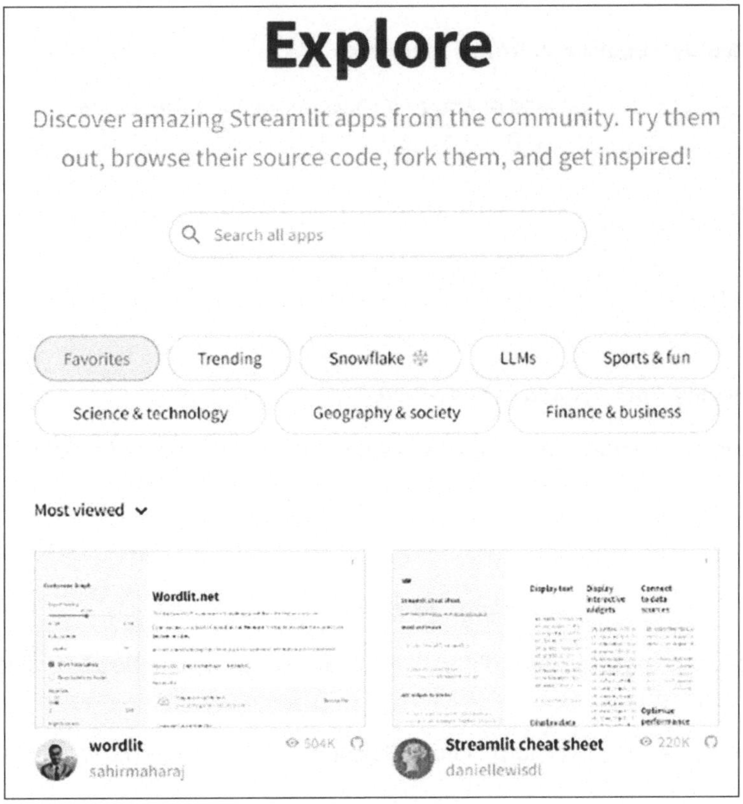

Figure 10.8: *Explore*

You can open the app by clicking on its preview or name, view the author's profile by clicking on the author's name, or view the app's source code on GitHub by clicking the GitHub icon.

Create App

The **`Create app`** button at the top right of the workspace allows us to create an app directly from the workspace. Clicking on it opens the new app page, as shown in *Figure 10.9*, where we can deploy a public app already on GitHub, deploy a **`public`** app from a template, or deploy a private app in Snowflake.

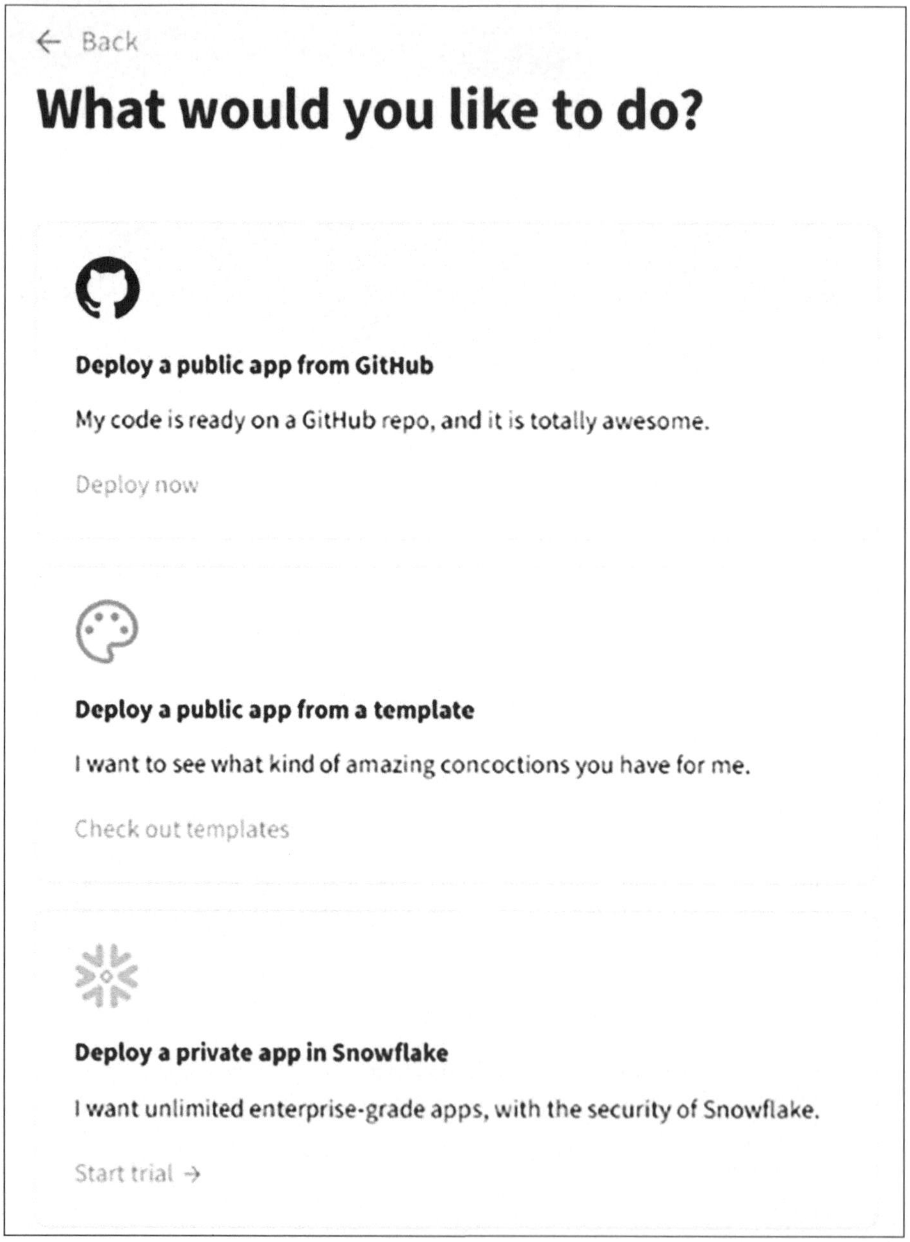

Figure 10.9: *New App Page*

1. Selecting **`Deploy a public app from a template`** opens the **`Deploy from a template page`**, as shown in *Figure 10.6*.
2. Selecting **`Deploy a public app from GitHub`** opens the **`Deploy an app`** page, as shown in *Figure 10.10*.

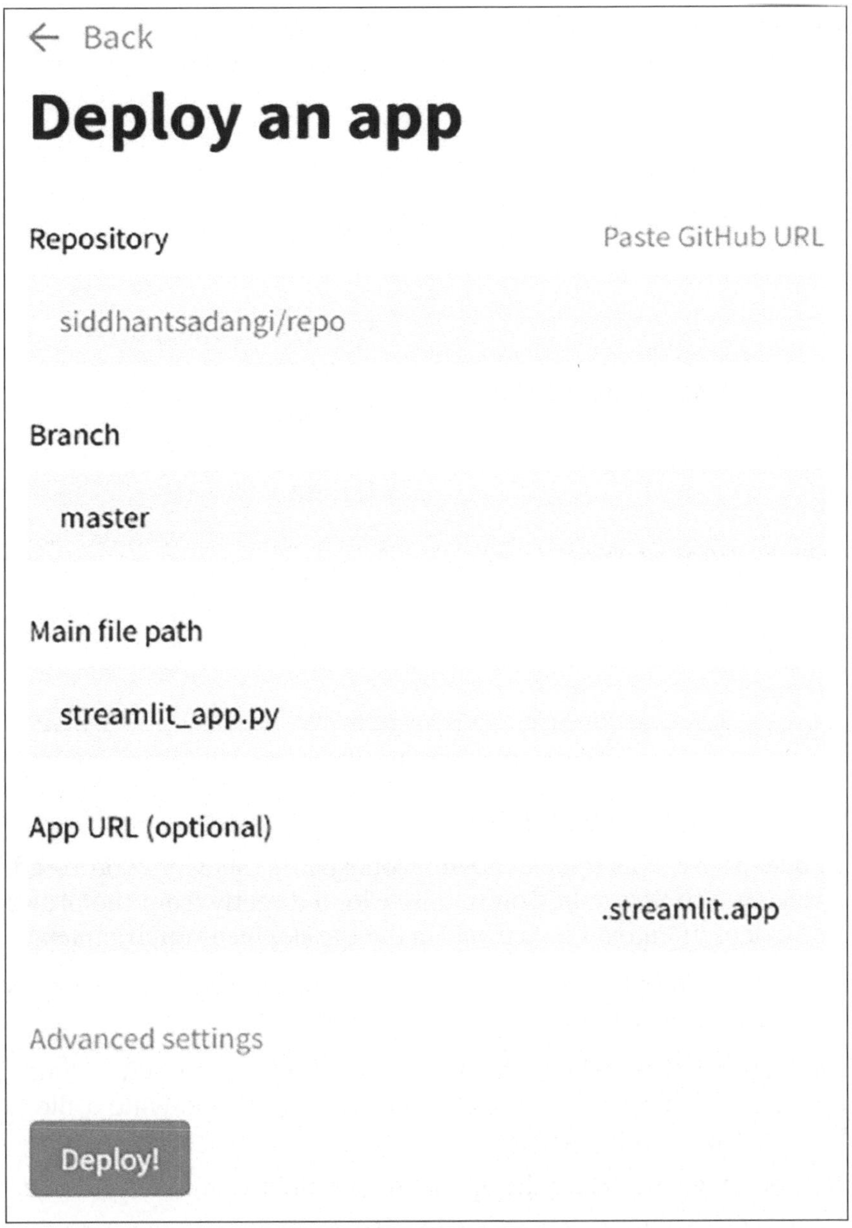

Figure 10.10: *Deploy an App*

This page allows us to enter the GitHub repository, branch, and main file path (relative to the repository root) of the Streamlit app. We can also customize the app URL in the `streamlit.app` domain, provided that the URL is available.

`Advanced settings` opens the Community Cloud Secrets Management Console. As discussed in *Chapter* 9, *Managing Secrets in Streamlit*, and shown in *Figure* 9.8, this modal lets you add secrets to your app, and select the version of Python the app will run on.

3. Selecting `Deploy a private app in Snowflake` opens the Snowflake signup page.

Managing an App from the Community Cloud Workspace

Now that we know how to navigate around and use the Streamlit Community Cloud Workspace, let us learn how to manage our app directly from the workspace itself.

As mentioned earlier in the *My apps* section, each app in the workspace has an app overflow menu (⋮) to the right that lets us manage the app. This menu contains various options, as shown in *Figure 10.11*.

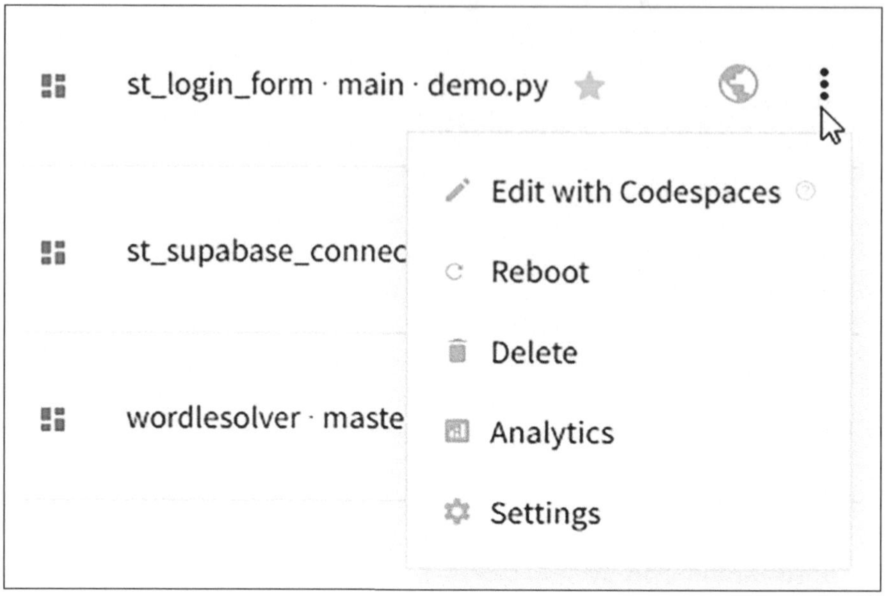

Figure 10.11: *App Overflow Menu*

Let us explore what each of these options does:

- **Edit with Codespaces:** This opens GitHub Codespaces, allowing you to edit the app's code, and deploy changes to Streamlit Community Cloud directly from the browser. We discussed GitHub Codespaces in *Chapter 2, Setting Up the Development Environment.*

Note: *Rebooting an app will interrupt any user currently using the app. Till the app is re-deployed, any visitor to the app will see a* **`Your app is in the oven`** *message.*[4]

- **Reboot:** This option lets us reboot the app on Streamlit Community Cloud. This is useful for clearing the app's memory or forcing a fresh build after modifying a file not monitored for changes by Streamlit Community Cloud.[5]
- **Delete:** This option lets us delete the app from Streamlit Community Cloud.

Note: *Deleting an app will make its custom subdomain immediately available for reuse. If you want to delete and redeploy your app, you might be unable to use the previous subdomain, if someone else has already taken it.*[6]

- **Analytics:** This opens a modal, as shown in *Figure* 10.12, that displays the app's total number of unique viewers (starting from April 2022), the 20 most recent viewers, and a relative timestamp of their last visit.[7]

---

[4] *https://docs.streamlit.io/deploy/streamlit-community-cloud/manage-your-app/reboot-your-app#reboot-your-app* (Accessed: 4 September 2024)

[5] *https://docs.streamlit.io/deploy/streamlit-community-cloud/manage-your-app/reboot-your-app#reboot-your-app* (Accessed: 4 September 2024)

[6] *https://docs.streamlit.io/deploy/streamlit-community-cloud/manage-your-app/delete-your-app* (Accessed: 4 September 2024)

[7] *https://docs.streamlit.io/deploy/streamlit-community-cloud/manage-your-app/app-analytics#app-analytics* (Accessed: 13 September 2024)

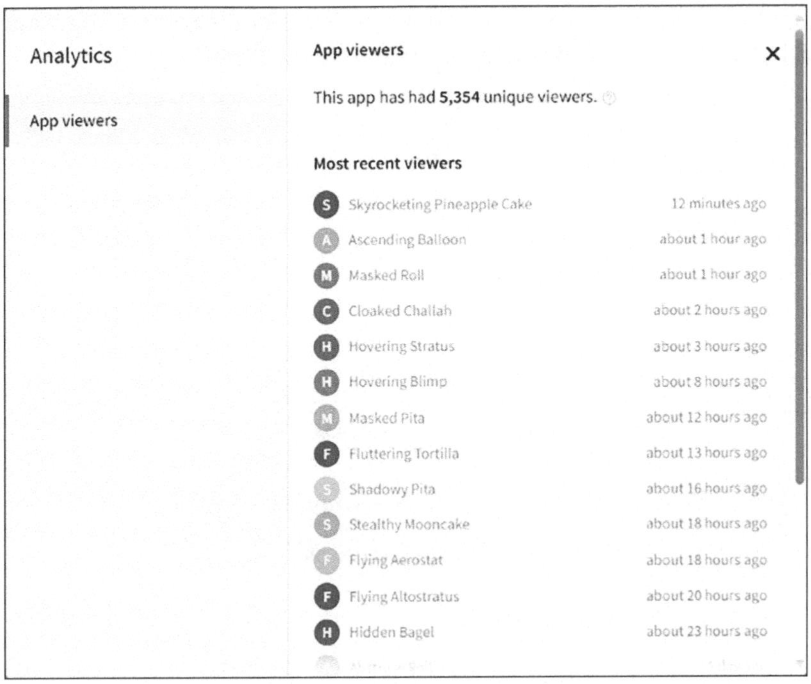

***Figure 10.12:** App Analytics*

Note: *Viewers outside our workspace are displayed as random pseudonyms for privacy reasons. We can see the email IDs of anyone in our workspace or viewers who have accepted an invitation.*[8]

- **Settings:** This opens the settings modal that lets us manage the following settings for the app:
    - **General:** As shown in *Figure* 10.13, this tab lets us choose a custom subdomain for the app as long as the subdomain is available, and the Python version to run the app.

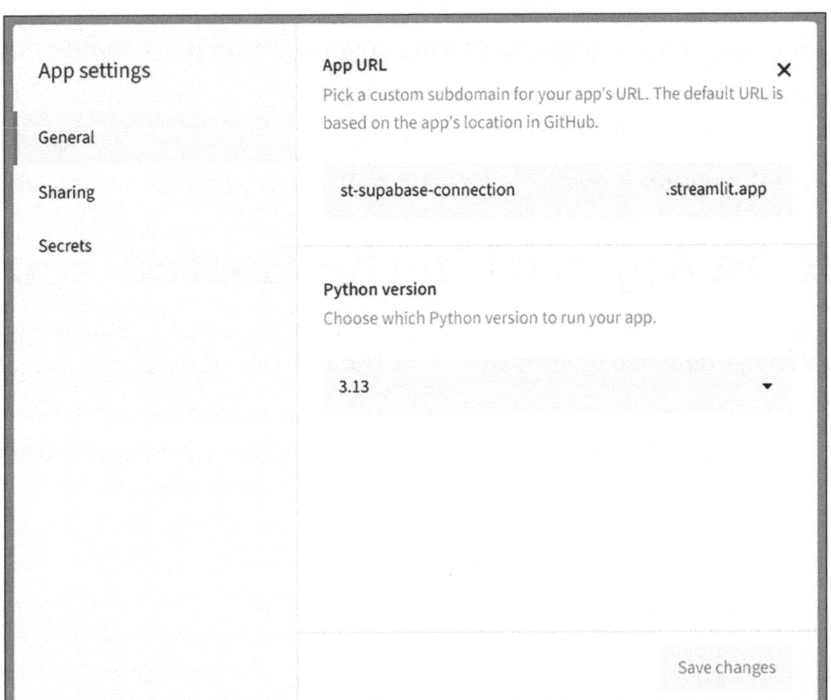

***Figure 10.13:** App URL*

[8] *https://docs.streamlit.io/deploy/streamlit-community-cloud/manage-your-app/app-analytics#app-viewers* (Accessed: 13 September 2024)

- **Sharing:** As shown in *Figure* 10.14, this tab lets us control who can manage and view the app, and also enables us to invite app viewers via email.

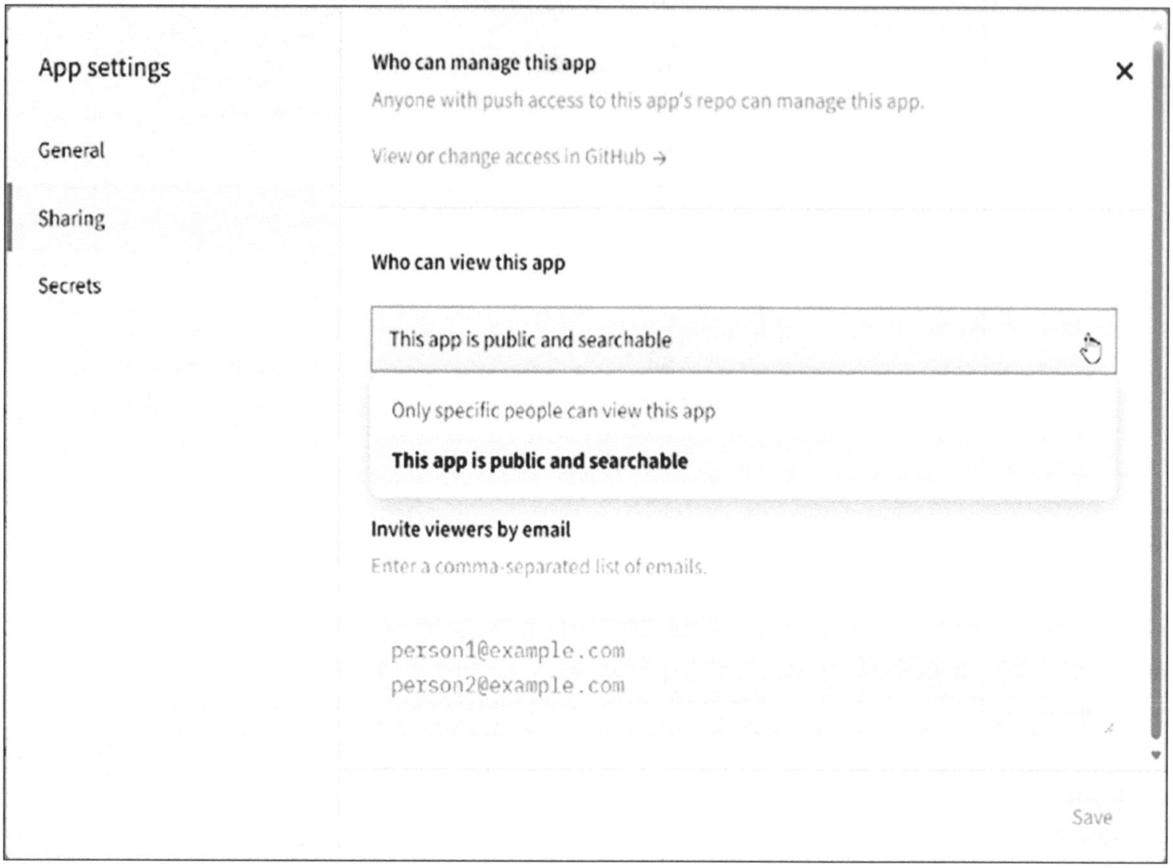

Figure 10.14: *Sharing Settings*

We will learn more about managing and sharing an app later in this chapter.

- **Secrets:** As discussed in *Chapter* 9, *Managing Secrets in Streamlit*, and shown in *Figure* 9.11, this section lets us manage the app's secrets.

Note: *Only the* **`Analytics`** *option is available for apps to which we have view-only access.*

Managing an App within the Hosted App

As long as we are signed in to the Streamlit Community Cloud, we can manage an app from the app itself through the **`Manage app`** expander available at the bottom right of the app, as shown in *Figure* 9.10.

Once opened, we can see the Streamlit Community Cloud logs for the app, as shown in *Figure* 10.15.

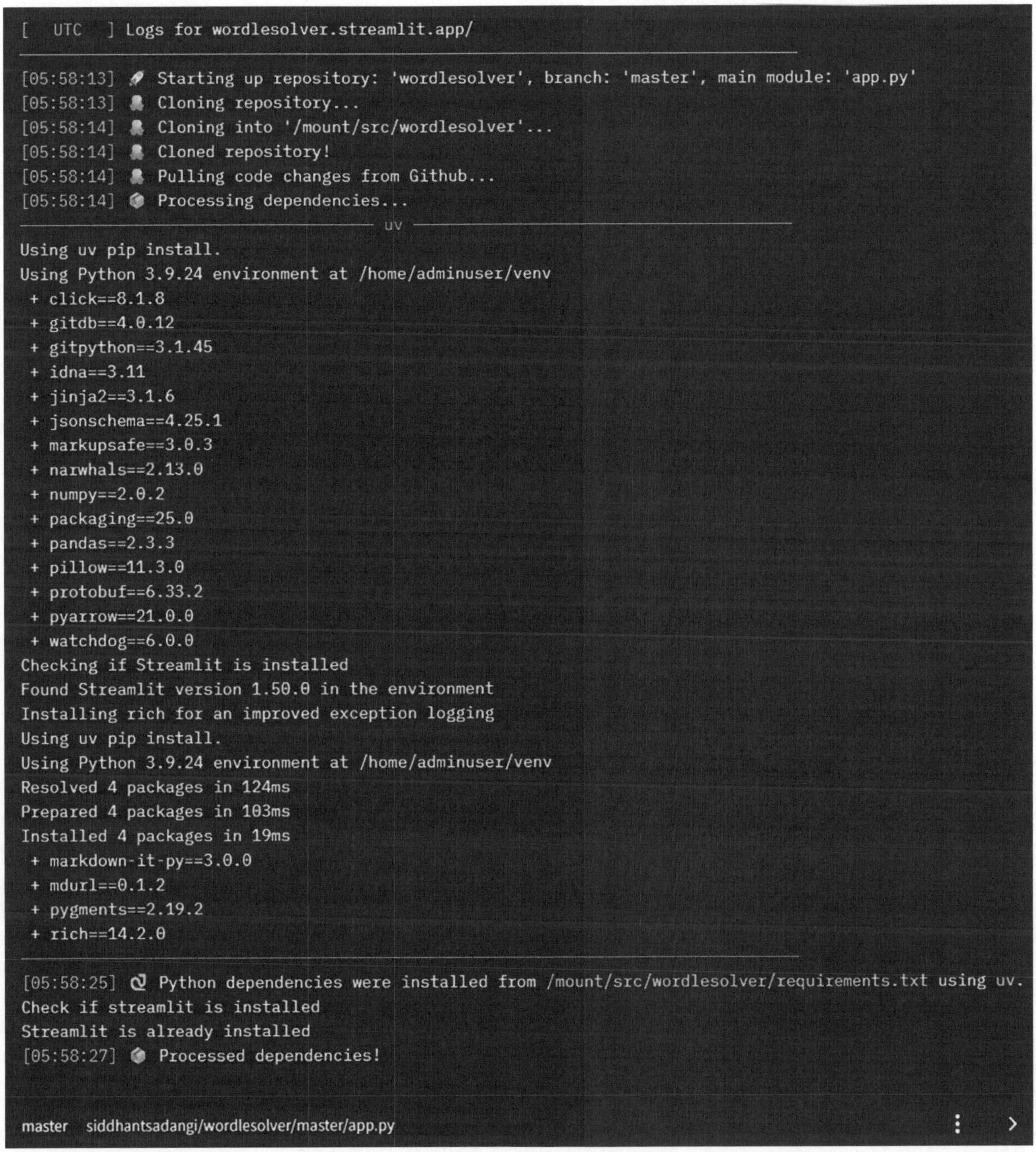

Figure 10.15: *Streamlit Community Cloud Logs*

These logs contain detailed deployment and execution information, including tracebacks for developers in case of any issues with the app. At the bottom, we can also see the branch the app was deployed from and the main file path of the app.

The overflow menu (⋮) opens more developer options in the bottom right, as shown in the following *Figure 10.16*.

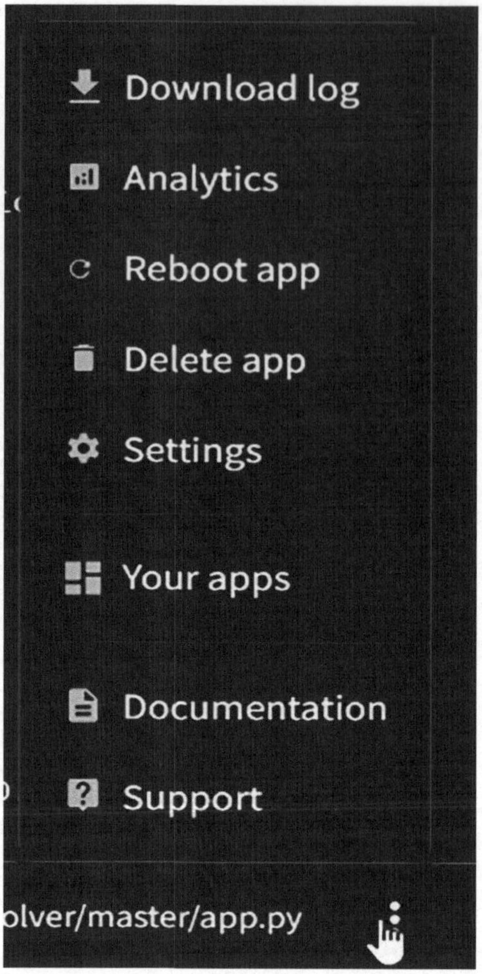

Figure 10.16: *Developer Options*

In addition to some of the options we discussed in the previous section – **`Analytics`**, **`Reboot app`**, **`Delete app`**, **`Settings`**, **`Documentation`**, and **`Support`** – it also contains two more options:

- **Download log:** This lets us download the Streamlit Community Cloud logs as a text file.
- **Your apps:** This takes us to our app workspace.

Sharing an App

Once an app is published, we might want to share it with other developers who can contribute to or manage it, or share it with viewers directly via email or social forums. This section will discuss how to do this.

Sharing with Developers

Streamlit Community Cloud inherits developer permissions from GitHub. To invite developers to contribute to or manage an app, we need to invite them to the GitHub repository hosting the app.[9] A shortcut to this setting in GitHub is available under the **`Sharing`** tab of the app settings, as shown in *Figure* 10.14.

This link takes us to the **`Collaborators`** setting of the GitHub repository, as shown in the following *Figure* 10.17.

[9] *https://docs.streamlit.io/deploy/streamlit-community-cloud/get-started/explore-your-workspace#invite-other-developers-to-your-workspace* (Accessed: 14 September 2024)

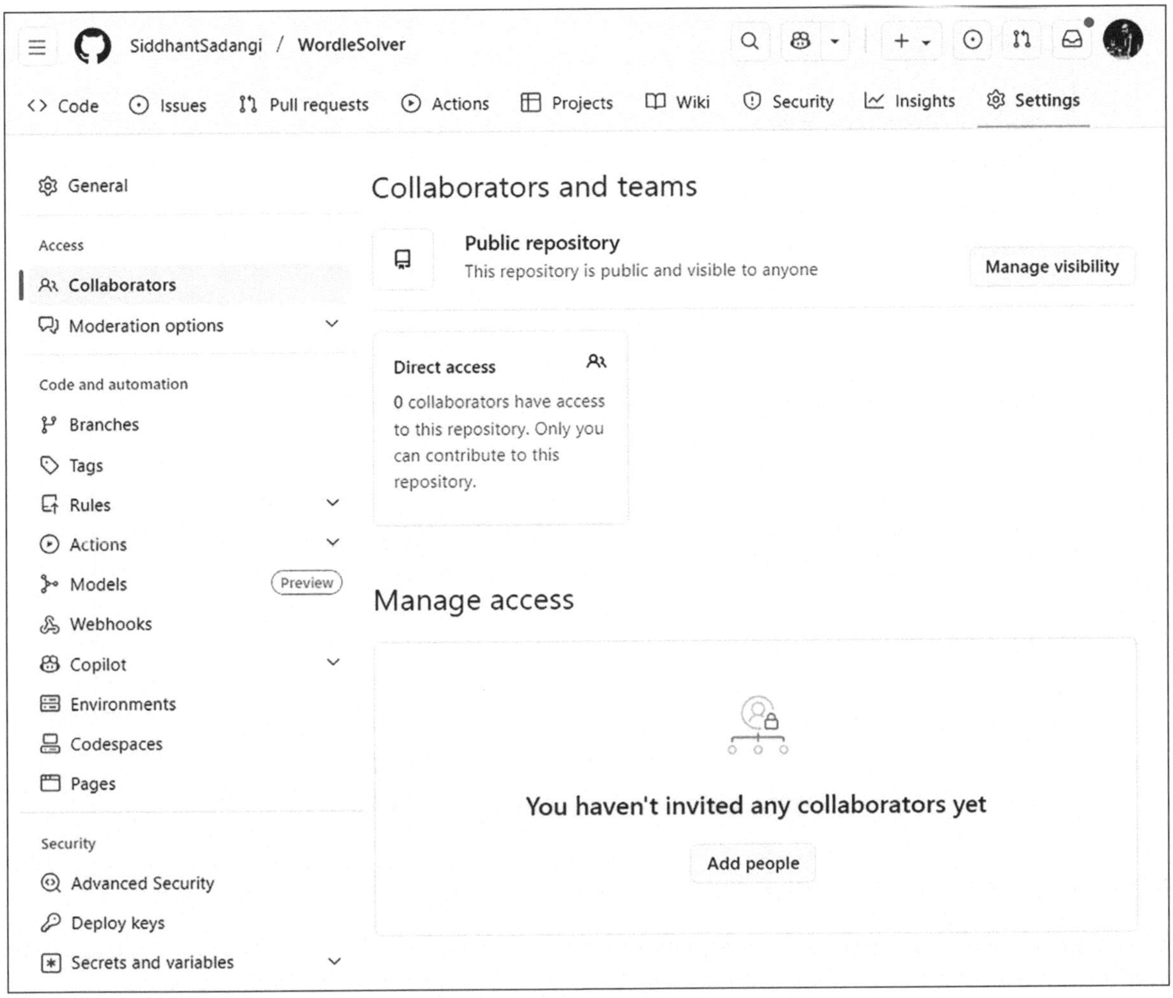

Figure 10.17: *GitHub Collaborators*

Here, we can add collaborators who we want to be able to make changes to the app code by clicking on **`Add people`**, as shown in *Figure 10.18*.

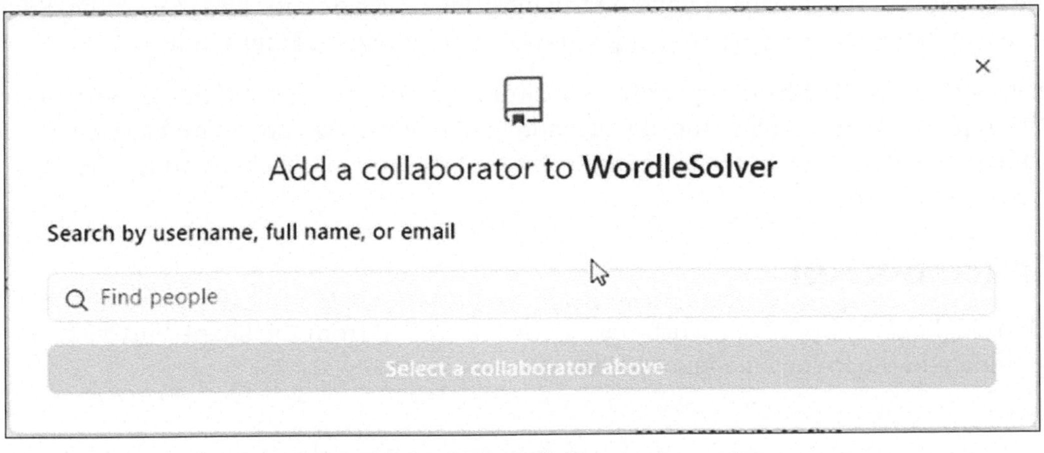

Figure 10.18: *Adding Collaborators to an App*

We can also make the repository private or public by clicking on **`Manage`**, scrolling down to **`Danger Zone`**, and clicking **`Change visibility`**, as shown in *Figure 10.19*.

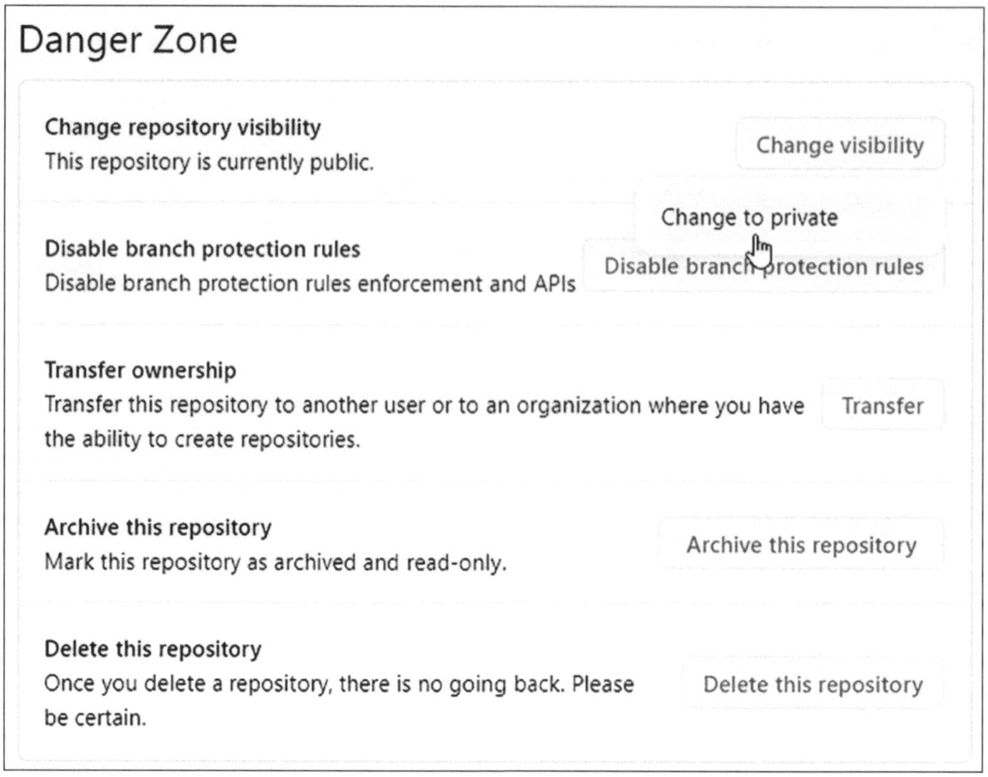

Figure 10.19: *Changing Repository Visibility*

Making a repository private will prevent anyone from seeing the Streamlit app's code, even if the app itself is public, unless they have been added to the repository as a collaborator.

Note: *At any time, we can have only one private app or app deployed from a private repository in the Streamlit Community Cloud. To make a new app private, we have to make a previous private app public.*

Sharing with Viewers

All apps published to the Streamlit Community Cloud from a public GitHub repository are public and searchable by default. This means anyone on the internet can search for and view them. Such viewers are visible as anonymous viewers in the app's analytics, as shown in *Figure* 10.12.

In contrast, apps published from a private repository are private, and cannot be viewed by anyone outside the app's workspace unless the app is made public or viewers are invited to view the app. Apps can be made public or private in the **`Sharing`** settings of the app in the Community Cloud Workspace, as shown in *Figure* 10.14.

The Share Button

From within the hosted app, an app's privacy can be controlled from the **`Share`** button at the top right corner, as shown in the following *Figure* 10.20.

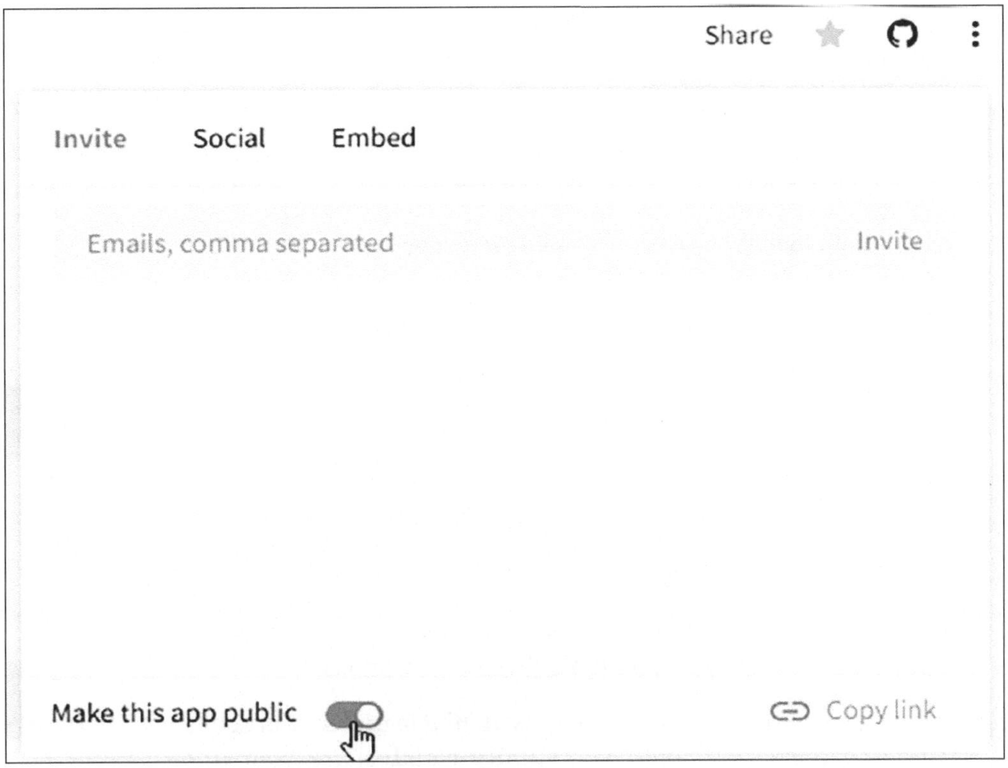

Figure 10.20: *Controlling Privacy from the Share Button*

This is also where we can invite viewers to private apps. Irrespective of the app being public or private, views by invited viewers are visible in the app's analytics, as shown in *Figure 10.12*, as long as the viewers are signed in to the Streamlit Community Cloud.

In addition to controlling app privacy, and inviting viewers to the app from the **`Invite`** tab, the **`Share`** button also has social sharing buttons in the **`Social`** tab, as shown in the following *Figure 10.21*.

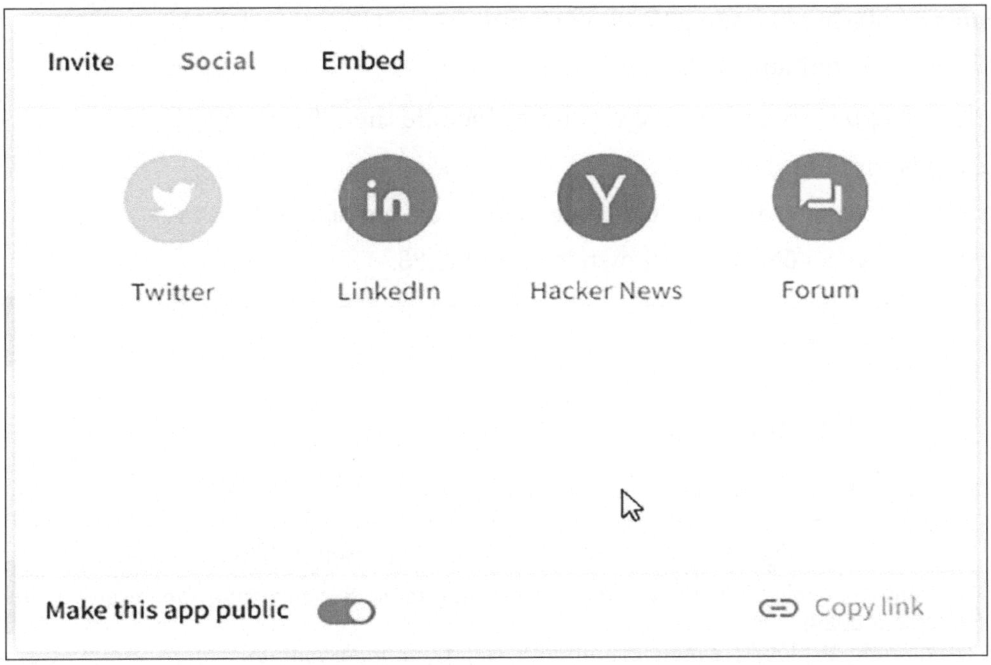

Figure 10.21: *Social Sharing Options*

Embedding options to embed the app on external sites are also available in the **`Embed`** tab, as shown in the following *Figure 10.22*.

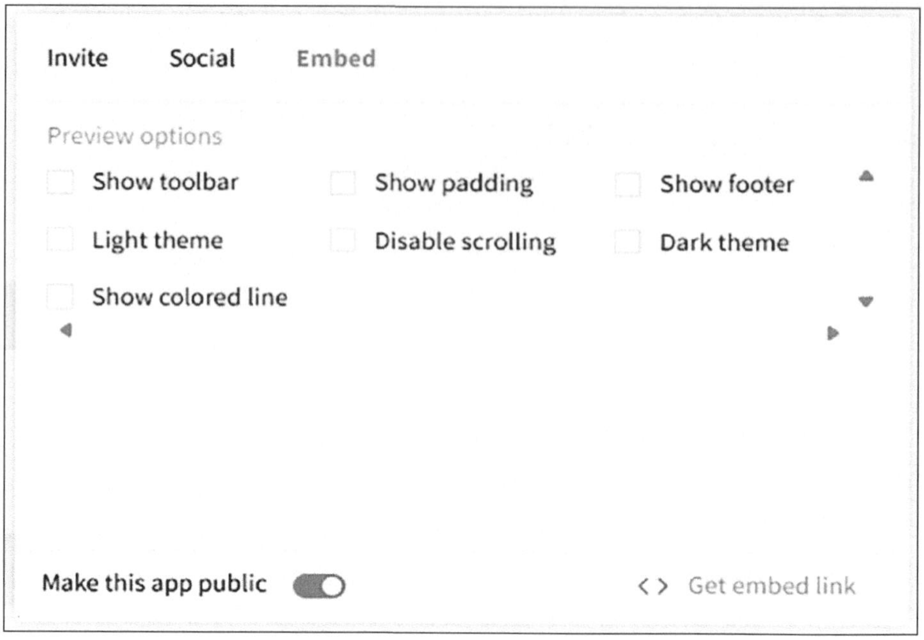

Figure 10.22: Embedding Options

Note: *You can further explore the sharing resources available and best practices in Streamlit's docs here: https://docs.streamlit.io/deploy/streamlit-community-cloud/share-your-app.*

App Resources and Limits

Since Streamlit Community Cloud is a free resource offered to developers to host and share their apps, it comes with a few limits on the resources available to hosted apps. *Figure* 10.3 shows the limits as of October 2025. In addition to the limits shown there, a few other limits are also as follows:[10]

- **CPU:** 0.078 cores minimum, 2 cores maximum
- **Memory:** 690MB minimum, 2.7GB maximum
- **Storage:** No minimum, 50GB maximum

Symptoms that an app is running out of resources include the following:

- The app is running slowly.
- The app displays · `This app has gone over its resource limits.`
- The app displays · `Oh no.`, as shown in *Figure* 10.23.

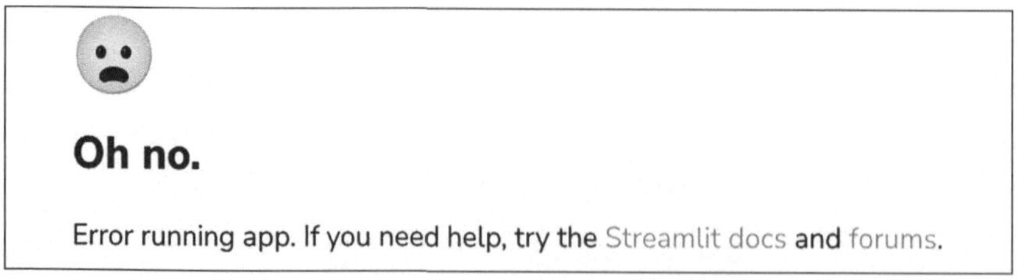

Figure 10.23: App Error on Exceeding Resource Limits[11]

[10] *https://docs.streamlit.io/deploy/streamlit-community-cloud/manage-your-app#app-resources-and-limits* (Accessed: 15 September 2024)
[11] *https://docs.streamlit.io/deploy/streamlit-community-cloud/manage-your-app#app-resources-and-limits* (Accessed: 15 September 2024)

Note: *Streamlit offers increased resources for apps used by educational institutes, non-profits, open-source projects, or any other good-for-the-world use case. This increase can be requested through this form: https://info.snowflake.com/streamlit-resource-increase-request.html.*[12]

Tip: *Best practices to optimize the app if it exceeds limits can be found in the Streamlit docs here: https://docs.streamlit.io/deploy/streamlit-community-cloud/manage-your-app#optimizing-your-app.*

Streamlit puts apps with no traffic for 12 hours to sleep to utilize shared resources best. On visiting such an app, viewers get a page, as shown in the following *Figure 10.24*.

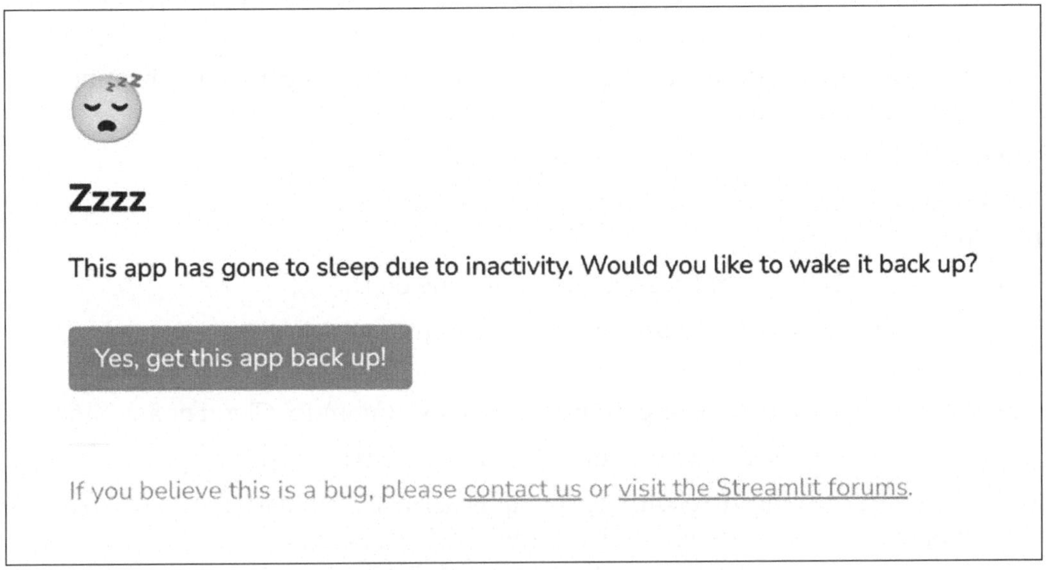

Figure 10.24: *App Sleeping Page*

The app can be woken up by anyone with view access to the app by clicking on Yes, get this app back up!

To prevent an app from going to sleep, visit it or commit to its repository at least once, every 12 hours.

Conclusion

In this chapter, we discussed app dependencies, and how to install them on the Streamlit Community Cloud server instance hosting our application. We then explored the Streamlit workspace and its various components. Following this, we learned how to manage and share our app, both from our workspace and directly from within the app itself, with viewers and developers. Finally, we covered the compute resources available for our app in Streamlit Community Cloud and their associated limits. In the next chapter, we will learn about the different app configuration options available in Streamlit, and the various ways to set those options.

Points to Remember

- The Streamlit Community Cloud server starts with a clean environment, so we must tell it which software our app requires.
- Streamlit recognizes several dependency files for installing Python packages, including **`uv.lock`**, **`Pipfile`**, **`environment.yml`**, **`requirements.txt`**, and **`pyproject.toml`**.
- Non-Python dependencies must be listed in a **`packages.txt`** file in the repository's root.

[12] *https://docs.streamlit.io/deploy/streamlit-community-cloud/manage-your-app#good-for-the-world* (Accessed: 15 September 2024)

- Streamlit Community Cloud is organized into workspaces, with group apps by the corresponding GitHub repository owner.
- The workspace menu allows switching between different workspaces and accessing settings, documentation, and support options.
- Users' Streamlit profiles are public, but the details to be included in the profile are optional.
- The `Create app` button allows for creating a new app from a template or deploying an existing app from GitHub.
- The `Manage app` expander within the hosted app provides access to logs, developer options, and settings.
- The `Share` button in the hosted app allows controlling app privacy, inviting viewers, and sharing the app on social media or embedding it.
- Rebooting an app clears the app's memory, and triggers a fresh build.
- The Streamlit Community Cloud logs contain the detailed deployment and execution logs of the app.
- Public apps are visible to and searchable by anyone on the internet.
- Private apps are visible only to users in the same Streamlit workspace or those invited to view the app.
- We can have only one private app in the Streamlit Community Cloud at any time.
- Developers can be added to a Streamlit app from its GitHub repository.
- Streamlit offers increased resources for apps used by educational institutes, non-profits, open-source projects, or other good-for-the-world use cases.
- Apps with no traffic for 12 hours are put to sleep, but can be woken up by anyone with view access.

Multiple Choice Questions

1. Which of the following statements regarding an app deployed to Streamlit Community Cloud is true?
   a. Both Python and Streamlit versions can be changed.
   b. Only the Python version can be changed.
   c. Only the Streamlit version can be changed.
   d. Neither Python nor Streamlit versions can be changed.
2. Which file is used to specify non-Python dependencies for a Streamlit app?
   a. `requirements.txt`
   b. `Pipfile`
   c. `packages.txt`
   d. `environment.yml`
3. How can you invite developers to contribute to a Streamlit app?
   a. By sending them an email invitation from the Streamlit app
   b. By adding them as collaborators in the GitHub repository

   c. By sharing the app URL with them
   d. By adding their GitHub username in the Streamlit settings
4. What happens to a Streamlit app with no traffic for 12 hours?
   a. It is deleted.
   b. It is archived.
   c. It is put to sleep.
   d. It is moved to a different workspace.
5. **True or False**: Rebooting an app on Streamlit Community Cloud will not interrupt any current users.

Answers

1. a
2. c
3. b
4. c
5. False

Questions

1. How can we specify the packages and software our app requires to run on the Streamlit Community Cloud server?
2. Describe the different components of a Streamlit Workspace.
3. What is the difference between public and private Streamlit apps?
4. How can you prevent viewers of a public Streamlit app from seeing the app's source code?
5. What are the resource limits for apps hosted on Streamlit Community Cloud?

Key Terms

- **`apt-get`:** A command-line tool for handling packages using the **A***dvanced* **P***ackaging* **T***ool* (APT) library.[13]
- **Workspace:** An organizational structure in Streamlit Community Cloud that groups apps by the corresponding GitHub repository owner.

[13] *https://linux.die.net/man/8/apt-get* (Accessed: 31 August 2024)

CHAPTER 11
App Configuration Options

Introduction

In most cases, launching a Streamlit app is as simple as importing Streamlit in the script, adding a few Streamlit widgets, and running **`streamlit run app.py`**. However, for more advanced usage and users, Streamlit provides many configuration options that control everything from app appearance to error logging and security. These are set to sensible defaults, so we do not have to worry about them most of the time.

In this chapter, we will discuss some of these options and the different ways of setting and reading them. We will also delve into app themes, exploring the different prebuilt themes available, and the various methods of setting custom themes.

Structure

In this chapter, we will discuss the following topics:

- Overview of Common Configuration Options
- Setting Configuration Options
    - Using Configuration Files
    - Using Environment Variables
    - Using Command Line Arguments
    - Using **`st.set_option`**
- Reading Configuration Options
- Order of Priority
- App Themes

Overview of Common Configuration Options

You can get all the configuration options available and their current values for a particular app by running **streamlit config show** in the command line.

For Streamlit version 1.50.0, the output appears as shown in *Figure 11.1*:

```
> streamlit config show

 # Below are all the sections and options you can have in
 ~/.streamlit/config.toml.


[global]

# By default, Streamlit displays a warning when a user sets both a widget
# default value in the function defining the widget and a widget value via
# the widget's key in `st.session_state`.

# If you'd like to turn off this warning, set this to True.

# Default: false
# disableWidgetStateDuplicationWarning = false

# If True, will show a warning when you run a Streamlit-enabled script
# via "python my_script.py".

# Default: true
# showWarningOnDirectExecution = true


[logger]

# Level of logging: 'error', 'warning', 'info', or 'debug'.

# Default: 'info'
# level = "info"

# String format for logging messages. If logger.datetimeFormat is set,
# logger messages will default to `%(asctime)s.%(msecs)03d %(message)s`. See
# [Python's documentation](https://docs.python.org/2.6/library/logging.html#formatter-objects)
# for available attributes.

# Default: "%(asctime)s %(message)s"
# messageFormat = "%(asctime)s %(message)s"


[client]

# Controls whether uncaught app exceptions and deprecation warnings
# are displayed in the browser. By default, this is set to True and
# Streamlit displays app exceptions and associated tracebacks, and
# deprecation warnings, in the browser.

# If set to False, deprecation warnings and full exception messages
# will print to the console only. Exceptions will still display in the
# browser with a generic error message. For now, the exception type and
# traceback show in the browser also, but they will be removed in the
```

Figure 11.1: *Configuration Options*

Let us discuss some of the most commonly used options. We shall learn how to set these options later.

- **`global.disableWidgetStateDuplicationWarning`**: As discussed in *Chapter 5, Persisting Data and State Using Session State* and shown in *Figure 5.10*, whenever you set a widget's value using **`Session State`** and the widget's **value** parameter, Streamlit will display a warning when the app is run for the first time. However, in some circumstances, you might need to use both the **`Session State`** and the **value** parameter. In such cases, it is better to hide this warning from users. You can set **`global.disableWidgetStateDuplicationWarning`** to `true` to turn off this warning.
- **`client.toolbarMode`**: This option determines the visibility of items in the **`App Menu`** (located at the top right of the app). [1]

[1] *https://docs.streamlit.io/develop/api-reference/configuration/config.toml#client* (Accessed: 24 September 2024)

- **Developer Mode:** Shows developer options like **`Clear cache`** or the **`Deploy`** button (if running locally), as shown in *Figure 11.2*.

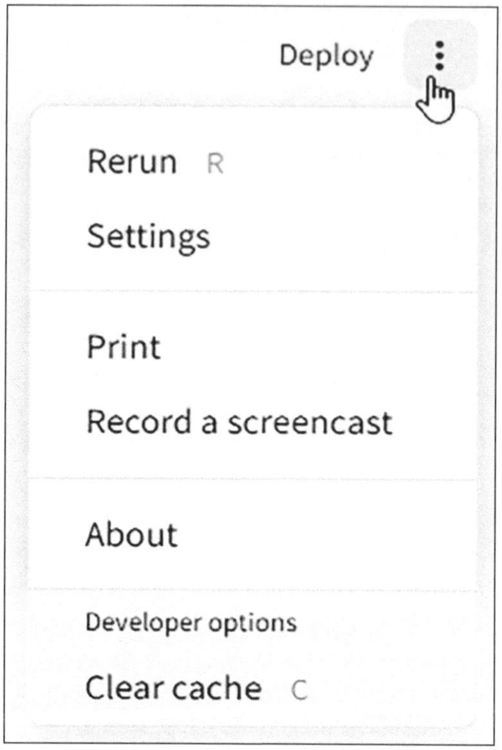

Figure 11.2: *Developer Toolbar Mode*

- **Viewer Mode:** Hides developer options, as shown in *Figure 11.3*.

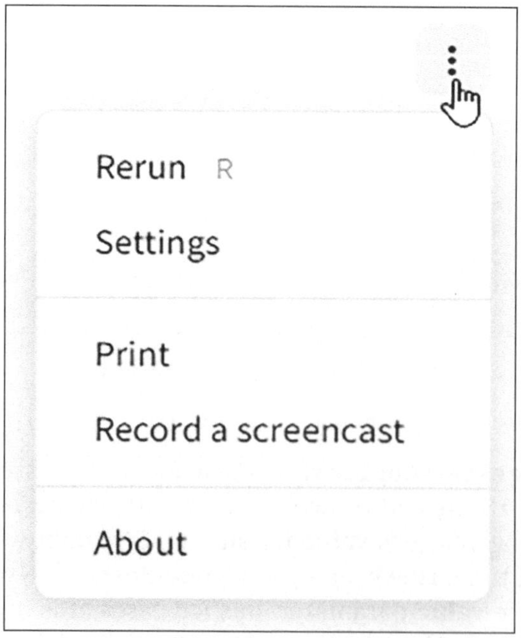

Figure 11.3: *Viewer Toolbar Mode*

- **Auto mode:** Automatically switches between the **`developer`** mode and **`viewer`** mode depending on whether the app is run locally or accessed by the developer on the Streamlit Community Cloud.

- **Minimal mode:** Shows only options that do not affect the app (like `About`), and hides the menu if no such options exist.

- **`server.headless`**: Set this to **`true`** to prevent a browser window from opening automatically whenever a Streamlit app is run.[2] The default value is **`false`**.
- **`server.runOnSave`**: Set this to ***`true`*** to automatically rerun the application when the source script is modified on disk.[3] The default value is **`false`**.

  Note: *The* **`Always rerun`** *option when Streamlit detects a change in the source file (as discussed in Chapter 3, Creating and Deploying Your First Streamlit App) sets this configuration option to* **`true`**.
- **`server.baseUrlPath`**: This sets the base URL path from where the app should be served.[4] For example, setting this to `mypath` will serve the app from `http://localhost:8501/mypath` as follows:

```
> streamlit run path/to/app.py --server.baseUrlPath="mypath"

  You can now view your Streamlit app in your browser.

  Local URL: http://localhost:8501/mypath
  Network URL: http://190.180.161.29:8501/mypath

   This is helpful if, for example, you want to serve multiple Streamlit apps
in the same domain with different paths.
```

- **`server.maxUploadSize`**: This sets the max size, in megabytes, for files uploaded using the **`file_uploader`** widget.[5] The default value is 200 MB.

  Note: *It can be increased to any required value, but remember to account for resource limits and restrictions on the server side (as discussed in Chapter 10, Advanced App Management Concepts) to prevent app crashes if the uploaded files in memory across all sessions are too large for the server to handle.*
- **`browser.gatherUsageStats`**: Set this to **`false`** to turn off sending telemetry data to Streamlit. The default value is **`true`**.[6]

  Note: *You can read more about telemetry in Streamlit's official docs here: https://docs.streamlit.io/develop/concepts/configuration/options#telemetry.*
- **`theme.*`**: Theme configuration options like **`base`**, **`primaryColor`**, **`backgroundColor`**, **`secondaryBackgroundColor`**, **`textColor`**, **`font`**, and so on are used to control the look and feel of the app. We will discuss these in more detail later in the chapter.
- **`secrets.files`**: As discussed in *Chapter 9, Managing Secrets in Streamlit*, by default, Streamlit looks for app secrets in a **`secrets.toml`** file in either the project directory or the user's home directory. Using the **`secrets.files`** configuration option, you can update the paths and filenames scanned for secrets by Streamlit. The default paths are **`[ "~/.streamlit/secrets.toml", "~/path/to/project/.streamlit/secrets.toml",]`**.

  Note: *Secrets in later files take priority over the earlier ones.*[7]

  Note: *A description of all the options is available in the Streamlit docs here: https://docs.streamlit.io/develop/api-reference/configuration/config.toml#available-configuration-options.*

---

[2] https://docs.streamlit.io/develop/api-reference/configuration/config.toml#server (Accessed: 22 September 2024)
[3] https://docs.streamlit.io/develop/api-reference/configuration/config.toml#server (Accessed: 22 September 2024)
[4] https://docs.streamlit.io/develop/api-reference/configuration/config.toml#server (Accessed: 22 September 2024)
[5] https://docs.streamlit.io/develop/api-reference/configuration/config.toml#server (Accessed: 22 September 2024)
[6] https://docs.streamlit.io/develop/concepts/configuration/options#telemetry (Accessed: 22 September 2024)
[7] https://docs.streamlit.io/develop/api-reference/configuration/config.toml#secrets (Accessed: 22 September 2024)

Setting Configuration Options

Streamlit provides multiple ways to set up the aforementioned configuration options. In this section, we will discuss the different methods and the priority order that applies if the same setting is configured through various modes.

Using Configuration Files

You can use a **config.toml** file to set configuration options. Like Streamlit Secrets, these options can be set at a project level or globally. Place the file in a **.streamlit** folder in the app's working directory for project-level settings. For global settings, put it in the **.streamlit** folder in your home directory (**~/.streamlit/** for macOS/Linux and **%userprofile%/.streamlit** for Windows).[8] Like Streamlit Secrets, the project-level configuration file takes priority, if both project-level and global configuration files are defined.

This file has the same format you see when you run **streamlit config show**. Any configuration option added to this file will override its default value, meaning you only need to include the configuration options that need to be customized.

Using Environment Variables

All the configuration options available in the **config.toml** file can also be set via environment variables. As a rule of thumb, to set a configuration option via an environment variable, convert it to upper snake case (including its section header) and add a **STREAMLIT_ prefix**.[9]

For example, the following setting in the **config.toml** file is the same as the **STREAMLIT_BROWSER_GATHER_USAGE_STATS = false** environment variable:

```
[browser]
gatherUsageStats = false
```

Using Command Line Arguments

The same configuration options can be passed as arguments when running **streamlit run** in the command line/terminal. The syntax is **streamlit run app.py --sectionHeader.configOption=value**, using the same case used in the **config.toml** file, but with the section header prefixed to the option, and separated by a period (**.**).[10]

For example, the **gatherUsageStats** configuration option from the previous example can be passed to **streamlit run** as:

```
streamlit run app.py --browser.gatherUsageStats=false
```

Using st.set_option

All the previously discussed methods can only be used to update configuration options before launching an app. Streamlit also provides a **set_option** method within its Python API to programmatically set a limited set of supported configuration options at runtime.

[8] *https://docs.streamlit.io/develop/api-reference/configuration/config.toml#file-location* (Accessed: 23 September 2024)

[9] *https://docs.streamlit.io/develop/concepts/configuration/options#available-options* (Accessed: 24 September 2024)

[10] *https://docs.streamlit.io/develop/concepts/configuration/options#available-options* (Accessed: 24 September 2024)

Here is an example script showing how to conditionally use **st.set_option** to turn on or off showing error details in the browser. The resulting app before and after the button is clicked, as shown in *Figure 11.4*:

```
import streamlit as st

st.set_option("client.showErrorDetails", True)

if st.button("Hide error details"):
    st.set_option("client.showErrorDetails", False)
    st.write("Error details are now hidden.")
else:
    st.write("Error details are now visible.")
raise RuntimeError("This is an error message.")
```

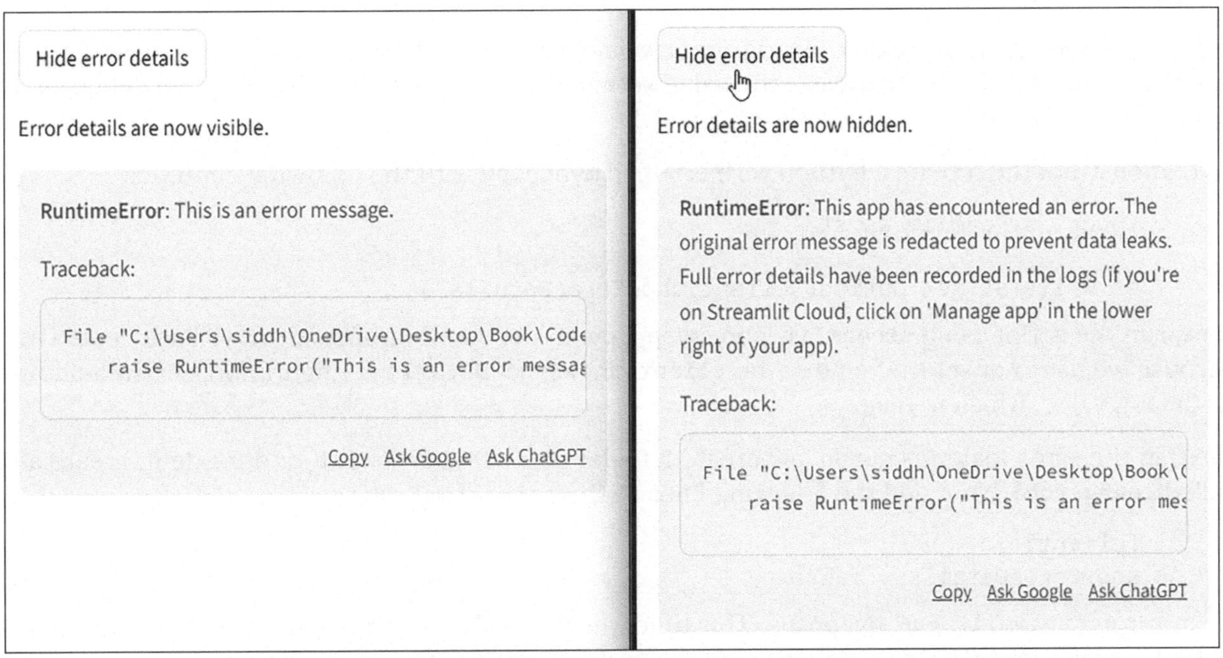

Figure 11.4: *Using st.set_option to Hide Error Details Conditionally*

As you can see, when the button is not clicked, the error message is visible (on the left). However, clicking the button sets the **client.showErrorDetails** configuration to False, hiding the error message (on the right).

As of Streamlit version 1.50, only the following configuration options can be set using **st.set_option**:

- **client.showErrorDetails**
- **client.toolbarMode**
- **client.showSidebarNavigation**

Reading Configuration Options

Streamlit provides the **get_option** method to return the current value of any configuration option.[11] Its syntax is as follows:

```
st.get_option("section.optionName")
```

[11] *https://docs.streamlit.io/develop/api-reference/configuration/st.get_option* (Accessed: 28 September 2024)

Order of Priority

Streamlit follows a specific order of priority to resolve conflicts if the same configuration option has different values set through different methods. The order of priority is as follows:

1. **st.set_option**
2. Command Line arguments
3. Environment Variables
4. Project-level config file
5. Global config file
6. Default value

Suppose a configuration option has different values set using **st.set_option** and the project and global level config files. In that case, the value set using **st.set_option** will take precedence as that has the highest priority.

To demonstrate this, create a Python script named **myapp.py** with the following contents:

```
import streamlit as st

st.write(st.get_option("client.showErrorDetails"))
```

Now, run the script using **streamlit run myapp.py**. In the app that opens, you will see **True**. This is because we have not set the value of the **client.showErrorDetails** configuration, so Streamlit uses its default value, which is **True**.

Next, in the same folder as myapp.py, create a folder named **.streamlit**, and inside it, create a file called **config.toml**. Now, add the following lines to the **config.toml** file:

```
[client]
showErrorDetails = false
```

Next, rerun **streamlit run myapp.py**. This time, the app will show **False** as we have set the value of **client.showErrorDetails** to **False** using the project-level configuration file.

Stop the app by pressing *Ctrl/Cmd* + C, and rerun it using:

```
streamlit run myapp.py --client.showErrorDetails=True
```

This time, the app shows **True** again as the value passed through the CLI argument overrides the value set using the project-level configuration file.

Finally, add the following line to **myapp.py** just above **st.write()**:

```
st.set_option("client.showErrorDetails", False)
```

On rerunning the app, you will see **False** as the value set using **st.set_option** overrides all other values, since it has the highest priority.

App Themes

So far, you have only seen the default white-themed Streamlit apps in this book. However, Streamlit also provides theme configuration options to control various aspects of the app's appearance, from the background color to the font.

Since themes are essential to the user experience (UX), we dedicate this section to discussing themes, and how to customize and set them.

To explore themes, create a sample Streamlit app with a few widgets and elements using the following script. Save the script as **theme_demo.py**.

```
import streamlit as st

with st.sidebar:
    st.subheader("Widgets")
    st.button("Sample Primary Button", type="primary")
    st.button("Sample Secondary Button")
    st.checkbox("Sample Checkbox")
    st.radio("Sample Radio", ["Option 1", "Option 2", "Option 3"])
    st.subheader("Dataframe")
    st.dataframe({"Column 1": [1, 2, 3], "Column 2": [4, 5, 6]})

st.title("Streamlit Theme Demo")
st.write("This is a simple app to demonstrate different theme options in Streamlit.")

st.header("Sample Content")
st.write("You can add any content here to see how it looks with different themes.")

st.subheader("Charts")
st.bar_chart([5, 4, 3, 2, 1])
```

When running this script using **streamlit run theme_demo.py**, the resulting app should look as shown in *Figure* 11.5 (assuming your browser uses the Light Mode).

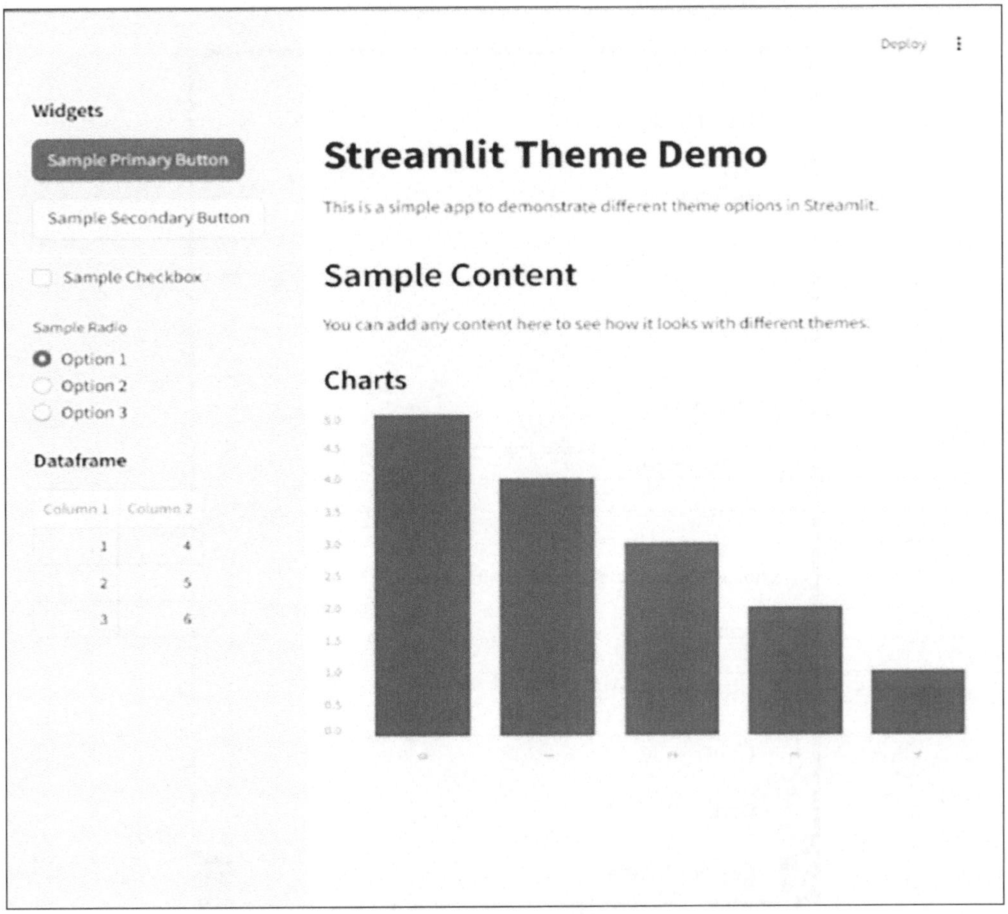

Figure 11.5: *Default Light Theme*

This is Streamlit's default *light theme*. The easiest way to change the theme is via **`Settings`** in the **`App`** menu at the app's top-right, as shown in *Figure 11.6*.

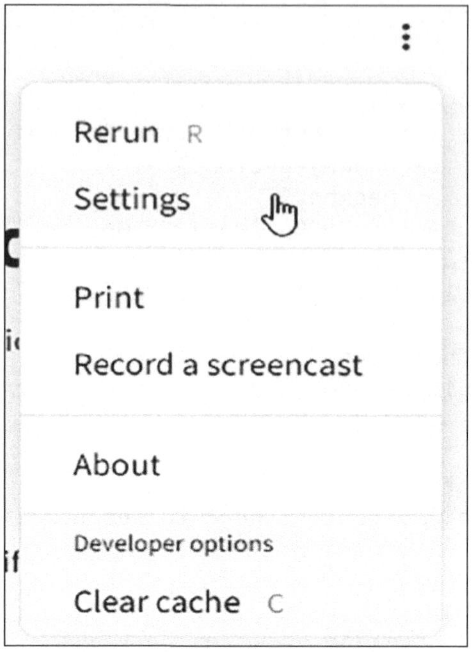

Figure 11.6: *Accessing Settings from the App Menu*

The active theme can be selected from the themes dropdown under **`Appearance`** in **`Settings`**, as shown in the following *Figure 11.7*.

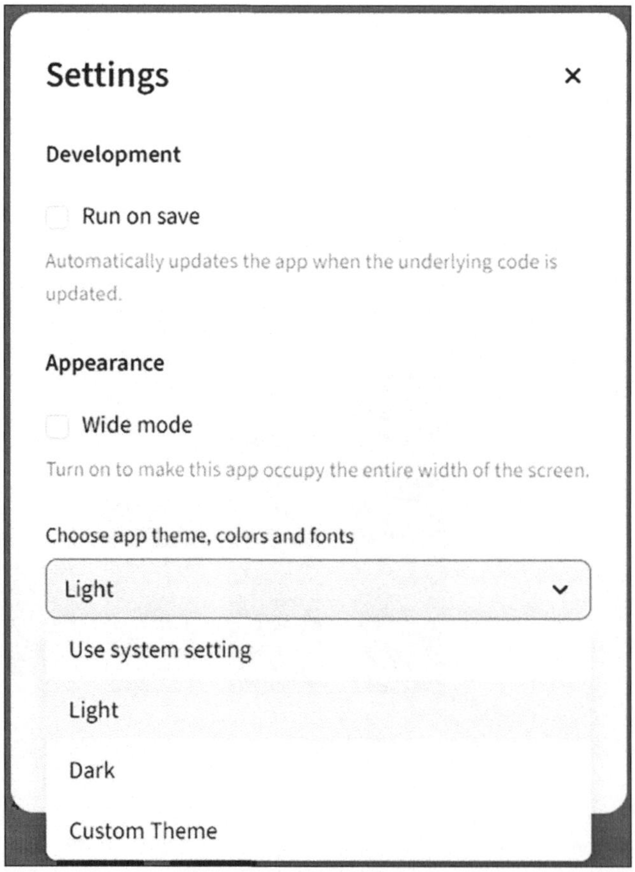

Figure 11.7: *Themes Dropdown*

- **Use System Setting:** The default mode, uses the **`Light`** or **`Dark`** theme depending on the client's settings.
- **Light:** Shows the app in a light background, as shown in *Figure* 11.5.
- **Dark:** Shows the app in a dark background, as shown in *Figure* 11.8.

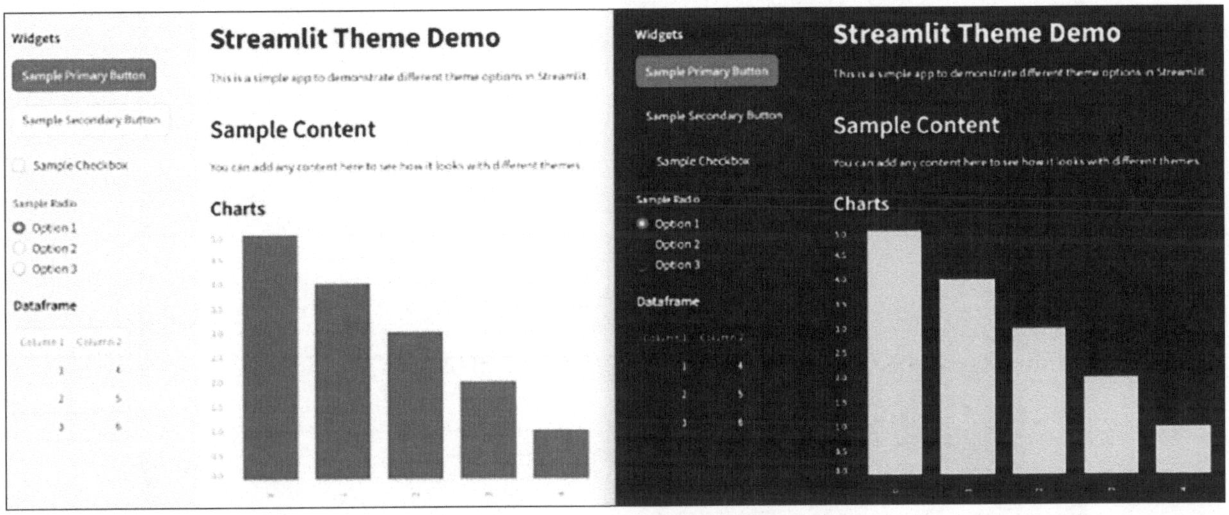

Figure 11.8: *Light Theme vs Dark Theme*

- **Custom Theme:** Applies a custom theme, as defined in the **`config.toml`** file.

The details of the active theme can be seen by clicking **`Edit active`** theme, as shown in *Figure* 11.9.

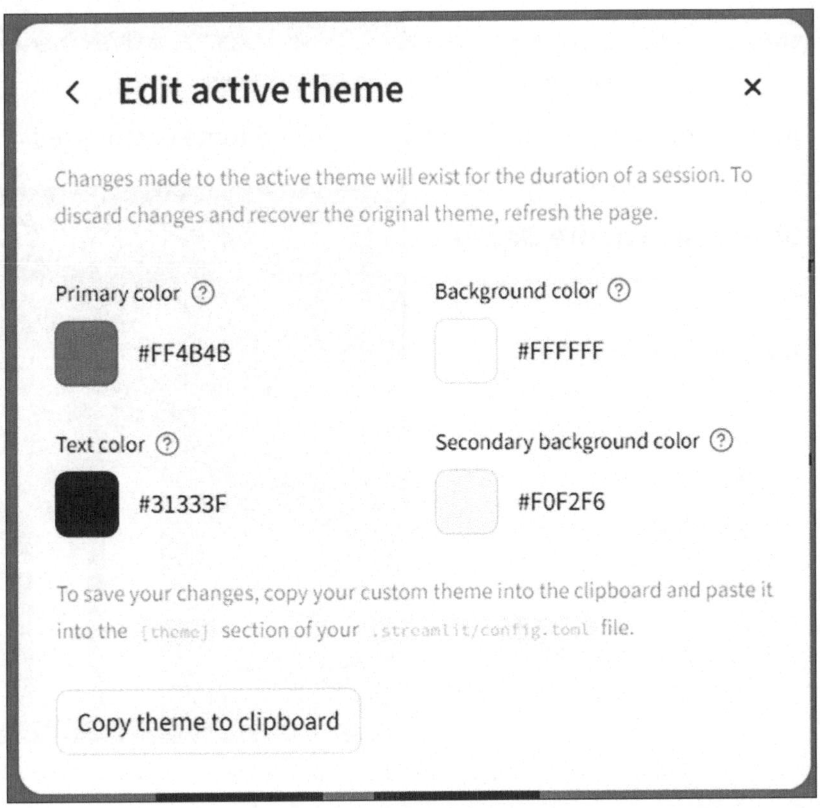

Figure 11.9: *Active Theme Details*

This modal shows you the primary color, background color, text color, and secondary background color used in the active theme. You can edit any of these elements by clicking on the respective element, as shown in the following *Figure* 11.10.

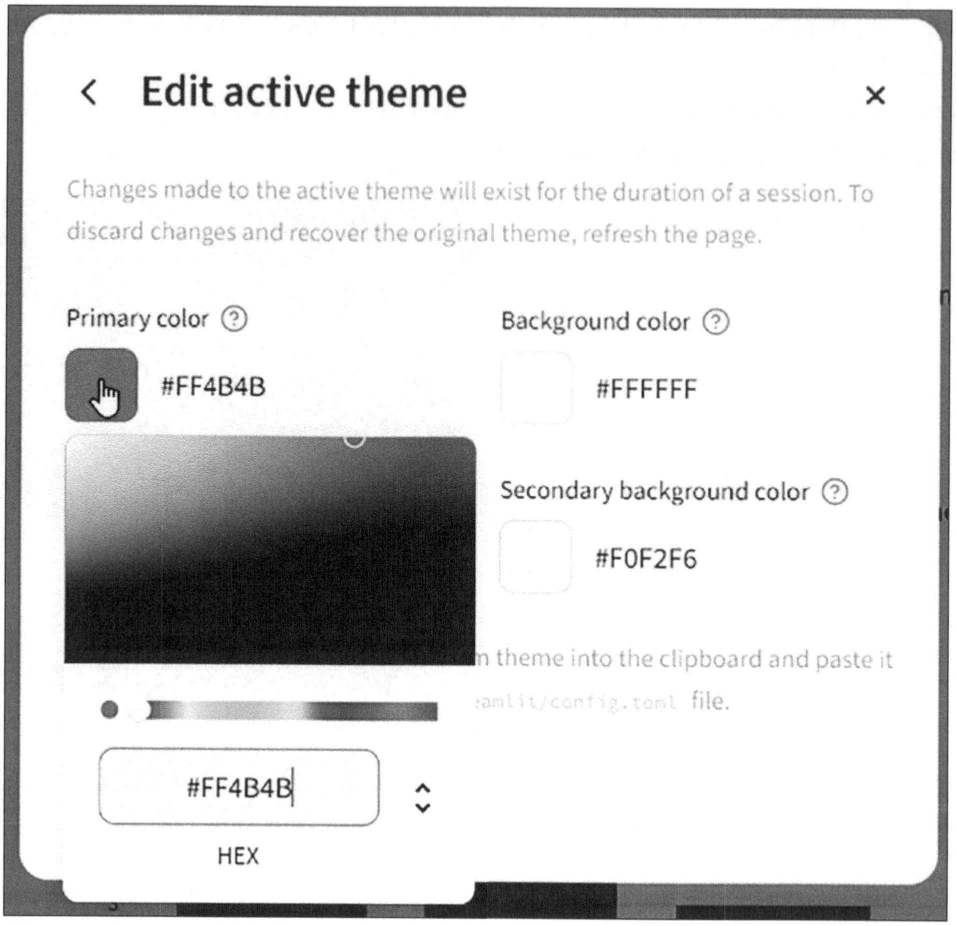

Figure 11.10: *Editing the Active Theme*

Figure 11.11 shows an app with a custom theme, with colors and fonts customized.

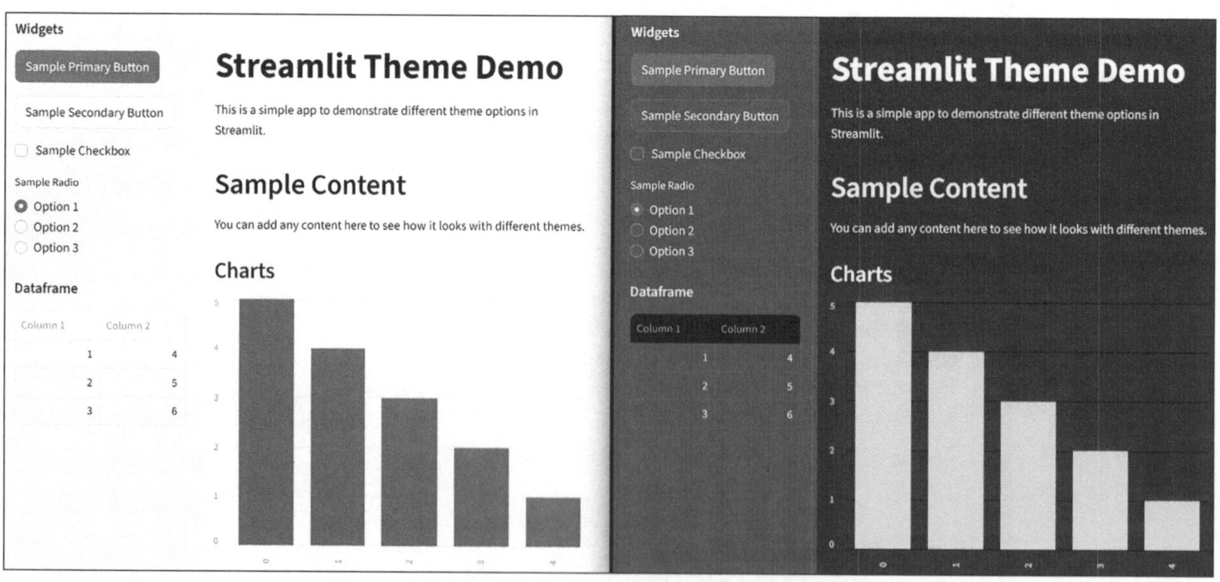

Figure 11.11: *Default Light Theme vs Custom Theme*

While updating the theme from the App menu settings is convenient, as mentioned in the **`Edit active theme`** modal, any changes made via this method will last only for the current session. Fortunately, Streamlit provides an easy way to copy the changes made to the theme to a configuration file using the **`Copy theme to clipboard`** button shown in *Figure 11.10*.

To see how it works, edit the active theme, then click **Copy theme to clipboard**. Now, create a **config.toml** file in a `.streamlit` folder in the same directory as the **theme_demo.py** script, and paste the copied configuration using *Ctrl/Cmd* + V.

The **config.toml** file would look like this (the values might change depending on your choices):

```
[theme]
primaryColor = "#9d4edd"
backgroundColor = "#5a189a"
secondaryBackgroundColor = "#7b2cbf"
textColor = "#ffffff"
```

Once this file is saved, any app using this configuration file will have the same theme as defined in the configuration file. You can test this by creating a new app in the same folder as the **theme_demo.py** script.

In addition to using the App menu and the configuration file, you can use command-line arguments to set the app's theme for that particular run.

For example, running **streamlit run theme_demo.py --theme.primaryColor="Green" --theme.font="monospace"** will override the primary color and font from the **config.toml** file to that set in the command line arguments, resulting in an app that looks like the one shown in *Figure* 11.12.

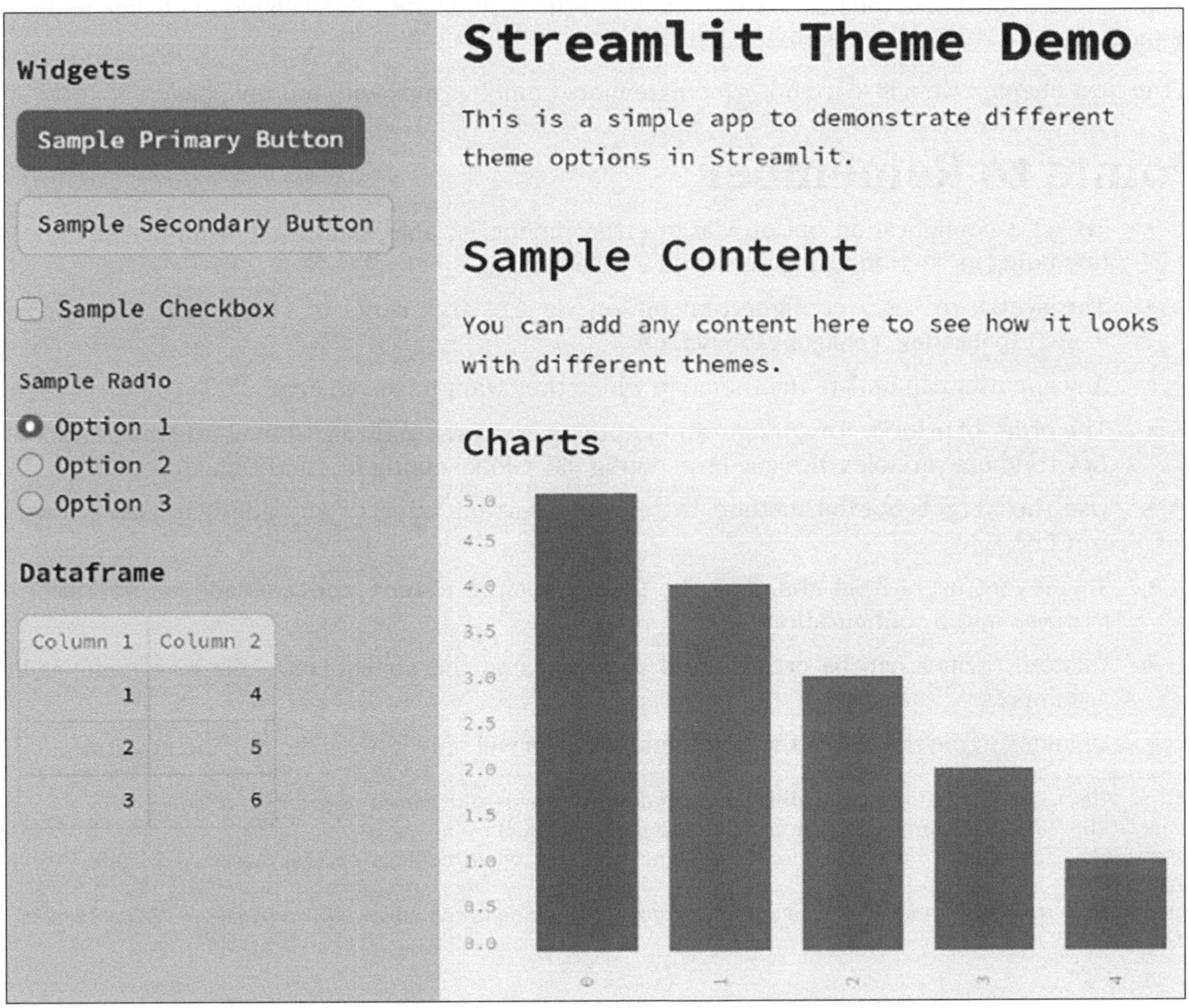

Figure 11.12: *Overriding Theme Set in config.toml Using CLI Arguments*

As you can see, only the primary color and font have been overridden, while all others remain as defined in **`config.toml`**, and as shown in *Figure 11.11*.

Tip: *Apps are generally designed with a particular theme in mind. An app designed for the dark theme might not render well in the light theme. This can lead to problems because the app menu is accessible to all users, allowing anyone to change the theme they want to see the app in.*

To prevent users from being able to change the theme themselves, you can set the **`client.toolbarMode`** *configuration to* **`minimal`** *in the configuration file.* [12] *This prevents users from being able to access the App menu, thereby preventing them from updating the theme.*

Conclusion

In this chapter, we have covered some of the most commonly used configuration options. We have also discussed the different methods of setting these configuration options, and the order of priority assigned to each of them in case of conflicting settings.

Additionally, we have learned how to read the current configuration options at runtime using **`st.get_option`**.

Finally, we have discussed app themes in detail, including the different base themes available, and how to customize and change themes. We also explored the various options available to change and set a theme.

In the next chapter, we will learn how to create more complex apps with multiple pages.

Points to Remember

- To set a configuration option via an environment variable, convert it to upper snake case (including its section header) and add a **`STREAMLIT_`** **prefix**.[13]
- The syntax to set a configuration option via CLI arguments is **`streamlit run app.py --sectionHeader.configOption=value`**.[14]
- Any app user can update the theme in which they want to see an app.
- The order of priority for configuration options is **`st.set_option`**, Command Line arguments, Environment variables, Project-level config file, Global config file, and Default value.
- Use the **`st.get_option`** method to read the current value of any configuration option at runtime.
- To prevent users from changing the theme, set the **`client.toolbarMode`** configuration to `minimal` in the configuration file.
- Custom themes can be created and applied using the **`config.toml`** file or command line arguments.
- Changes to the theme via the App menu settings will only last for the current session.

[12] *https://discuss.streamlit.io/t/launching-pdf-workdesk-an-open-source-web-app-for-your-pdf-needs/70163/16?u=siddhantsadangi* (Accessed: 28 September 2024)
[13] *https://docs.streamlit.io/develop/concepts/configuration/options#available-options* (Accessed: 24 September 2024)
[14] *https://docs.streamlit.io/develop/concepts/configuration/options#available-options* (Accessed: 24 September 2024)

Multiple Choice Questions

1. Which command shows you all the different configuration options available?
   a. `streamlit config help`
   b. `streamlit config show`
   c. `streamlit get config`
   d. `streamlit config list`
2. Which **`toolbarMode`** can hide the `App menu` from users?
   a. Developer
   b. Viewer
   c. Auto
   d. Minimal
3. Which configuration option controls Streamlit's automatic rerun of the app when the source file is updated?
   a. `server.runOnSave`
   b. `server.runOnChange`
   c. `browser.runOnSave`
   d. `client.runOnSave`
4. Which configuration option should be `false` to turn off sending telemetry data to Streamlit?
   a. `browser.sendTelemetry`
   b. `client.disableTelemetry`
   c. `browser.gatherUsageStats`
   d. `client.gatherUsageStats`
5. If **`secrets.files = [ "secrets1.yaml", "secrets2.toml", "secrets3.toml" "secrets.config", ]`**, which file will have the highest priority?
   a. `secrets1.yaml`
   b. `secrets3.toml`
   c. `secrets.config`
   d. Error
6. Where should the **`config.toml`** file be placed for global configuration settings on a Windows system?
   a. C:\Streamlit\config.toml
   b. %userprofile%\.streamlit\config.toml
   c. C:\Users\Streamlit\config.toml
   d. %userprofile%\Streamlit\config.toml

7. Which of the following options is the correct environment variable representation of the **`client.toolbarMode`** configuration?
    a. `CLIENT_TOOLBARMODE`
    b. `STREAMLIT_TOOLBARMODE`
    c. `STREAMLIT_CLIENT_TOOLBAR_MODE`
    d. `Streamlit_Client_ToolbarMode`
8. Which method can set configuration options programmatically at runtime?
    a. config.toml
    b. Environment Variables
    c. Command Line Arguments
    d. `st.set_option`
9. Which of the following methods of setting a configuration option has the highest priority?
    a. Global configuration file
    b. Project-level configuration file
    c. CLI arguments
    d. `st.set_option`
10. Which method allows you to read the current value of any configuration option at runtime?
    a. `st.read_option`
    b. `st.get_config`
    c. `st.get_option`
    d. `st.read_config`
11. How can you change the theme of an app during runtime?
    a. Using a configuration file
    b. Using command-line arguments
    c. Using the `App` menu settings
    d. Using `st.update_theme`

Answers

1. b
2. d
3. a
4. c
5. d
6. b
7. c

8. d
9. d
10. c
11. c

Questions

1. What different methods can you use to set Streamlit configurations? What is their order of priority?
2. How can you use the `config.toml` file to set project-level and global configuration options? What is the difference between the two?
3. How can you prevent users from being able to change the theme they see an app in? Why would you want to do so?
4. Explain how to set a configuration option using an environment variable. Provide an example.
5. What is the purpose of the `st.get_option` method? Provide an example of its usage.
6. Describe the process of creating and applying a custom theme to a Streamlit app.

Key Terms

- **App Theme:** A set of configuration options that control the appearance of a Streamlit app, including colors, fonts, and other visual elements.
- **Command Line Argument:** An argument passed to a program during execution to modify its behavior.
- **Upper Snake Case:** Upper Snake Case is a naming convention used in programming where words are separated by an underscore (_), and each letter is capitalized.
- **Telemetry:** In software development, telemetry refers to collecting software usage statistics to monitor the software's performance and health, and for analytical purposes.[15]

[15] *https://www.techtarget.com/whatis/definition/telemetry* (Accessed: 22 September 2024)

CHAPTER 12
Building Multipage Streamlit Apps

Introduction

Until now, we have only created Streamlit apps with a single page. A single-page app is adequate for small-scale applications. However, as apps grow, organizing them into multiple pages becomes beneficial. This organization aids both the developer in managing and constructing the app, and the user in navigating the various components.

Streamlit offers two straightforward methods for creating multipage apps.

In this chapter, we will explore multipage apps in Streamlit, including their rationale, the associated terminology, and the process of building them.

We will then explore advanced topics like individual page configuration and navigation customization.

Finally, we will discuss nuances in the behavior of widgets in multipage apps that should be considered during the design process.

Structure

In this chapter, we will cover the following topics:

- Motivation behind Streamlit Pages
- Page Terminology
- Building a Multipage App
    - Using the **`pages/Directory`**
    - Using **`st.Page`** and **`st.navigation`**
        - Creating Pages from Source Files
        - Creating Pages from Functions
- Page Configuration Options
- Customizing Navigation
    - Grouping Pages by Sections
    - Building Dynamic Navigation Menus
    - Building a Custom Navigation Menu from Scratch
    - Programmatically Switching Pages
- Widget Behavior in Multipage Apps

Motivation behind Streamlit Pages

Perhaps, the best app to introduce the concept of **`Pages`** in Streamlit is the **`Streamlit Hello`** app. Let us open it again by running **streamlit hello**. It looks as shown in *Figure* 12.1.

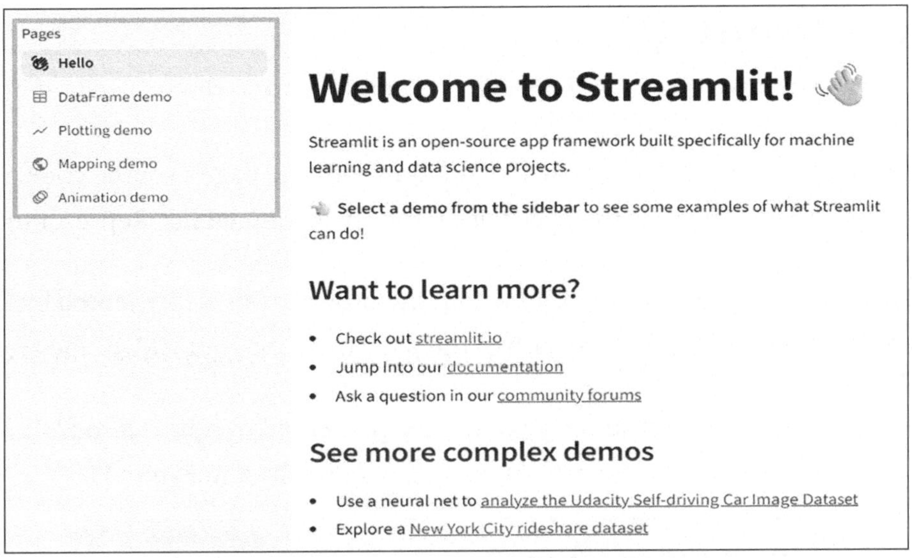

Figure 12.1: *Streamlit Hello App, with Pages Highlighted*

At the top of the left sidebar, you can see this app's different pages. Clicking on any of those takes you to the respective page.

As you can see, on the UI side, pages help divide the app into manageable sections. All the pages you see above could also have been part of the same page, with branching applied to display the relevant content. However, maintaining such a structure would be extremely difficult. To illustrate this, the team at Streamlit has shared the motivation behind adding pages, which can be accessed at https://docs.streamlit.io/get-started/tutorials/create-a-multipage-app#motivation. *Figure* 12.2 shows how this app looked before **`Pages`** were added.

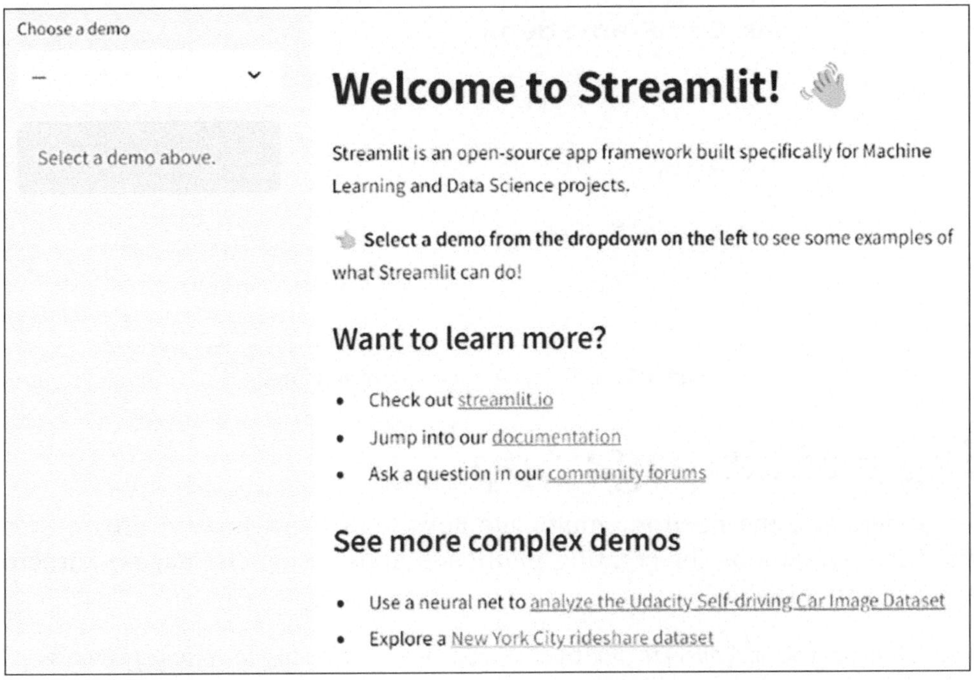

Figure 12.2: *Streamlit Hello App, before Pages were Introduced*

Initially, this app was a single 230-line-long Python file. After migrating to **Pages**, the app was broken into five separate files, each for a different **Page**. This resulted in a better UI, and made managing the code more straightforward, as updating one page would not accidentally introduce errors in another.

Page Terminology

Following are some terms associated with a page of a multipage app that we will refer to throughout the chapter:[1]

- **Page Source:** The Python file or callable function with the page's source code.
- **Page Label:** The identifier for the page within the navigation menu. Represented by 1 in *Figure* 12.3.
- **Page Title:** The identifier for the page within the browser tab. Represented by 2 *in Figure* 12.3.
- **Page URL Pathname:** The relative path of the page from the root URL of the app. Represented by 3 in *Figure* 12.3.
- **Page Favicon:** The icon next to the page title. Represented by 4 in *Figure* 12.3.
- **Page Icon:** The icon next to the page label. Represented by 5 in *Figure* 12.3.

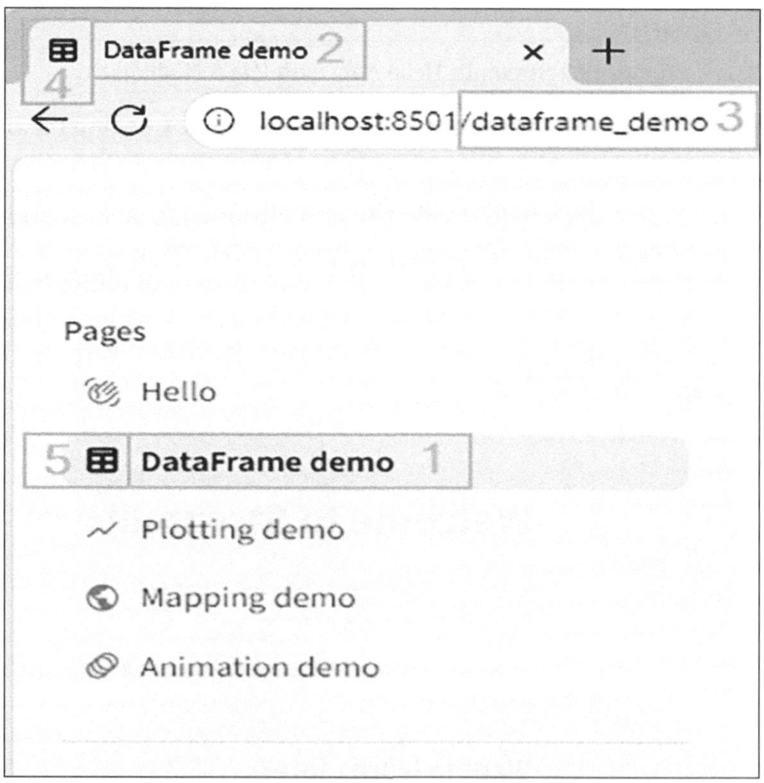

***Figure* 12.3:** *Terms Associated with a Page*

Building a Multipage App

Now that we understand the need for multipage apps, let's learn how to create them. Streamlit provides two distinct methods for creating multipage apps: using the `pages/` directory or using **`st.Page`** and **`st.navigation`**.

[1]*https://docs.streamlit.io/develop/concepts/multipage-apps/overview#page-terminology* (Accessed: 13 October 2024)

Using the Pages/Directory

This method is the original approach for creating multipage apps and is suitable for quick and straightforward implementations. It involves creating Python (`.py`) files for each page in a `pages` folder located in the same directory as the main script (also called the `entrypoint`). Streamlit automatically recognizes the presence of multiple pages, and generates the necessary navigation based on the content of these files.

Let us see how this works in practice by following these steps:

1. Create a **`main.py`** file with the following content:
   ```
   import streamlit as st

   st.title("Main Page")
   ```
   This file is the **`entrypoint`** and corresponds to the app's main page.
2. Run the command **`streamlit run main.py`**. The app will initially display only the title **`Main Page`**.
3. In the same directory as **`main.py`**, create a **`pages`** folder.
4. Inside the pages folder, create a **`page_one.py`** file.
5. Once the file is created, the app will update to include the new page, as shown in *Figure 12.4*.

Figure 12.4: *Adding Page One*

   Congratulations! You have just created your first multipage app. However, since the **`page_one.py`** file is empty, so is the corresponding page in the app. Add the following content to **`page_one.py`**:
   ```
   import streamlit as st
   st.title("Page One")
   ```
6. Now, clicking on **`page one`** in the sidebar will show its content, as shown in *Figure 12.5*.

Figure 12.5: *Populating Pages*

   Feel free to add multiple pages by repeating the previous steps. Here, we have created three pages, resulting in the directory structure shown in *Figure 12.6*.

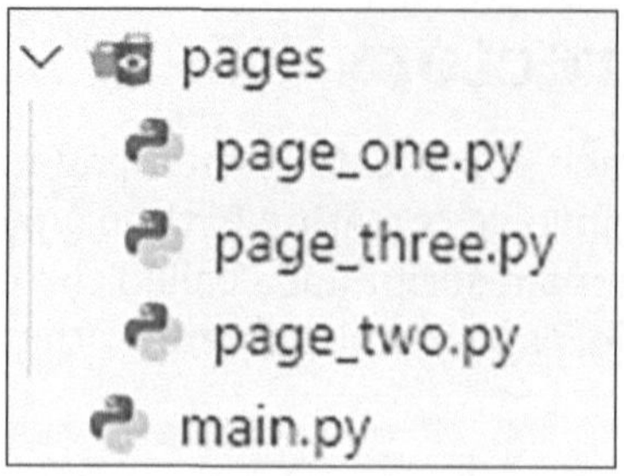

Figure 12.6: *Directory Structure When Using the Pages/Directory Method*

The app will look like this in *Figure* 12.7.

Figure 12.7: *Crude Multi-page App*

Notice that the pages are listed in order of their filename, ignoring underscores. This is why **`page three`** appears above **`page two`**. We can add numerical prefixes to the filenames to correct this, as shown in *Figure* 12.8.

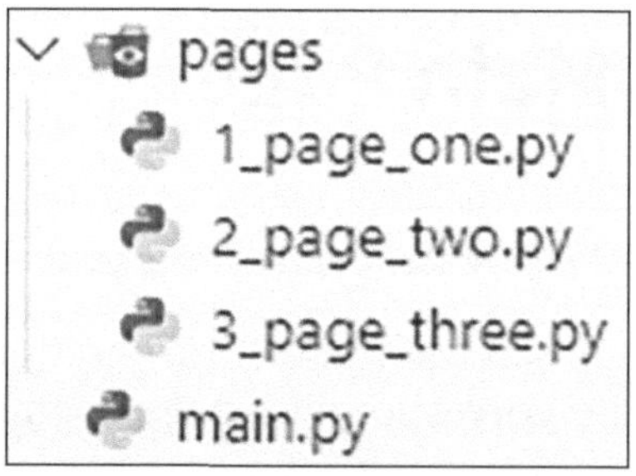

Figure 12.8: *Adding Numerical Prefixes to Pages to Sort Them*

The order of pages in the app is now correct, as shown in *Figure* 12.9.

Figure 12.9: *Correct Order of Pages in a Multi-page App*

Note that Streamlit ignores the numerical prefixes **1_**, **2_**, etc. from the filenames when displaying page labels.

Tip: *Filenames can also contain emojis. These can enhance the user experience by making page labels more visually appealing, similar to the Streamlit Hello app.*

The order in which pages are displayed follows these rules:[2]

1. The **entrypoint** file is always displayed first.
2. Files with a numerical prefix appear before those without.
3. Files are sorted based on the number, followed by the filename.

Note: *For a detailed guide on how pages are sorted in the sidebar, refer to the Streamlit documentation here: https://docs.streamlit.io/develop/concepts/multipage-apps/pages-directory#how-pages-are-sorted-in-the-sidebar.*

Using st.Page and st.navigation

This newer method offers greater flexibility for creating multipage apps. In addition to building pages from different source files, it allows you to create pages from Python functions within the same source file. This section will explore both methods.

Creating Pages from Source Files

Unlike the **pages/** directory method, this approach does not require the source files for pages to be in a **pages** folder. Instead, you can create a page from any Streamlit-compatible **.py** file using **st.Page**, and link it to your **entrypoint** using **st.navigation**. Here is how:

1. Create an **entrypoint.py** file and three other **.py** files named **page_one.py**, **page_two.py**, and **page_three.py**. You can place the page source files wherever you want in the same directory as the **entrypoint.py** file. Here, we have placed **page_one.py** and **page_three.py** in the same folder, while **page_two.py** is placed inside a subfolder called **some_folder**, as shown in Figure 12.10.

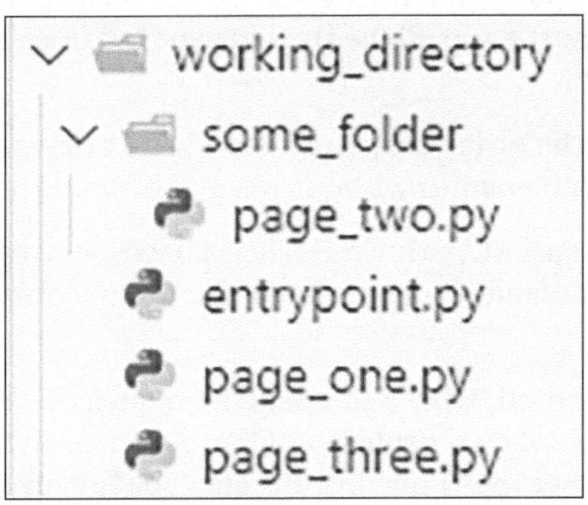

Figure 12.10: *Example Folder Structure of a Multi-page App*

2. Add the following lines to the page source files, replacing **Page One** with **Page Two** and **Page Three** for **page_two.py** and **page_three.py**, respectively:

```
import streamlit as st
st.title("Page One")
```

[2] *https://docs.streamlit.io/develop/concepts/multipage-apps/pages-directory#how-pages-are-sorted-in-the-sidebar* (Accessed: 12 October 2024)

3. Add the following lines to **entrypoint.py**, replacing the paths to the page source files with your paths:

```
import streamlit as st

st.title("Main Page")

pg = st.navigation(
    [
        st.Page("page_one.py"),
        st.Page("some_folder/page_two.py"),
        st.Page("page_three.py"),
    ]
)
pg.run()
```

4. Run the **entrypoint.py** file using **streamlit run entrypoint.py**. Your app will look like *Figure 12.11*.

Figure 12.11: *Multipage App Using st.Page and st.navigation*

You might have noticed some differences already. First, the titles **Main Page** and **Page One** both appear on **page one**, and there is no **entrypoint** page in the navigation. This is because, when using **st.navigation**, the entrypoint file acts as a page router, not a separate page.[3] Any Streamlit elements or widgets included in the **entrypoint** file will be shared across all pages. Navigate to the other pages; you will always see **Main Page** at the top. Since the **entrypoint** does not behave like a separate page, it is not visible in the navigation.

Second, the pages are listed in the order they were added to **st.navigation** and not by the filename. This allows more flexibility with filenames without worrying about the order in the navigation.

Finally, **page one** does not have a URL pathname. This is because, when using **st.navigation**, unless another page is defined as the default, using **st.Page**, the first page is assumed to be the default and, therefore, the app's root.

Unlike the **pages/** directory method, where the page icon, favicon, label, etc., are inferred from the page source filename, **st.Page** allows explicit configuration of these elements using parameters. Replace the **st.Page("page_three.py")** line in your **entrypoint.py** file with:

```
st.Page(
    "page_three.py",
    title="Page Three",
    icon=":material/timer_3:",
    url_path="third_page",
)
```

[3] *https://docs.streamlit.io/develop/concepts/multipage-apps/page-and-navigation#app-structure* (Accessed: 13 October 2024)

Reload the app and navigate to the third page. It should look as shown in *Figure 12.12*.

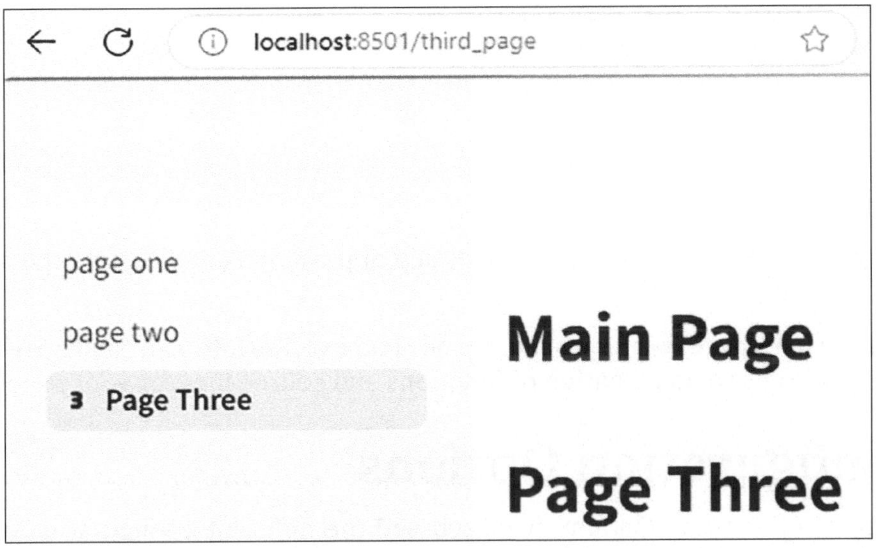

***Figure 12.12:** Customizing Page Using st.Page*

What differences do you observe between **page three** and the other pages? First, unlike **page one** and **page two**, where the page label was inferred from the page source, **Page Three** has a customized title passed to **st.Page**. Second, **Page Three** has an icon next to it, thanks to the emoji passed to **st.Page's icon** parameter. Finally, **Page Three** has a custom URL pathname **third_page**, taken from **st.Page's url_path** argument.

In addition to customizing the page using **st.Page**, we can also customize the navigation by hiding the default navigation and building one ourselves. We will discuss this in the *Customizing Navigation* section of this chapter. These customization options are not available in the **pages/** directory method, which is why using **st.Page** and **st.navigation** is recommended for most apps.

Creating Pages from Functions

This method is similar to creating pages using Python source files, but we use Python functions instead of a source file and pass these functions to **st.Page** instead of a path to a source file.

Let us recreate the previous app using a single **app.py** file:

```
import streamlit as st

st.title("Main Page")

def page_one():
    st.title("Page One")

def page_two():
    st.title("Page Two")

def page_three():
    st.title("Page Three")

pg = st.navigation(
    [
        st.Page(page_one),
        st.Page(page_two),
        st.Page(
```

```
                page_three,
                title="Page Three",
                icon=":material/timer_3:",
                url_path="third_page",
            ),
        ]
    )

    pg.run()
```

Run this using **`streamlit run app.py`**. The resulting app will look and behave the same as the one previously shown in *Figure 12.12*.

Each function—**`page_one`**, **`page_two`**, and **`page_three`**—is converted into a Streamlit page using **`st.Page`**. Of course, you can also use a combination of functions and source files for your pages. Give it a try!

Page Configuration Options

In *Chapter 11, App Configuration Options*, we discussed the different configuration options available for the app as a whole. In addition to app configuration options, Streamlit allows you to configure individual pages of an app using **`st.set_page_config`**. These configuration options can be used to customize page elements unavailable in **`st.Page`**, such as the favicon, page title, and menu options. This section will explore these configuration options, and see how they affect the page.

Note: **`st.set_page_config`** *can only be used with pages created from a source file, not a function.*

Let us use the same scripts we created in the *Creating Pages from Source Files* section as the starting point, and make some modifications as well as observations described as follows:

1. Spin up the app as before using **`streamlit run entrypoint.py`**.
2. Remove the **`st.title("Main Page")`** line from **`entrypoint.py`**. This is no longer needed.
3. Add **`st.caption([i for i in range(100)])`** to the bottom of **`page_one.py`**. The app should look as shown in the following *Figure 12.13*.

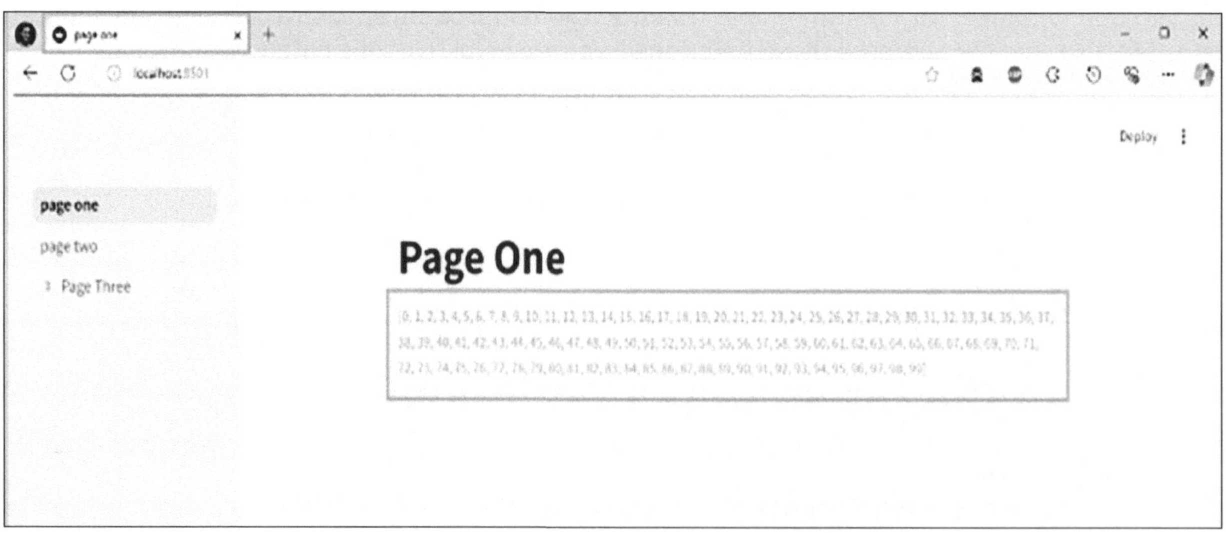

Figure 12.13: *Default Page Favicon, Title, and Width*

4. Note the page favicon and title in the browser tab. The favicon will be the default Streamlit dark logo, and the page title will be the same as the page label. Also, observe the horizontal space occupied by the contents of the main section. In *Figure 12.13*, we can fit 37 numbers in the first line.

5. Note the options available under the App Menu at the top right. The default options are shown in *Figure 12.14*.

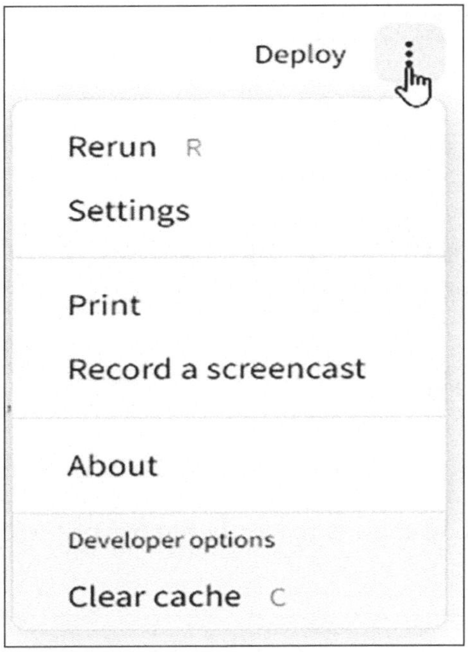

Figure 12.14: *Default App Menu*

Now, let us use **`st.set_page_config`** to update all these elements by following these steps:

1. Add the following lines to **`page_one.py`**, just below the import statement:

```
st.set_page_config(
    page_title="Welcome",
    page_icon=":wave:",
)
```

Note: **`st.set_page_config`** *must always be the first Streamlit element being called in a page, even before* **`st.title`**.[4]

After rerunning, the page's favicon and title will change to · and **`Welcome`**, respectively, as shown in the following *Figure 12.15*.

[4] *https://docs.streamlit.io/develop/api-reference/configuration/st.set_page_config* (Accessed: 23 October 2024)

Figure 12.15: *Updated Favicon and Page Title*

2. Now, add **layout="wide"** in **st.set_page_config** as follows:

```
st.set_page_config(
    page_title="Welcome",
    page_icon=":wave:",
    layout="wide",
)
```

This increases the width of the main area to almost fit the entire screen width, as shown in *Figure 12.16*.

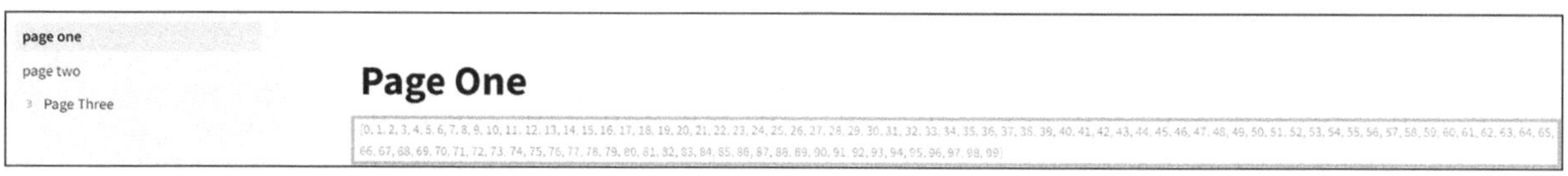

Figure 12.16: Wide Layout

Note: ***Wide*** *mode can also be accessed under* ***Settings*** *in the App Menu at the app's top-right.*

As shown in *Figure 12.16*, we can now fit more numbers than in *Figure 12.13*. The actual width will depend on your screen and window size.

3. Similarly, add **initial_sidebar_state="collapsed"** to **st.set_page_config.** This will collapse the sidebar when the page is opened.

4. Finally, let us explore the **menu_items** parameter. This is used to configure the **App** Menu at the app's top-right. It is a dictionary that can take three keys to control the respective menu items:

   - **Get help:** A URL or email address
   - **Report a bug:** A URL or email address
   - **About:** A markdown string

   The following code snippet shows an example of how this can be used:

```
st.set_page_config(
  page_title="Welcome",
  page_icon=":wave:",
  layout="wide",
  initial_sidebar_state="collapsed",
  menu_items={
```

```
        "Get help": "mailto:awesome.reader@example.com",
        "Report a Bug": "https://github.com/SiddhantSadangi/AwesomeApp/issues/
new",
        "About": ":fire: Awesome App! Developer: [Awesome Reader]
(mailto:awesomereader@example.com)",
    },
)
```

This makes the **App** Menu look as shown in the following *Figure* 12.17.

Figure 12.17: *Updated App Menu*

Notice the new **Report a bug** and **Get help** sections previously missing in *Figure* 12.5. The **About** section has also been updated, as shown in *Figure* 12.18.

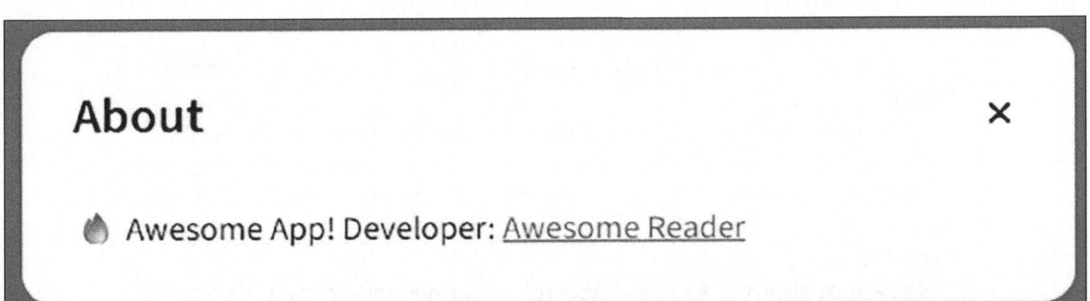

Figure 12.18: *Updated About*

It is important to note that although the element is named **st.set_page_config**, the **menu_items** and **layout** parameters affect the entire app, and not just the page where **st.set_page_config** was used. In case multiple pages have **st.set_page_config** with conflicting **menu_items** and **layout** parameters, the most recent page takes precedence.

Customizing Navigation

We have seen how Streamlit automatically builds a navigation section for multipage apps, and how we can customize the page logo, label, and position in the navigation section. This section will explore additional ways to customize the navigation section, including building dynamic navigation menus (menus that change during the app's execution depending on user action) and building a navigation menu from scratch.

Note: *These customizations require* **`st.navigation`**, and cannot be used with the ***pages/*** *directory method to build multipage apps.*

Grouping Pages by Sections

Pages can be grouped into sections in the navigation menu for easier organization. In addition to accepting a list of **`StreamlitPage`** objects, which are the returned values from **`st.Page`**, **`st.navigation`** can also accept a dictionary with the section header as the key and a list of pages in the section as the value. Here is an example **`app.py`**:

```
import streamlit as st

def login():
    st.title("Log in")

def logout():
    st.title("Log out")

def profile():
    st.title("User Profile")

def home():
    st.title("Home Page")

def about():
    st.title("About")

def contact():
    st.title("Contact details")

pg = st.navigation(
    {
        "": [st.Page(home, title="Home", icon=":material/home:")],
        "User": [
          st.Page(login, title="Log in", icon=":material/login:"),
          st.Page(profile, title="Profile", icon=":material/account_circle:"),
          st.Page(logout, title="Log out", icon=":material/logout:"),
        ],
        "Info": [
          st.Page(about, title="About", icon=":material/info:"),
           st.Page(contact, title="Contact", icon=":material/contact_
support:"),
        ],
    }
)

pg.run()
```

Running this script using **`streamlit run app.py`** opens an app that looks like the following *Figure 12.19*.

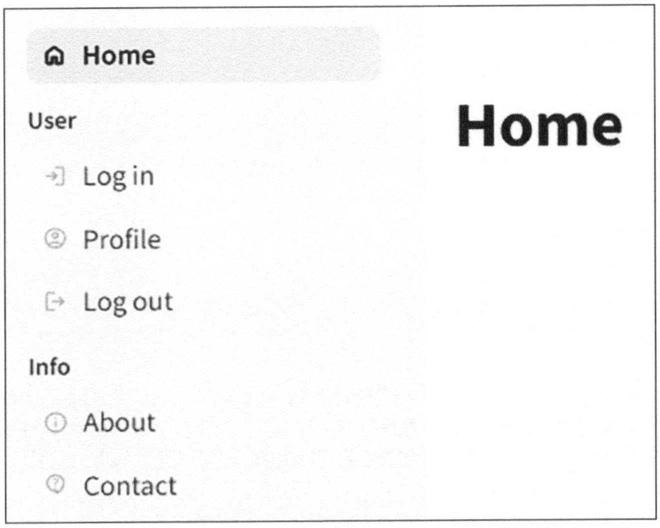

Figure 12.19: *Page Sections*

As you can see, the pages are grouped under the **`User`** and **`Info`** sections in the navigation menu. All we had to do was to pass the section headers and list of pages in the section to **`st.navigation`** as key-value pairs of a dictionary. Since the **`Home`** page does not need to be in a section, we have passed it to a blank key as a blank section header.

Building Dynamic Navigation Menus

Since Streamlit reruns the script on any user interaction, we can use this behavior to change the list of pages passed to **`st.navigation`** on each rerun, and create a dynamic navigation menu that responds to user actions. Take, for example, the app we created in the previous section, as shown in *Figure 12.19*. All pages are visible by default, regardless of whether the user is logged in. This is not ideal, as we would want the user to log in before showing the **`Home`**, **`Profile`**, and **`Log out`** pages.

This can be done by passing a different list of pages to **`st.navigation`** depending on whether the user has logged in. Let us update the **`app.py`** script to handle this.

First, to make things easier, create **`StreamlitPage`** objects that can be easily passed to **`st.navigation`**, similar to creating variables in Python:

```
home_page = st.Page(home, title="Home", icon=":material/home:")
login_page = st.Page(login, title="Log in", icon=":material/login:")
profile_page = st.Page(profile, title="Profile", icon=":material/account_
circle:")
logout_page = st.Page(logout, title="Log out", icon=":material/logout:")
about_page = st.Page(about, title="About", icon=":material/info:")
contact_page = st.Page(contact, title="Contact", icon=":material/contact_
support:")
```

Add these lines after the function definitions and before **`st.navigation`** in **`app.py`**. Once done, pass these objects to **`st.navigation`**, as follows:

```
import streamlit as st

def login():
    st.title("Log in")
```

```
def logout():
    st.title("Log out")

def profile():
    st.title("Profile")

def home():
    st.title("Home")

def about():
    st.title("About")

def contact():
    st.title("Contact details")

home_page = st.Page(home, title="Home", icon=":material/home:")
login_page = st.Page(login, title="Log in", icon=":material/login:")
profile_page = st.Page(profile, title="Profile", icon=":material/account_
circle:")
logout_page = st.Page(logout, title="Log out", icon=":material/logout:")
about_page = st.Page(about, title="About", icon=":material/info:")
contact_page = st.Page(contact, title="Contact", icon=":material/contact_
support:")

pg = st.navigation(
    {
        "": [home_page],
        "User": [login_page, profile_page, logout_page],
        "Info": [about_page, contact_page],
    }
)

pg.run()
```

As you can see, this makes **st.navigation** cleaner, and the pages easier to reuse.

Now, we have to implement a login mechanism. We will use a login button linked to a **logged_in** session state under the **login** function to simplify things. Do not forget to initialize the **logged_in** session state, as discussed in Chapter 5, *Persisting Data and State Using Session State*. Add the initialization to the script, and update the **login** function as follows:

```
if "logged_in" not in st.session_state:
    st.session_state.logged_in = False

def login():
    if st.button("Log in"):
        st.session_state.logged_in = True
```

Then, check if the user is logged in. If not, only show the **Log in** and **Info** pages in the navigation. Once the user logs in, the **Log in** page is no longer needed. This is done as follows:

```
if st.session_state.logged_in:
    pg = st.navigation(
        {
            "": [home_page],
            "User": [profile_page, logout_page],
            "Info": [about_page, contact_page],
        }
    )
```

```
else:
    pg = st.navigation(
        {
            "User": [login_page],
            "Info": [about_page, contact_page],
        }
    )

pg.run()
```

Now, if you clear the cache and rerun the app, you will only see the **Log in** and **Info** pages. However, if you click the **Log in** button, the app reloads, but nothing else happens until you perform another action (like clicking again or navigating to another page). Why? This is a consequence of Streamlit's app execution flow, as discussed in Chapter 4, *Exploring Streamlit's Flow and Architecture*. When the button is clicked, the app reloads before the **logged_in** is set to **True**. In the next run, the **logged_in** is set to **True**, but only after if st.session_state.logged_in has been executed. So, to satisfy the condition, the app needs to be rerun. We can do this programmatically by adding **st.rerun()** after we set **logged_in** to **True**, as follows:

```
def login():
    if st.button("Log in"):
        st.session_state.logged_in = True
        st.rerun()
```

Clear the cache and rerun the app. Now, you can see the hidden pages immediately after clicking **Log in**.

Similarly, we can add a **Log out** button to the **Log out** page to set **logged_in** to **False** and hide pages, once the user logs out. The final script looks like this:

```
import streamlit as st

if "logged_in" not in st.session_state:
    st.session_state.logged_in = False

def login():
    if st.button("Log in"):
        st.session_state.logged_in = True
        st.rerun()

def logout():
    if st.button("Log out"):
        st.session_state.logged_in = False
        st.rerun()

def profile():
    st.title("Profile")

def home():
    st.title("Home")

def about():
    st.title("About")

def contact():
    st.title("Contact details")

home_page = st.Page(home, title="Home", icon=":material/home:")
login_page = st.Page(login, title="Log in", icon=":material/login:")
```

```
profile_page = st.Page(profile, title="Profile", icon=":material/account_circle:")
logout_page = st.Page(logout, title="Log out", icon=":material/logout:")
about_page = st.Page(about, title="About", icon=":material/info:")
contact_page = st.Page(contact, title="Contact", icon=":material/contact_
support:")

if st.session_state.logged_in:
    pg = st.navigation(
        {
            "": [home_page],
            "User": [profile_page, logout_page],
            "Info": [about_page, contact_page],
        }
    )
else:
    pg = st.navigation(
        {
            "User": [login_page],
            "Info": [about_page, contact_page],
        }
    )

pg.run()
```

This example was a simple way of implementing role or user-based access control using a dynamic navigation menu.

Building a Custom Navigation Menu from Scratch

For even more customization of the navigation menu, we can use **st.page_link**. **st.page_link** combines some functionalities of **st.Page** and **st.navigation**, and adds some of its own.

Similar to **st.Page**, it can create a Streamlit page from a Python file, and add labels and icons. Unlike **st.Page**, it can also link to the external sites.

Like **st.navigation**, **st.page_link** can create a navigation link to a Streamlit (or external) page. Unlike **st.navigation**, it can accept only one page at a time (not a list or dictionary of pages), and can be placed anywhere in the app (not limited to the sidebar).

Let us recreate the app from the previous section using **st.page_link**. For each page to be displayed, add an **st.page_link**, as follows:

```
import streamlit as st

if "logged_in" not in st.session_state:
    st.session_state.logged_in = False

def login():
    if st.button("Log in"):
        st.session_state.logged_in = True
        st.rerun()

def logout():
    if st.button("Log out"):
        st.session_state.logged_in = False
        st.rerun()

def profile():
```

```
    st.title("Profile")

def home():
    st.title("Home")

def about():
    st.title("About")

def contact():
    st.title("Contact details")

home_page = st.Page(home, title="Home", icon=":material/home:")
login_page = st.Page(login, title="Log in", icon=":material/login:")
profile_page = st.Page(profile, title="Profile", icon=":material/account_circle:")
logout_page = st.Page(logout, title="Log out", icon=":material/logout:")
about_page = st.Page(about, title="About", icon=":material/info:")
contact_page = st.Page(contact, title="Contact", icon=":material/contact_
support:")

if st.session_state.logged_in:
    pg = st.navigation(
        {
            "": [home_page],
            "User": [profile_page, logout_page],
            "Info": [about_page, contact_page],
        }
    )

    st.page_link(home_page, icon=":material/home:")
    st.page_link(profile_page, icon=":material/account_circle:")
    st.page_link(logout_page, icon=":material/logout:")
    st.page_link(about_page, icon=":material/info:")
    st.page_link(contact_page, icon=":material/contact_support:")

else:
    pg = st.navigation(
        {
            "User": [login_page],
            "Info": [about_page, contact_page],
        }
    )

    st.page_link(login_page, icon=":material/login:")
    st.page_link(about_page, icon=":material/info:")
    st.page_link(contact_page, icon=":material/contact_support:")

pg.run()
```

The resultant app looks as shown in *Figure* 12.20.

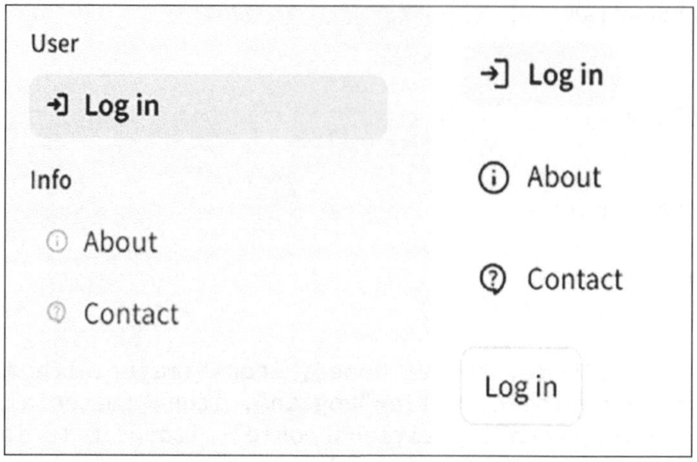

Figure 12.20: *Using st.page_link to Create a Custom Navigation Menu*

To move the new navigation to the sidebar, use **`st.sidebar`** as a context manager, and add the section headers manually using **`st.write`**. Both of these are as follows:

```
    if st.session_state.logged_in:
    pg = st.navigation(
        {
            "": [home_page],
            "User": [profile_page, logout_page],
            "Info": [about_page, contact_page],
        }
    )

    with st.sidebar:
        st.page_link(home_page, icon=":material/home:")
        st.write("User")
        st.page_link(profile_page, icon=":material/account_circle:")
        st.page_link(logout_page, icon=":material/logout:")
        st.write("Info")
        st.page_link(about_page, icon=":material/info:")
        st.page_link(contact_page, icon=":material/contact_support:")

else:
    pg = st.navigation(
        {
            "User": [login_page],
            "Info": [about_page, contact_page],
        }
    )

    with st.sidebar:
        st.write("User")
        st.page_link(login_page, icon=":material/login:")
        st.write("Info")
        st.page_link(about_page, icon=":material/info:")
        st.page_link(contact_page, icon=":material/contact_support:")

pg.run()
```

The app now looks as shown in the following *Figure* 12.21.

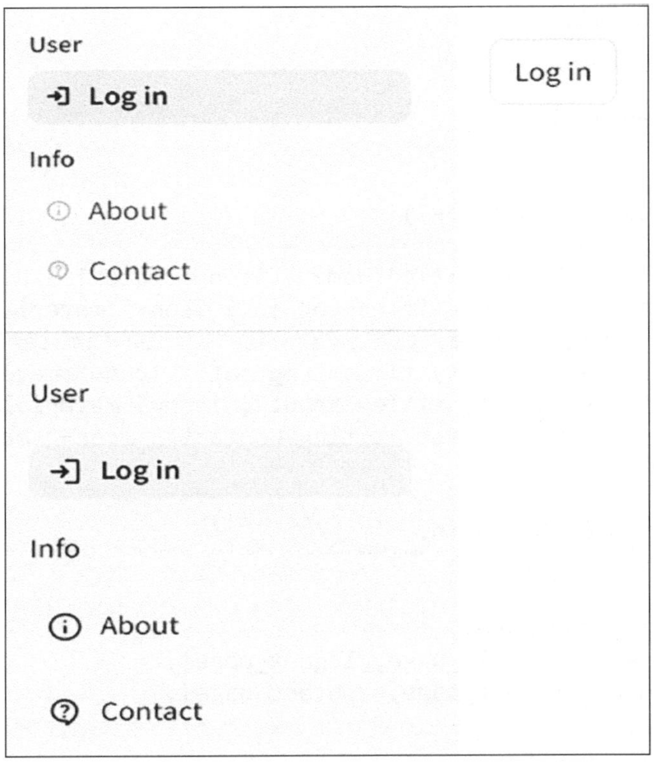

Figure 12.21: *Moving the Custom Navigation Menu to the Sidebar*

The upper navigation menu is the default menu created by **`st.navigation`**. Whenever **`st.navigation`** is visible, it will always be at the top of the sidebar. Since we no longer need it, we can hide it by passing **`position="hidden"`**.

Note: **`st.navigation`** *is required to build the navigation menu, and define the actual paths to the pages. Hence, although it can be hidden if not required, it must still be included in the app, if navigating between multiple pages is necessary.*

Since **`st.page_link`** can also be disabled, you can show all the pages every time, but only enable certain pages after the user has logged in. This way, **`st.page_link`** can be moved outside the **`if`** condition. Also, since **`st.page_link`** can link to external pages, you can add a link to the Streamlit website (www.streamlit.io) under the **`Info`** section. The updated script is as follows:

```
import streamlit as st

if "logged_in" not in st.session_state:
    st.session_state.logged_in = False

def login():
    if st.button("Log in"):
        st.session_state.logged_in = True
        st.rerun()

def logout():
    if st.button("Log out"):
        st.session_state.logged_in = False
        st.rerun()

def profile():
    st.title("Profile")

def home():
```

```
    st.title("Home")

def about():
    st.title("About")

def contact():
    st.title("Contact details")

home_page = st.Page(home, title="Home", icon=":material/home:")
login_page = st.Page(login, title="Log in", icon=":material/login:")
profile_page = st.Page(profile, title="Profile", icon=":material/account_circle:")
logout_page = st.Page(logout, title="Log out", icon=":material/logout:")
about_page = st.Page(about, title="About", icon=":material/info:")
contact_page = st.Page(contact, title="Contact", icon=":material/contact_
support:")

if st.session_state.logged_in:
    pg = st.navigation(
        {
            "": [home_page],
            "User": [profile_page, logout_page],
            "Info": [about_page, contact_page],
        },
        position="hidden",
    )

else:
    pg = st.navigation(
        {
            "User": [login_page],
            "Info": [about_page, contact_page],
        },
        position="hidden",
    )

with st.sidebar:
    st.page_link(
        home_page,
        icon=":material/home:",
        disabled=not st.session_state.logged_in,
    )
    st.write("User")
    st.page_link(
        login_page,
        icon=":material/login:",
        disabled=st.session_state.logged_in,
    )
    st.page_link(
        profile_page,
        icon=":material/account_circle:",
        disabled=not st.session_state.logged_in,
    )
    st.page_link(
        logout_page,
        icon=":material/logout:",
        disabled=not st.session_state.logged_in,
    )
```

```
    st.write("Info")
    st.page_link(about_page, icon=":material/info:")
    st.page_link(contact_page, icon=":material/contact_support:")
    st.page_link(
        "https://www.streamlit.io",
        label="Streamlit",
        icon=":material/open_in_new:",
    )

pg.run()
```

The app now appears as shown in the following *Figure 12.22*.

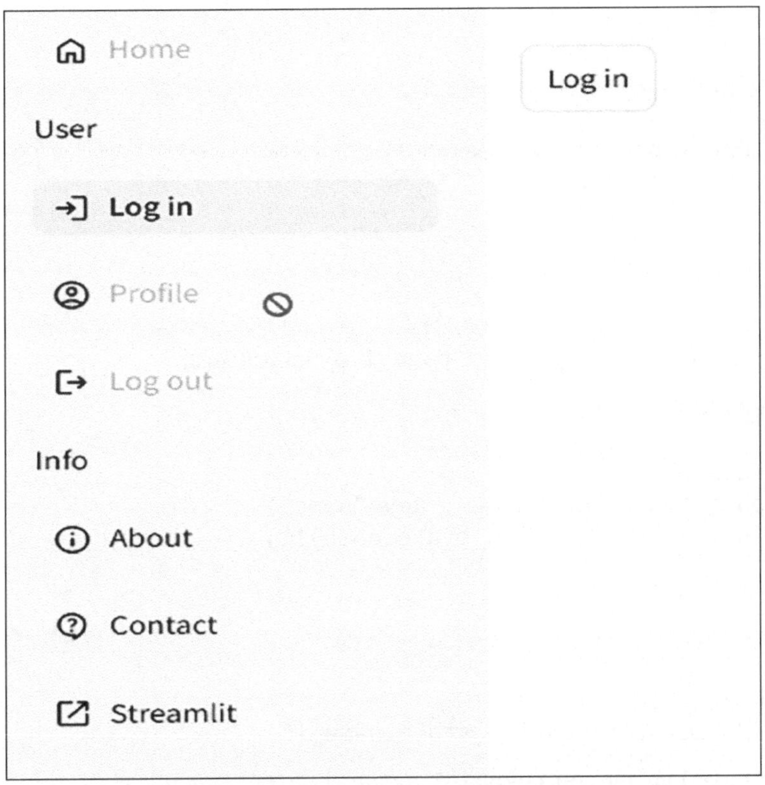

Figure 12.22: *Enhanced Customized Navigation Menu*

Initially, all pages are visible, but the user must log in to access any disabled pages. Besides the internal pages, the navigation menu includes a link to the external Streamlit website, which opens in a new browser tab.

Programmatically Switching Pages

The final navigation customization feature offered by Streamlit is **`st.switch_page`**. This can be used to programmatically switch pages without needing the user to click on a page link.

For instance, if we want the **`About`** page to automatically open when the user logs out instead of the first accessible page (**`Log in`**, in this case), we can add **`st.switch_page(about_page)`** to the **`Log out`** button, as follows:

```
def logout():
    if st.button("Log out"):
        st.session_state.logged_in = False
        st.switch_page(about_page)
```

Widget Behavior in Multipage Apps

When a user navigates to a new page by clicking on the navigation menu or page link, the app reruns and loads the selected page.[5] This impacts widgets because, as discussed in *Chapter* 7, *Widget Keys and Callbacks*, the widget ID also depends on the page where a widget has been created,[6] and Streamlit cleans up data for widgets not rendered on the screen at the end of the script run.[7] This means that widgets created on the page being navigated from can lose their state, if not rendered on the new page. Additionally, if identical widgets are defined on two different pages, the widget will reset to its default value when switching between pages.[8]

Let us see this in practice using a simple example. Create an **entrypoint.py** file as follows:

```
import streamlit as st

pg = st.navigation(
    [
        st.Page("page_1.py"),
        st.Page("page_2.py"),
    ]
)

pg.run()
```

In the same folder as **entrypoint.py**, create **page_1.py** as follows:

```
import streamlit as st

st.title("Page 1")
st.text_input("Enter your name", key="name")
st.write(f"Hello, {st.session_state.name}!")
```

And **page_2.py** as follows:

```
import streamlit as st

st.title("Page 2")
st.write(f"Hello, {st.session_state.name}!")
```

Run the app using **streamlit run entrypoint.py**, and enter your name on **page 1**. The app will look as shown in the following *Figure* 12.23.

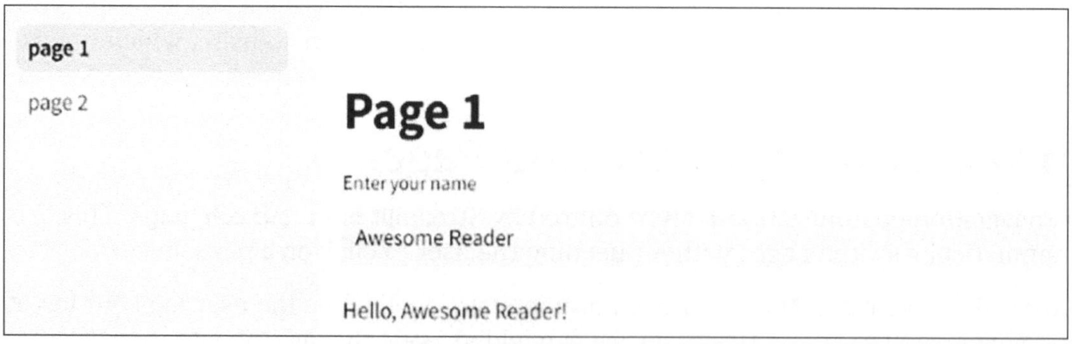

Figure 12.23: *After Entering the Name on Page 1*

---

[5] *https://docs.streamlit.io/develop/concepts/multipage-apps/overview#navigating-between-pages* (Accessed: 27 October 2024)
[6] *https://docs.streamlit.io/develop/concepts/architecture/widget-behavior* (Accessed: 27 October 2024)
[7] *https://docs.streamlit.io/develop/concepts/architecture/widget-behavior#widget-clean-up-process* (Accessed: 27 October 2024)
[8] *https://docs.streamlit.io/develop/concepts/multipage-apps/widgets* (Accessed: 27 October 2024)

However, when navigating to **page 2**, you will encounter a **st.session_state that has no attribute "name"** error. Why? This is because the **name text_input** widget is not rendered on **page 2**; and hence, Streamlit deletes it from **session_state**.

There are two ways to solve this issue:

- **Add the widget to the entrypoint file:** This method works because the **entrypoint i**s always executed, regardless of the page the user is on.[9] However, this method makes the widget visible on all pages, and cannot be used with the **pages/**directory method.
- **Interrupt the widget cleanup process** (discussed in *Chapter 7, Widget Keys and Callbacks*):

  By adding the following code block to the top of each page, we can prevent Streamlit from cleaning up **name** in **session_state**:

  ```
  if "name" in st.session_state:
      st.session_state.name = st.session_state.name
  ```

  If there are multiple such keys, the preceding block can be updated to:

  ```
  for key in st.session_state:
      st.session_state[key] = st.session_state[key]
  ```

  This will prevent Streamlit from cleaning up any **session_state** key. When using the **st.Page** and **st.navigation** method, this block can be included only in the entrypoint file before the pages are executed.

Conclusion

In this chapter, we explored the world of multipage apps in Streamlit. We began by understanding the motivation behind creating multipage apps, and familiarizing ourselves with common terminologies associated with pages. We then built multipage apps using various methods available in Streamlit.

Next, we took a deeper dive into different page configuration options, customized the page navigation menu, and discussed the nuances of widget behavior in multipage apps.

In the next chapter, we will learn how to test Streamlit apps, and explore different strategies for automating testing and alerting.

Points to Remember

- As the size of an app grows, dividing it into multiple pages improves the user experience and the developer's maintainability.
- Streamlit automatically creates pages for each **.py** file in the **pages** directory.
- Pages are listed in order of their filename, ignoring underscores and numerical prefixes.
- The **menu_items** and **layout** parameters of **st.set_page_config** affect the entire app, not just the page where **st.set_page_config** was called.
- To create sections of pages in the navigation menu, pass a dictionary to **st.navigation** with section headers as keys, and the list of pages in the section as values.
- **st.page_link** can be used with both Streamlit pages and external websites.
- **st.navigation** is needed to render the default navigation menu, and create the path to the linked pages. Therefore, it has to be used even when customizing the navigation menu using **st.page_link**.

[9] *https://docs.streamlit.io/develop/concepts/multipage-apps/widgets#option-1-preferred-execute-your-widget-command-in-your-entrypoint-file* (Accessed: 27 October 2024)

- **`st.switch_page`** is used to switch the current page in a multipage app programmatically.[10]
- The **`entrypoint`** file is always executed when using the **`st.Page`** and **`st.navigation`** method of building multipage apps.
- Widgets do not retain their state across pages, unless visible on the open page.
- To retain the state of widgets across pages, even if they are not visible on the open page, they can either be defined in the **`entrypoint`** file, or the Streamlit widget clean-up process can be interrupted by manually assigning **`session_state`** key-value pairs.

Multiple Choice Questions

1. What will be the name of a page in the sidebar if its corresponding file is named `_01_Page One_1.py`?
   a. `01 Page One 1`
   b. `Page One 1`
   c. `page one`
   d. `_01_Page One_1`
2. What is the icon next to the page title within a browser tab?
   a. Source
   b. Label
   c. Favicon
   d. Icon
3. What happens if different pages have different `menu_items` in `st.set_page_config`?
   a. The `menu items` of the first opened page are used.
   b. The `menu items` of the most recently opened page are used.
   c. The default `menu items` are used.
   d. Error. There can be only one `st.set_page_config` in the app.
4. What is the drawback of defining widgets in the `entrypoint` file to preserve their state across pages?
   a. The widgets will be rendered on all pages.
   b. This method does not work with the `pages/` directory method.
   c. All of the above.
   d. None of the above.

[10] *https://docs.streamlit.io/develop/api-reference/navigation/st.switch_page* (Accessed: 27 October 2024)

Answers

1. b
2. c
3. b
4. c

Questions

1. Why do we need multipage apps in Streamlit?
2. What different terms are associated with a page in a multipage app? Draw a labeled diagram showing them.
3. What are the different ways of creating multipage apps? What arc their respective advantages and disadvantages?
4. Create a multipage app using the `pages/directory` method.
5. How is customizing a page using **`st.Page`** different from using **`st.set_page_config`**?
6. Show an example of using **`st.set_page_config`** to customize a page's favicon, title, and menu items.
7. Create a multipage app using source files and functions to create pages in the **`st.Page`** and **`st.navigation`** method. Group the pages under relevant sections in the navigation menu.
8. Use **`st.page_link`** to create the navigation menu for an app that requires a user to log in with their name, and opens a new page greeting them with their name, once the user has logged in. The navigation menu should also link to the Streamlit website, and be accessible only once the user has logged in. If the user logs out, they should be directed to the login page, and no other page should be accessible.

   Why do widgets not retain their state across pages of a multipage app? What are the methods available to deal with this behavior? Explain each with an example.

Key Terms

- **Entrypoint:** The main file of a Streamlit app, passed to **streamlit run**.
- **Page Source:** This is the Python file or callable function with the page's source code.
- **Page Label:** This is how the page is identified within the `navigation` menu.
- **Page Title:** This is how the page is identified within a browser tab.
- **Page URL Pathname:** This is the relative path of the page from the root URL of the app.
- **Page Favicon:** This is the icon next to the page title.
- **Page Icon:** This is the icon next to the page label.[11]

[11] *https://docs.streamlit.io/develop/concepts/multipage-apps/overview#page-terminology* (Accessed: 13 October 2024)

CHAPTER 13
Testing Streamlit Apps

Introduction

You have now learned to build complex and powerful Streamlit apps using caching, connections, secrets, and spanning across multiple pages. A Streamlit app is a software project, and as such, like any other piece of software, as apps grow in complexity, it becomes challenging to ensure that a code change does not break other functionality.

Streamlit has a native testing framework that can programmatically and deterministically test its various components and automate those tests with other test frameworks and platforms.

In this chapter, you will learn about the importance of testing Streamlit apps and be introduced to Streamlit's native testing framework. You will then learn how to use Streamlit's testing framework to test Streamlit apps and, finally, use it with **pytest**, pre-commit hooks, and GitHub Actions to automate those tests.

Note: *Prior knowledge and experience working with* **pytest***, pre-commit, and GitHub Actions, although beneficial, are not mandatory. You will be introduced to all required concepts in this chapter.*

Note: *We shall use Streamlit version 1.51.0 from this chapter onwards. Streamlit's app testing framework is still experimental and not widely supported as of this version. It might change drastically in a future release or be deprecated altogether. However, it is essential to learn about testing in general.*

Structure

In this chapter, we will cover the following topics:

- Importance of Testing Streamlit Apps
- Introduction to Streamlit's Native Testing Framework
    - Building and Testing the Login Page
        - Creating and Using a Dummy User Database
        - Testing the Login Component
- Automating Tests Using **pytest**
    - Converting the Login Tests to **pytest** Format
        - Optimizing the Login Tests Using Parametrization
- Adding and Testing a Logout Button
- Creating and Testing Role-Based Pages
    - Manage Users
    - Bells and Whistles

- Adding Role-Based Pages to the App
- Testing Role-Based Access Control to Pages
- Testing before Pushing to Repo Using Pre-commit Hooks
- Continuous Testing Using GitHub Actions

Importance of Testing Streamlit Apps

Thorough testing is necessary for any mature software project, including Streamlit applications, to ensure all components behave as intended. While manual testing can be viable for simpler apps or those that do not require frequent updates, it becomes impractical, and prone to errors as the app evolves and expands. The complexity of numerous interconnected components and the variety of potential user interactions make it challenging to verify every aspect of the app across multiple scenarios manually.

Automated testing provides a robust solution to this challenge. By developing a comprehensive suite of automated test cases, you can systematically verify the functionality of your app, each time code changes are made. This approach allows developers to identify and address issues early in development, minimizing the risk of introducing bugs. Additionally, automated testing provides consistency, enabling tests to be run quickly and repeatedly, ensuring that previously functioning features remain intact after modifications.

This is particularly critical in Python projects, where the landscape of dependencies can lead to unexpected breaking changes. Python's ecosystem is rich and varied, meaning that updates or modifications in one library can inadvertently affect others. Such cascading changes can have a domino effect on your application, potentially causing significant disruptions. By implementing automated tests, you can safeguard your application against these vulnerabilities, ensuring that it remains reliable and functional as it grows and evolves.

Introduction to Streamlit's Native Testing Framework

Due to Streamlit's architecture, writing automated tests can be challenging as the app needs to run, and user input or actions need to be simulated to test, if the results are as expected. Thankfully, Streamlit's built-in testing framework addresses this challenge. It simulates running the app, declares user input, and examines the results.[1] Additionally, the framework can be used with Python testing frameworks such as **pytest** and automated using platforms like GitHub Actions.

In this section, we will create an app, and then use Streamlit's testing framework. Our sample app will be a multipage app with a homepage that requires users to log in, and then provides access to additional pages and functionalities based on their role – **admin**, **editor**, or **viewer**.

The tests will cover the login functionality, ensuring that the pages shown correspond to what should be visible for each role, and verifying that the components on the respective pages behave as they should. We will create tests in parallel with the app features to make the concepts easier to understand, and ensure that we cover all the required test cases.

---

[1] *https://docs.streamlit.io/get-started/fundamentals/additional-features#app-testing* (Accessed: 30 October 2024)

Building and Testing the Login Page

Let us start by building the login page. This will be the first page users see, featuring only a title and a login form. Upon successful login, the username and role should be visible in the sidebar, and other pages should be made visible, based on the user's role (this will be added later).

The initial script, named **login.py**, is as follows.

```
import streamlit as st

st.title("A Well-Tested App!")

if not st.session_state.get("role"):
    with st.form("login_form"):
        st.session_state.username = st.text_input("Username")
        password = st.text_input("Password", type="password")
        if st.form_submit_button(
            "Login",
            use_container_width=True,
            type="primary",
            icon=":material/login:",
        ):
            if st.session_state.username == "test" and password == "1234":
                st.session_state.role = "admin"
                st.rerun()
            else:
                st.error(
                    "Login failed. Incorrect username/password.",
                    icon=":material/lock:",
                )
else:
    with st.sidebar:
        st.success(
            f"Welcome **{st.session_state.get('username')}** ({st.session_
state.get('role')}) :wave:"
        )
```

Running this script using **streamlit run login.py** opens an app, as shown in the following *Figure* 13.1.

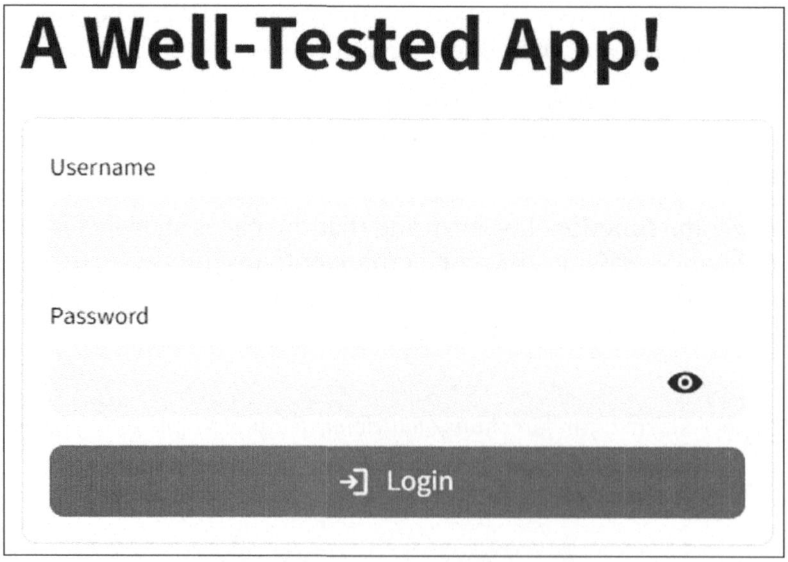

Figure 13.1: *Login Page Empty State*

We have used a dummy username and password here. To make the login process more realistic, we will create a sample JSON file with usernames, passwords, and roles to represent our user database.

Creating and Using a Dummy User Database

To simulate a user database, we can create a **users.json** file in the same directory as the app. An example is shown as follows:

```
{
  "johndoe": {
    "password": "password123",
    "role": "admin"
  },
  "janedoe": {
    "password": "securepass456",
    "role": "editor"
  },
  "viewer01": {
    "password": "viewonly789",
    "role": "viewer"
  }
}
```

It consists of three users – **johndoe**, **janedoe**, and **viewer01** – having the roles of **admin**, **editor**, and **viewer** respectively. It also contains their passwords, which are stored as plaintext.

Warning: *This is a highly simplified example. For production use cases, passwords should never be stored as plain text. Use Streamlit components like* **st-login-form** *to handle authentication securely for your apps. You can read more about* **st-login-form** *here: https://github.com/SiddhantSadangi/st_login_form.*

Next, we can load the users from the JSON file, validate the username and password, and fetch the user's role by adding the **highlighted** lines to **login.py**.

```
import json

import streamlit as st

with open("users.json", "r") as file:
    users = json.load(file)

st.title("A Well-Tested App!")

if not st.session_state.get("role"):
    with st.form("login_form"):
        st.session_state.username = st.text_input("Username")
        password = st.text_input("Password", type="password")
        if st.form_submit_button(
            "Login",
            use_container_width=True,
            type="primary",
            icon=":material/login:",
        ):
            if (
                st.session_state.username in users
                and users[st.session_state.username]["password"] == password
            ):
```

```
                st.session_state.role = users[st.session_state.username]
["role"]
                st.rerun()
            else:
                st.error(
                    "Login failed. Incorrect username/password.",
                    icon=":material/lock:",
                )
else:
    with st.sidebar:
        st.success(
            f"Welcome **{st.session_state.get('username')}** ({st.session_
state.get('role')}) :wave:"
        )
```

The app UI and behavior will not change, and a successful login of the **johndoe** admin will look as shown in the following *Figure* 13.2.

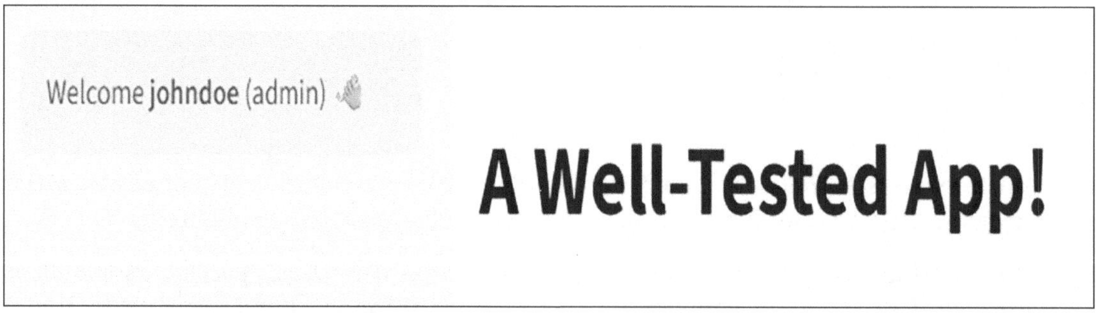

Figure 13.2: *Successful Admin Login*

Testing the Login Component

Now that the login component is ready, we can start creating tests using Streamlit's native testing framework. This framework is included with Streamlit's default installation, and can be accessed using the **AppTest** class.

First, create a new **tests** folder in the same directory as the app source files. This folder will contain all the scripts used for testing. Next, create a **test_login.py** script in the tests folder to test the login functionality.

Import **AppTest**, and run a simulated app from the **login.py** file as follows:

```
from streamlit.testing.v1 import AppTest

at = AppTest.from_file("login.py").run()
```

Note: *While simulating an app run from a file is recommended, it can also be done from a function or a string using the* **from_function** *or* **from_string** *methods. Detailed examples are available in the Streamlit docs: https://docs.streamlit.io/develop/api-reference/app-testing/st.testing.v1.apptest.*

Next, we simulate the possible user actions and their desired results. We will create two negative and three positive test cases for this example. The negative test cases will check if the login fails and displays an error for an incorrect username-password combination. The positive test cases will verify if the login component assigns the correct role for valid username-password input.

To create the first negative test case, enter the wrong username but the correct password and attempt to log in. This state of the app is displayed in *Figure* 13.3.

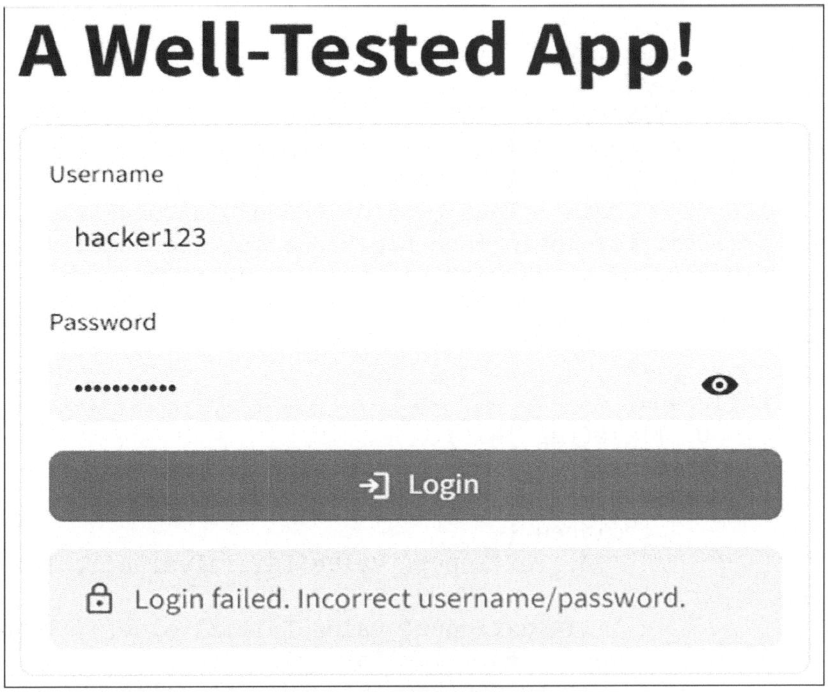

Figure 13.3: *Incorrect Username but Correct Password*

In this case, an error message is displayed in the login form itself. The test case should check if the login form is still visible to users to correct the inputs, and if the fourth element (or child) of the form is an error message starting with **`Login failed`**. To simulate the wrong inputs, add the following lines to **`test_login.py`**:

```
at.text_input[0].set_value("hacker123").run()
at.text_input[1].set_value("password123").run()
at.button[0].click().run()
```

To check for the correct behavior, add the following **`if`** condition:

```
if at.get("form")[0].children[3].value.startswith("Login failed"):
    print("Username test passed")
else:
    print("Username test failed")
```

If these conditions are satisfied, the script will print **`Username test passed`**; otherwise, it will print **`Username test failed`**.

Note: *In addition to being retrieved by index, elements can also be retrieved by key. A detailed guide on how to retrieve, manipulate, and inspect elements and widgets is available in the Streamlit docs here: https://docs.streamlit.io/develop/concepts/app-testing/get-started#how-to-retrieve-elements.*

Run this script using **`python tests/test_login.py`**. You should see the following message:

```
2024-11-02 17:15:02.264 WARNING streamlit.runtime.scriptrunner_utils.script_
run_context: Thread 'MainThread': missing ScriptRunContext! This warning can
be ignored when running in bare mode.
Username test passed
```

You can ignore the warning, but as you can see, the test has been passed.

Task: *Create the second negative test case – correct username but incorrect password.*

Note: *You can use* **`print()`** *statements to debug and inspect elements. For example,* **`print(at)`** *will display all the elements and session states active at that point in the simulated app* (**`at`**). *For the first test case, the* **`at`** *object should look something like this:*

```
AppTest(
    _script_path='login.py',
    default_timeout=3,
    session_state={$$STREAMLIT_INTERNAL_KEY_SCRIPT_RUN_WITHOUT_ERRORS:
True, $$ID-4837de3479c389258af5a3c35834b33d-None: 'password123', $$STREAM-
LIT_INTERNAL_KEY_TESTING: {'$$ID-20d6be2b0a200c458f112ccd83e26c60-Form-
Submitter:login_form-Login': True}, $$ID-20d6be2b0a200c458f112c-
cd83e26c60-FormSubmitter:login_form-Login: False, username: 'hacker123',
$$ID-fb748f9249934947af245123c2fd05c1-None: 'hacker123'},
    _tree={
        0: SpecialBlock(
            type='main',
            children={
                0: Title(tag='h1'),
                1: Block(
                    type='form',
                    children={
                        0: TextInput(_value=InitialValue(), label='Username',
form_id='login_form'),
                        1: TextInput(_value=InitialValue(), label='Password',
autocomplete='new-password', form_id='login_form'),
                        2: Button(key='FormSubmitter:login_form-Login',
label='Login', form_id='login_form'),
                        3: Error(icon=':material/lock:')
                    }
                )
            }
        ),
        1: SpecialBlock(
            type='sidebar'
        ),
        2: SpecialBlock(
            type='event'
        )
    }
)
```

Now, let us move on to the positive test cases. The app state for the correct login of an admin user, **johndoe**, is shown in *Figure* 13.2 in the previous section. In this case, the login form should disappear, and there should be a success message saying **Welcome johndoe (admin)** 👋 in the sidebar.

To ensure that each test case starts from a clean state, reinitialize the simulated app before each test case, and then simulate the correct user inputs as follows:

```
at = AppTest.from_file("login.py").run()
at.text_input[0].set_value("johndoe").run()
at.text_input[1].set_value("password123").run()
at.button[0].click().run()
```

The test case is shown as follows:

```
if at.sidebar.get("success")[0].value == "Welcome **johndoe** (admin) :wave:":
    print("Admin login test passed")
else:
    print("Admin login test failed")
```

Note: *Although the test case requires the login form to disappear after a successful login, we cannot test for this scenario due to a bug in the Streamlit* **AppTests** *class as of version 1.51.0 that does not properly clean up widgets. The test condition, if this bug is fixed, will be as follows:*

```
    if (
        len(at.get("form")) == 0  # Check that there is no form visible
        and at.sidebar.get("success")[0].value == "Welcome **johndoe** (admin)
:wave:"
    ):
```

We check that the success message is displayed, and has the expected username and role.

Can you finish the `test_login.py` script with the two remaining positive test cases for editors and viewers? Try it yourself before referring to the solution as follows:

```
# Test that login succeeds and editor role is assigned for correct editor user-
name-password combination
    at = AppTest.from_file("login.py").run()

    at.text_input[0].set_value("janedoe").run()
    at.text_input[1].set_value("securepass456").run()
    at.button[0].click().run()

    if at.sidebar.get("success")[0].value == "Welcome **janedoe** (editor) :wave:":
        print("Editor login test passed")
    else:
        print("Editor login test failed")

    # Test that login succeeds and viewer role is assigned for correct viewer
    username-password combination
    at = AppTest.from_file("login.py").run()

    at.text_input[0].set_value("viewer01").run()
    at.text_input[1].set_value("viewonly789").run()
    at.button[0].click().run()

    if at.sidebar.get("success")[0].value == "Welcome **viewer01** (viewer)
    :wave:":
        print("Viewer login test passed")
    else:
        print("Viewer login test failed")
```

Provided that the app was coded correctly, adding the previous code snippet to **`test_login.py`** and running it will show that all five tests – **`Username`**, **`Password`**, **`Admin login`**, **`Editor login`**, and **`Viewer login`** – have passed.

Automating Tests Using pytest

The previous testing script provides a good introduction to Streamlit's native testing function and how you can use it to simulate running an app, user interactions, and test for expected results. However, relying on manually running Python scripts to test apps and **`print`** statements to examine the results is not ideal. This method also cannot be used for automation, as the script always returns a zero code, indicating that it has passed, even though a **`print`** statement might suggest that a test has failed.

This issue can be resolved by raising errors in **`try`** and **`except`** blocks so that the script continues to run even though there are errors. However, this adds a lot of boilerplate code to the script. This is where a proper test framework like **`pytest`**, which takes care of all this automatically, can help.

pytest is a simple and powerful framework for writing and running tests for Python applications and libraries.[2] **pytest** uses a naming convention for files and functions to execute tests conveniently.[3] By convention, test files are placed under a **tests** folder within the application's root folder to be tested. Each test file should either start with **test_** or end with **_test**. This is the same folder and file naming convention we followed, shown in *Figure* 13.4. Each test case within the file is written as a separate function starting with **test_**.[4]

Figure 13.4: *Directory Structure for pytest*

Note: *We shall cover* **pytest** *basics as required in this chapter. However, going through its documentation is highly recommended to get a deeper understanding of how pytest works: https://docs.pytest.org/en/stable/.*

Since **pytest** is not included with the Python standard library, it must be installed separately. You can do this by running **pip install pytest** in your virtual environment.

Note: *We have used* **pytest** *version 8.4.2 in this chapter.*

Once **pytest** is installed, we can change the **test_login.py** script to make it **pytest** compliant.

Converting the Login Tests to pytest Format

The first step is wrapping each test case within its function, starting with **test_**. For example, the first test for the incorrect username can be wrapped within a **test_incorrect_username()** function as follows:

```
def test_incorrect_username():
    """Test that login fails when the username is incorrect"""
    at = AppTest.from_file("login.py").run()

    at.text_input[0].set_value("hacker123").run()
    at.text_input[1].set_value("password123").run()
    at.button[0].click().run()

    if at.get("form")[0].children[3].value.startswith("Login failed"):
        print("Username test passed")
    else:
        print("Username test failed")
```

Then, instead of using **if-else** and **print** statements, we use **assert** to check if the results are as expected. This reduces the length of the test function as follows:

```
def test_incorrect_username():
    """Test that login fails when the username is incorrect"""
    at = AppTest.from_file("login.py").run()
```

[2] *https://docs.pytest.org/en/stable/* (Accessed: 3 November 2024)

[3] *https://docs.streamlit.io/develop/concepts/app-testing/get-started#how-pytest-is-structured* (Accessed: 3 November 2024)

[4] *https://medium.com/@shingurding/automated-testing-for-streamlit-apps-with-pytest-a0dd6e56c86d* (Accessed: 11 November 2024)

```
    at.text_input[0].set_value("hacker123").run()
    at.text_input[1].set_value("password123").run()
    at.button[0].click().run()

    assert at.get("form")[0].children[3].value.startswith("Login failed")
```

Task: *Write a function to test for an incorrect password before proceeding.*

Tests can be executed by running **pytest** in your application's root directory. ***pytest*** will automatically run every file starting with **test_** or ending with **_test** in the current and **tests** directories. The results should look as shown in *Figure* 13.5.

```
● > pytest
===================== test session starts =====================
platform win32 -- Python 3.10.11, pytest-8.3.3, pluggy-1.5.0
rootdir:
plugins: typeguard-4.3.0
collected 2 items

tests\test_login.py ..                                    [100%]

===================== 2 passed in 0.48s =====================
```

Figure 13.5: *pytest Output When Tests Pass*

If a test were to fail, **pytest** displays the details of the failed test case and the assertion that failed. For example, if we update the **test_incorrect_username** assertion to assert that a success message is displayed, the output will look as shown in *Figure* 13.6.

```
⊗ > pytest
========================================= test session starts =========================================
platform win32 -- Python 3.10.11, pytest-8.3.3, pluggy-1.5.0
rootdir: C:\Users\siddh\OneDrive\Desktop\Book\Code\Chapter_13
plugins: typeguard-4.3.0
collected 1 item

tests\test_login.py F                                                                            [100%]

============================================== FAILURES ==============================================
_______________________________________ test_incorrect_username _______________________________________

    def test_incorrect_username():
        """Test that login fails when the username is incorrect"""
        at = AppTest.from_file("login.py").run()

        at.text_input[0].set_value("hacker123").run()
        at.text_input[1].set_value("password123").run()
        at.button[0].click().run()

>       assert at.get("form")[0].children[3].value.startswith("Success")
E       AssertionError: assert False
E        +  where False = <built-in method startswith of str object at 0x000002517BFC1950>('Success')
E        +    where <built-in method startswith of str object at 0x000002517BFC1950> = 'Login failed. In
correct username/password.'.startswith
E        +      where 'Login failed. Incorrect username/password.' = Error(icon=':material/lock:').value

tests\test_login.py:13: AssertionError
--------------------------------------- Captured stderr call ----------------------------------------
2024-12-07 16:09:06.447 WARNING streamlit.runtime.scriptrunner_utils.script_run_context: Thread 'MainThr
ead': missing ScriptRunContext! This warning can be ignored when running in bare mode.
====================================== short test summary info ======================================
FAILED tests/test_login.py::test_incorrect_username - AssertionError: assert False
======================================== 1 failed in 0.50s ========================================
```

Figure 13.6: *pytest Output When a Test Fails*

To see each test case's status, the output's verbosity can be increased using the **-v** flag. The output then looks as shown in *Figure 13.7*.

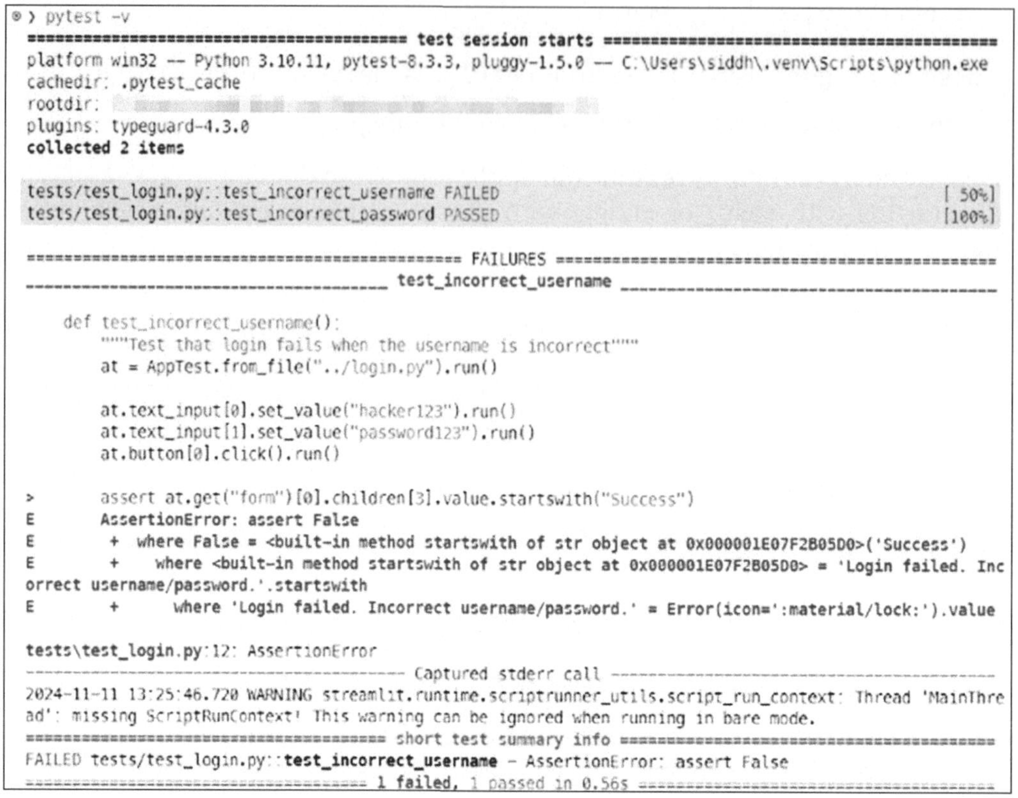

Figure 13.7: *Verbose pytest Output*

Another advantage of using **pytest** is that you can select which tests to run instead of running the entire test script. This is done by using the **-k** flag when running **pytest**. For example, to run just the **test_incorrect_password** test, you can run **pytest -k test_incorrect_password**.

Note: ***pytest****, by default, hides* **stdout** *if all the test cases pass. If you use* **print()** *statements to debug or inspect an element, run* **pytest** *with the* **-s** *flag to display the output of* **print()** *statements.*

Optimizing the Login Tests Using Parametrization

You may have noticed that, except for the different inputs, the incorrect username and password tests are the same. Instead of duplicating the code, we can pass the various inputs to the same function to test for both cases. **pytest** allows us to do this using parametrization.

Note: *You can learn more about parametrizing tests using* **pytest** *in the* **pytest** *docs: https://docs.pytest.org/en/stable/example/parametrize.html.*

To parametrize the login negative test cases, create a **test_incorrect_username_password()** function that accepts **username** and **password** as arguments. The function's body is the same as **test_incorrect_username()** or **test_incorrect_password()** but with the hardcoded username and password replaced with the **username** and **password** variables. The function is as follows:

```
def test_incorrect_username_password(username: str, password: str):
    at = AppTest.from_file("login.py").run()

    at.text_input[0].set_value(username).run()
    at.text_input[1].set_value(password).run()
```

```
        at.button[0].click().run()

        assert at.get("form")[0].children[3].value.startswith("Login failed")
```

To pass different combinations of usernames and passwords, use the **@pytest.mark.parametrize** decorator. This takes the names of the arguments to parametrize as a comma-separated string as the first parameter, and the list of different combinations of the arguments as the second parameter.

Note: *The complete API reference of parametrize is available here: https://docs.pytest.org/en/stable/reference/reference.html#pytest.Metafunc.parametrize.*

To recreate the inputs of the **test_incorrect_username()** and **test_incorrect_password()** tests, the parametrization decorator looks as follows:

```
import pytest

@pytest.mark.parametrize(
    "username, password",
    [["hacker123", "password123"], ["viewer01", "password"]],
)
```

This effectively creates two test cases using the same **test_incorrect_username_password()** function.

Task: *Create a third test case for when both the username and password are incorrect.*

The previous **test_incorrect_username()** and **test_incorrect_password()** functions can now be removed from **test_login.py** as they are redundant.

Running the tests in verbose mode using **pytest -v** gives an output, as shown in *Figure 13.8*.

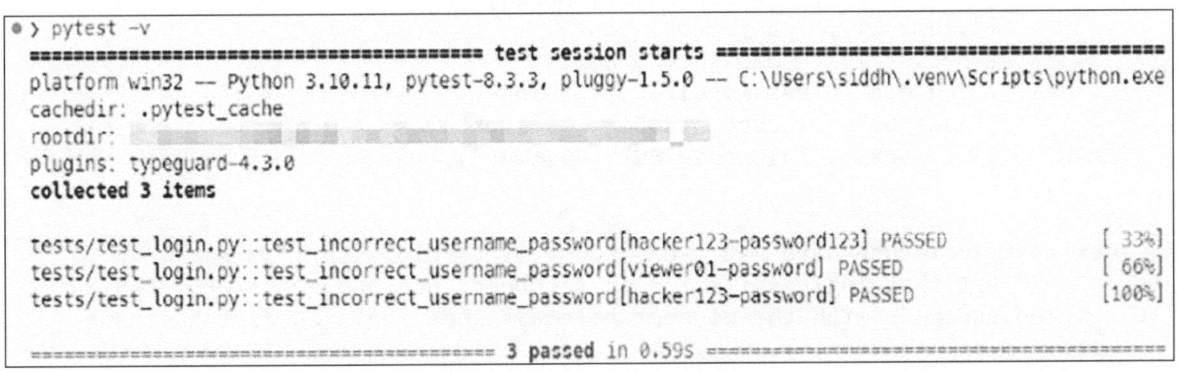

Figure 13.8: Parametrized Tests

As can be seen, the same function, **test_incorrect_username_password()**, was run thrice with three different sets of inputs – effectively behaving as three different test cases.

Can you similarly parametrize the three positive test cases to see if the correct role is assigned for the correct username-password input? In this case, the expected **role** will also need to be added to the test function in addition to the **username** and **password**. The parametrized function is as follows:

```
@pytest.mark.parametrize(
    "username, password, role",
    [
        ["johndoe", "password123", "admin"],
        ["janedoe", "securepass456", "editor"],
        ["viewer01", "viewonly789", "viewer"],
    ],
)
```

```
def test_correct_login(username: str, password: str, role: str):
    at = AppTest.from_file("login.py").run()

    at.text_input[0].set_value(username).run()
    at.text_input[1].set_value(password).run()
    at.button[0].click().run()

    assert (
        at.sidebar.get("success")[0].value == f"Welcome **{username}**
({role}) :wave:"
    )
```

This creates three test cases to test if the **admin**, **editor**, and **viewer** roles are assigned correctly on successful login.

Notice that both parametrized functions are similar except for the **assert** statement. We can use the same function to test for both the positive and negative test cases by having the **role** as **None** for the negative test cases and branching to the relevant assertion, depending on the **role** passed as the input.

Note: *While acceptable for the purposes of this chapter, branching in test cases is generally not a good practice as it introduces some drawbacks. You can read more about this at https://8hob.io/posts/assertions-if-clauses-tests/.*

This function is as follows:

```
@pytest.mark.parametrize(
    "username, password, role",
    [
        ["hacker123", "password123", None],
        ["viewer01", "password", None],
        ["hacker123", "password", None],
        ["johndoe", "password123", "admin"],
        ["janedoe", "securepass456", "editor"],
        ["viewer01", "viewonly789", "viewer"],
    ],
)
def test_login(username: str, password: str, role: str | None):
    """Test that login fails for an incorrect username-password combination
    and succeeds with the correct role assigned for a correct username-
password combination.

    Args:
        username (str): The username to test
        password (str): The password to test
        role (str | None): The expected role
    """
    at = AppTest.from_file("login.py").run()

    at.text_input[0].set_value(username).run()
    at.text_input[1].set_value(password).run()
    at.button[0].click().run()

    if role is None:
        # Login failed
        assert at.get("form")[0].children[3].value.startswith("Login failed")
    else:
        # Login successful
```

```
            assert (
                at.sidebar.get("success")[0].value
                == f"Welcome **{username}** ({role}) :wave:"
            )
```

This creates six test cases – three positive and three negative – that all run using the **`test_login()`** function. The **`role`** is **`None`** for the negative test cases. Depending on the value of **`role`** passed, we either check the negative login failed assertion or the login successful assertion.

Running this using **`pytest -v`** gives the output shown in the following *Figure 13.9*.

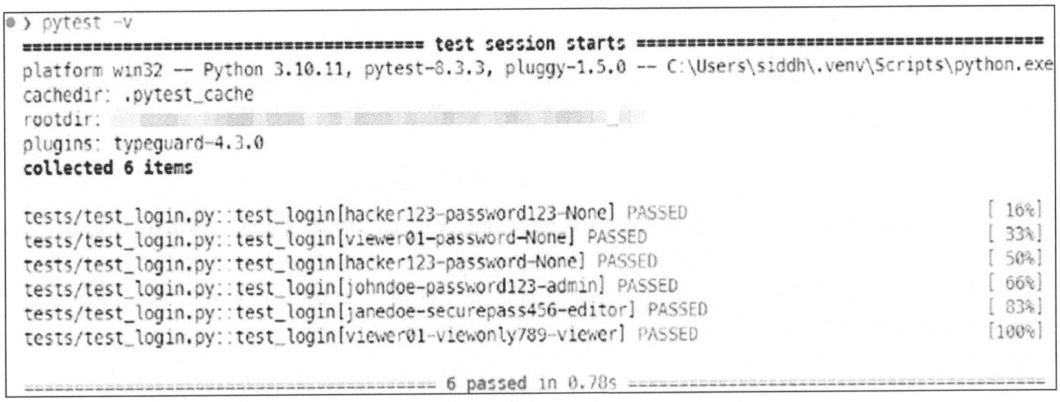

```
> pytest -v
========================= test session starts =========================
platform win32 -- Python 3.10.11, pytest-8.3.3, pluggy-1.5.0 -- C:\Users\siddh\.venv\Scripts\python.exe
cachedir: .pytest_cache
rootdir:
plugins: typeguard-4.3.0
collected 6 items

tests/test_login.py::test_login[hacker123-password123-None] PASSED        [ 16%]
tests/test_login.py::test_login[viewer01-password-None] PASSED            [ 33%]
tests/test_login.py::test_login[hacker123-password-None] PASSED           [ 50%]
tests/test_login.py::test_login[johndoe-password123-admin] PASSED         [ 66%]
tests/test_login.py::test_login[janedoe-securepass456-editor] PASSED      [ 83%]
tests/test_login.py::test_login[viewer01-viewonly789-viewer] PASSED       [100%]

========================= 6 passed in 0.78s =========================
```

Figure 13.9: *Parametrized Test for Both Positive and Negative Test Cases*

Adding and Testing a Logout Button

Now that we have implemented and tested the login functionality, let us extend our app by including a **`Logout`** button for all logged-in users, irrespective of their role. This button should clear the **`username`** and **`role`** session states as well as show the login form again.

Figure 13.10 shows how the app should look with the **`Logout`** button implemented, if the **`johndoe`** admin logs in.

Figure 13.10: *App with a Logout Button*

To add this feature, make the relevant changes to the **`login.py`** script. For reference, add the following lines at the end of the **`st.sidebar`** block:

```
if st.button("Logout", icon=":material/logout:", use_container_width=True):
    st.session_state.clear()
    st.rerun()
```

Now, let us add tests for it. The test cases are as follows:

1. The **`Logout`** button should not be displayed unless the user has logged in.
2. The **`Logout`** button should be displayed as soon as a user logs in.
3. Clicking **`Logout`** should display the login form in its initial (clear) state.

The first two tests are an extension of the Login form and can be added to the **test_login()** function. The required assertion is that there should not be any button in the sidebar unless a user has logged in, and the **Logout** button should be the first button displayed in the sidebar once a user has logged in. These assertions to be added to **test_login()** are **highlighted** as follows:

```
if role is None:
    # Login failed
    assert at.get("form")[0].children[3].value.startswith("Login failed")
    assert at.sidebar.get("button") == []
else:
    # Login successful
    assert (
        at.sidebar.get("success")[0].value == f"Welcome **{username}**
({role}) :wave:"
    )
    assert at.sidebar.button[0].label == "Logout"
```

The third test case requires a successful login, but we do not want to duplicate the steps we have already used to test the login functionality or run the login tests every time we want to test the logout button. Instead of simulating a login by entering the **username** and **password**, we will hardcode the role session state to **viewer** and rerun the app. This will be added as a new **test_logout()** function to the **test_login.py** file, as follows:

```
def test_logout():
    """Test that clicking the Logout button shows the login form and hides the
Logout button."""
    at = AppTest.from_file("login.py")

    # Simulate a successful login
    at.session_state.role = "viewer"
    at.run()

    # Click the Logout button
    at.sidebar.button[0].click().run()

    # Check that the login form is displayed
    login_form_elements = at.get("form")[0].children

    # Check that the Username text input is empty
    assert login_form_elements[0].label == "Username"
    assert login_form_elements[0].value == ""

    # Check that the Password text input is empty
    assert login_form_elements[1].label == "Password"
    assert login_form_elements[1].value == ""

    # Check that the Login button is displayed
    assert login_form_elements[2].label == "Login"
```

Running **pytest -v** now gives us the results for both **test_login()** and **test_logout()**, as shown in the following *Figure 13.11*.

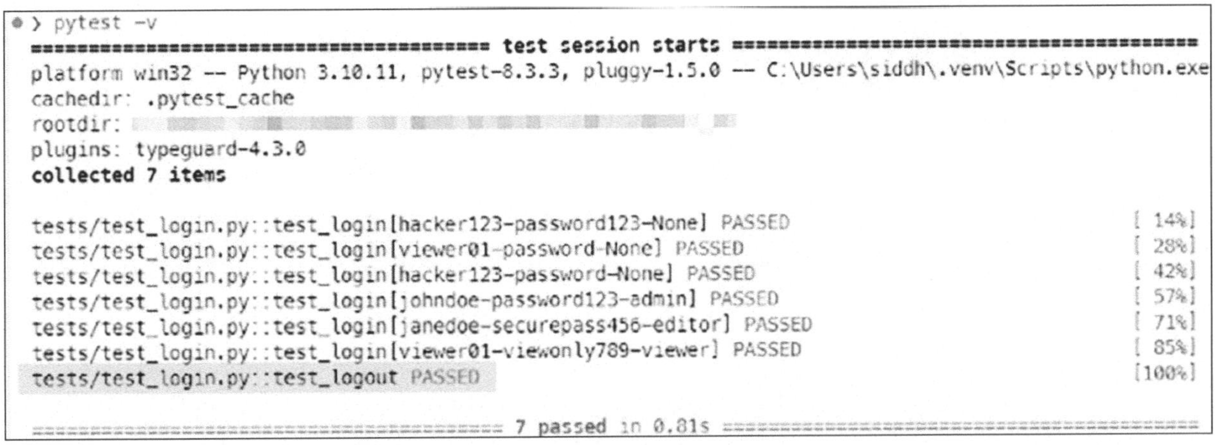

Figure 13.11: *test_login() and test_logout() Results*

As discussed before, to run only **`test_logout()`**, you can run **`pytest -k test_logout`**.

Creating and Testing Role-Based Pages

Now that we have login and logout functionality, let us start creating a few pages that app users can access based on their roles. For simplicity, we will have only two pages:

- **Manage Users**: A page showing the username and role of all users. This page will be accessible only to app admins.
- **Bells and Whistles**: This page will let admins and editors update a few widgets, while viewers can only see the widgets but not make any changes. This simulates a read-only page for viewers.

Manage Users

This page will show the username and role of all app users to app admins. In real-world scenarios, such a page would also let admins conduct actions like adding and removing users, resetting passwords, changing roles, and so on. But we are limiting the action to just seeing a list of users for simplicity. You can consider adding these advanced features to the app as homework.

The page source itself is pretty simple. Just read from the **`users.json`** file and display the **`username`** and **`role`** from the file in a table. We do not display the **`password`** as a best practice for security reasons, even though this is just a demo app. The script, named **`manage_users.py`**, is as follows:

```
import json

import pandas as pd
import streamlit as st

with open("users.json", "r") as file:
    users = json.load(file)

st.header("Manage Users :material/people:")

users_df = pd.DataFrame(users).T.reset_index()
users_df.columns = ["Username", "Password", "Role"]
st.table(users_df[["Username", "Role"]])
```

To see how it looks, you can run this page using **`streamlit run manage_users.py`**. It should look as shown in the following *Figure 13.12*.

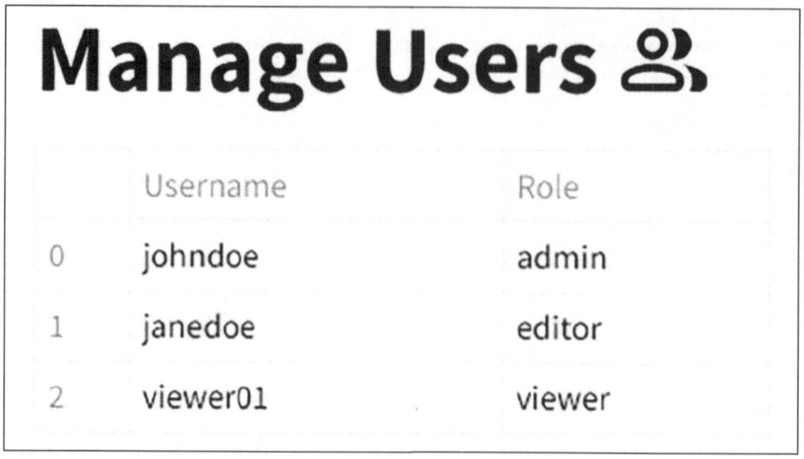

Figure 13.12: *Manage Users Page*

Before adding it to the main app, let us add tests to ensure that this page behaves as expected. This way, once the page has been added to the main app, we only need to test how it is displayed to relevant users without writing tests for its functionality. Since it is a different page, the best practice is to have a different test script, in this case, **`test_manage_users.py`**. And since this page only displays data, we only need to ensure that all the data displayed is the same as the source. The test looks almost the same as the app source itself, and is as follows:

```
import json

import pandas as pd
from streamlit.testing.v1 import AppTest

def test_displayed_users():
    at = AppTest.from_file("manage_users.py").run()

    with open("users.json", "r") as file:
        users = json.load(file)

    users_df = pd.DataFrame(users).T.reset_index()
    users_df.columns = ["Username", "Password", "Role"]

    assert all(at.table[0].data == users_df[["Username", "Role"]])
```

`test_displayed_users()` checks if the page has a table, and if the data in the table matches that of the **`users.json`** file (excluding the **`password`**). It can be run independently from the other tests using **`pytest -k test_displayed_users`**.

Bells and Whistles

This page is a random collection of Streamlit input widgets. **`Admins`** and **`editors`** should be able to interact with these widgets, while **`viewers`** should not.

We will use a **`bells_and_whistles.py`** file as the source for this page, and add the title:

```
import streamlit as st

st.header("Bells and Whistles :material/engineering:")
```

Since edits are allowed only by **`admins`** and **`editors`**, create a **`disabled`** flag that is **`True`** when the **`role`** is not **`admin`** or **`editor`**:

```
disabled = st.session_state.get("role", "viewer") not in ["admin", "editor"]
```

Here, as a cybersecurity best practice following the **Principle of Least Privilege**, we pass **viewer** as the default role as this has the least access.

Then, create a bunch of random widgets. Remember to pass the **disabled** argument to prevent **viewers** from making any changes. A sample page is shown in *Figure* 13.13.

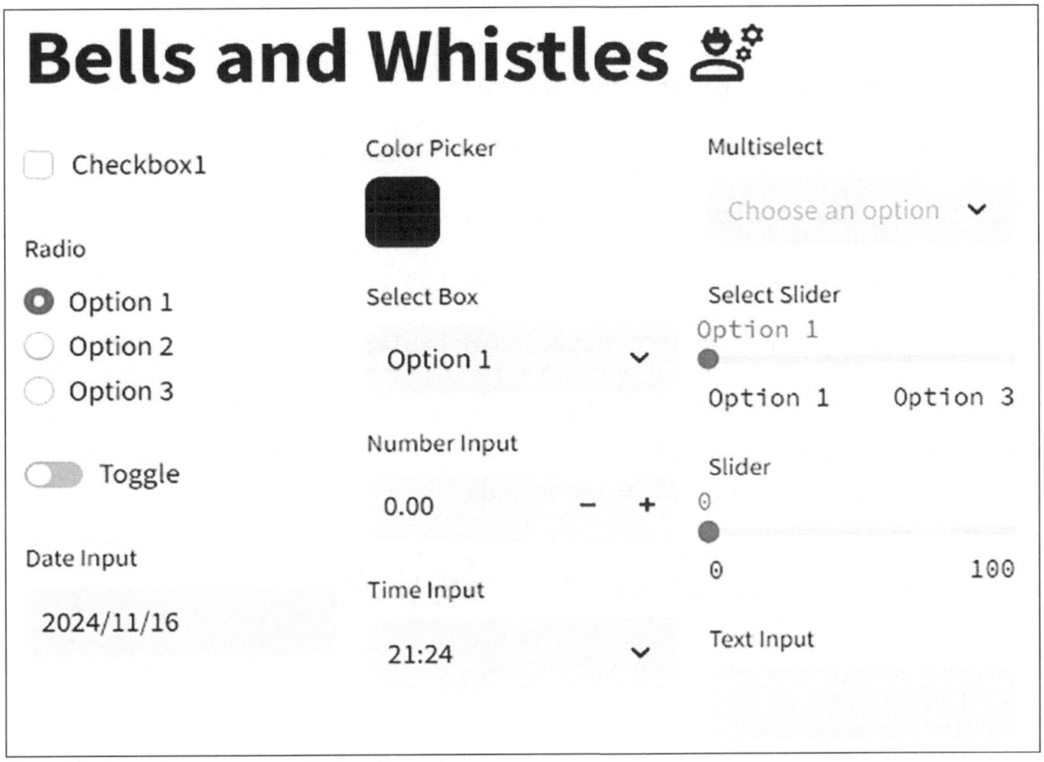

***Figure 13.13:** Bells and Whistles Page for Admins and Editors*

The complete page source is as follows:

```
import streamlit as st

st.header("Bells and Whistles :material/engineering:")

disabled = st.session_state.get("role") == "viewer"

lcol, mcol, rcol = st.columns(3)

lcol.checkbox("Checkbox1", disabled=disabled)

mcol.color_picker("Color Picker", disabled=disabled)

rcol.multiselect(
    "Multiselect",
    ["Option 1", "Option 2", "Option 3"],
    disabled=disabled,
)

lcol.radio("Radio", ["Option 1", "Option 2", "Option 3"], disabled=disabled)

mcol.selectbox(
    "Select Box",
    ["Option 1", "Option 2", "Option 3"],
    disabled=disabled,
```

```
)

rcol.select_slider(
    "Select Slider",
    ["Option 1", "Option 2", "Option 3"],
    disabled=disabled,
)

lcol.toggle("Toggle", disabled=disabled)

mcol.number_input("Number Input", disabled=disabled)

rcol.slider("Slider", disabled=disabled)

lcol.date_input("Date Input", disabled=disabled)

mcol.time_input("Time Input", disabled=disabled)

rcol.text_input("Text Input", disabled=disabled)
```

For a **viewer**, all these widgets are disabled, and the page looks as shown in *Figure* 13.14. This can be simulated by temporarily hardcoding **disabled** to **True**.

Figure 13.14: *Bells and Whistles Page for Viewers*

Like the **Manage Users** page, this page gets its **test_bells_and_whistles.py** test script. For now, we have a single parametrized function that accepts the **role** and tests, whether the **disabled** flag of each widget is set as per the role. An implementation of this is as follows:

```
import pytest
from streamlit.testing.v1 import AppTest

@pytest.mark.parametrize("role", ["admin", "editor", "viewer"])
def test_bells_and_whistles(role: str):
    at = AppTest.from_file("bells_and_whistles.py")
    at.session_state.role = role
    at.run()
```

```
    disabled = role == "viewer"

    widgets = [
        at.checkbox,
        at.color_picker,
        at.multiselect,
        at.radio,
        at.selectbox,
        at.select_slider,
        at.toggle,
        at.number_input,
        at.slider,
        at.date_input,
        at.time_input,
        at.text_input,
    ]

    for widget in widgets:
        assert widget[0].disabled == disabled
```

The above tests ensure that each expected widget is populated, and is disabled if the **role** is **viewer**. Running this using **pytest -v -k test_bells_and_whistles** runs three tests on the **test_bells_and_whistles()** function, one each for each role, as shown in the following *Figure* 13.15.

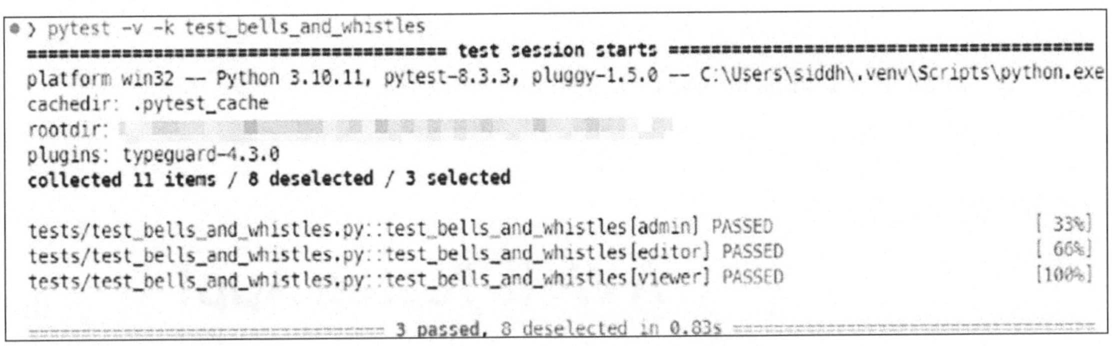

Figure 13.15: *Testing Bells and Whistles*

Adding Role-Based Pages to the App

Now that we have tested the pages independently, we can add them to the main app using **st.navigation** and **st.Page** as well as test the app as a whole.

Starting with the **Manage Users** page, since this page is visible only to admins, we need to add a guard clause before **st.navigation**. The following snippet can be added to the bottom of **login.py**, outside the sidebar context:

```
if st.session_state.role == "admin":
    pg = st.navigation(
        [
            st.Page(
                "manage_users.py",
                title="Manage Users",
                icon=":material/people:",
            ),
        ]
    )
    pg.run()
```

Then, we add the **Bells and Whistles** page. This page should be visible to all users, irrespective of their role, so it needs to be added to both the if clause of the recently added block, and a new else clause that will contain just this page, as follows, with the addition to the **admin** block **highlighted**:

```
bells_and_whistles_page = st.Page(
    "bells_and_whistles.py",
    title="Bells and Whistles",
    icon=":material/engineering:",
)

if st.session_state.role == "admin":
    pg = st.navigation(
        [
            st.Page(
                "manage_users.py",
                title="Manage Users",
                icon=":material/people:",
            ),
            bells_and_whistles_page,
        ]
    )
else:
    pg = st.navigation([bells_and_whistles_page])

pg.run()
```

Running the app and logging in as an **admin** will render both pages, as shown in the following *Figure* 13.16.

Figure 13.16: *Admin View*

Logging in as an **editor** or **viewer** will render the app, as shown in the *Figure* 13.17.

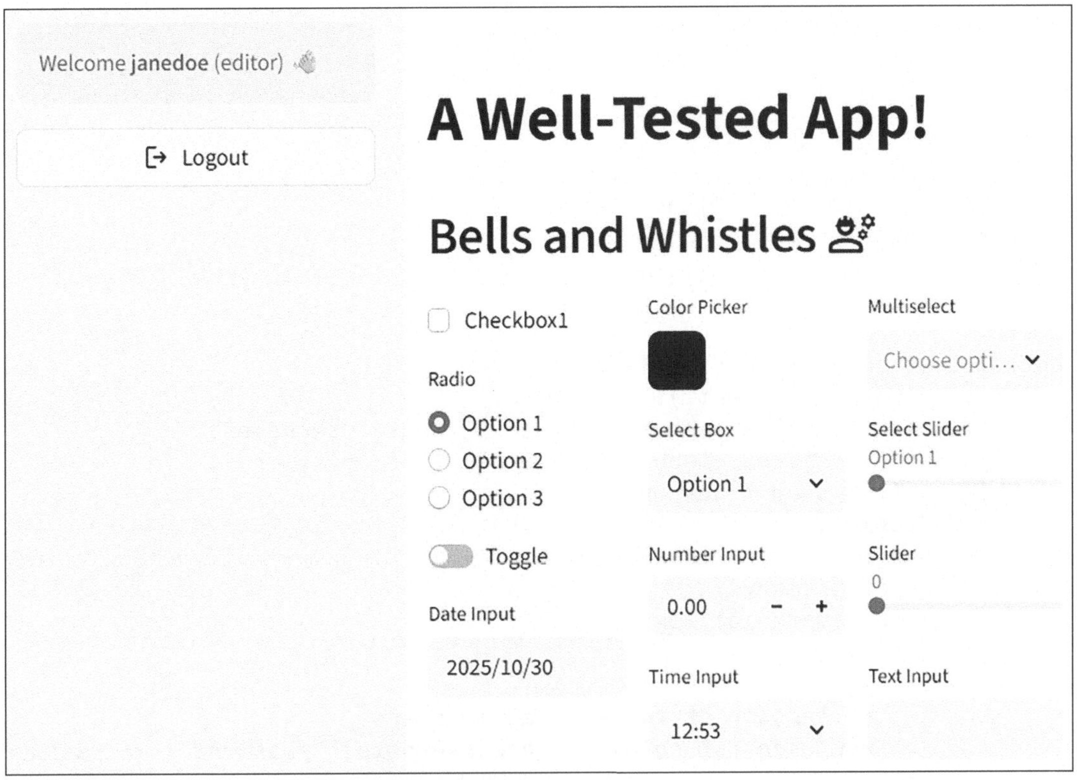

Figure 13.17: *Editor/Viewer View*

There is no navigation menu in this case, as it is hidden if only a single page is rendered.

Clicking Logout works as expected for **editors** and **viewers**. However, for **admins**, it opens the login page with the navigation menu still visible, as shown in *Figure 13.18*:

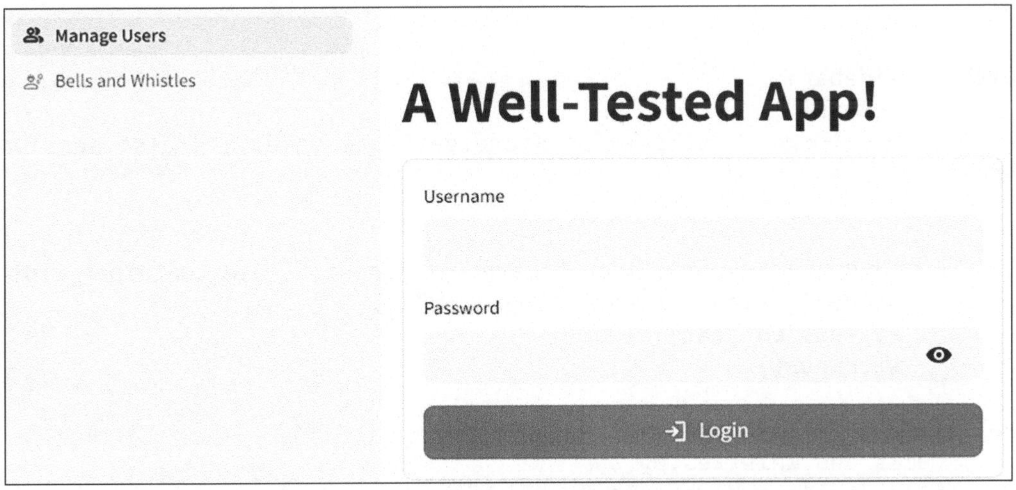

Figure 13.18: *Persistent Navigation Menu after Admin Logout*

Although the navigation does not work unless a user has logged in, we might want to hide the list of pages for security reasons unless a user with the appropriate access has logged in. This can be done by passing just the **Login** page to **st.navigation** in the **Logout** block, as follows:

```
if st.button("Logout", icon=":material/logout:", use_container_width=True):
    st.navigation([st.Page("login.py")])
    st.session_state.clear()
    st.rerun()
```

Now, when an **admin** logs out, the app returns to its original state with no navigation menu visible.

The complete **login.py** script is as follows for reference:

```
import json

import streamlit as st

with open("users.json", "r") as file:
    users = json.load(file)

st.title("A Well-Tested App!")

if not st.session_state.get("role"):
    with st.form("login_form"):
        st.session_state.username = st.text_input("Username")
        password = st.text_input("Password", type="password")
        if st.form_submit_button(
            "Login",
            use_container_width=True,
            type="primary",
            icon=":material/login:",
        ):
            if (
                st.session_state.username in users
                and users[st.session_state.username]["password"] == password
            ):
                st.session_state.role = users[st.session_state.username]["role"]
                st.rerun()
            else:
                st.error(
                    "Login failed. Incorrect username/password.",
                    icon=":material/lock:",
                )
else:
    with st.sidebar:
        st.success(
            f"Welcome **{st.session_state.get('username')}** ({st.session_state.
get('role')}) :wave:"
        )

        if st.button("Logout", icon=":material/logout:", use_container_width=True):
            st.navigation([st.Page("login.py")])
            st.session_state.clear()
            st.rerun()

    bells_and_whistles_page = st.Page(
        "bells_and_whistles.py",
        title="Bells and Whistles",
        icon=":material/engineering:",
    )

    if st.session_state.role == "admin":
        pg = st.navigation(
            [
                st.Page(
                    "manage_users.py",
                    title="Manage Users",
                    icon=":material/people:",
```

```
                ),
                bells_and_whistles_page,
            ]
        )
    else:
        pg = st.navigation([bells_and_whistles_page])

    pg.run()
```

Testing Role-Based Access Control to Pages

Note: *As of version 1.51.0, Streamlit's* **AppTest** *class only supports testing of a single page of an app per instance, and is not yet compatible with multipage apps using* **st.navigation** *and* **st.Pages**.[5] *While we have already tested the pages independently, it is impossible to test how the role-based access control works in our current setup with these restrictions. However, it is good practice to list the test cases you would have if you could test for this. As an added challenge, you can update the app to use the* **pages/** *directory method, instead of* **st.navigation** *and* **st.Page** *and test that approach.*

The expected behavior of the login form is to show the relevant pages on a successful login and for the logout button to hide all pages other than the login page.

For the login component, this can be broken down into three test cases:

1. Pages should not be visible on unsuccessful login.
2. Only **Bells and Whistles** should be visible on an **editor** or **viewer** login.
3. Both **Manage Users** and **Bells as well as Whistles** should be visible on the **admin** login.

For the logout component, the test case is:

- Neither **Manage Users** nor **Bells and Whistles** should be visible, once the user has logged out.

Under ideal circumstances, all these test cases could be added to the existing **test_login()** and **test_logout()** functions. However, if you inspect the contents of the **at** object that simulates a running app, you will see that no elements from a page other than the entry point are displayed at any point, even though they are visible in the running app. This limitation of the Streamlit's app testing framework makes testing impossible for multiple pages as of version 1.51.0.

Testing before Pushing to Repo Using Pre-commit Hooks

We now have the app source ready and the tests for (most of) the components in place. While **pytest** does an excellent job of collating all tests and running them together or individually when required, running **pytest** itself is manual. To ensure that our code is tested correctly, we need an automated solution that runs the tests before committing any code changes to the repository. This is where pre-commit hooks come into the picture.

Pre-commit hooks are custom scripts executed before a commit is made in a repository.[6] If these scripts are testing scripts, you can be sure that the code passed the tests, before it was committed.

Pre-commit is a framework for managing and maintaining multi-language pre-commit hooks.[7] It is beneficial if you run multiple hooks in multiple languages – a common scenario in production use cases.

[5] *https://docs.streamlit.io/develop/api-reference/app-testing/st.testing.v1.apptest#stAppTest* (Accessed: 30 October 2025)
[6] *https://git-scm.com/book/en/v2/Customizing-Git-Git-Hooks* (Accessed: 18 November 2024)
[7] *https://pre-commit.com/* (Accessed: 19 November 2024)

To use **pre-commit**, you first need to be in a **git** repo. If not done already, initialize a **git** repo. For guidance, refer to Chapter 3, *Creating and Deploying Your First Streamlit App*, Section- *Deploying the Application to Streamlit Community Cloud*. Once done, you can start installing **pre-commit**.

Thus, **Pre-commit** is not included in the Python standard library. It has to be installed separately by running **pip install pre-commit** in your Python virtual environment.

Note: *We have used* **pre-commit** *version 4.3.0 in this chapter.*

Once installed, verify the installation by running **pre-commit --version**. It should display the version of **pre-commit** installed.

Once verified, create a file named **.pre-commit-config.yaml** in the repo's root directory with the following content:

```
repos:
  - repo: local
    hooks:
      - id: pytest
        name: pytest
        entry: pytest
        language: system
        types: [python]
```

Note: *There are many other helpful pre-commit hooks available that you can add to* **.pre-commit-config.yaml**. **Pre-commit** *also includes some hooks out-of-the-box, which can be found here: https://github.com/pre-commit/pre-commit-hooks.*

Once the **.pre-commit-config.yaml** has been saved, you can install pre-commit by running **pre-commit install** in your terminal. By default, it will be installed in a **.git/hooks/pre-commit** folder under the repo's root directory.

Once done, commit all the required changes. This will trigger the pre-commit hooks, and the output should look as shown in the following *Figure* 13.19.

```
● > git commit -m "Initial commit"
 pytest.................................................................Passed
 [main (root-commit) 1e24188] Initial commit
  8 files changed, 250 insertions(+)
  create mode 100644 .pre-commit-config.yaml
  create mode 100644 bells_and_whistles.py
  create mode 100644 login.py
  create mode 100644 manage_users.py
  create mode 100644 tests/test_bells_and_whistles.py
  create mode 100644 tests/test_login.py
  create mode 100644 tests/test_manage_users.py
```

Figure 13.19: *Running pytest as a Pre-commit Hook*

If a hook fails, the commit will also fail. This ensures that all hooks have to pass on all modified files for them to be committed, and subsequently pushed to the repo.

Note: *You can read more about pre-commit at https://pre-commit.com/.*

Continuous Testing Using GitHub Actions

We have now build a framework that can be used to test Streamlit apps locally and mandatorily, before pushing code changes to GitHub. However, sometimes changes might be external to our codebase. If the app requirements are not pinned, a change in an external dependency could cause the app to break, even without any code change in the app source itself. Even if the requirements are pinned, changes in the upstream data pipelines can cause an app to break without any change in the source code or dependencies. While we have no control over such external changes, we can continuously test the app to be notified of any failures, and take corrective actions. This is where GitHub Actions help.

GitHub Actions is a platform that allows us to create workflows to build, test, and deploy code to production.[8] These workflows generally run on GitHub's infrastructure using compute provided by GitHub for free (with limits), or they can also be run on your infrastructure. Workflows can be triggered on-demand, based on specific events (like running whenever a pull request is created), or scheduled to run at particular intervals.

Like pre-commit, GitHub Actions are configured using **YAML** files, with one file for each action placed in a **.github/workflows** folder within the repo's root directory. Let us build an action that can be run manually, on a schedule, and every push and pull request to the main branch.

First, create a **streamlit-app-test.yml** file in the **.github/workflows** folder in the repo's root directory.

Add the following content to the file. The comments are added to explain what the line does, so that they can be ignored.

```
name: Streamlit App Test  # Name of the GitHub Action

on:
  workflow_dispatch:  # Manually trigger the workflow
  schedule:
  - cron: "30 21 * * *"  # Run the workflow at 2130hrs [UTC] every day
  push:
    branches: [main]  # Run when code is pushed to the main branch
  pull_request:
    branches: [main]  # Run for pull requests that target the main branch

permissions:
  contents: read  # Read the contents of the repository

jobs:
  test:  # Name of the job
    runs-on: ubuntu-latest  # Operating system for the job
    steps:  # Steps to run in the job
    - uses: actions/checkout@v4  # Check out the repository
    - uses: actions/setup-python@v5
      with:
        python-version: "3.12"  # Setup Python 3.12
    - uses: streamlit/streamlit-app-action@v0.0.3  # Use the Streamlit App
Action
      with:
        app-path: login.py  # Path to the Streamlit app
### Optional steps to display the test results summary
        pytest-args: -v --junit-xml=test-results.xml  # Run pytest with
verbose output and save the results in test-results.xml
    - if: always()  # Always run the following steps
      uses: pmeier/pytest-results-action@v0.6.0  # Use the pytest-results-
action
      with:
        path: test-results.xml  # Path to the test results
        summary: true  # Display a summary of the test results
        display-options: fEsp  # Display the failed, errored, skipped, and
passed tests
```

[8] *https://docs.github.com/en/actions/about-github-actions/understanding-github-actions#overview* (Accessed: 21 November 2024)

A few sections deserve additional explanation:

- **Scheduling Workflows:** GitHub uses the POSIX cron syntax to schedule workflows at UTC times.[9] The schedule event can be delayed during high loads of GitHub actions, like midnight or the start of every hour. This is why we have scheduled the workflow to run at 2130 hrs (9:30 PM) UTC. This can be changed to meet your needs.

  Note: *You can learn more about the POSIX cron syntax here: https://pubs.opengroup.org/onlinepubs/9699919799/utilities/crontab.html#tag_20_25_07.*
- **Events That Trigger Workflows:** In addition to manual (**`workflow_dispatch`**), **`scheduled`**, **`push`**, and **`pull_request`**, GitHub also provides many other events that can be used to trigger workflows. All such events, usage syntax, and rules are here: https://docs.github.com/en/actions/writing-workflows/choosing-when-your-workflow-runs/events-that-trigger-workflows.

Streamlit provides the **`Streamlit App Action`** as an easy way to add automated testing using GitHub Actions.[10] In addition to installing all requirements specified in the **`requirements.txt`** file, setting up **`pytest`**, and running **`pytest`** on all tests specified, it also runs a **`smoke test`** on each app page. More details about the **`Streamlit App Action`** can be found here: https://github.com/marketplace/actions/streamlit-app-action.

The optional steps are needed only to see the test results summary. We can still see the test result details without them.

Once the file is ready, commit it and push it to GitHub. When done, you can head to the **`Actions`** tab of the GitHub repo, which shall show a test running under the name of the latest commit message. *Figure* 13.20 shows what this page looks like.

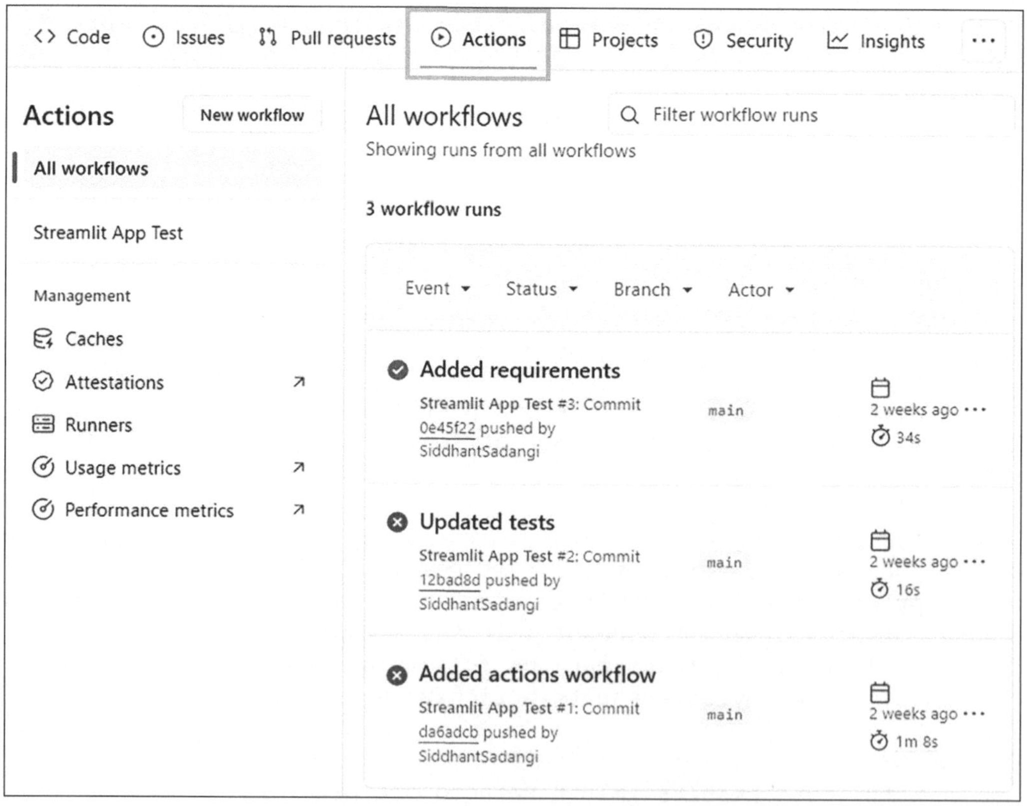

Figure 13.20: GitHub Actions Tab

[9] *https://docs.github.com/en/actions/writing-workflows/choosing-when-your-workflow-runs/events-that-trigger-workflows#schedule* (Accessed: 23 November 2024)

[10] *https://docs.streamlit.io/develop/concepts/app-testing/automate-tests#streamlit-app-action* (Accessed: 23 November 2024)

As you can see, there were two failures here. To inspect a run and see more details, click on the run to open its summary, as shown in the following *Figure 13.21*.

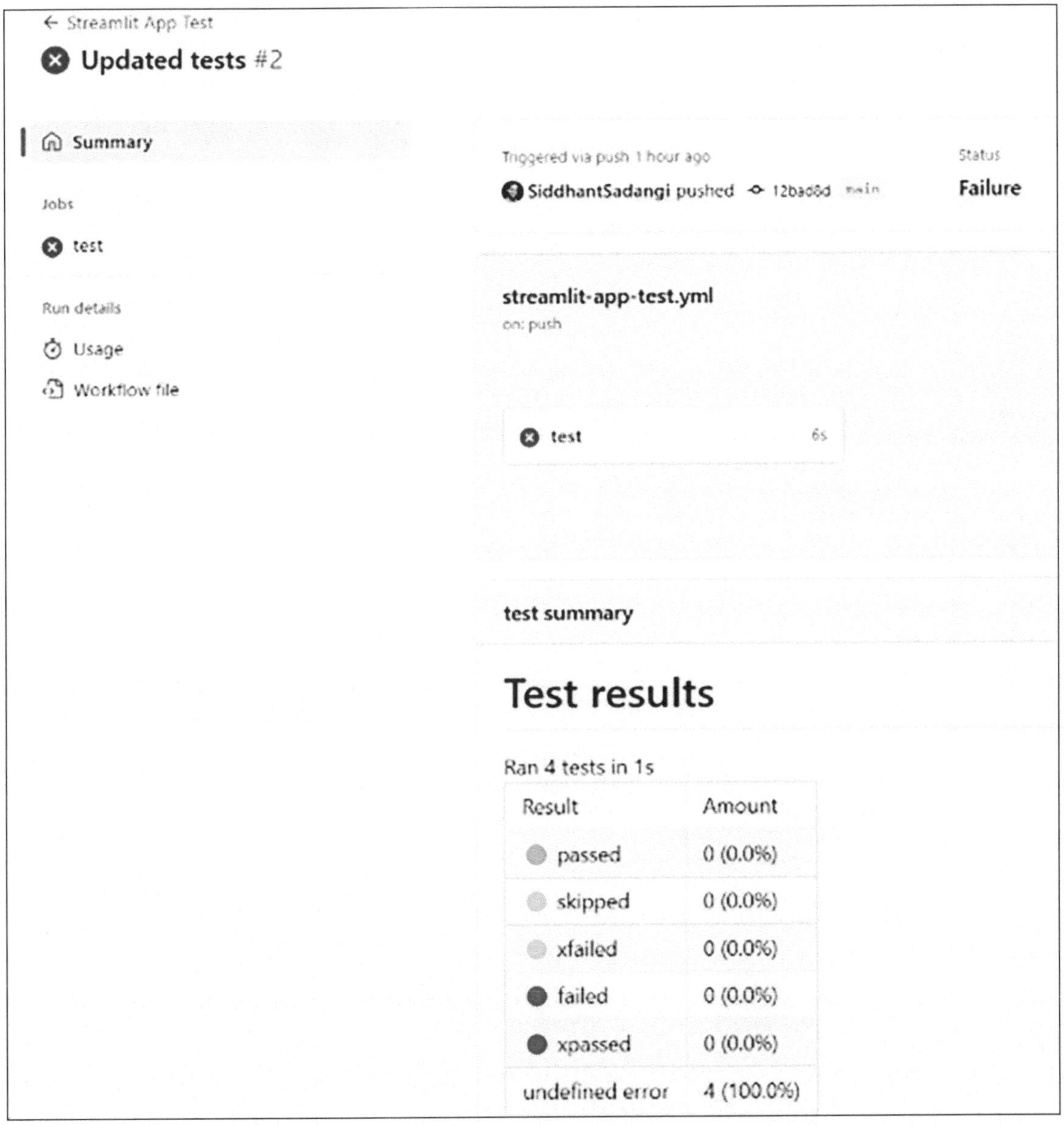

Figure 13.21: *Run Details*

The test summary section will only be visible if the optional steps are added to the workflow **YAML** file. You can scroll down to see the details of the errors, which, in this case, are shown in *Figure 13.22*.

```
error

▼ .st_smoke_test

ImportError while importing test module '/home/runner/work/app-test/app-test/st_smoke_test.py'.
Hint: make sure your test modules/packages have valid Python names.
Traceback:
/opt/hostedtoolcache/Python/3.12.7/x64/lib/python3.12/importlib/__init__.py:90: in import_module
    return _bootstrap._gcd_import(name[level:], package, level)
st_smoke_test.py:5: in <module>
    from streamlit.testing.v1 import AppTest
E   ModuleNotFoundError: No module named 'streamlit'

▼ .tests.test_bells_and_whistles

ImportError while importing test module '/home/runner/work/app-test/app-test/tests/test_bells_and_whistles.p
Hint: make sure your test modules/packages have valid Python names.
Traceback:
/opt/hostedtoolcache/Python/3.12.7/x64/lib/python3.12/importlib/__init__.py:90: in import_module
    return _bootstrap._gcd_import(name[level:], package, level)
tests/test_bells_and_whistles.py:2: in <module>
    from streamlit.testing.v1 import AppTest
E   ModuleNotFoundError: No module named 'streamlit'

▼ .tests.test_login

ImportError while importing test module '/home/runner/work/app-test/app-test/tests/test_login.py'.
Hint: make sure your test modules/packages have valid Python names.
Traceback:
/opt/hostedtoolcache/Python/3.12.7/x64/lib/python3.12/importlib/__init__.py:90: in import_module
    return _bootstrap._gcd_import(name[level:], package, level)
tests/test_login.py:2: in <module>
    from streamlit.testing.v1 import AppTest
E   ModuleNotFoundError: No module named 'streamlit'

▼ .tests.test_manage_users

ImportError while importing test module '/home/runner/work/app-test/app-test/tests/test_manage_users.py'.
Hint: make sure your test modules/packages have valid Python names.
Traceback:
/opt/hostedtoolcache/Python/3.12.7/x64/lib/python3.12/importlib/__init__.py:90: in import_module
    return _bootstrap._gcd_import(name[level:], package, level)
tests/test_manage_users.py:3: in <module>
    import pandas as pd
E   ModuleNotFoundError: No module named 'pandas'
```

Figure 13.22: *Error Details in Test Summary*

If the test summary is not visible, you can click on the **`test`** job to see the status of each step, and expand the steps to see their details, as shown in the following *Figure 13.23*.

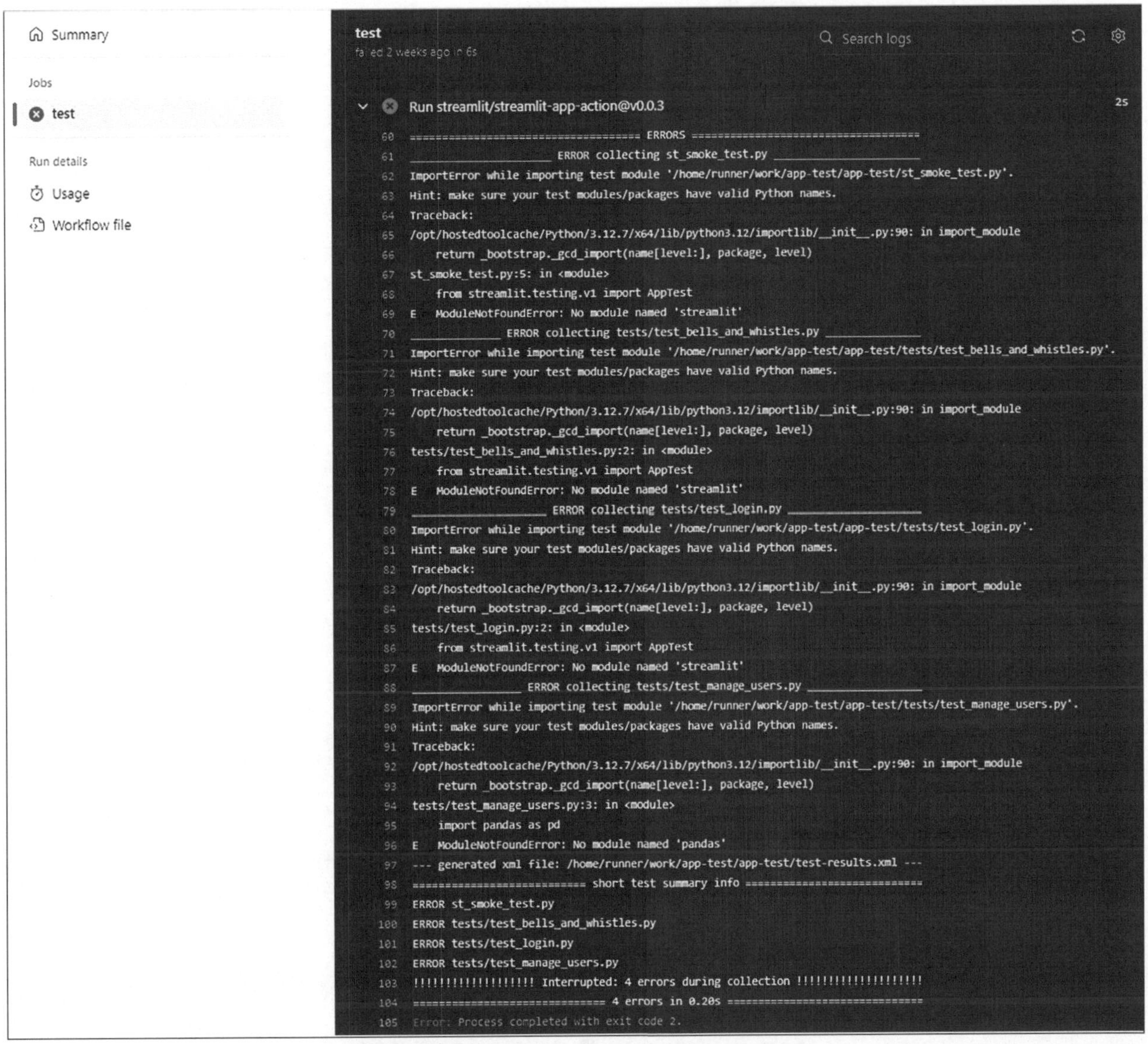

Figure 13.23: *Error Details in the Job*

There are four errors here. We again forgot to add a **`requirements.txt`** file, so the **`Streamlit App Action`** could not install **`streamlit`** and **`pandas`** in the testing environment. This would have caused an error while deploying the app to Streamlit Community Cloud, but thanks to the automated test, we found the issue before attempting to deploy the app. This is why tests are essential!

All the tests succeed after adding the required **`requirements.txt`** file, as shown in the following *Figure* 13.24.

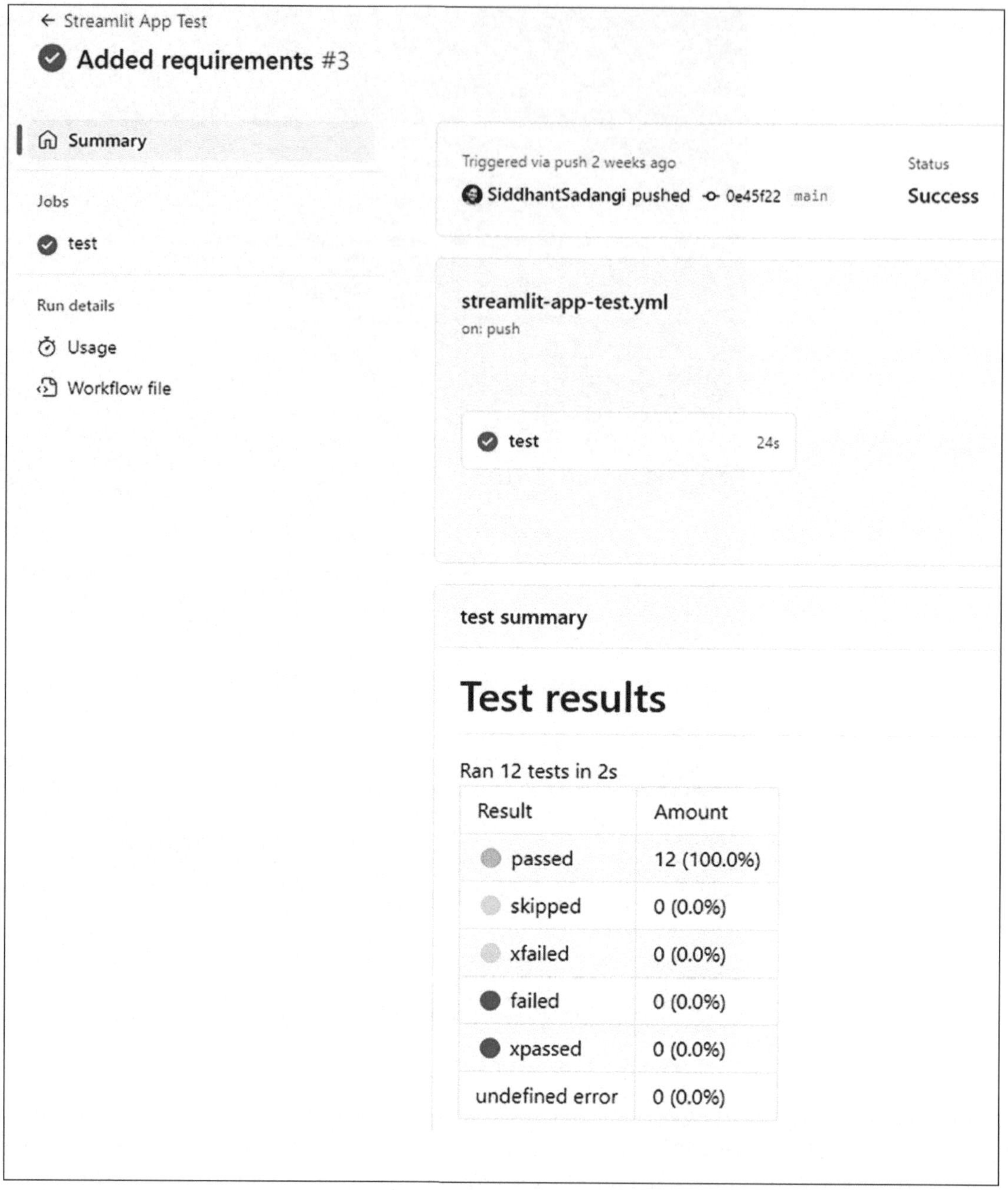

Figure 13.24: *Successful Tests*

This workflow will also run at the scheduled time and whenever changes are pushed to the **`main`** branch or a pull request targeting the **`main`** branch is created. GitHub Actions trigger an email once a workflow has been completed, and so we are always aware of the status of our app and code changes.

Note: *You can read more about GitHub Actions at https://docs.github.com/en/actions/about-github-actions.*

Conclusion

In this chapter, we explored the critical role of software testing, particularly within Python and Streamlit applications. We demonstrated how to utilize Streamlit's native testing framework alongside powerful tools like **`pytest`**, **`pre-commit`**, and GitHub Actions to automate our testing processes. Through practical examples, we showcased how to ensure our applications maintain their functionality as they grow in complexity.

Software testing is a comprehensive subject that extends far beyond what we have covered here. For those eager to delve deeper, the blog post on automated testing for Streamlit apps provides valuable insights, especially on pytest fixtures, mocking, and patching: https://medium.com/@shingurding/automated-testing-for-streamlit-apps-with-pytest-a0dd6e56c86d.

In the upcoming chapters, we will put our acquired knowledge into practice by developing and deploying real-world applications that encompass data analysis, machine learning, and chatbot functionalities. These exercises will solidify your understanding and showcase the robustness of the testing frameworks, we have discussed.

Points to Remember

- As software applications grow in size and complexity, manual testing becomes time-consuming and prone to errors.
- Testing early and often helps identify and address issues during development, minimizing disruptions later.
- A change in any dependencies of a Python project can break the project, without any change in the project itself.
- Automated testing ensures consistency, enabling tests to be run quickly and repeatedly, reducing the risk of introducing bugs.
- Streamlit's native testing framework simulates running the app, declaring user input, setting session states, and examining the results.
- Streamlit's native testing framework does not support testing multipage apps using **`st.navigation`** and **`st.Page`** as of version 1.51.0.
- **`pytest`** will automatically run every file starting with **`test_`** or ending with **`_test`** in the current working and **`tests`** directories.
- Tests can be run automatically before pushing the code to a repository using pre-commit hooks.
- GitHub Actions can run workflows on-demand, on a schedule, or based on specified events.
- Continuous testing, such as using GitHub Actions, helps to monitor and maintain app functionality even when external changes occur, ensuring proactive maintenance.

Multiple Choice Questions

1. Which of the following can be used as the app source by the `AppTest` class?
    a. File
    b. Function
    c. String
    d. All of the above
2. Considering a `text_input` widget with key `name`, which of the following statements will assign it the value of `Awesome Reader`?
    a. `at.get("name") = "Awesome Reader"`
    b. `at.text_input("name").set_value("Awesome Reader")`
    c. `at.text_input("name") == "Awesome Reader"`
    d. `at.get("name").set("Awesome Reader")`

3. For the same `text_input` widget as in Q2, which of the following statements will check if its value is `Awesome Reader`?
    a. `at.get("name") = "Awesome Reader"`
    b. `at.text_input("name") = "Awesome Reader"`
    c. `at.text_input("name").value == "Awesome Reader"`
    d. `at.get("name").assert("Awesome Reader")`
4. Which `pytest` flag lets you display `stdout` even when all tests pass?
    a. v
    b. k
    c. s
    d. p
5. How can you run all tests using `pytest`?
    a. `pytest`
    b. `pytest run all`
    c. `pytest *`
    d. `pytest run *`
6. How can you run all tests in a `test_app.py` file in the `tests` folder using `pytest`?
    a. `pytest tests/test_app.py`
    b. `pytest -k test_app`
    c. `Both a and b`
    d. None of the above
7. How can you run a `test_app()` function in the previous `test_app.py` file using `pytest`?
    a. `pytest test_app`
    b. `pytest tests/test_login.py::test_app`
    c. `pytest -k test_app`
    d. Both b and c

Answers

1. d
2. b
3. c
4. c
5. a
6. c
7. d

Questions

1. What is software testing, and why is it important, especially for Python applications?
2. How does Streamlit's native testing framework aid in testing applications? What are its limitations, particularly concerning multipage apps?
3. Discuss the importance of parameterization in **`pytest`**. Provide an example of how it can reduce redundancy in test code.
4. Given the following function, how can it be parameterized using **`pytest`** to test for two usernames – **`johndoe`** and **`janedoe`**? **`johndoe`** is an **`admin`**, and **`janedoe`** is a **`viewer`**.

```
def test_something():
    """Test if the app runs and displays the username and role after input is
provided."""

    at = AppTest.from_file("app.py").run()

    at.text_input[0].set_value("johndoe").run()

    assert at.text[0].value == "Name: johndoe, Role: admin"
```

5. Explain the use of pre-commit hooks in software testing. How do they contribute to maintaining code quality?
6. What is the significance of continuous testing using platforms like GitHub Actions? Provide an example scenario where continuous testing could prevent a potential issue.
7. How can the combination of **`pytest`**, pre-commit hooks, and GitHub Actions create a robust testing pipeline for a software project?

Key Terms

- **Software Testing**: This refers to accessing the functionality of a software program, and validating that it is free of bugs as well as meets the technical and user requirements.[11]
- **Test Case:** In software engineering, a test case specifies the inputs, execution conditions, steps, and expected results of a test that evaluates a single behavior of the software being tested.[12]
- **Manual Testing**: This is a software testing process in which the tester executes test cases manually, without using any scripting or automation tool.[13]
- **Automation Testing**: It is a software testing process in which test cases are executed automatically on predefined test cases, using specialized software and automation tools.[14]
- **JSON**: JavaScript Object Notation (**JSON**) is a lightweight data-interchange format that is both human and machine-readable.[15]
- **Positive Test Cases**: These test cases test if a system produces the expected output on valid inputs.[16]

---

[11] *https://www.geeksforgeeks.org/software-testing-basics/* (Accessed: 31 October 2024)
[12] *Systems and software engineering* -- Vocabulary. Iso/Iec/IEEE 24765:2010(E). 2010-12-01. *pp.* 1–418. *doi*:10.1109/IEEESTD.2010.5733835. ISBN 978-0-7381-6205-8
[13] *https://www.javatpoint.com/manual-testing* (Accessed: 31 October 2024)
[14] *https://artoftesting.com/automation-testing* (Accessed: 31 October 2024)
[15] *https://www.w3schools.com/whatis/whatis_json.asp* (Accessed: 2 November 2024)
[16] *https://www.geeksforgeeks.org/positive-vs-negative-vs-destructive-test-cases/* (Accessed: 2 November 2024)

- **Negative Test Cases**: These cases are designed to test if the system fails as expected on invalid input.[17]
- **Try and Except**: `try` and `except` code blocks are used to handle exceptions in Python. `try` checks for an exception in its block, and executes the code in the `except` block if an exception matching the `except` block's type is encountered.[18]
- **Parameterization**: This is a `pytest` feature that enables running the same test with different sets of inputs to prevent code duplication, and cover as many test cases as possible.
- **Principle of Least Privilege**: The Principle of Least Privilege (PoLP), also known as the *Least Access Principle*, is the concept that a user should only have access to what they absolutely need to perform their responsibilities and no more.[19]
- **Pre-commit Hooks:** These are custom scripts executed before a commit is made in a repository.[20]
- **Pre-commit:** It is a framework for managing and maintaining multi-language pre-commit hooks.[21]
- **YAML:** This stands for YAML *Ain't Markup Language*, but it originally stood for *Yet Another Markup Language*. It is a human-readable data serialization language, such as `JSON` and `TOML`.[22]
- **Continuous Testing**: This involves running tests automatically as part of the development process to ensure that code changes do not break the existing functionality.
- **GitHub Actions:** It is a platform that allows developers to create workflows to build, test, and deploy code to production, often used for Continuous Integration and Continuous Delivery (CI/CD).[23]
- **POSIX:** This stands for Portable Operating System Interface. It is a family of standards specified by the IEEE (Institute of Electrical and Electronics Engineers) to maintain compatibility between operating systems.[24]
- **Cron:** This is a job scheduler utility in Unix-like operating systems that automates the execution of scripts, and commands at specified times and dates.[25]
- **Smoke Testing**: This is a type of software testing performed to quickly identify and fix any major issue with the software, before more detailed testing is performed.[26]

[17] *https://www.geeksforgeeks.org/positive-vs-negative-vs-destructive-test-cases/* (Accessed: 2 November 2024)
[18] *https://www.geeksforgeeks.org/python-try-except/* (Accessed: 4 November 2024)
[19] *https://www.cloudflare.com/learning/access-management/principle-of-least-privilege/* (Accessed: 25 November 2024)
[20] *https://git-scm.com/book/en/v2/Customizing-Git-Git-Hooks* (Accessed: 18 November 2024)
[21] *https://pre-commit.com/* (Accessed: 19 November 2024)
[22] *https://www.freecodecamp.org/news/what-is-yaml-the-yml-file-format/* (Accessed: 26 November 2024)
[23] *https://docs.github.com/en/actions/about-github-actions/understanding-github-actions#overview* (Accessed: 26 November 2024)
[24] *https://itsfoss.com/posix/* (Accessed: 26 November 2024)
[25] *https://www.howtogeek.com/devops/what-is-a-cron-job-and-how-do-you-use-them/* (Accessed: 26 November 2024)
[26] *https://www.guru99.com/smoke-testing.html* (Accessed: 23 November 2024)

CHAPTER 14
Building a Data Analysis Streamlit App

Introduction

You have now acquired the foundational and advanced skills necessary to create and deploy Streamlit applications. It is time to apply this knowledge by developing practical, real-world applications that a wider audience can access. In the upcoming chapters, you will progressively build a multipage Streamlit application. This application will allow users to analyze a dataset of their choice, train models to make predictions based on that data, and interact with a chatbot regarding the dataset. Each component will be modular, enabling incremental deployment to the Streamlit Community Cloud.

This chapter will focus on creating the first component: the analysis module. This module will enable users to upload a dataset of their choice, and generate descriptive charts as well as insights for thorough analysis.

Note: *These chapters are designed to consolidate and reinforce your existing knowledge, while guiding you in integrating concepts from previous chapters into a production-grade application. The design decisions and features presented here should serve as recommendations, rather than strict rules. You are encouraged to develop your own designs and implementations.*

Structure

This chapter will cover the following topics:

- Creating the Entrypoint
  - Providing sample datasets
  - Caching datasets for efficient performance
  - Displaying dataset information
  - Adding a reset button
  - Adding page navigation links
- Creating the analyze page
  - Preview and description of the dataset
  - Cleaning the dataset
    - Handling missing values
    - Managing outliers
  - Adding data analysis tools
    - Generating the profile report
    - Creating custom plots

Creating the Entrypoint

As this will be a multipage app, we first create an entrypoint that will serve as a frame around all other pages. This entrypoint shall have the app's title, a concise caption, a file upload button for viewers to upload their own datasets, and a section for selecting a sample dataset.

A navigation menu will become visible once a dataset has been uploaded or selected, enabling users to move between the various app pages.

Figure 14.1 illustrates the initial design when no dataset is available.

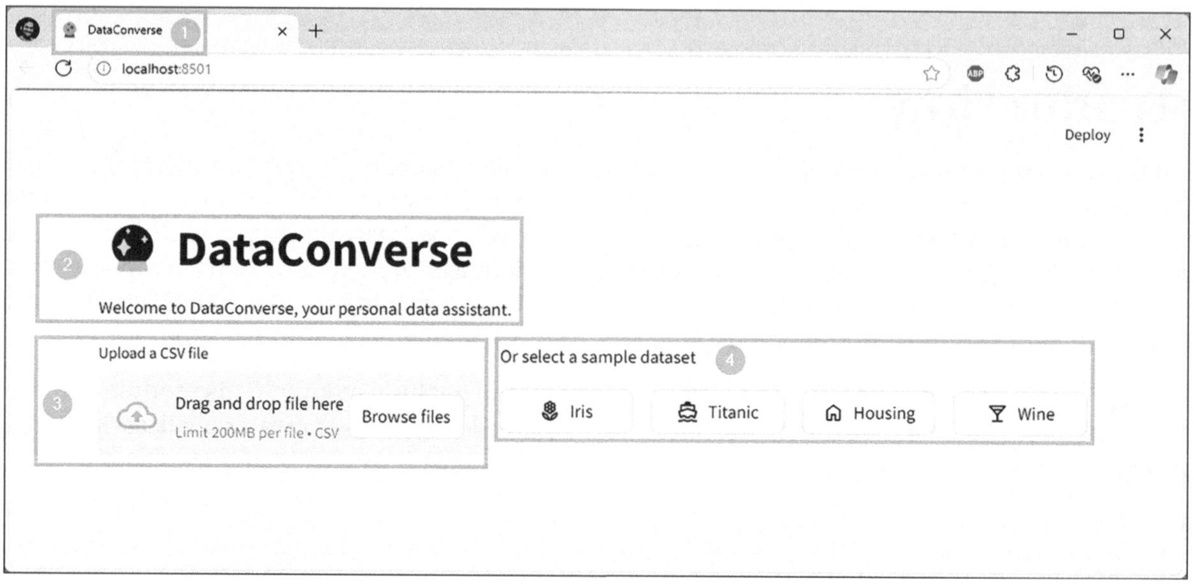

***Figure* 14.1:** *Initial State of the Entrypoint*

As shown in the screenshot, the entrypoint consists of four key sections in this state:

1. Page favicon and title
2. App logo, title, and description
3. File upload functionality
4. Sample dataset selection

Given the app's multipage structure, and the need to manage multiple source and data files, creating separate folders for better organization is recommended. For instance:

- An `app` folder for housing all source files (`.py` files)
- A `data` folder for storing all dataset files.

To begin, try creating an **`entrypoint.py`** file within the `app` folder. This task should be manageable, if you have been following the book up to this point. Use the following hints to guide your implementation:

1. **Configure the page:** Use **`st.set_page_config()`** to set the favicon, title, and layout. Note that the app adopts a wide layout.
2. **Set up the header:** Use **`st.title()`** and **`st.write()`** to display the app's logo, title, and description.
3. **Enable file upload:** Use **`st.file_uploader()`** for the file upload functionality, ensuring that only CSV files are allowed. The uploaded data should be stored in the session state to allow access across multiple scripts for different app pages.

Refer to the code example provided only if necessary. Treat the code, and design as inspiration rather than strict guidelines.

```
import pandas as pd
import streamlit as st

# Section 1: Page favicon and title
st.set_page_config(
    page_icon=":crystal_ball:",
    page_title="DataConverse",
    layout="wide",
)

# Section 2: App logo, title, and description
st.title(":crystal_ball: DataConverse")
st.write("Welcome to DataConverse, your personal data assistant.")

# Section 3: Data upload section
col1, col2 = st.columns([2, 3])
with col1:
    file = st.file_uploader("Upload a CSV file", type=["csv"])
    if file:
        st.session_state["data"] = pd.read_csv(file)
```

Providing Sample Datasets

This section is optional. However, providing sample datasets for users to try the application can significantly enhance the initial user experience. Let us discuss how this functionality has been implemented. There are numerous ways to implement this feature, and you are encouraged to develop your own approach.

As illustrated in *Figure 14.1*, the design includes four buttons, each corresponding to a sample dataset. When a button is clicked, the associated sample dataset is selected. Each button requires the path of the sample dataset to load. For simplicity, the sample datasets have been downloaded as CSV files into the `data` folder, and their relative paths are referenced from the entrypoint file. Alternatively, you could use a URL or even a database connection and query to access the datasets.

Let us detail the implementation for the `Iris` and `Wine` datasets. You can apply the same principles to configure the remaining buttons.

Note: *These, and many more, datasets can be downloaded from the UCI Machine Learning Repository at https://archive.ics.uci.edu/.*

The first step is to specify the dataset's path. As mentioned, the datasets have been saved as **`iris.csv`** and **`wine.csv`** files within the `data` folder. You could also use URLs linking to online versions of the datasets. However, note that changes to the online file might adversely impact the application's functionality.

To streamline the management of multiple datasets, a nested **`SAMPLE_DATASETS`** dictionary is created in the following format:

```
{
    "DATASET_NAME":
        {
            "path": "PATH_TO_DATASET",
            "icon": "DATASET_ICON"
        },
```

```
    ..., # Add more datasets here
}
```

This approach allows all dataset details, such as the name, path, and icon, to be managed centrally in one place.

Now, we can start working on the `Section 4` code.

Next, the buttons are arranged in a columnar format, with the number of columns matching the number of sample datasets. This can be achieved by defining a list of columns as follows:

```
columns = st.columns(len(SAMPLE_DATASETS))
```

For each sample dataset, a button is created within its dedicated column. The button's label matches the dataset name, and the icon is specified in the **`SAMPLE_DATASETS`** dictionary. When a button is clicked, the dataset is read from the specified path and stored in the session state for use across different application pages.

Following is an example of the implementation for this section:

```
# Section 4: Sample data selection
SAMPLE_DATASETS = {
    "Iris": {"path": "data/iris.csv", "icon": ":material/local_florist:"},
    "Wine": {"path": "data/wine.csv", "icon": ":material/local_bar:"},
    # Add more sample datasets here
}

with col2:
    st.text("Or select a sample dataset")
    columns = st.columns(len(SAMPLE_DATASETS))
    for i, (dataset_name, dataset_info) in enumerate(SAMPLE_DATASETS.items()):
        if columns[i].button(
            dataset_name,
            icon=dataset_info["icon"],
            use_container_width=True,
        ):
            st.session_state["data"] = pd.read_csv(dataset_info["path"])
```

Note: *To verify if the data has been loaded correctly, you can temporarily write and review the contents of* **`st.session_state["data"]`**.

Caching the Datasets for Efficient Performance

When uploading potentially large files, caching can help reduce upload times. Streamlit's **`st.cache_data()`** function provides an efficient way to cache datasets. However, different approaches are required for user-uploaded files and sample datasets.

- **User-uploaded files**: These files are typically relevant only to the specific user who uploads them, and usually for a limited duration. To prevent unnecessary cache storage usage, you can use the **`ttl`** parameter of **`st.cache_data()`** to cache the file for a fixed period.
- **Sample datasets**: These datasets are likely to be used more frequently and by multiple users. Hence, they can be cached indefinitely.

You can implement caching for both use cases using the concepts introduced in *Chapter 8, Introduction to Streamlit Caching and Connections*. Following is the implementation for the user-file upload section:

```
# Section 3: Data upload section
@st.cache_data(ttl="1h")
def cached_upload_data(file):
```

```
        return pd.read_csv(file)

    col1, col2 = st.columns([2, 3])
    with col1:
        file = st.file_uploader("Upload a CSV file", type=["csv"])
        if file:
            st.session_state["data"] = cached_upload_data(file)
            st.session_state["dataset_name"] = file.name
            st.rerun()
```

Task: *Implement indefinite caching for the sample datasets*

Once the data has been uploaded, you will want the application to transition to the Analyze page. This state of the app is demonstrated in the following *Figure 14.2*.

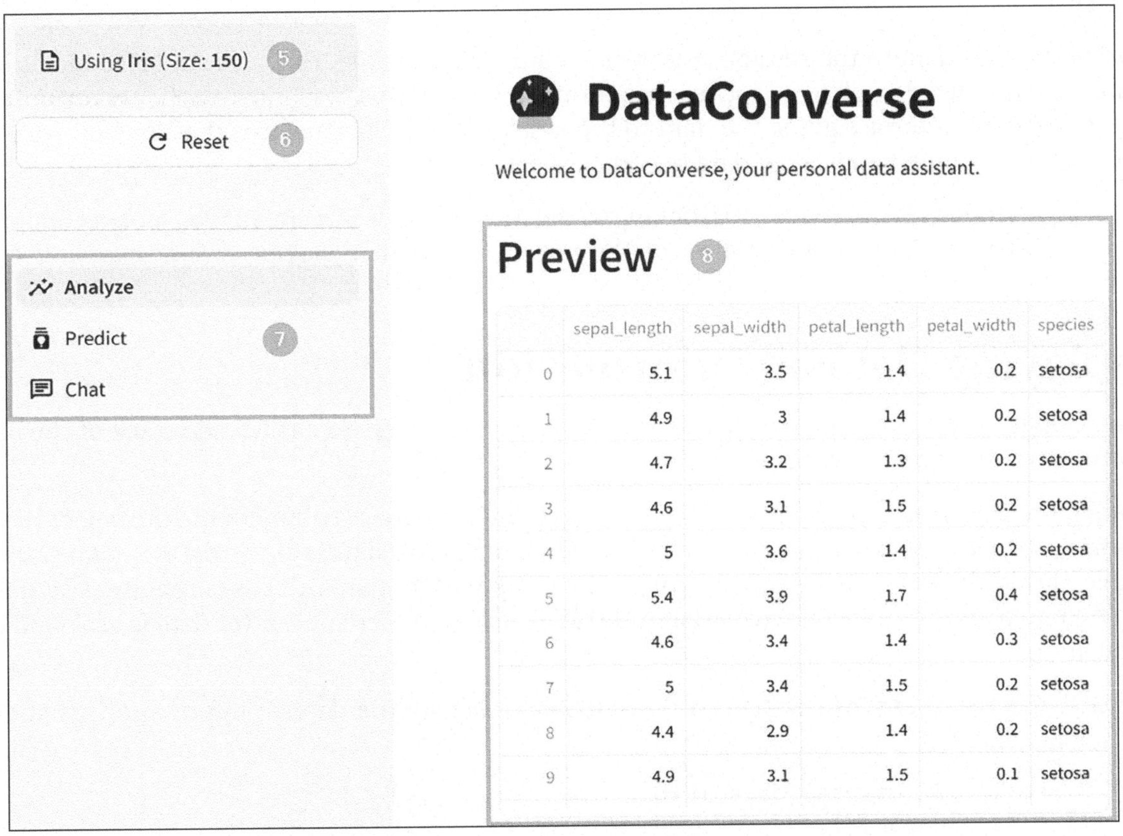

Figure 14.2: *App State after a File has been Uploaded*

This interface is composed of four sections:

1. An **`st.info()`** widget displaying the dataset, name, and size.
2. A **`Reset`** button to return the app to its initial state.
3. Page navigation links to the three main pages: **`Analyze`**, **`Predict`**, and **`Chat`**.
4. A preview of the dataset, as shown on the **`Analyze`** page.

To control visibility, ensure that the data upload section is displayed only when no data is present in the session state, and the post-upload interface is shown when the data is available. Use an **`if-else`** block as a guard clause to manage these states:

```
# Section 2: App logo, title, and description
...
```

```
if "data" not in st.session_state:
    # Section 3: Data upload section
    ...

    # Section 4: Sample data selection
    ...

else:
    # Section 5: Display data info
    ...
```

However, you may notice that the app does not automatically transition to the next state when data is uploaded or a sample dataset is selected, unless there is another interaction. This behavior occurs due to Streamlit's execution flow, as discussed in *Chapter 4, Exploring Streamlit's Flow and Architecture.*

The **if** block adds data to the session state when data is unavailable. However, the **else** block cannot be entered without a complete script re-execution. To resolve this, you must explicitly rerun the app using **st.rerun()**, after assigning the data to the session state. This ensures that the app transitions to the next state immediately after data becomes available.

Additionally, Sections 5 and 6 appear to belong to the Analyze page but are, in fact, global components visible on all pages. They should, therefore, be added to the **entrypoint**, rather than any specific page.

Displaying Dataset Information

This section is optional, but it provides a valuable feature for users to easily keep track of the dataset they are currently working with.

To implement this, you need the dataset's name and size. The **name** attribute of the file object returned by **st.file_uploader()** can be used for uploaded files. For sample datasets, the dataset name is already available within the loop that iterates through the sample datasets. Both cases require assigning the dataset name to a new session state variable, **dataset_name**, immediately after data is assigned to the session state.

Afterward, use the **st.info()** widget in the sidebar to display the dataset information, as shown in the following code:

```
# Section 5: Display data info
with st.sidebar:
    st.info(
        f"Using **{st.session_state[‹dataset_name›]}** (Size: **{len(st.
session_state[‹data›])}**)",
        icon=":material/description:",
    )
```

Adding a Reset Button

To reset the app to its initial state, you can clear all session state keys using **st.session_state.clear()**, and rerun the app with a clear session state by invoking **st.rerun()**. A simple implementation might look like this:

```
with st.sidebar:
    ...

    # Section 6: Reset Button
    if st.button(
```

```
            "Reset",
            use_container_width=True,
            icon=":material/refresh:",
        ):
            st.session_state.clear()
            st.rerun()
```

However, this straightforward approach introduces a significant UX issue: accidental clicks on the `Reset` button could unintentionally reset the app. A confirmation dialog modal can be added to ask for user confirmation before resetting the app. This can be achieved using the **`@st.dialog`** decorator.

A function decorated with **`@st.dialog`** becomes a dialog function. When the function is called, Streamlit inserts a modal dialog into the app, and any Streamlit elements within this function are rendered inside the modal dialog.

Note: *The* **`st.dialog`** *element was not covered in Chapter 6, Exploring Streamlit's Page Elements, as it was introduced after the chapter was written. For more information about* **`st.dialog`**, *refer to its API reference: https://docs.streamlit.io/develop/api-reference/execution-flow/st.dialog.*

Figure 14.3 provides an example of such a confirmation dialog modal.

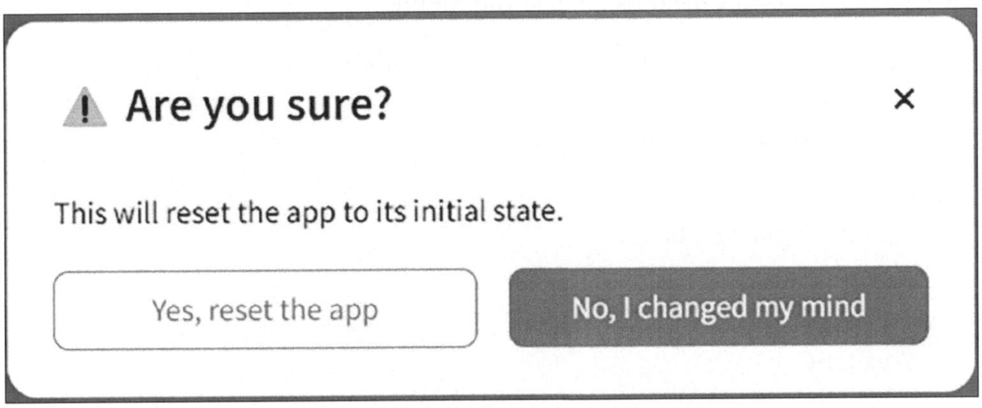

Figure 14.3: *App Reset Confirmation Dialog Modal*

Here is the implementation:

```
# Section 6: Reset Button
@st.dialog("⚠ Are you sure?")
def reset():
    st.write("This will reset the app to its initial state.")
    col1, col2 = st.columns(2)
    if col1.button("Yes, reset the app", use_container_width=True):
        st.session_state.clear()
        st.rerun()
    elif col2.button(
        "No, I changed my mind",
        use_container_width=True,
        type="primary",
    ):
        st.rerun()

st.button(
    "Reset",
    use_container_width=True,
    icon=":material/refresh:",
    on_click=reset,
)
```

In this approach:

- The `Reset` button triggers the **`reset()`** dialog function.
- Within the dialog, users can confirm or cancel their action using two buttons: **`Yes, reset the app`** or **`No, I changed my mind`**.
- If confirmed, the app clears the session state and restarts. If canceled, the app continues without changes.

Adding Page Navigation Links

Since the application has three different pages, it requires three separate source files: **`analyze.py`**, **`predict.py`**, and **`chat.py`**. Place these files in the same folder as **`entrypoint.py`** for ease of organization.

As shown in *Figure 14.2*, the navigation section is positioned below the dataset information. However, using **`st.navigation()`** to display the page links would place the navigation section at the top of the sidebar. To adhere to the desired design, use **`st.page_link()`** instead. Nonetheless, as covered in *Chapter 12, Building Multipage Streamlit Apps*, **`st.navigation()`** is still required to construct the navigation menu, even if it is not used to display the menu.

The following is the implementation of the navigation component:

```
with st.sidebar:
    # Section 5: Display data info
    ...

    # Section 6: Reset Button
    ...

    # Section 7: Page Navigation
    st.divider()

    analyze_page = st.Page("analyze.py", title="Analyze")
    predict_page = st.Page("predict.py", title="Predict")
    chat_page = st.Page("chat.py", title="Chat")

    page = st.navigation(
        [analyze_page, predict_page, chat_page],
        position="hidden",
    )

    st.page_link(analyze_page, icon=":material/insights:")
    st.page_link(predict_page, icon=":material/batch_prediction:")
    st.page_link(chat_page, icon=":material/chat:")

page.run()
```

Once implemented, the application will resemble the layout as shown in the *Figure 14.2*, with the navigation section appropriately positioned below the dataset information. **`Section 8`**, which provides a dataset preview, will be implemented within the **`Analyze`** page in the **`analyze.py`** file.

Creating the Analyze Page

This page allows users to analyze datasets effectively. Since data analysis is a comprehensive subject often taught as an entire University course, this section will focus on implementing a few basic features. These features serve as a guide, encouraging you to extend your app creatively, and tailor it to your needs.

All functionalities for this page will be implemented in the **analyze.py** file.

Preview and Description of the Dataset

The first sections include a simple preview and description of the dataset. These features can be implemented using **st.dataframe()** for both tasks, as demonstrated in the following code:

```
import streamlit as st

data = st.session_state.get("data")

st.header(":material/preview: Preview")
st.dataframe(data)

st.header(":material/description: Description")
st.dataframe(data.describe())
```

Once added to **analyze.py**, the page layout will resemble the following *Figure* 14.4.

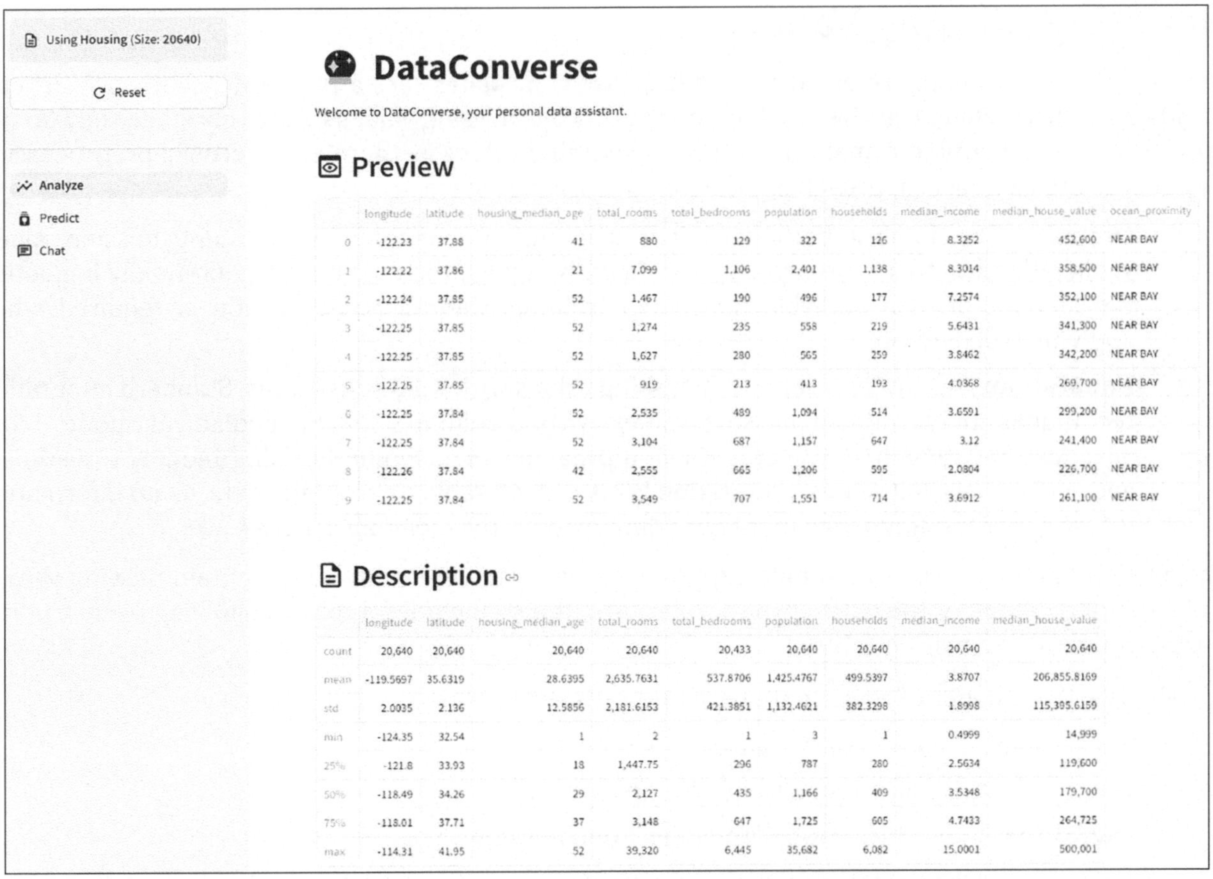

Figure 14.4: *Housing Dataset Preview and Description*

- **Preview**: Displays the entire dataset.
- **Description**: Provides summary statistics of the numerical columns using the DataFrame's **describe()** method.

Cleaning the Dataset

Any data scientist will agree that cleaning the data is the most crucial (and often the least enjoyable) part of their job. The sample datasets provided in this application are curated and mostly clean. However, real-world data is usually messy, and requires significant preprocessing before insights can be derived.

Data cleaning encompasses various steps and techniques, many of which are taught in specialized courses. This section focuses on implementing a couple of fundamental steps: handling missing values and removing outliers. Adding more advanced techniques will be straightforward once you understand how to incorporate these basics.

Note: *Numerous tutorials on data cleaning are available online. For a comprehensive introduction, consider exploring the guide by DataCamp: https://www.datacamp.com/tutorial/guide-to-data-cleaning-in-python.*

To start, add a heading for the data cleaning section:

```
st.header(":material/mop: Data Cleaning")
```

This will serve as the foundation for incorporating subsequent data-cleaning steps.

Handling Missing Values

Missing values—commonly referred to as **`NULLs`**, **`NaNs`**, or **`Nones`**—are a frequent occurrence in real-world datasets. Machine learning models cannot process missing values effectively since they do not provide any meaningful information. Addressing missing values is, therefore, a crucial preprocessing step. There are two basic approaches for handling missing values:

- **Dropping:** The simplest method involves dropping rows or columns containing missing values. While effective, this approach can significantly reduce the dataset size, potentially impacting the amount of data available for model training. Careful consideration is required when applying this method.
- **Imputation:** This involves replacing missing values with valid substitutes. Standard imputation techniques include filling missing values with a column's mean, median, or mode. More advanced methods may use statistical approaches or machine learning models to estimate and replace missing values. Imputation is often preferable to dropping data, as no information is lost. However, it introduces added complexity to the cleaning process.

This implementation displays a simple caption summarizing how many rows contain missing values, and what percentage of the dataset they constitute. It also includes a button allowing users to drop rows containing the missing values.

To calculate the number of rows containing missing values:

```
null_count = data.isna().any(axis=1).sum()
```

- **`isna()`** identifies all missing values in the dataset.
- **`any(axis=1)`** identifies rows with at least one missing value.
- **`sum()`** provides the total count of such rows.

To calculate the percentage of rows with missing values:

```
null_percentage = null_count / len(data)
```

Based on whether the dataset contains the missing values, the interface either displays:

- A success message indicating that no missing values are found, or

- A warning message showing the count and percentage of missing rows, and a button to drop them.

The implementation is as follows:

```
if null_count > 0:
    col1, col2 = st.columns(2)
    with col1:
        st.warning(
            f"Found **{null_count}** rows with NULL values
(**{null_percentage:.2%}** of the dataset)"
        )
    with col2:
        if st.button(
            "Drop NULL values",
            icon=":material/warning:",
            use_container_width=True,
            help="This will remove all rows with **any** NULL values",
        ):
            data.dropna(inplace=True)
            st.session_state["data"] = data
            st.rerun()
else:
    st.success("No NULL values found", icon=":material/check_circle:")
```

If missing values are found, the warning highlights their count and percentage. The button uses the **dropna()** method to remove rows with missing values. The cleaned dataset is reassigned to the session state, ensuring subsequent operations reference the updated dataset. The **st.rerun()** function forces the app to rerun, applying these updates immediately.

Once implemented, the data cleaning section will resemble the following *Figure* 14.5.

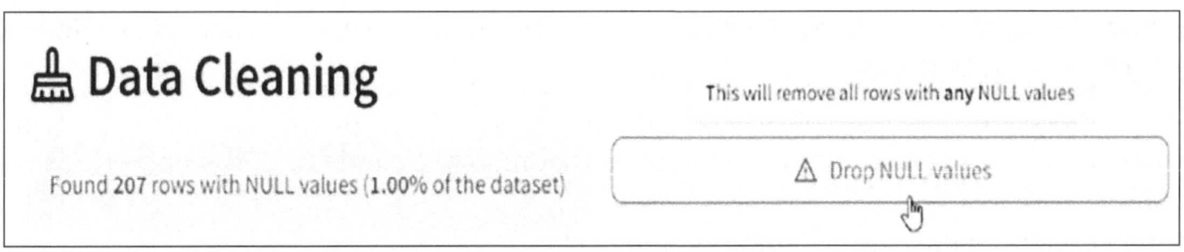

***Figure* 14.5:** *Handling* NULL *Values*

When the user clicks **Drop NULL values**:

- Rows containing NULL values are removed from the dataset.
- The app reruns, reflecting the reduced dataset size in the dataset information section.
- The data description updates accordingly, and a **No NULL values found** success message replaces the earlier warning.

Task: *To optimize performance, cache the calculation of rows with missing values. This prevents recalculating these numbers every time the script is rerun, improving efficiency.*

Handling Outliers

With the dataset now cleaned of missing values, the next step is to handle outliers. An outlier is a data point that deviates significantly from the rest of the data. For instance, an age of 200 in a demographic dataset is likely an outlier. Outliers often result from data entry errors, and should be handled to ensure that they do not skew the dataset analysis.

Note: *Not all outliers are errors. Some may represent genuine anomalies that highlight critical insights about a system. Such outliers should be investigated by Subject Matter Experts (SMEs).*

There are various methods for identifying and handling outliers. For a detailed overview, refer to this guide: https://www.geeksforgeeks.org/detect-and-remove-the-outliers-using-python/. In this app, we adopt a straightforward process of detecting outliers using the **`z-score`**.

Steps to Calculate Outliers:

1. **Filter Numeric Columns:** As the **`z-score`** applies only to numeric data, first filter the dataset to include only numeric columns:

   ```
   numeric_data = data.select_dtypes(include=["number"])
   ```

2. **Calculate Z-scores:** Use the **`stats`** module from the **`scipy`** package to compute the absolute **`z-score`** for each numeric value in the dataset:

   ```
   from scipy import stats

   z_scores = abs(stats.zscore(numeric_data, nan_policy="omit"))
   ```

3. **Identify Outliers:** Rows with **`z-scores`** greater than or equal to 3 (the default threshold) are considered outliers. Calculate the count and percentage of outliers:

   ```
   outliers = numeric_data[(z_scores >= 3).any(axis=1)]
   outlier_pct = len(outliers) / len(data)
   ```

   Note: *A **`z-score`** threshold of 3 is a common convention but is not absolute. You may adjust the threshold depending on the domain, dataset size, and distribution. For example:*

   - `z-score ≥ 2 captures ~95% of normally distributed data.`
   - `z-score ≥ 3 captures ~99.7%.`
   - `z-score ≥ 4 captures ~99.99%.`

   Task: *To improve flexibility, allow users to customize the z-score threshold via a slider. Refer to Figure 14.6 for inspiration.*

4. If outliers are detected, display a warning message, and provide a button to drop them. Dropping outliers involves excluding rows that match the indices of the outliers, as shown in the following code:

   ```
   data[~data.index.isin(outliers.index)]
   ```

The complete implementation is as follows:

```
col1, col2, col3 = st.columns(3)
numeric_data = data.select_dtypes(include=["number"])
z_scores = abs(stats.zscore(numeric_data, nan_policy="omit"))
outliers = numeric_data[
    (z_scores >= col1.slider("Z-score threshold", min_value=1, max_value=10,
value=3)).any(axis=1)
]
outlier_pct = len(outliers) / len(data)

if outlier_pct > 0:
    col2.warning(
        f"Found **{len(outliers)}** rows with outliers (**{outlier_pct:.2%}**
of the dataset)"
    )
    if col3.button(
        "Drop outliers",
        icon=":material/warning:",
```

```
        use_container_width=True,
        help="This will remove all rows with outliers",
    ):
        st.session_state["data"] = data[~data.index.isin(outliers.index)]
        st.rerun()
else:
    col2.success("No outliers found", icon=":material/check_circle:")
```

After cleaning the data, allow users to download the updated dataset. This can be achieved using **`st.download_button()`**:

```
st.download_button(
    "Download cleaned data",
    data.to_csv(),
    file_name=f"{st.session_state[‹dataset_name›]}_cleaned.csv",
    mime="text/csv",
    icon=":material/download:",
)
```

The following *Figure* 14.6 shows what the cleaning section of the `Analyze` page looks like.

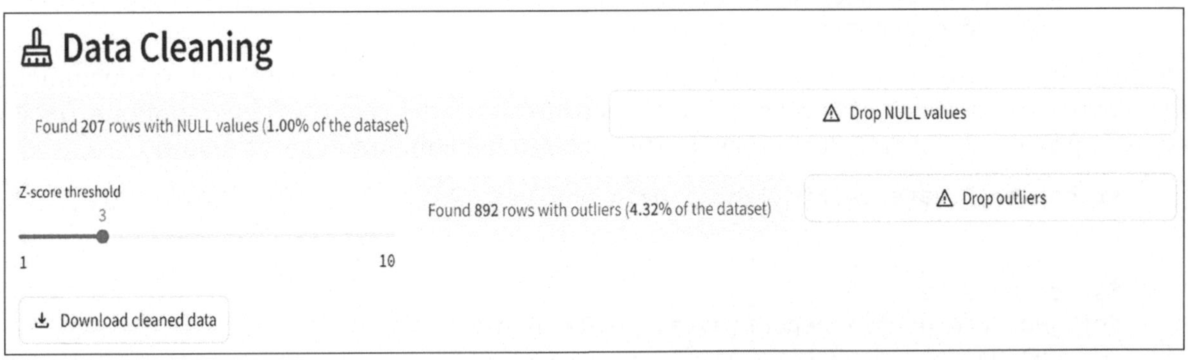

Figure 14.6: *Data Cleaning Section*

As users adjust the **`z-score`** threshold, fewer points are identified as outliers, as more values fall within the specified range. This dynamic approach gives users greater control over the cleaning process. However, unlike the `Drop NULL values` button, dropping outliers will not immediately remove all outliers from the data. Why? Because the **`z-scores`** are calculated based on the current state of the data. Once outliers are dropped, the variance of the dataset decreases, and some points previously within the threshold are now considered outliers.

Task: *Cache the calculation of outliers so that the numbers do not have to be recalculated every time the script is rerun.*

Adding Data Analysis Tools

With the dataset cleaned, it is time to conduct a more detailed and sophisticated analysis.

Generating the Profile Report

A powerful automated, in-depth data analysis tool is **`ydata-profiling`** (previously known as **`pandas-profiling`**). This package simplifies and standardizes the creation of comprehensive data profiling reports. These reports include detailed statistics and visualizations, all generated with just a single line of code.[1]

[1] *https://docs.profiling.ydata.ai/latest/* (Accessed: 23 March 2025)

Note: *You can explore the complete documentation for* **ydata-profiling** *here: https://docs.profiling.ydata.ai/latest/.*

To use **ydata-profiling** within your Streamlit app, you must install **ydata-profiling** and its Streamlit integration, **streamlit-pandas-profiling**. You can install these packages using the following command:

```
pip install -U 'ydata-profiling<5.0' 'streamlit-pandas-profiling<1.0'
```

Once installed, generating a profile report becomes straightforward. A sample implementation is as follows:

```
import ydata_profiling
from streamlit_pandas_profiling import st_profile_report

if st.button(
    "Generate Dataset Report",
    icon=":material/insights:",
    type="primary",
):
    pr = data.profile_report()
    st_profile_report(pr)
```

Since generating a profile report can be resource-intensive and time-consuming, it is recommended to cache the process using **st.cache_data**. This ensures that the report is generated only once per session, improving the overall performance. The updated implementation is as follows:

```
st.header(":material/insights: Data Analysis")


@st.cache_data
def generate_profile_report(data: pd.DataFrame)
    return data.profile_report()


if st.button(
    "Generate Dataset Report",
    icon=":material/insights:",
    type="primary",
):
    pr = generate_profile_report(data)
    st_profile_report(pr)
```

This addition lets users generate interactive, detailed profile reports directly within the app. The following *Figure* 14.7 demonstrates an example of the profile report generated in the app.

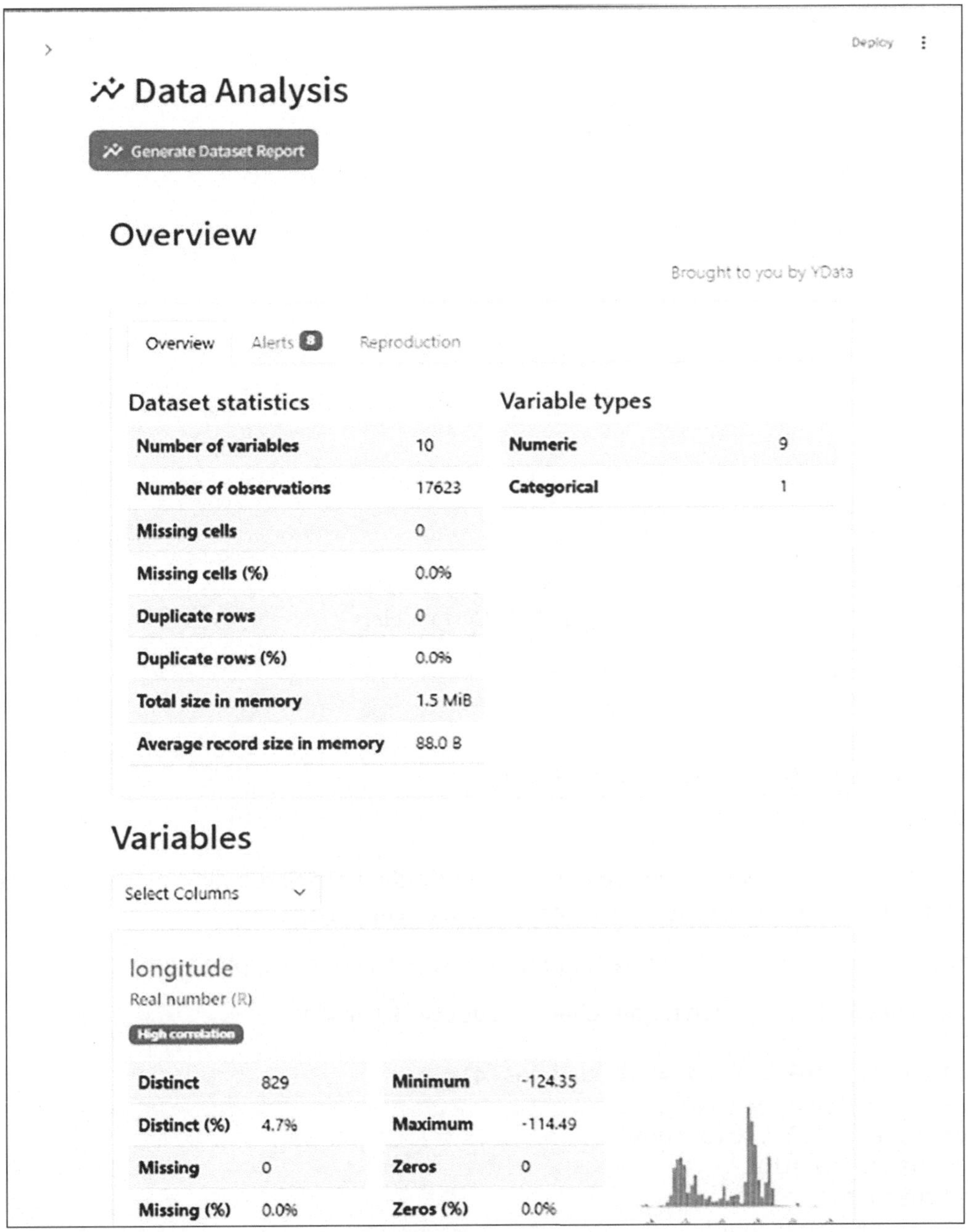

Figure 14.7: *Profile Report*

Creating Custom Plots

In addition to the numerous plots generated by **ydata-profiling**, Streamlit's built-in chart elements can be leveraged to add custom visualizations (as described in *Chapter 6, Exploring Streamlit's Page Elements*). This section implements the **Custom Plots** feature on the `Analyze` page, enabling users to select plot types and columns for visualization.

Figure 14.8 provides a preview of what this section looks like.

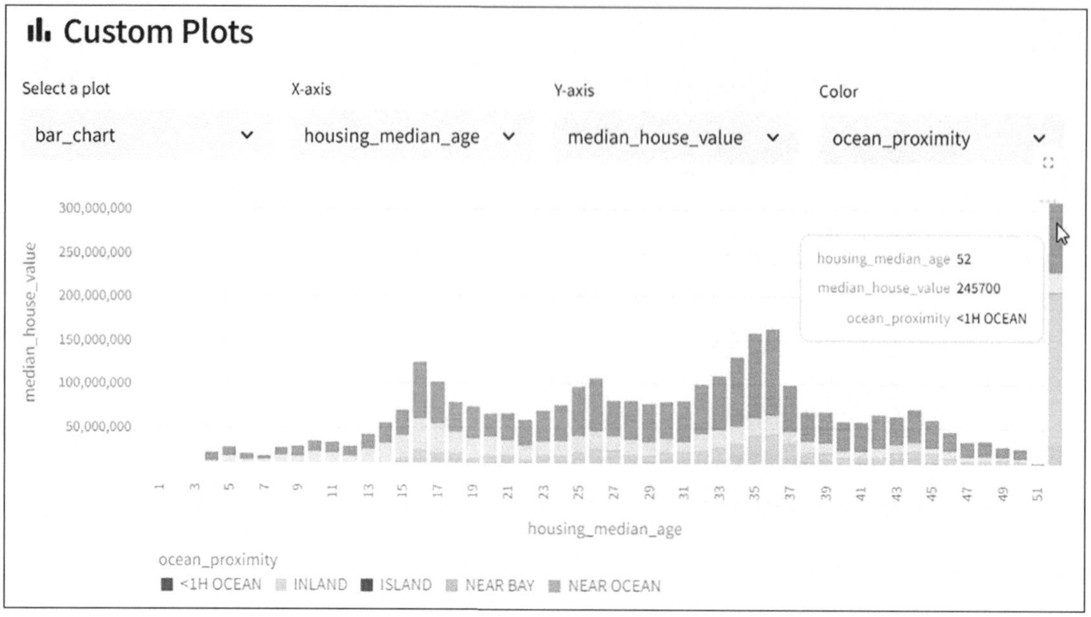

Figure 14.8: *Custom Plots*

The section consists of three major components:

1. **Selecting a plot type**
2. **Choosing columns for the axes and color**
3. **Rendering the plot**

The implementation supports simple chart elements available in Streamlit such as: **`st.area_chart`**, **`st.bar_chart`**, **`st.line_chart`**, **`st.map`**, and **`st.scatter_chart`**.

Start with a **`subheader`** and a **`selectbox`** that allows users to choose a plot type:

```
st.subheader(":material/bar_chart: Custom Plots")

col1, col2, col3, col4 = st.columns(4)

plot_type = col1.selectbox(
    "Select a plot",
    options=[
        st.area_chart,
        st.bar_chart,
        st.line_chart,
        st.map,
        st.scatter_chart,
    ],
    format_func=lambda x: x.__name__,
)
```

- The **`options`** parameter lists chart methods rather than strings.
- The **`format_func`** parameter extracts the method name to populate the **`selectbox`**.

Since most charts (except **`st.map`**) accept similar parameters, check the selected plot type and pass parameters accordingly. For map plots, latitude and longitude columns must be specified, while other plots require x-axis, y-axis, and color columns.

```
if plot_type.__name__ == st.map.__name__:
    latitude = col2.selectbox("Select Latitude Column", data.columns)
    longitude = col3.selectbox("Select Longitude Column", data.columns)
```

```
        plot_type(data, latitude=latitude, longitude=longitude)
    else:
        x_axis = col2.selectbox("Select X-axis Column", options=data.columns)
        y_axis = col3.selectbox("Select Y-axis Column", options=data.columns)
        color = col4.selectbox("Select Color Column", options=data.columns)
        plot_type(data, x=x_axis, y=y_axis, color=color)
```

- The `__name__` attribute is used to compare the selected method with **`st.map`**.
- For map plots, `latitude`, and `longitude` columns are chosen, while other charts utilize the `x-axis`, `y-axis`, and `color` columns.

This implementation provides the basic structure for the `Analyze` page. As mentioned, this is a starting template that can be expanded upon. Refer to the **Additional Tasks** section later in the chapter for inspiration on features you might add to enhance your app further.

Conclusion

In this chapter, we developed the **`entrypoint`** for our application, enabling users to upload their datasets or select from predefined sample datasets. Additionally, we implemented a `Reset` button to return the app to its initial state, and added navigation links for seamless access to different pages within the app.

In the `Analyze` section, we delved into workflows for data cleaning and analysis using Streamlit. This included handling missing values and outliers, generating comprehensive data profiles with **`ydata-profiling`**, and creating custom plots using Streamlit's built-in chart elements.

In the next chapter, we will focus on building the `Predict` page. This addition will empower users to train machine learning models on their datasets, and generate predictions efficiently.

Additional Tasks

1. Expand `Section 3` of the entrypoint to support loading Excel files in addition to CSV files. Note that additional packages such as **`openpyxl`** or **`xlrd`** might be required to handle Excel files.
2. Now that you know how to handle missing values and outliers, here are a few more advanced techniques to add to the app:
    a. Drop dataset columns with more than 30% missing values. Allow users to customize the threshold (for example, 20%, 50%) through the app interface.
    b. Impute missing values using the mean, median, or mode (selected by the user). Refer to the scikit-learn imputation guide for techniques and examples: https://scikit-learn.org/stable/modules/impute.html.
    c. Clip outlier values to the maximum or minimum value of the column instead of dropping them. Refer to the **clip()** method documentation for implementation details: https://pandas.pydata.org/pandas-docs/stable/reference/api/pandas.DataFrame.clip.html
    d. Add more advanced data cleaning techniques such as deduplication, normalization, and encoding categorical variables.
3. Update the app so that the original dataset remains untouched during data cleaning. Provide users an option to reset the dataset to its original state, without resetting the entire app.
4. Expand the range of custom plots using more advanced Streamlit-supported chart elements such as **`st.pyplot`** (for Matplotlib plots) and **`st.plotly_chart`** (for Plotly interactive charts).

5. Implement dynamic filtering and grouping of data for visualization, allowing users to drill down into specific subsets of the data for analysis.
6. Personalize the app with a custom theme, based on what you have learned in Chapter 11: *App Configuration Options.*
7. Deploy and share your app on the Streamlit Community Cloud as per *Chapter 3, Creating and Deploying Your First Streamlit App* and *Chapter 10, Advanced App Management Concepts.* Ensure that your **`requirements.txt`** file includes all external dependencies needed by the app.
8. Create a comprehensive test suite for the app, based on the knowledge gained in *Chapter 13, Testing Streamlit Apps.* Automate the test suite deployment using GitHub Actions.
9. Add tooltips or help sections throughout the app to provide contextual information about each feature, improving usability for new users.

Key Terms

- **Imputation:** Refers to techniques for filling missing values in a dataset with valid substitutes such as mean, median, or mode.
- **Outlier:** A data point that differs significantly from the rest of the dataset, either too high or too low compared to other observations.
- **Z-score:** A statistical measure that quantifies how far a data point is from the mean of the dataset, expressed in standard deviations.

CHAPTER 15
Building a Machine Learning Streamlit App

Introduction

Now that you have learned how to create a data analysis and cleaning application, the next logical step is to utilize that data to train a model and generate predictions.

This chapter will focus on the prediction module. This module enables users to train Machine Learning (ML) models on their data, evaluate model performance, and generate predictions using the trained models.

Note: *As stated in the previous chapter, the design decisions and features presented here should serve as recommendations rather than strict rules. You are encouraged to develop your own designs and implementations.*

Note: *From this chapter onward, we will use Streamlit version 1.46.1.*

Structure

This chapter will cover the following topics:

- Introduction to AutoML
- Preparing for Model Training
    - Customizing AutoGluon Parameters
    - Resetting AutoGluon Parameters
    - Training the Models
- Exploring Model Details
- Making Predictions

Introduction to AutoML

Machine Learning development is very technical and time-consuming. Numerous different architectures can be used, and various parameters for each. Given that the app is intended for both technical and non-technical users, it is reasonable to assume that they will not have the time, patience, or knowledge required to train an effective model on their data independently. This holds even for experienced Machine Learning developers due to the significant time investment needed to experiment with various combinations of architectures and parameters.

This is where Automated Machine Learning (AutoML) comes to the rescue. AutoML simplifies the Machine Learning development process by automating steps like feature engineering, hyperparameter tuning, model selection, and fine-tuning. This simplification of Machine Learning development for individuals with limited technical expertise comes at the expense of reduced flexibility and potentially lower performance compared to models trained by experts.

Various open-source AutoML tools are available in the Python ecosystem, like auto-sklearn, Auto-PyTorch, AutoKeras, AutoGluon, and so on.

We will implement the `Predict` module using AutoGluon, but you are also welcome to experiment with any tool of your choice.

Preparing for Model Training

Before starting work on the `Predict` module, it is important to ensure that the AutoML library intended for use has been installed. In this example, we have used AutoGluon version 1.4.0.

```
pip install autogluon==1.4.0
```

We shall mostly work on the `predict.py` file in this module. The initial step involves determining the target column that the model will be trained to predict. For example, we want to predict the species for the `Iris` dataset, and for the `Housing` dataset, we would like to predict the house value. However, because the dataset the user will utilize is unknown beforehand, selecting the target column will be delegated to the user through the **`selectbox()`** widget, as shown in the following code.

```
import streamlit as st

data = st.session_state["data"]
target = st.selectbox("Select the target column", options=data.columns)
```

The options in the **`selectbox()`** are populated based on the columns available in the dataset, accessed using the **`.columns`** attribute of the pandas DataFrame.

After this code snippet is added to the **`predict.py`** script and the entry point is executed, a page similar to the one shown in *Figure 15.1* will appear when the **`Housing`** dataset is selected, and the user navigates to the **`Predict`** page.

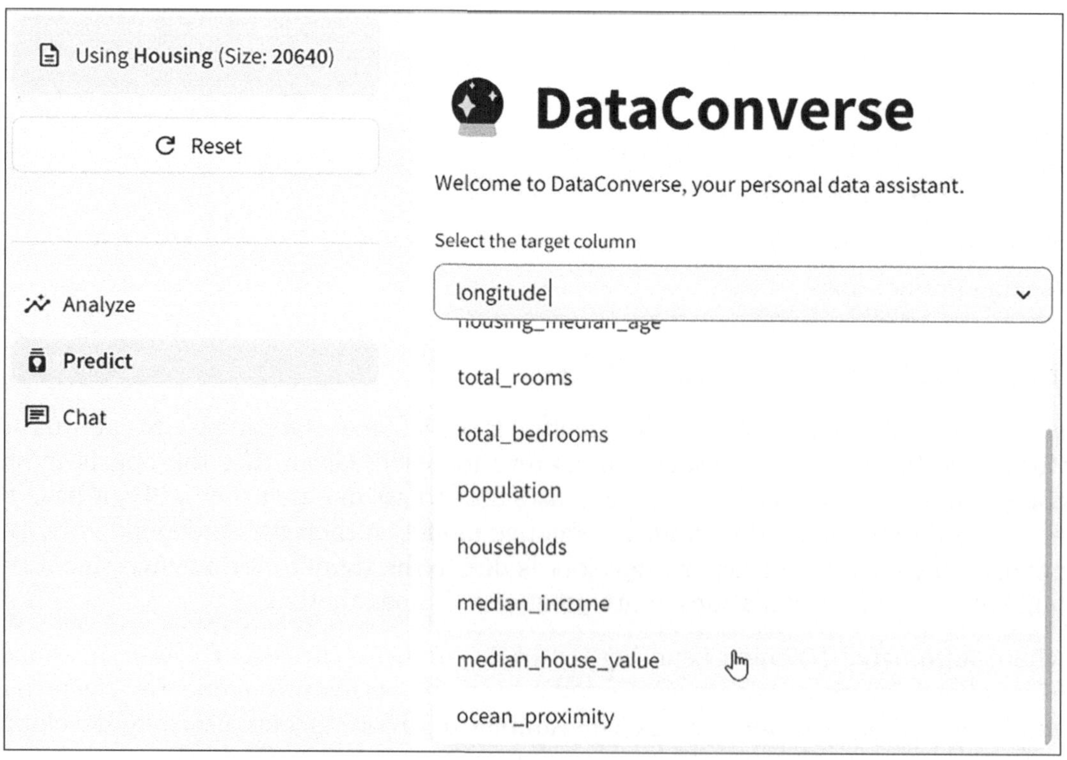

Figure 15.1: *Target Column Selection Dropdown in the Predict Page*

Note: *The California Housing dataset can be downloaded from Kaggle at https://www.kaggle.com/datasets/dhirajnirne/california-housing-data.*

Customizing AutoGluon Parameters

The target column is the minimum requirement for AutoGluon to train a model on the provided data. Nevertheless, AutoGluon also offers configuration options that can be employed to improve performance or tailor the training process to specific use cases.

These options are intended for advanced users with Machine Learning development experience, so that they can be kept hidden within an **expander()** widget. This approach offers other users a cleaner and less cluttered interface, as demonstrated in the following code.

```
with st.expander("Model Parameters", icon=":material/settings:"):
    ...
```

All the configuration options can now be organized within the **expander()** widget. A sample configuration section with the expander is shown in the following *Figure* 15.2.

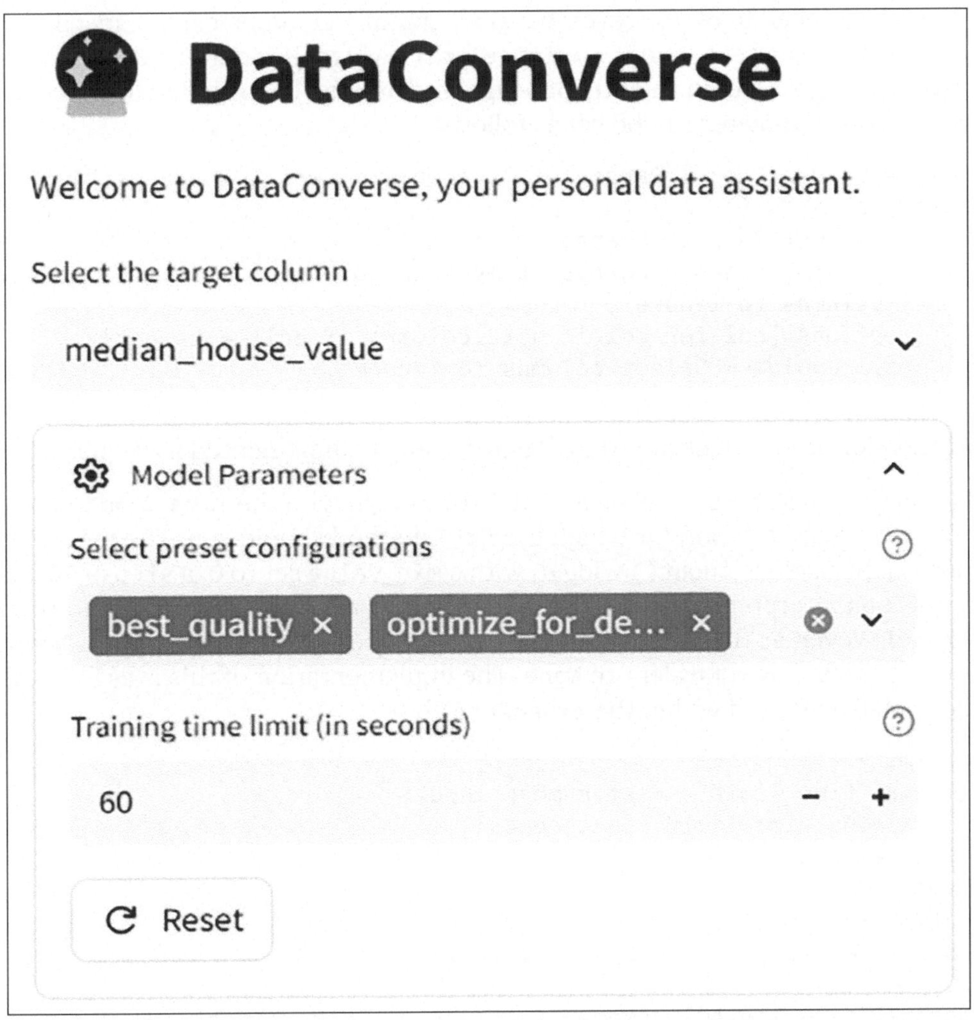

Figure 15.2: *Sample Model Configuration Section*

It is now possible to add configuration widgets within the **expander()**. Given that the datasets will be tabular, the parameters available for AutoGluon's **TabularPredictor** class will be utilized. Three categories of parameters can be customized: the **TabularPredictor** class initialization parameters, the **fit()** method parameters, and the **predict()** method parameters. Comprehensive documentation for these parameters is available in the AutoGluon documentation at https://auto.gluon.ai/stable/api/autogluon.tabular.TabularPredictor.html.

As this list is quite extensive, only a selection of these parameters will be used in this tutorial. However, readers are encouraged to experiment with a broader range of parameters.

To simplify the process of passing parameters to AutoGluon, all parameters will be passed as keyword arguments (**kwargs**). These will be stored as key-value pairs within a dictionary, with distinct dictionaries for initialization, **fit**, and **predict** parameters.

Let us begin with the initialization parameters. Among the initialization parameters, **ignored_columns** is particularly important. This parameter enables the user to exclude specific dataset columns during the model training process. This can be beneficial when the dataset contains columns with no predictive value, such as ID fields or names. Because **ignored_columns** is a learner keyword argument, it is necessary first to initialize an empty dictionary named **init_params**. Subsequently, an empty nested dictionary named **learner_kwargs** must be created within **init_params** before the value of this parameter can be stored.

As this parameter also accepts a list of DataFrame columns, the same logic employed for the target **selectbox()** can be applied here. However, because multiple columns can be specified as **ignored_columns** (unlike the single target column), a **multiselect()** widget is required instead of a **selectbox()**. Furthermore, as the target column should not be ignored, it must be excluded from the list of options. The **ignored_columns** parameter can be set as follows:

```
with st.expander("Model Parameters", icon=":material/settings:"):
    init_params = {}
    init_params["learner_kwargs"] = {}
    init_params["learner_kwargs"]["ignored_columns"] = st.multiselect(
        "Columns to ignore",
        options=[col for col in data.columns if col != target],
        placeholder="Select columns to ignore",
    )
```

Additional widgets for other initialization parameters can be implemented as required.

Next, the **fit()** method parameters will be added. Let us begin with the **time_limit** parameter, which determines the maximum duration for which the **fit()** method should run. The most suitable widget for this purpose is the **number_input()** widget, with a **min_value** set to 0, a **step** of 10, and a **default** value of 0. AutoGluon interprets a value of **None** for **time_limit** as an instruction to run without any time constraint. However, as the **number_input()** widget does not directly support **None** as an input, a value of 0 will be treated as equivalent to **None**. The implementation of this is as follows. Please note that this code should be placed within the **expander()** block:

```
fit_params = {}
fit_params["time_limit"] = st.number_input(
    "Training time limit (in seconds)",
    min_value=0,
    value=0,
    step=10,
    help="`0` will remove any time limit",
)
fit_params["time_limit"] = None if fit_params["time_limit"] == 0 else fit_
params["time_limit"]
```

Another significant and highly useful **fit()** parameter is **presets**. This is a list of preset configurations for various arguments in **fit()**, such as **best_quality**, **optimize_for_deployment**, and **ignore_text**, among others. A comprehensive list of all available presets, along with their descriptions, can be found in the **fit()** method's API reference at https://auto.gluon.ai/stable/api/autogluon.tabular.TabularPredictor.fit.html.

This also necessitates the use of a **multiselect()** widget. Given that the list of presets is predefined, a static list of options can be provided. As the application will be deployed in the cloud, having the **best_quality** and **optimize_for_deployment** presets as defaults is advisable to generate an optimized model with high performance and a minimal size.

The code to generate the presets widget is as follows:

```
fit_params["presets"] = st.multiselect(
    "Select preset configurations",
    options=[
        "best_quality",
        "high_quality",
        "good_quality",
        "medium_quality",
        "experimental_quality",
        "optimize_for_deployment",
        "interpretable",
        "ignore_text",
    ],
    default=["best_quality", "optimize_for_deployment"],
    help="List of preset configurations.",
    placeholder="Select preset configurations",
)
```

Regarding the **predict()** method parameters, these typically do not require modification.

However, should you wish to explore these further, a complete list of available parameters can be found here: https://auto.gluon.ai/stable/api/autogluon.tabular.TabularPredictor.predict.html.

Resetting AutoGluon Parameters

In this example, only three parameters have been customized; however, more can be added as needed. Having many such widgets can make it challenging for users to revert these parameters to their default values. A Reset button should be provided to facilitate this, similar to the global Reset button located at the top of the sidebar, but specifically for model parameters.

There are multiple ways this can be done. One seemingly straightforward method involves updating a widget's value to its default setting by explicitly assigning this value to the associated session state, as discussed in *Chapter 7, Widget Keys and Callbacks*. Although functional, this method can become cumbersome and lead to more complex code, particularly when dealing with many widgets.

A more straightforward solution, which is also scalable to any number of widgets, is to modify the widget's key entirely. As detailed in *Chapter 7, Widget Keys and Callbacks*, each widget possesses a unique identifier determined by the widget's page, its parameters, and the key assigned by the user. Altering any of these attributes results in an updated identifier, causing Streamlit to recognize it as a completely new widget. This behavior can be leveraged to update the widget key when clicking the Reset button. This action prompts Streamlit to generate new but structurally similar widgets with their default values.

One method to implement this approach is to append an incrementing suffix to the widget key each time the **Reset** button is activated. To achieve this, it is first necessary to assign a widget key to each of the parameter widgets, incorporating a suffix stored within the session state. For instance, the key for the **ignored_columns** widget can be defined as **f"ignored_columns_{st.session_state.get('key_suffix', 0)}"**.

Assign a similar key to all parameter widgets, and then create a code block for the `Reset` button within the parameters, **`expander()`** as follows:

```
if st.button("Reset", icon=":material/refresh:"):
    st.session_state["key_suffix"] = st.session_state.get("key_suffix", 0) + 1
    st.rerun()
```

Initially, before the `Reset` button has been clicked, the **`key_suffix`** session state does not exist, and all widget keys implicitly have a suffix of `0`. Upon clicking the `Reset` button, the **`key_suffix`** session state is initialized (if it does not already exist), and its value is incremented by `1`. Consequently, each click of the `Reset` button increments the widget key by `1`, prompting Streamlit to replace the existing widget with a new but structurally identical widget that retains its default values, thereby effectively resetting the parameters.

At this point, the `Model Parameters` section will resemble *Figure* 15.3.

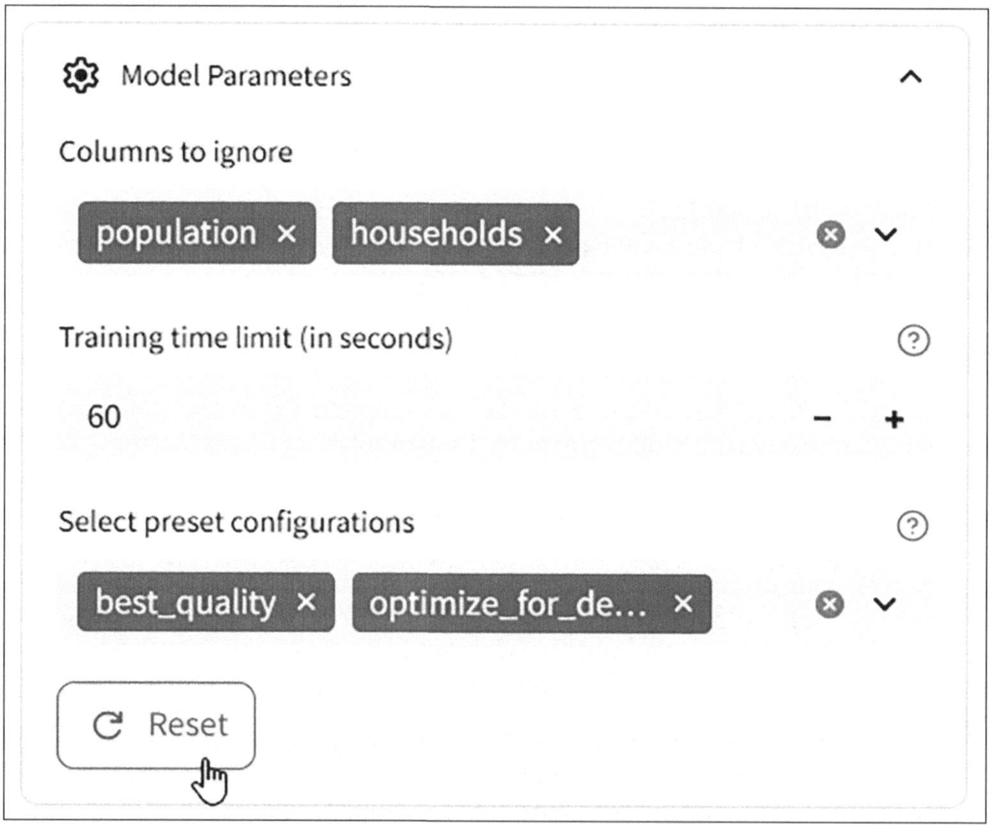

Figure 15.3: *Model Parameters Section*

Upon clicking `Reset`, the widgets will be reset to their default values.

Tasks:

1. *All the widgets are currently arranged vertically in one column. This results in a significant amount of wasted space, and can be inconvenient when there are numerous parameters. Arrange the layout so that the widgets are spread across multiple columns. Note that all widgets do not need to have the same width.*
2. *Add a confirmation dialog to the model parameters reset button as was done for the global reset button in the previous chapter.*

Training the Models

With the AutoGluon parameters now configured, the next step is to train the model. Behind the scenes, AutoGluon trains multiple models concurrently, and subsequently selects and returns the best-performing one.

First, it is necessary to import the **`TabularPredictor`** class from the **`autogluon.tabular`** module, as shown in the following code:

```
from autogluon.tabular import TabularPredictor
```

Next, a **`Train Model`** button is created. Activating this button will initiate the model training process. For the training process, the **`TabularPredictor()`** is initialized by providing the target column and the initialization parameters stored in the **`init_params`** dictionary, which were configured in the preceding section. Subsequently, the model is trained using the **`fit()`** method on the training data, which is stored in the session state, and utilizing the fit parameters defined in the **`fit_params`** dictionary in the previous section. This is done as follows:

```
if st.button("Train Model", icon=":material/model_training:", type="primary"):
    predictor = TabularPredictor(
        label=target,
        verbosity=0,
        **init_params,
    ).fit(train_data=data, **fit_params)
```

The `predictor` variable here refers to the best model identified and returned by AutoGluon. The **`verbosity`** parameter is set to `0` to suppress the display of console logs during the training process.

This method can be used directly. However, model training can be time-consuming. If implemented in this manner, the model will need to be retrained every time there is interaction with the application that causes the script to rerun. This is where the **`session_state`** feature can be utilized.

By leveraging **`session_state`**, the trained model can be stored within the session, thus making it possible to use the trained model in other places, without calling the training method every time. Replace the `predictor` variable with **`st.session_state["predictor"]`**.

Nevertheless, this approach addresses only a portion of the challenge. Consider the scenario where the user clicks the **`Train Model`** button again. Alternatively, what happens if the user experiments with different parameter settings, and then reverts to an initial set of parameters to train the model? In both situations, the application will initiate the model training process from the beginning, even if a model has already been trained using the same set of parameters and data. This is where the **`cache_resource`** decorator can be employed.

To cache the training functionality, it is necessary to encapsulate it within a function decorated with **`@st.cache_resource`**. It is expected that the same output will be produced given the same target column, training data, and parameters. Therefore, the inputs to this cached function will be the target column, the training data, and all the customized parameters. The output of this function will be the trained model.

Note: *Due to the non-deterministic nature inherent in some machine learning models, which is further amplified by the use of AutoML, it is possible to obtain different models for the same input data and even different predictions for identical inputs applied to the same model. However, this inherent randomness can be disregarded for the purposes of this application. Further information regarding the non-deterministic nature of machine learning can be found in this blog post: https://yetiai.com/is-machine-learning-deterministic/.*

The implementation of the cached training function is presented in the following code:

```
@st.cache_resource(show_spinner="Training model...")
def train_model(
    target: str, data: pd.DataFrame, init_params: dict, fit_params: dict
):
    predictor = TabularPredictor(
        label=target,
        verbosity=0,
        **init_params,
    ).fit(data, **fit_params)

    return predictor
```

The spinner provides visual feedback to the user, indicating that the application is actively running in the background, and has not encountered any issues.

Based on the preceding explanation, the following code snippet the `Train Model` button should be updated to utilize this function. The updated code snippet is presented as follows:

```
if st.button("Train Model", icon=":material/model_training:", type="primary"):
    st.session_state["predictor"] = train_model(
        target=target,
        data=data,
        init_params=init_params,
        fit_params=fit_params,
    )
```

To indicate that the model training has been completed successfully, a success message can be added:

```
if st.session_state.get("predictor"):
    st.success("Model trained successfully!", icon=":material/check_circle:")
    predictor = st.session_state["predictor"]
```

With the model now trained, the following steps involve exploring its details, and utilizing it to make predictions.

Exploring Model Details

This section is optional and intended for advanced users who wish to inspect the details of the models that AutoGluon trains manually.

While numerous methods and attributes of the **`TabularPredictor`** class can be used to examine the models, this section will focus on three specific ones: **`leaderboard()`**, **`feature_importance()`**, and **`info()`**. Readers are encouraged to explore other available methods and attributes to expand this section further. The complete documentation is available at this link: https://auto.gluon.ai/stable/api/autogluon.tabular.TabularPredictor.html#autogluon.tabular.TabularPredictor.

As this section is optional, it can be organized within an **`expander()`** widget, similar to the **`Model Parameters`** section. Furthermore, because retrieving some of the model details can take time, these methods should be called only when explicitly requested by the user, rather than automatically. This can be achieved by using a **`button()`** widget.

A sample implementation is as follows, and the resulting section with details for the `Titanic` dataset is shown in the following *Figure* 15.4:

```
with st.expander("Model Details", icon=":material/info:"):
    if st.button("Fetch Model Details", icon=":material/info:"):
        st.subheader(":material/leaderboard: Model Leaderboard")
```

```
st.dataframe(predictor.leaderboard(data))
st.subheader(":material/bar_chart: Feature Importance")
st.dataframe(predictor.feature_importance(data))
st.subheader(":material/info: Model Info")
st.write(predictor.info())
```

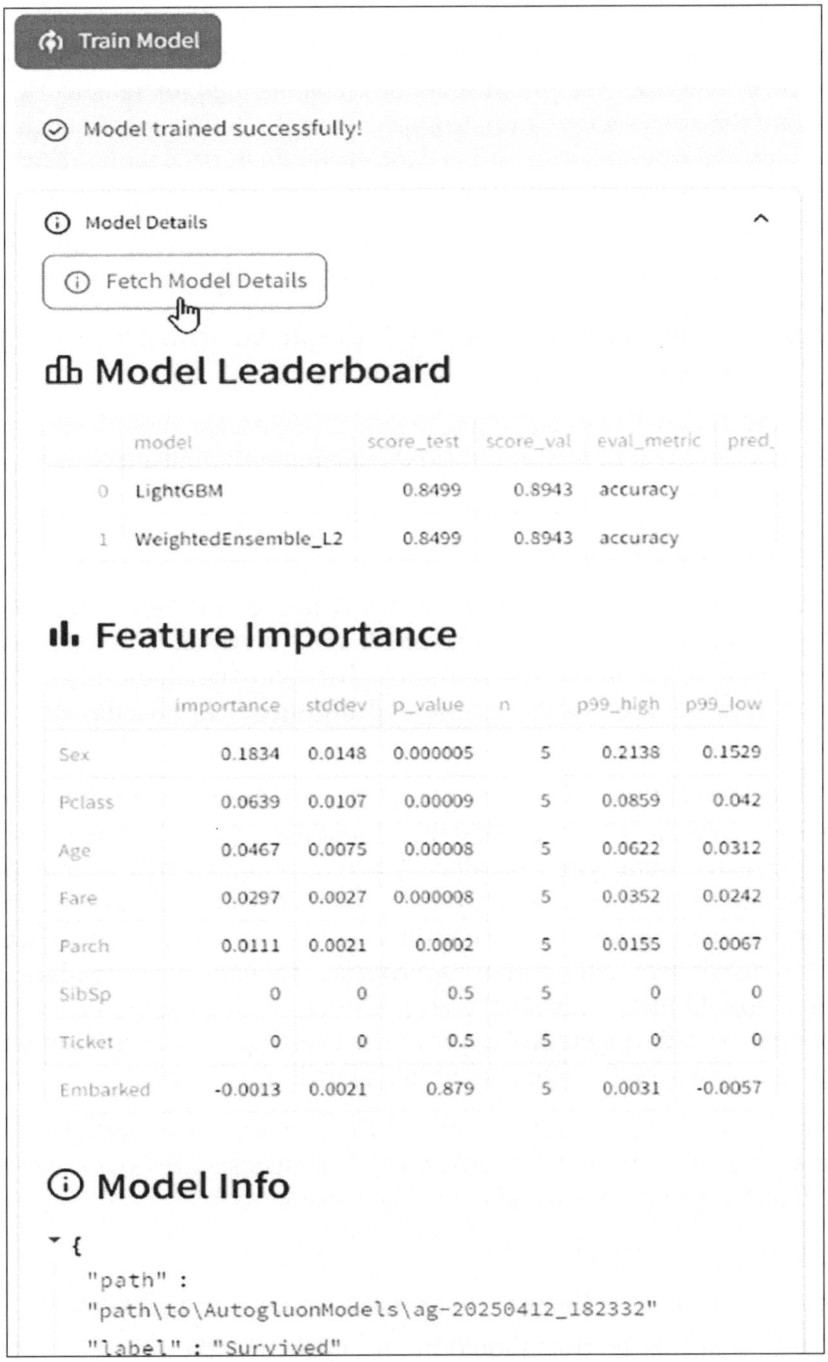

Figure 15.4: *Model Details*

Here, the **`Model Leaderboard`** displays all the models generated during the **`fit()`** process, their respective performance scores, training and inference times, and other relevant details.

The **`Feature Importance`** functionality calculates the importance of scores for each feature in the best model trained by AutoGluon. The feature importance score quantifies how much each feature (or variable) influences the model's output, with higher scores indicating more significant importance. For the example shown in *Figure 15.4*, it can be observed that `Sex` and `Age` were important factors in determining whether a passenger survived. This observation aligns with the historical fact that women and children were given priority for boarding lifeboats.

This method accepts several parameters that can be used to control its behavior. A complete list of these parameters is available at https://auto.gluon.ai/stable/api/autogluon.tabular.TabularPredictor.feature_importance.html.

Note: *For the sake of simplicity in this tutorial, the original training data has been passed to the* `feature_importance()` *method. This practice is not recommended for real-world applications, as it can introduce bias into the scores due to overfitting. The original data should be divided into training and test datasets for optimal results. The training dataset should be used with the* `fit()` *method, and the test dataset should be used with the* `feature_importance()` *method.*

More details about splitting data into training and test sets are available at https://machinelearningmastery.com/train-test-split-for-evaluating-machine-learning-algorithms/.

`Model Info` provides all the metadata associated with the predictor, including comprehensive details of all trained models, presented in a dictionary format.

This detailed information can assist advanced users in adjusting model parameters to enhance performance, and can also aid in understanding and explaining the outputs of the models.

Making Predictions

The model can now be used to generate predictions based on data provided by users. While this might seem as straightforward as calling `predict()` method, it is important to remember that obtaining user input is the initial requirement. The primary challenge in this section lies in developing a user-friendly method for data input, without prior knowledge of the specific dataset the user will employ.

Although utilizing a `textbox()` for all columns might seem the most straightforward approach, it is not particularly user-friendly and necessitates manual data type conversion and validation. This is crucial to ensure that the data type provided by the user for each field matches the input data type on which the model was trained. Failure to ensure data type compatibility could result in errors during the prediction process. To provide an optimal user experience, the application should allow users to input data using widgets that are most appropriate for each column's data type. For instance, a categorical column should utilize a `selectbox()` widget, while a numerical column should use a `number_input()` widget. These widgets will improve the user experience, and simplify data validation, as they only accept data of a specific type and within a particular range.

This presents a complication because, as the user chooses the original dataset, the number of columns and their respective data types are initially unknown. This necessitates the dynamic creation of the appropriate number and type of input widgets during runtime.

Let us begin by creating a subheading for this section:

```
st.subheader(":material/input: Enter data to get prediction")
```

It is important to note that this section should be placed within the initial `if st.session_state.get("predictor")` block, as it should only be visible after a model has been successfully trained.

The initial step here involves identifying the columns for which input widgets are required. This is a relatively straightforward process. The goal is to include all columns in the dataset, excluding those ignored in the `Model Parameters` section and the target column itself.

Next, the data type of each column is checked to determine if it is an **object** type. If the column's data type is an **object**, a **selectbox()** widget is created. Otherwise, a **number_input()** widget is used.

```
st.subheader(":material/input: Enter data to get prediction")
input_columns = [
    col
    for col in data.columns
    if col not in init_params["learner_kwargs"]["ignored_columns"] and col !=
target
]
```

The **input_columns** list can be iterated through to generate the input widgets, and their respective values can be assigned to a **user_input** dictionary, as shown in the following code:

```
user_input = {}
for column in input_columns:
    if data[column].dtype == "object":
        user_input[column] = st.selectbox(
            column,
            options=sorted(data[column].fillna("").unique()),
            accept_new_options=True,
        )
    else:
        user_input[column] = st.number_input(
            column,
            min_value=data[column].min(),
            max_value=data[column].max(),
        )
```

For the **selectbox()** widget, all the unique values in the column are displayed as options. These options are sorted to enable easier data discovery. As sorting is not effective when the column contains **Null** values, the **fillna("")** method is used to replace any **Null** values with an empty string before sorting. The **accept_new_options** parameter lets users enter data that the model has not seen during training.

For the **number_input()** widget, the minimum and maximum values from the data within the column are used as the **min_value** and **max_value** for the widget. This constraint is necessary for certain models, such as decision-tree-based models, as they cannot process input values outside the range observed in the training data. However, if the models used do not have this requirement, such as regression models, the minimum and maximum value constraints can be removed, allowing users to enter any desired value.

For the Titanic dataset, with the **PassengerId** and Name columns ignored, the resulting section on the app is shown in the following *Figure* 15.5:

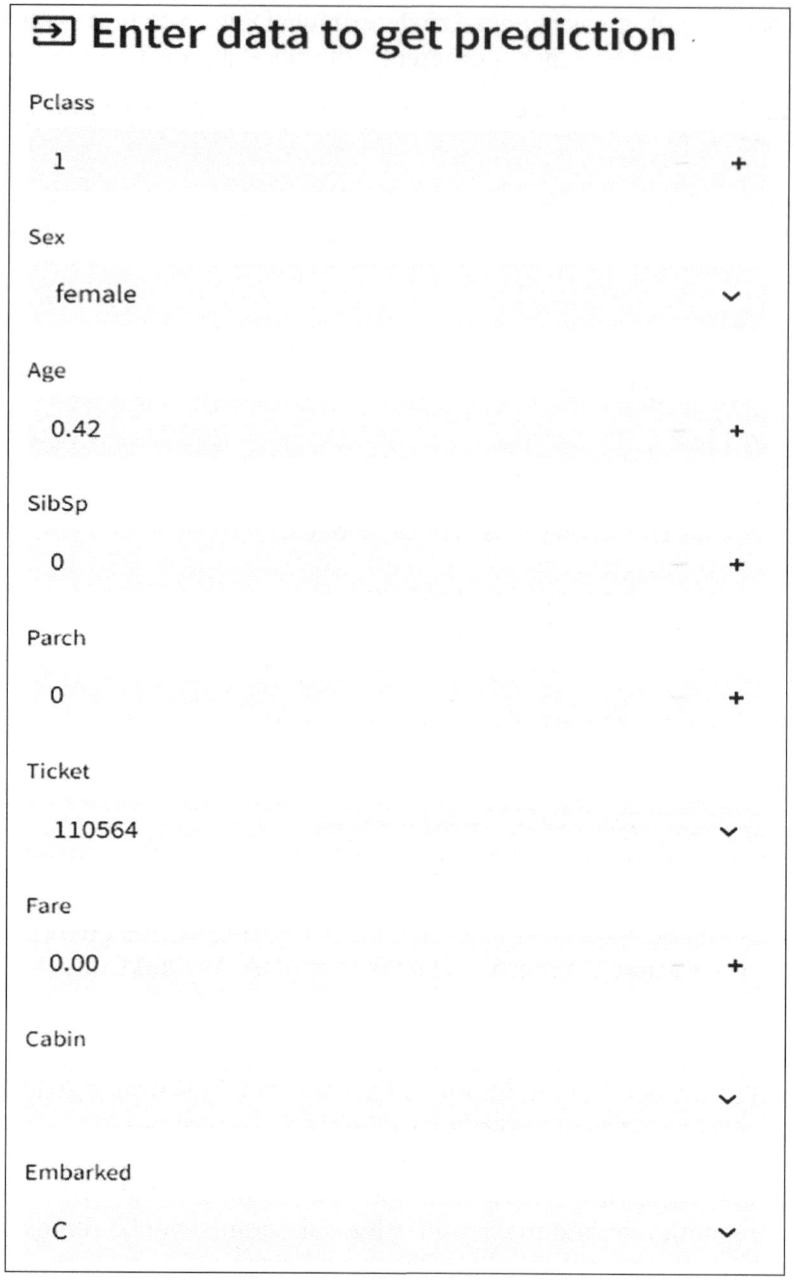

Figure 15.5: *Data Entry Section*

While functional, this layout presents certain inconveniences:

- The widgets are not ordered, making it difficult for users to locate a specific widget.
- All widgets are arranged vertically in a single column. This results in significant wasted horizontal space, as the widgets do not require such width, and can lead to excessive vertical scrolling, if many input fields are present.

The columns can be sorted alphabetically, and then distributed across three layout columns to address these issues. This can be achieved by updating the previous code block as follows, with the modifications highlighted:

```
layout_columns = st.columns(3)
for idx, column in enumerate(sorted(input_columns)):
    if data[column].dtype == "object":
        user_input[column] = layout_columns[idx % 3].selectbox(
            column,
```

```
            options=sorted(data[column].fillna(" ").unique()),
        )
    else:
        user_input[column] = layout_columns[idx % 3].number_input(
            column,
            min_value=data[column].min(),
            max_value=data[column].max(),
        )
```

The resulting layout is shown in the following *Figure* 15.6:

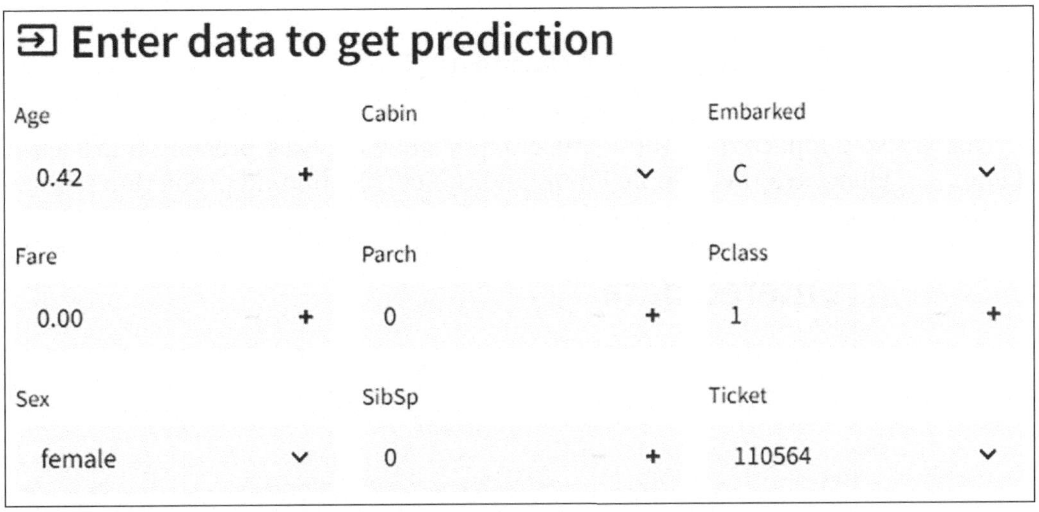

Figure 15.6: *Organized Data Entry Section*

As can be observed, this arrangement is significantly more organized and user-friendly than the previous one.

The mechanism by which this code evenly distributes the widgets across the three columns is explained as follows.

Initially, a list of three **`layout_columns`** is created using **`st.columns(3)`**. Next, the **`enumerate()`** function is used to iterate through the sorted **`input_columns`**, returning both the index (**`idx`**) and the name of each input column.

Subsequently, this index is divided by 3, and the column whose index matches the remainder of this division (**`idx % 3`**) is selected to render the corresponding input widget.

For example, considering the first column, **`Age`**, its index (**`idx`**) is `0`. The remainder of 0 divided by 3 (**`idx`** `% 3`) is also 0. Therefore, **`column[0]`**, which represents the first column, is used to render the input widget for `Age`.

Similarly, the index (**`idx`**) is 4 for the fifth column, `Parch`. The remainder of 4 divided by 3 is 1. Consequently, the input widget for `Parch` is rendered in the second column, **`column[1]`**.

This demonstrates an efficient method for dynamically arranging widgets, even when the total number of widgets is unknown beforehand.

Once the user has provided all the necessary input, a simple table can be used to display a summary of the entered data for validation purposes:

```
st.subheader("Entered data")
st.table(user_input)
```

Finally, to generate predictions, a **Predict** button is added. Upon activation, this button calls the **.predict()** method of the trained **predictor** object, passing the **user_input** data, which is first converted into a DataFrame format to match the format of the training dataset.

The prediction result can then be displayed by accessing the first element of the array returned by the **.predict()** method.

```
if st.button("Predict", icon=":material/rocket:", type="primary"):
    prediction = predictor.predict(
        pd.DataFrame([user_input]),
        as_pandas=False,
    )
    st.subheader(f"{target}: {prediction[0]}")
```

For a sample input with a low **Age** and **female Sex**, historical evidence suggests a high likelihood of survival. This is also supported by the feature importance analysis presented in *Figure* 15.4. The following *Figure* 15.7 illustrates this sample input, and the corresponding prediction result generated by the model:

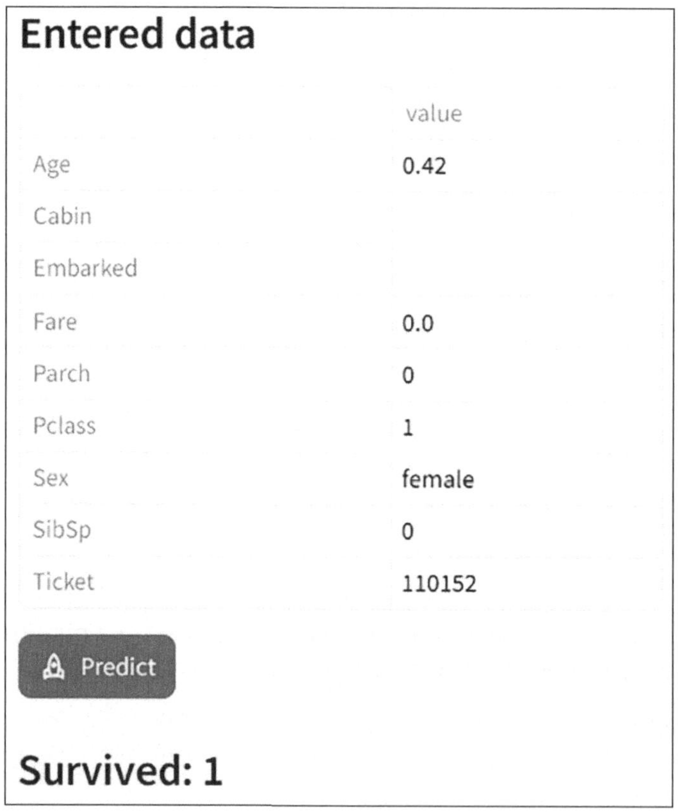

Figure 15.7: *Summary of User Input and Prediction Results*

As anticipated, the model predicts that this passenger would have survived the event.

Conclusion

This chapter has expanded upon the **DataConverse** application by incorporating prediction capabilities within the `Predict` page.

This page enables users to train an AutoML model using their own data, and subsequently generate predictions on new data using the trained model. Additionally, for advanced users, sections have been included to allow for adjusting the model's default parameters, and the detailed exploration of model characteristics for debugging and explainability purposes.

Throughout this process, we have also learned how to reset the values of multiple widgets using a button and their associated widget keys, and how to create as well as arrange widgets dynamically during runtime. These skills will prove highly valuable in developing user-friendly, production-grade applications where all necessary parameters might not be known or predictable beforehand.

The next and final chapter will conclude the development of the application by building a chatbot that will allow users to interact with their data through conversation.

Advanced Assignments

1. Discuss the advantages and disadvantages of using AutoML tools such as AutoGluon compared to manually building and tuning Machine Learning models. When might using AutoML be the most appropriate approach, and when might manual development be preferred?
2. Currently, the chapter focuses on training and prediction. Extend the app to display relevant model evaluation metrics (for example, accuracy, precision, recall, F1-score for classification; RMSE, MAE for regression) after the model is trained. Allow users to select which metrics they want to see. A summary of the different model evaluation metrics available in scikit-learn is available here: https://coderzcolumn.com/tutorials/machine-learning/model-evaluation-scoring-metrics-scikit-learn-sklearn.
3. Integrate visualizations (for example, confusion matrix for classification, scatter plot of predicted vs. actual values for regression) to provide a more intuitive understanding of the model's performance. Use Streamlit's charting capabilities for this.
4. The current implementation handles **`object`** and numerical data types. Extend it to handle other common data types like dates and booleans for prediction input, using appropriate Streamlit widgets (for example, **`st.date_input()`**, **`st.checkbox()`**).
5. The current version of the application only allows users to generate predictions for a single row of data at a time. Implement functionality that will enable users to upload a CSV file with the same format as the training dataset, and generate predictions for all rows within the file. The prediction results should be displayed within the application alongside the uploaded data, and available for download as a CSV file.

Key Terms

- **Automated Machine Learning (AutoML):** The process of automating the end-to-end process of applying machine learning to real-world problems.[1]
- **Overfitting:** This occurs when a model learns the training data too well, capturing noise and details that do not generalize to new data.[2]

[1] *Spears, Taylor; Bondo Hansen, Kristian (2023-12-18), "The Use and Promises of Machine Learning in Financial Markets", The Oxford Handbook of the Sociology of Machine Learning, Oxford University Press, doi:10.1093/oxfordhb/9780197653609.013.6,* ISBN 978-0-19-765360-9, *retrieved* 2024-06-10

[2] *https://www.geeksforgeeks.org/underfitting-and-overfitting-in-machine-learning/* (Accessed: 13 April 2025)

CHAPTER 16
Building a Chatbot on Streamlit

Introduction

We have journeyed through data loading, analysis, and predictive modeling. Now, we will bring our application to life by integrating a conversational AI, transforming it from a static analysis tool into an interactive data partner.

This chapter begins with a brief introduction to various Large Language Model (LLM) providers available for use.

Using Google's Gemini API, you will employ techniques such as prompt engineering to enable users to chat with the LLM about their data. While doing so, you will learn about the **`system prompt`** and how it can be used to control an LLM's responses. Additionally, you will learn how to authenticate users using the Gemini API key, create a new chat, using any of the available models, learn about the role **`temperature`** plays in generating responses, display streaming responses, and add additional features to the app, like being able to download conversations in markdown format.

You will finally be equipped to create and deploy your own GenAI Chat Applications.

Note: *As stated in the previous chapters, the design decisions and features presented here should serve as recommendations rather than strict rules. You are encouraged to develop your own designs and implementations.*

Structure

This chapter will cover the following topics:

- Brief Exploration of LLM Providers
- Gemini API Prerequisites
- User Authentication
- Chatting with the Chatbot
    - Selecting a Model
    - Starting a Chat
    - Sending and Receiving Messages
    - Providing Context to the Chatbot
        - Using the System Prompt
    - Displaying the Conversation History

- Additional Features
  - Tuning Responses Using the Temperature
  - Downloading the Conversation
  - Streaming Responses

Brief Exploration of LLM Providers

To create a natural, non-robotic user experience in a chatbot, it is highly effective to use LLMs. There are many different providers, such as OpenAI, DeepSeek, Perplexity, Google, Anthropic, and Cohere, that offer access to their LLMs hosted on their servers via an Application Programming Interface (API). While proprietary chat applications like chatgpt.com are often available free of charge (within certain limits), programmatic access to these models typically requires payment to cover development and hosting costs. To use their models in our application, we will need programmatic access. While you are free to pay for and use any API you prefer, we aim to avoid paid services to ensure accessibility for all readers.

Then there are open-source LLM developers such as Meta, Google, Mistral, and DeepSeek, among others. These companies make some of their LLMs available for free download and hosting on your computers using platforms like Ollama. However, running models locally requires relatively high-end devices. Since this approach requires a local Ollama server, it cannot be used for apps deployed to the Streamlit Community Cloud.

This leaves us with providers that host models, and allow us to access them programmatically via an API for free, at least within limits. Some providers that do this are Google and OpenRouter. As of writing, Google provides limited free API access to its Gemini models, while OpenRouter has an assortment of open-source models, you can access for free with their API, again within limits. OpenRouter's advantage is being able to use the same API for models from different developers, allowing you to easily switch without making any code changes. However, Google's Gemini API is more user-friendly, and the Gemini models are generally better than the free ones provided by OpenRouter. We will use the Gemini API in this chapter, but you are encouraged to explore and use any API you prefer.

Gemini API Prerequisites

Using the Gemini API requires a Google account and a Gemini API token, both of which are free to create. If you do not have one already, you can create a Gemini API token at https://aistudio.google.com/app/apikey. This page will also guide you through the process of creating a Google account, if you do not already have one.

Once the API key is created, you can copy it from the same page.

Note: *The API key is your identifier. Keep it secured by not sharing it, adding it to public code, or committing it to public repositories.*

The **`google-genai`** Python library is also required. Install it using **`pip install -U google-genai`**.

Remember to add it to your **`requirements.txt`** file.

Note: *In this chapter, we have used **`google-genai`** version 1.47.0.*

There are rate limits applied to free-tier use of the Gemini API. These limits depend on the model being used and change over time. Up-to-date limits are available at https://ai.google.dev/gemini-api/docs/rate-limits#current-rate-limits. These rates are generous enough to allow for most individual learning use. However, if you feel you would need higher rate limits, you can upgrade to a higher tier.

If you want to only use your app locally, on your machine, you can use Ollama. A comprehensive video tutorial is available at https://youtu.be/bAI_jWsLhFM. Remember that Ollama does not work with Streamlit Community Cloud, so apps built on it cannot be uploaded to the Community Cloud.

The concepts explained in this chapter will be relevant, irrespective of the API being used, although there may be slight differences in the implementation.

User Authentication

Note: *Unless mentioned otherwise, all the codes in this chapter applies to the* **`chat.py`** *file.*

The first step for using the Gemini API is to create a **`client`** using the Gemini API key. As mentioned earlier, this key identifies a user and should be treated with the same security considerations as a password. As convention, and for a streamlined User Experience (UX), we should let users enter their API key in a password-style text box in the sidebar, as follows:

```
import streamlit as st

with st.sidebar:
    st.divider()
    st.session_state["gemini_api_key"] = st.text_input(
        "Enter your Gemini API Key",
        type="password",
        help="API key will not be stored in the app.",
        value=st.session_state.get("gemini_api_key", ""),
    )

if st.session_state.get("gemini_api_key") == "":
    st.warning(
        "Enter your Gemini API Key to start chatting."
        " You can create a free Gemini API Key [here](https://aistudio.google.
com/app/api-keys).",
        icon=":material/warning:",
    )
    st.stop()
```

The text input accepts the key, and hides it as a password. When no key has been entered, its value defaults to blank (**`""`**), and the text box is empty. In this condition, the app prompts the user to do so. It also includes a link to the page from which a free Gemini API key can be generated.

If a key has been entered, it is stored in the **`gemini_api_key`** session state, and becomes the default value of the text input box. This provides visual feedback to the user that an API key has been entered. Without this implementation, the text input would appear blank after an app rerun, even though the key was correctly saved in the session state.

The state of the app, without the API key entered, is shown in *Figure* 16.1.

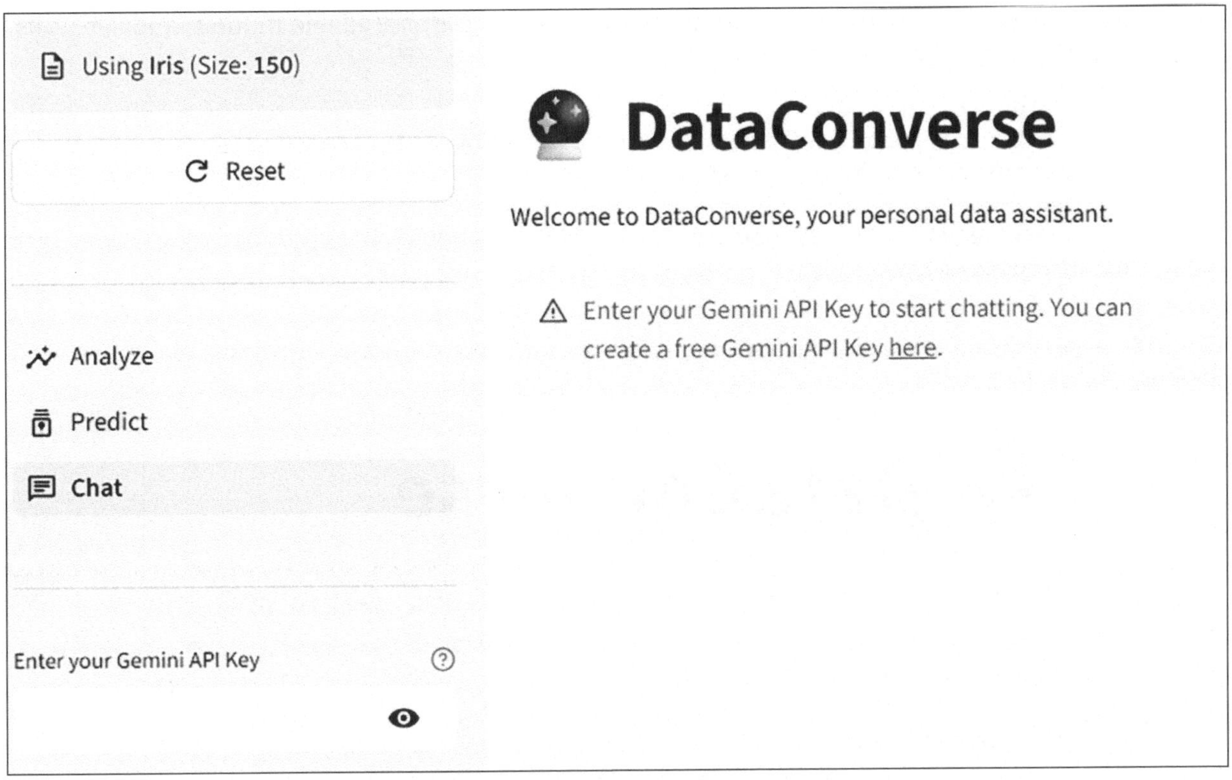

Figure 16.1: *Chat Page before Entering the Gemini API Key*

Chatting with the Chatbot

Once the API key has been entered, you can start chatting with the chatbot. The first step is to initialize the genai **`client`** using the API key and cache this process so that the **`client`** is reused for the same API key. This can be done as follows:

```
from google import genai
...

@st.cache_resource
def get_client(api_key: str):
    return genai.Client(api_key=api_key)


client = get_client(st.session_state["gemini_api_key"])
```

Once the client has been created, you can create a new **`chat`**. A **`chat`**, in Google terminology, is a collection of multiple rounds of prompts and responses.[1] This enables the model to remember the whole conversation history for more contextual responses.

Selecting a Model

To start a new **`chat`**, you first need to select a relevant Gemini **`model`**. There can be multiple approaches to this. The approach we take is to show a **`New Chat`** dialog that lets users choose a model, and start a new chat.

[1] *https://ai.google.dev/gemini-api/docs/text-generation?authuser=1#multi-turn-conversations* (Accessed: 10 July 2025)

To start, add a **selectbox** that lets users pick a model from a list of available models, and save this in the **model** session state, as follows:

```
st.session_state["model"] = st.selectbox(
    ":material/robot: Select a model to use for this chat",
    options=client.models.list(),
    index=None,
    help="Details of all models can be found [here](https://ai.google.dev/gem-
ini-api/docs/models).",
)
```

This adds a **selectbox** with all available models populated as dropdown options, as shown in the following *Figure 16.2*.

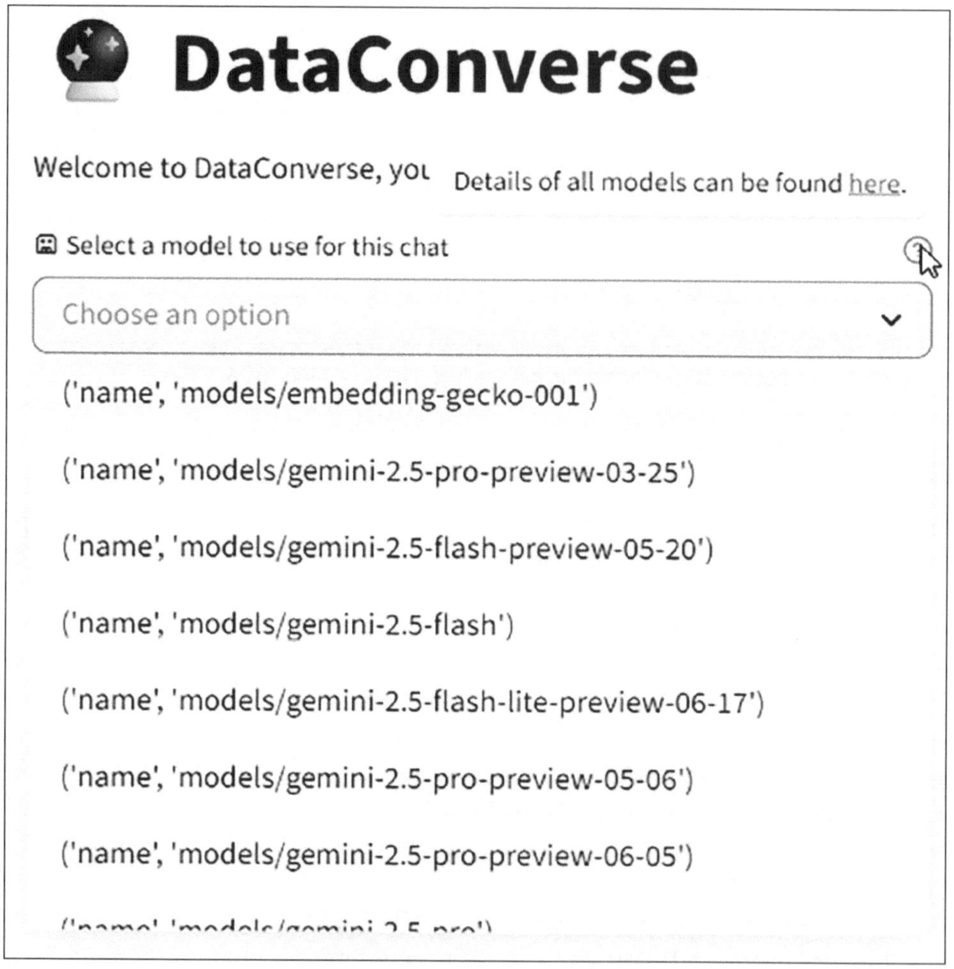

Figure 16.2: *Model Selection Options*

There are a couple of issues with this:

- The options are unsorted, making it harder to find a particular model, without already knowing its name. They are also not in a format accepted by the chat API.
- The options can include old models that have been deprecated. A lot of models are also not relevant to the task. For example, the **imagen** models are used to generate images, not text.
- There is no description of the model to help users select an appropriate model.

To be able to address these concerns, you need to know the output format of **`client.models.list()`**. You can write the contents of a single item from the list using **`st.write(client.models.list()[0])`**. The output will be something as follows (note that the structure and results might change over time):

```
{
        "name":"models/embedding-gecko-001"
        "display_name":"Embedding Gecko"
        "description":"Obtain a distributed representation of a text."
        "version":"001"
        "endpoints":NULL
        "labels":NULL
        "tuned_model_info":"TunedModelInfo()"
        "input_token_limit":1024
        "output_token_limit":1
        "supported_actions":[
               0:"embedText"
               1:"countTextTokens"
        ]
        "default_checkpoint_id":NULL
        "checkpoints":NULL
}
```

As you can see, it is a dictionary containing model details. The important details here are **`name`**, **`description`**, and **`supported actions`**. These are the ones we shall use to address the concerns mentioned previously.

Formatting the Options

As seen in the output sample, we can access the name of the model through its **`name`** attribute. This can then be sorted using the **`sorted()`** function, and the redundant **`models/`**prefixes can be removed from the results using the **`replace()`** method. All of this can be done in one line, using list comprehension, as highlighted in the following code snippet:

```
st.session_state["model"] = st.selectbox(
    ":material/robot: Select a model to use for this chat",
    options=sorted([model.name.replace("models/", "") for model in
client.models.list()]),
    index=None,
    help="Details of all models can be found [here](https://ai.google.dev/
gemini-api/docs/models).",
)
```

This shows only the names of the models, in alphabetical order, as shown in the following *Figure* 16.3.

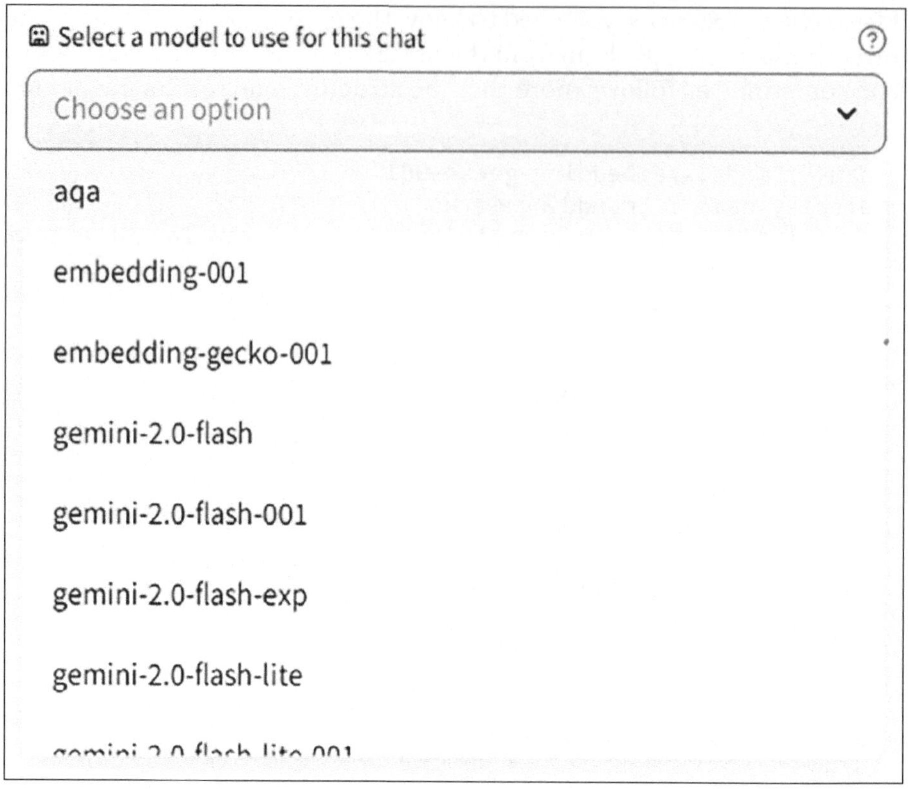

Figure 16.3: *Model Names in Sorted Order*

Showing Only Relevant Models

Now that the options have been formatted, the next step is to display only relevant models. There are two parts to this: showing only models from an appropriate model family, that is, a new series of models that have better performance and have not been deprecated, and showing only models that can generate text.

Since the model dictionary does not contain any details around its release or deprecation date, or which family it belongs to, you have to fetch the latest model from the model name itself. This can easily be done by adding an `if` condition in the list comprehension that checks if the model name ends with **`the latest`**, as highlighted in the following code snippet:

```
st.session_state["model"] = st.selectbox(
    ":material/robot: Select a model to use for this chat",
    options=sorted(
        [
            model.name.replace("models/", "")
            for model in client.models.list()
            if model.name.endswith("latest")
        ]
    ),
    index=None,
    help="Details of all models can be found [here](https://ai.google.dev/
gemini-api/docs/models).",
)
```

Once this filter is added, only the latest models will be available in the dropdown, as shown in the following *Figure 16.4*.

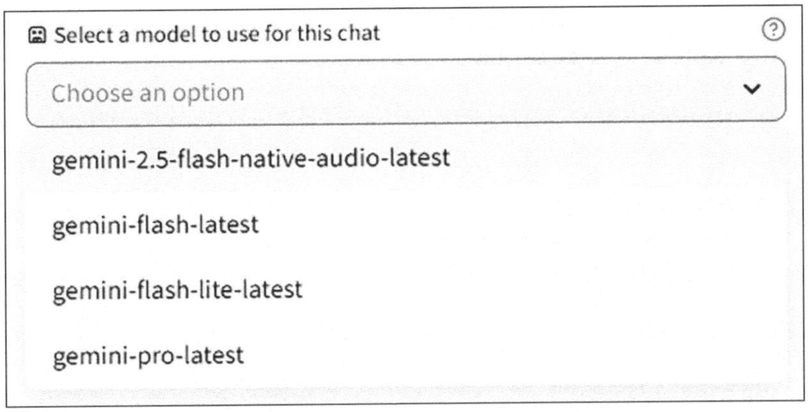

Figure 16.4: *Filtering Only the Latest Models*

As you can see in this list, there is a **gemini-2.5-flash-native-audio-latest** model (might not be available for you depending on when you are reading this), which is not relevant to our use case of building a text chatbot. To see only models that can generate text, you have to filter models that support the **generateContent** action. This requires checking the model's **supported_actions** attribute for the **generateContent** item, and can be done as highlighted in the following code snippet:

```
st.session_state["model"] = st.selectbox(
    ":material/robot: Select a model to use for this chat",
    options=sorted(
        [
            model.name.replace("models/", "")
            for model in client.models.list()
            if model.name.endswith("latest")
            and "generateContent" in getattr(model, "supported_actions", [])
        ]
    ),
    index=None,
    help="Details of all models can be found [here](https://ai.google.dev/
gemini-api/docs/models).",
)
```

Once added, only models that can generate text will be displayed, as shown in the following *Figure* 16.5.

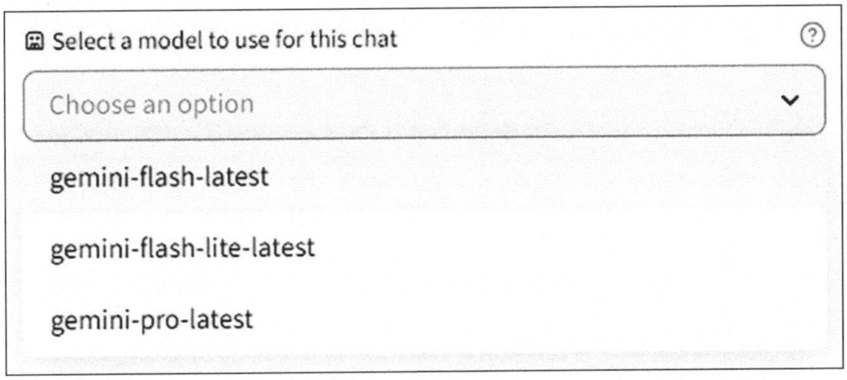

Figure 16.5: *Filtering Only the Latest Models That Can Generate Text*

Showing Model Description

You have now filtered the models to include only the latest model family, and models that can generate text, but users still do not know anything about the models yet. To help users make a selection, you can display the model description. It can be accessed through the model's

description attribute. Once a model has been selected, you can show the description of the model in the following code in the **selectbox** as follows:

```
st.info(
    next(
        (
            model.description
            for model in client.models.list()
            if model.name.replace("models/", "") == st.session_state["model"]
        ),
        "Select model to see description",
    ),
    icon=":material/info:",
)
```

next() returns the next item from the iterator. If no match is found, it returns the **default.** In this case, if no model has been selected, the **info** shows **Select model to see description**.

The name of the selected model can also be displayed in the sidebar for reference. The code snippet for this is as follows:

```
if st.session_state.get("model"):
    with st.sidebar:
        st.markdown(
            f"**:material/robot: Chat Model:** {st.session_state['model']}",
            help="""
The model to use for this chat. Start a new chat to change the model.

Details of all models can be found [here](https://ai.google.dev/gemini-api/
docs/models).
""",
        )
```

This will display the details of the model as shown in the following *Figure* 16.6.

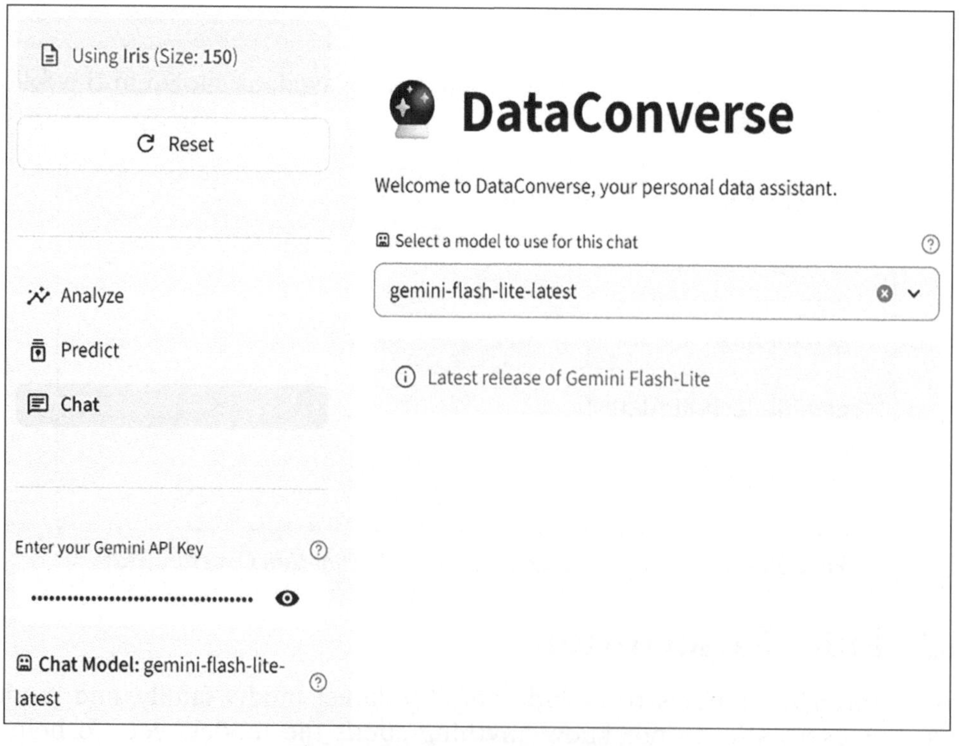

Figure 16.6: *Showing Model Details*

Creating a Model Selection Dialog

One issue with the current design is that the model selection section is always visible at the top. This gives the impression that the model can be changed in the middle of a chat, which is not possible with the Gemini API, at least the latest version of the API at the time this was written. Since the model needs to be selected only once, before starting the chat, this section can be converted to a dialog box that is displayed after the user clicks on a **New Chat** button, after the API token has been entered.

To do this, wrap the **selectbox** and **info** components used for model selection under a **select_model()** function, and decorate the function with **st.dialog**, as highlighted in the following code:

```
@st.dialog("New Chat")
def select_model():
    st.session_state["model"] = st.selectbox(
        ":material/robot: Select a model to use for this chat",
        options=sorted(
            [
                model.name.replace("models/", "")
                for model in client.models.list()
                if model.name.endswith("latest")
                and "generateContent" in getattr(
                  model, "supported_actions", []
                )
            ]
        ),
        index=None,
        help="Details of all models can be found [here](https://ai.google.dev/
gemini-api/docs/models).",
    )

    st.info(
        next(
            (
                model.description
                for model in client.models.list()
                if model.name.replace("models/", "") == st.session_state
["model"]
            ),
            "Select model to see description",
        ),
        icon=":material/info:",
    )
```

Call this function when the **New Chat** button has been clicked. This button is visible in the sidebar only after the API key has been entered, and can be created after the **select_model()** function as follows:

```
st.sidebar.button(
    "New Chat",
    icon=":material/chat:",
    use_container_width=True,
    on_click=select_model,
)
```

The following *Figure* 16.7 shows what this button looks like in the sidebar.

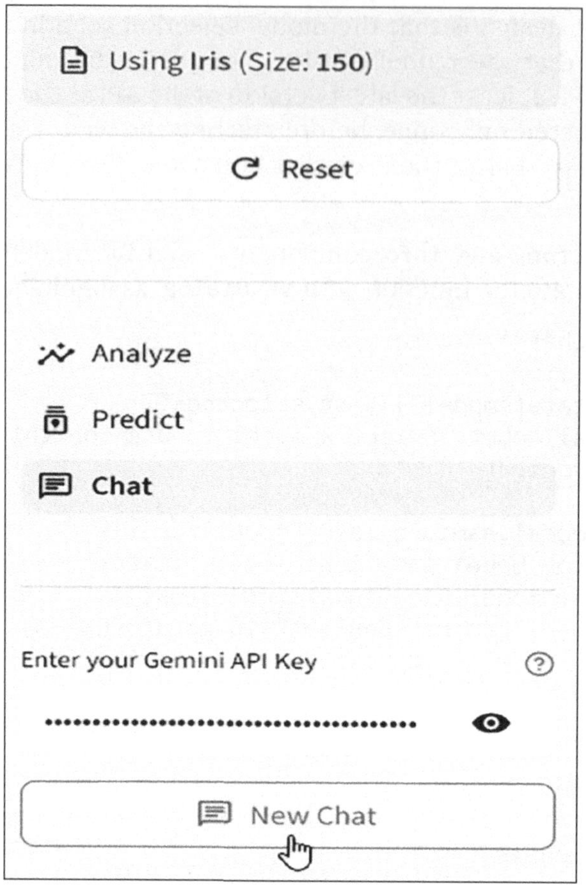

Figure 16.7: *New Chat Button*

On clicking this button, the **`New Chat`** dialog is displayed, as shown in *Figure* 16.8.

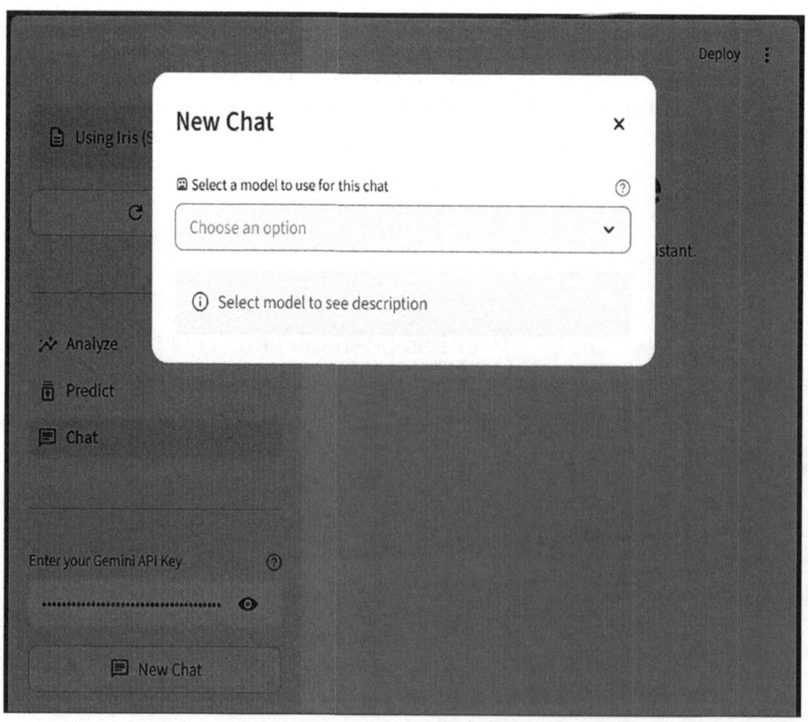

Figure 16.8: *New Chat Dialog Box*

Creating a Chat

A chat can be created using the **client.chats.create()** method. This method returns an instance of the **chat** that can be saved in the session state to be reused across app reruns. Since a chat can be created only once a model has been selected, add this to the **select_model()** function itself under a button, as follows:

```
@st.dialog("New Chat")
def select_model():
    …
    if st.button(
        "Start Chat",
        icon=":material/chat:",
        use_container_width=True,
        type="primary",
        disabled=st.session_state.get("model") is None,
    ):
        st.session_state["chat"] = client.chats.create(
            model=st.session_state["model"]
        )
        st.rerun()
```

This adds a button to the dialog as shown in the following *Figure* 16.9.

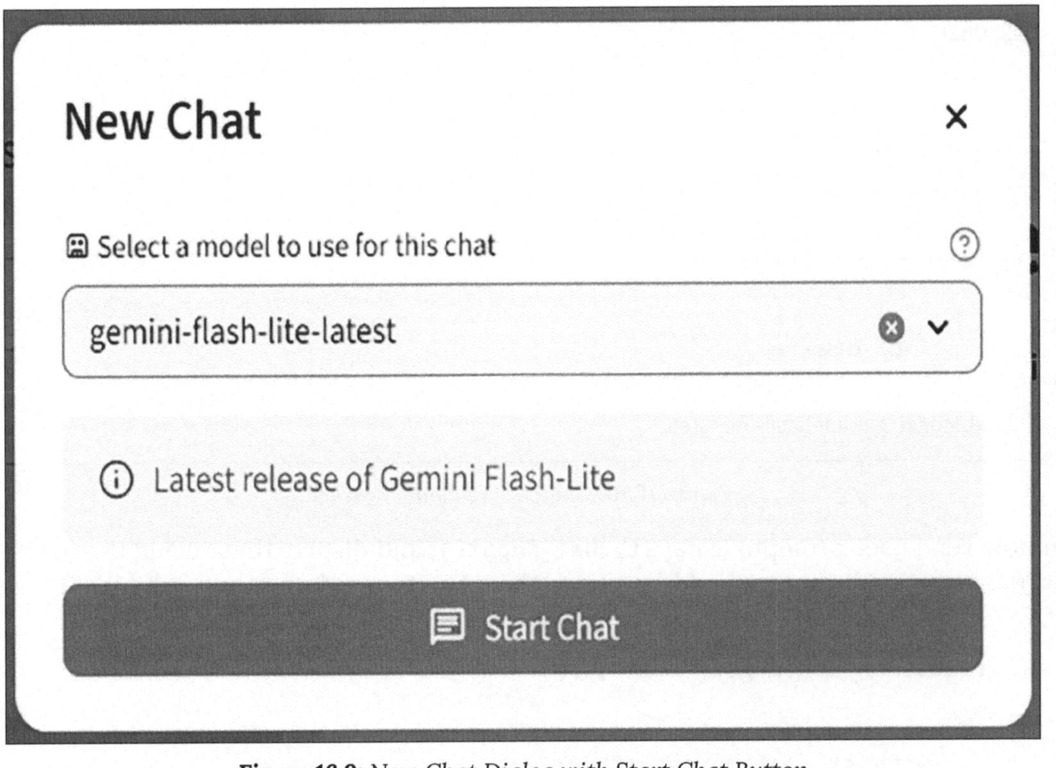

Figure 16.9: *New Chat Dialog with Start Chat Button*

This button is enabled only when a model has been selected, and clicking on it creates a new chat instance as well as saves it to the session state so that it can be reused across app reruns.

Sending and Receiving Messages

Once a chat has been created, you can start using **st.chat_input()** to send user prompts to the chatbot, and **st.chat_message()** to write user prompts as well as chatbot responses to the screen.

First, show a welcome message from the chatbot to the user to indicate that the chatbot has now been initialized, and the user can start chatting. Since this message is from the chat assistant, use the **assistant** role with **st.chat_message()**, as follows:

```
if st.session_state.get("chat"):
    with st.chat_message("assistant"):
        st.write(f"""Hello! I am the DataConverse Assistant.\n
Ask me anything about the __{st.session_state["dataset_name"]}__ data.""")
```

This displays the welcome message as shown in the following *Figure 16.10*.

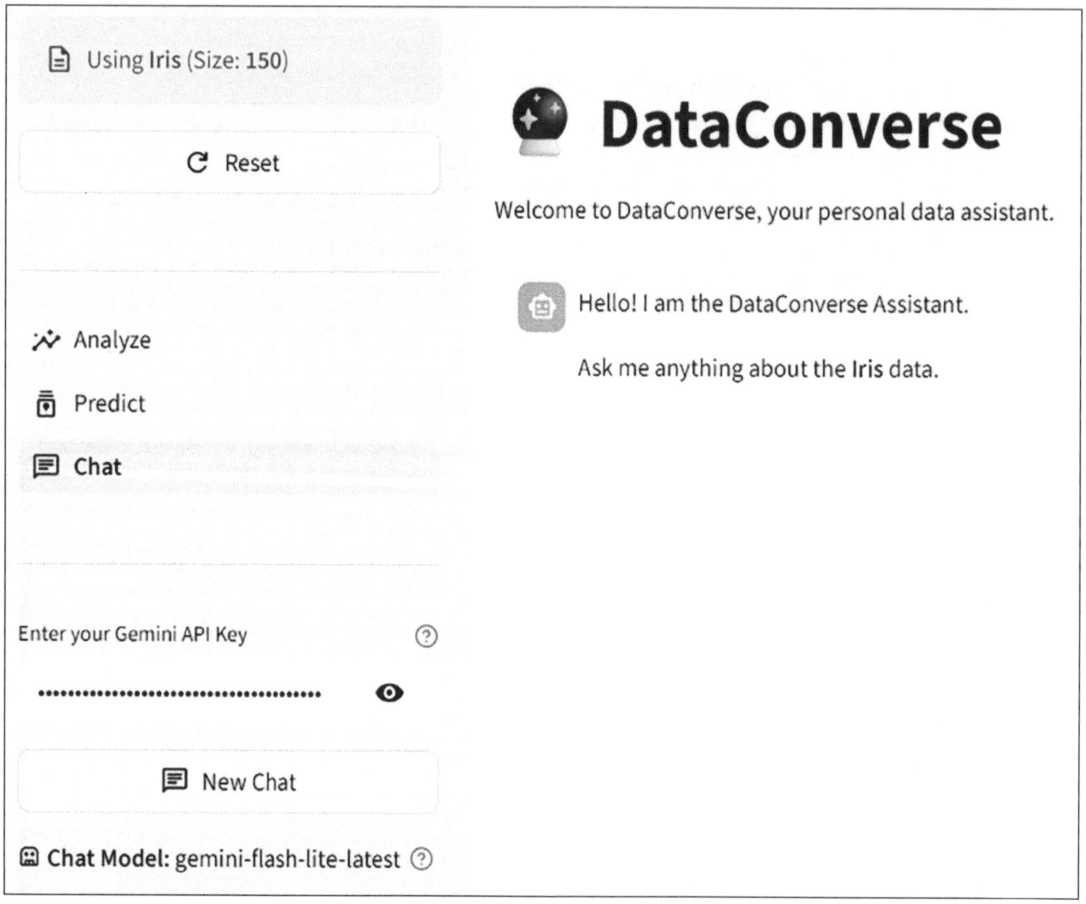

Figure 16.10: *Chatbot Welcome Message*

You can now send user prompts using **st.chat_input()**, and display them using the **user** role with **st.chat_message()**. All these should be under the **if st.session_state.get("chat")** guard, as follows:

```
if st.session_state.get("chat"):
    ...
    if user_prompt := st.chat_input("Ask me anything about the data..."):
        with st.chat_message("user"):
            st.markdown(user_prompt)
```

This adds a **chat_input** widget at the bottom of the app. Sending a message through the widget displays it under the chatbot's welcome message, with the user's persona, as shown in the following *Figure 16.11*.

Figure 16.11: *Sending and Displaying User Prompts*

User prompts can be sent to the chatbot using the **`chat.send_message()`** method. This sends the prompt to the chatbot, and returns the response. This response can be written under a **`chat_message()`** block with the **`assistant`** role, as follows:

```
if user_prompt := st.chat_input("Ask me anything about the data..."):
    ...
    with st.chat_message("assistant"):
        with st.spinner("Thinking...", show_time=True):
            response = st.session_state["chat"].send_message(user_prompt)
            st.write(response.text)
```

The spinner provides a visual clue to users that a response is being processed, and looks as shown in the following *Figure* 16.12.

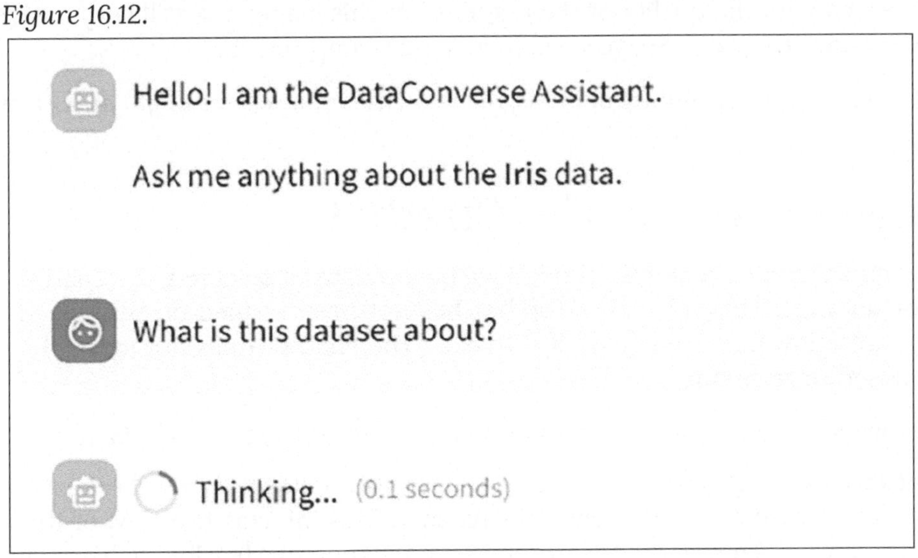

Figure 16.12: *Waiting for a Response from the Chatbot*

Once a response is received, it is displayed as shown in *Figure 16.13*.

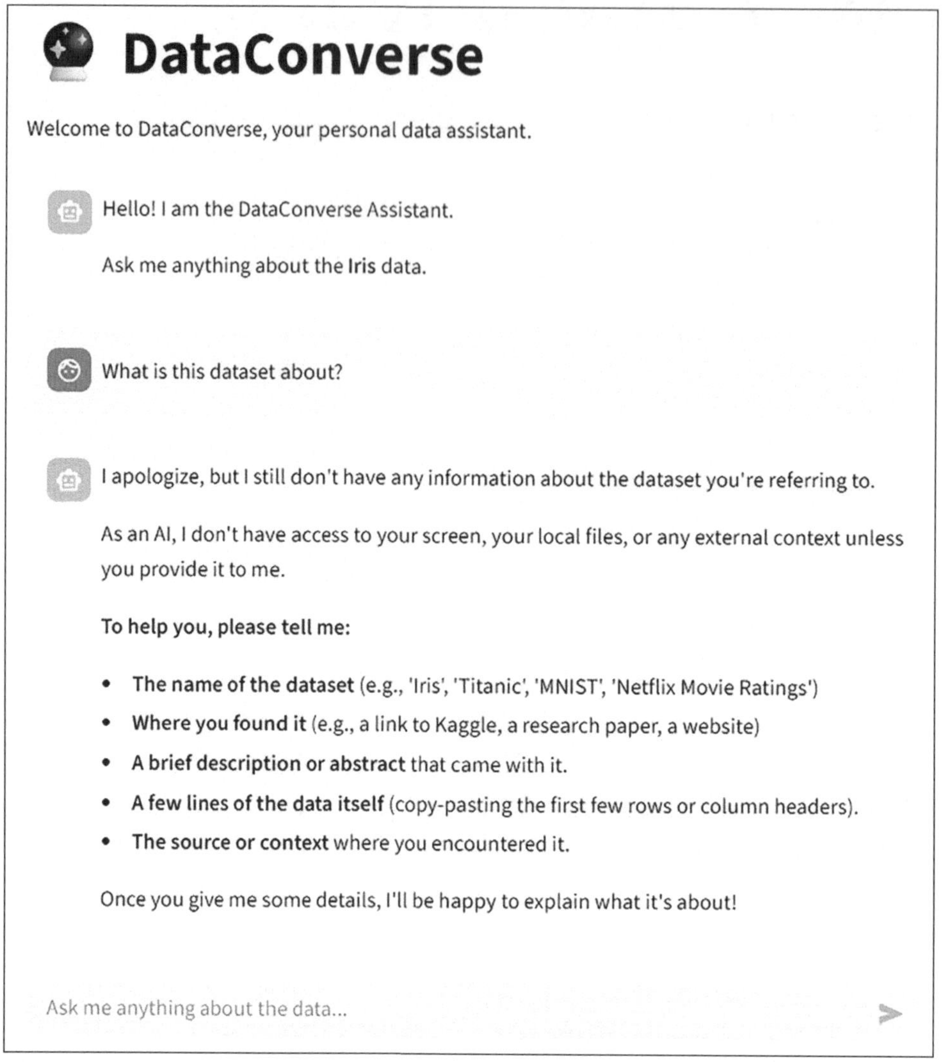

Figure 16.13: *Displaying Chatbot Response*

If you receive a response from the chatbot, congratulations – you have built your very own chatbot! Do not be concerned with the quality of the response at this stage; it is still very basic, and does not have any context about the data. So, you will now need to improve it.

Note: *Due to the indeterministic nature of LLMs, the responses you receive might differ from those shown in this chapter.*

Providing Context to the Chatbot

In *Figure 16.13*, you will notice that even though we have a dataset selected, the chatbot does not have any information about it. This is because the bot has not been trained on this specific dataset and, therefore, does not know how to refer to it. Basically, the chatbot does not know the context under which it is supposed to respond.

There are three ways, you can make a pretrained LLM more contextually relevant:

- **Prompt Engineering:** In this method, you pass your dataset as a system prompt to the LLM chatbot, and instruct it to use only this dataset. This informs the LLM of the context to use while responding. This method is simple to implement, but feasible only for simple use-cases where the datasets are very limited.

- **Retrieval Augmented Generation (RAG):** In this method, an LLM is provided access to a domain-specific knowledge base that it can refer to (retrieve information from) while generating responses. This method is more complicated than prompt engineering, but generalizes better across a larger dataset or domain.
- **Fine-tuning:** Fine-tuning refers to retraining a pre-trained model on a domain-specific dataset to improve model performance in that domain. This is the most complicated method of making an LLM contextually aware, but it offers the best results on very large datasets and wide domains.

We will not delve into the details of prompt engineering, RAG, or fine-tuning in this chapter, as each of these topics can easily be an entire book in itself. *Table 16.1* elaborates on some high-level differences between these approaches, and a more detailed summary of differences is available at https://www.intersystems.com/resources/rag-vs-fine-tuning-vs-prompt-engineering-everything-you-need-to-know/#summary.

Criteria	**Prompt Engineering**	**RAG**	**Fine-tuning**
Implementation	Easy	Medium	Complex
Cost	Low	Medium	High
Accuracy	Variable	High	High
Maintenance	Low	Medium	High

Table 16.1: *Differences between Prompt Engineering, RAG, and Fine-tuning*[2]

RAG and fine-tuning are complex to implement within a Streamlit application, and are not compatible with deployment on Streamlit Community Cloud. In addition to this technical limitation, our chatbot needs to have the context around only a single CSV file, so using prompt engineering by passing the entire file to the system prompt of the chatbot will be by far the easiest method of making the chatbot contextually relevant.

Using the System Prompt

Since we have a relatively small dataset in CSV format, we can easily add it to the chatbot's system prompt. The system prompt can also be used to control the tone of the model, and provide additional instructions to it.

To create a system prompt with the dataset added to it, we can convert the dataset to string format as follows:

```
SYSTEM_PROMPT = f"""
You are a helpful data analyst. Answer the user's questions in markdown format
based on the following data.

Data:
{st.session_state["data"].to_string()}
"""
```

Here, the system prompt specifies the tone and persona of the chatbot - **`helpful data analyst`**, instructions - **`Answer the user's questions`**, the output format - **`in markdown format`**, and the context - **`based on the following data`**.

Note: *Google's guide on system instructions is a helpful resource for learning more about the best practices and use cases for system instructions. It is available at https://cloud.google.com/vertex-ai/generative-ai/docs/learn/prompts/system-instruction-introduction.*

[2] *https://www.intersystems.com/resources/rag-vs-fine-tuning-vs-prompt-engineering-everything-you-need-to-know/#headline* (Accessed: 13 July 2025)

Task: *Experiment with different tones and personas of the chatbot to match your style. Some examples include a patient high-school teacher, a curious university student, a thorough statistician, and a frustrated data scientist. You can also go one step ahead and let the end-users choose their own tone and persona using input widgets in the app.*

The system prompt needs to be included in the **`send_message()`** call, as follows:

```
from google.genai import types
...
        with st.chat_message("assistant"):
            with st.spinner("Thinking...", show_time=True):
                response = st.session_state["chat"].send_message(
                    user_prompt,
                    config=types.GenerateContentConfig(
                        system_instruction=SYSTEM_PROMPT,
                    ),
                )
                st.write(response.text)
```

Once the system prompt has been added to the chatbot, the chatbot will have the relevant context available, and asking it about the data now generates an appropriate response, as shown in the following *Figure 16.14*.

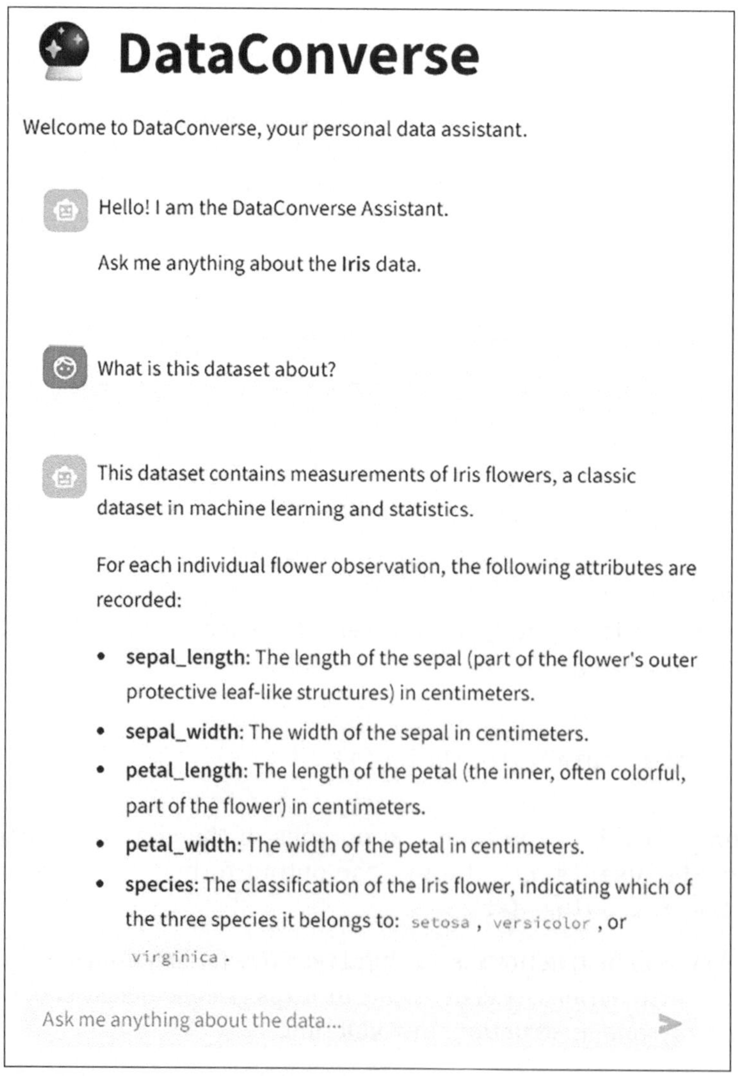

Figure 16.14: *Contextually Relevant Response after Prompt Engineering*

Displaying the Conversation History

The current implementation of the chatbot does not show the entire conversation history. You can verify this behavior by asking the chatbot to summarize the conversation. You will notice that although the chatbot remembers the conversation history, and can summarize the conversation, the previous messages will be deleted, as shown in *Figure 16.15*:

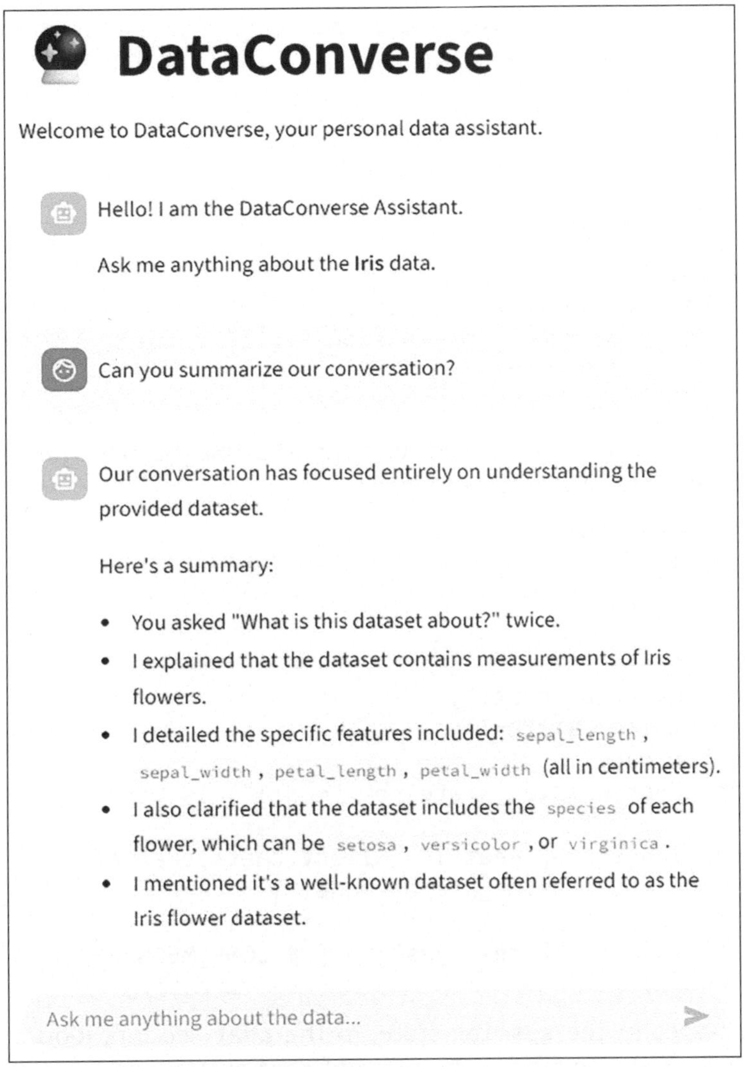

Figure 16.15: *Previous Messages Overwritten*

Most modern chatbots display the conversation history, making it easier for users to refer back to the conversation at any point in time. Our chatbot should also do this to provide a good user experience.

The reason the history is not displayed is that each new user prompt overwrites the previous prompt saved in the **`user_prompt`** variable and triggers a script rerun. This causes the last response of the chatbot to be overwritten by the new response to the latest user prompt. Not only does a new user prompt clear the entire history, but any action, such as navigating to another page of the app, also clears the entire history. The reason why the welcome message is always visible is that it is static and remains the same, even after the script is rerun.

To prevent the previous user prompts and assistant responses from being overwritten, you need to use the session state to store all the messages, and then retrieve them in sequence to display whenever the script is rerun.

To do this, you can create a **messages** session state as a list of dictionaries, with the role as the key and the message as the value.

The first message will always be the assistant's welcome message with the **assistant** role. Then, when the user enters a prompt, it is appended to this dictionary with the **user** role, and the assistant's response is appended with the **assistant** role. This process then continues for the entire conversation, saving all prompts to the session state so that they are not lost when the script is rerun.

To begin, initialize the message session state with the welcome assistant prompt. To make it easier to organize, we can store the welcome assistant prompt under a **WELCOME_MESSAGE** dictionary, below the **SYSTEM_PROMPT**, as follows:

```
SYSTEM_PROMPT = …

WELCOME_MESSAGE = {
    "role": "assistant",
    "content": f"""
Hello! I am the DataConverse Assistant.\n
Ask me anything about the __{st.session_state["dataset_name"]}__ data.
    """,
}
```

The **messages** session state can be initialized with the **WELCOME_MESSAGE** just after a chat has been created in the **select_model()** function, as follows:

```
@st.dialog("New Chat")
def select_model():
    …
    if st.button(
        "Start Chat",
        icon=":material/chat:",
        use_container_width=True,
        type="primary",
        disabled=st.session_state.get("model") is None,
    ):
        st.session_state["chat"] = client.chats.create(
            model=st.session_state["model"]
        )
        st.session_state["messages"] = [WELCOME_MESSAGE]
        st.rerun()
```

To display all the messages in the **session** state, in the **chat** section, loop through the **messages** session state, fetching the **role** to display the relevant **chat** avatar, and the content. This is shown in the following code snippet, with the code block to be deleted in red, and the one to be added in green, as follows:

```
if st.session_state.get("chat"):
    with st.chat_message("assistant"):
        st.write(f"""Hello! I am the DataConverse Assistant.\n
Ask me anything about the __{st.session_state["dataset_name"]}__ data.""")

    for message in st.session_state.messages:
        with st.chat_message(message["role"]):
            st.markdown(message["content"])
```

The relevant avatar is displayed using the role assigned to the message (**message["role"]**), and the message content is displayed in a **Markdown** widget (which supports markdown formatting, unlike a text widget) within the chat context (**message["content"]**).

This takes care of displaying previous messages. To add new user prompts to the **messages** session state, append them to the dictionary with the **user** role, as follows:

```
if user_prompt := st.chat_input("Ask me anything about the data..."):
    st.session_state["messages"].append(
        {"role": "user", "content": user_prompt}
    )
    with st.chat_message("user"):
        ...
```

The chatbot's response is also appended to the **messages** session state under the **assistant** role, as follows:

```
with st.chat_message("assistant"):
    ...
        st.write(response.text)
        st.session_state.messages.append(
            {
                "role": "assistant",
                "content": response.text,
            }
        )
```

Once this is done, the entire conversation history will be displayed in the app (after clearing the cache and rerunning). This enhances the user experience, and makes the chatbot's responses more relevant to the conversation, as shown in *Figure 16.16*.

Note: *If expected changes are not visible on app rerun, try clearing the app cache and rerunning.*

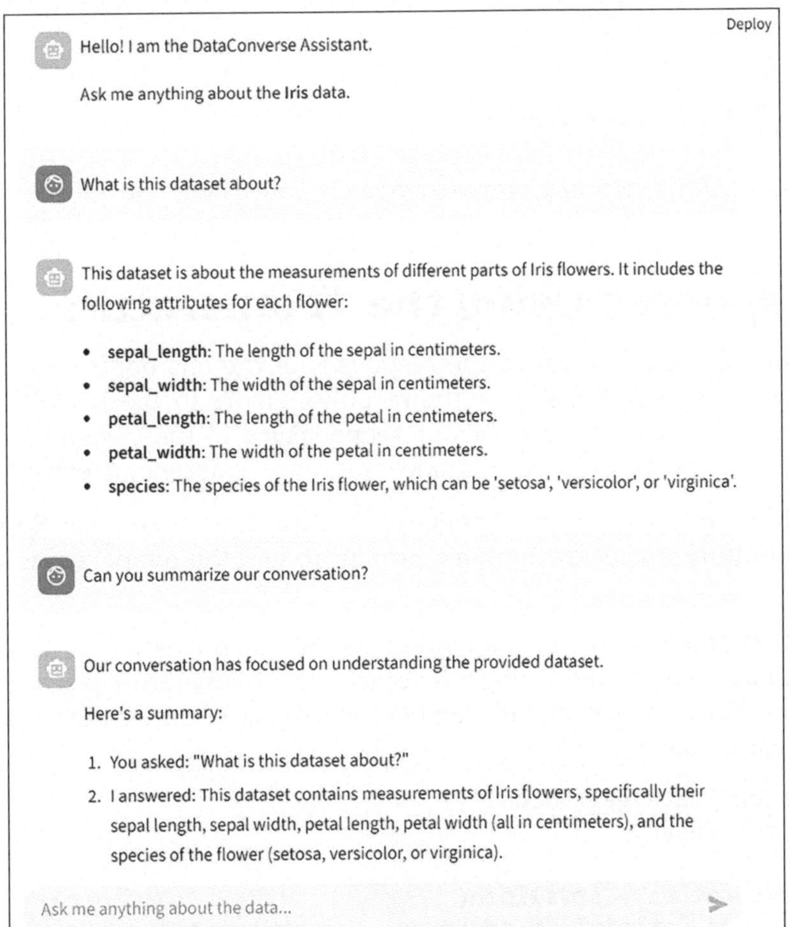

Figure 16.16: *Entire Conversation History Visible and Remembered by the Chatbot*

For reference, the complete section that handles sending and receiving messages is as follows:

```
if st.session_state.get("chat"):

    for message in st.session_state["messages"]:
        with st.chat_message(message["role"]):
            st.markdown(message["content"])

    if user_prompt := st.chat_input("Ask me anything about the data..."):
        st.session_state["messages"].append(
            {"role": "user", "content": user_prompt}
        )
        with st.chat_message("user"):
            st.markdown(user_prompt)
        with st.chat_message("assistant"):
            with st.spinner("Thinking...", show_time=True):
                response = st.session_state["chat"].send_message(
                    user_prompt,
                    config=types.GenerateContentConfig(
                        system_instruction=SYSTEM_PROMPT,
                    ),
                )
                st.write(response.text)
                st.session_state.messages.append(
                    {
                        "role": "assistant",
                        "content": response.text,
                    }
                )
```

Additional Features

While the chatbot is already functional, you can add a few more bells and whistles to improve the user experience.

Tuning Responses Using the Temperature

You can control how focused or creative the responses of the chatbot are using the **temperature** setting. Lower values of **temperature** make the responses more focused, while higher values make them more creative. You can learn more about **temperature** in the Google docs at https://cloud.google.com/vertex-ai/generative-ai/docs/model-reference/inference#temperature.

Unlike the model, the temperature can be changed for each message of the chat. So, you can experiment with different temperature values for the same prompt to find the temperature value that best suits your use case.

Since the temperature should be visible and modifiable for each message, it should be visible in the sidebar once a chat has been created. Using a slider to select temperature provides good control over its values. The temperature widget can be added to the sidebar just after the markdown that displays the selected model, as follows:

```
if st.session_state.get("model"):
    with st.sidebar:
        ...
        temperature = st.slider(
            "**:material/thermometer: Temperature**",
            min_value=0.0,
```

```
            max_value=2.0,
            value=1.0,
            step=0.1,
            help="""Temperature controls the randomness of the model›s output.
    Lower values make the output more focused and deterministic, while higher
    values make it more creative and varied.
    Learn more about temperature [here](https://cloud.google.com/vertex-ai/
    generative-ai/docs/multimodal/content-generation-parameters#temperature).

    You can change the temperature for each message in the chat.""",
        )
```

The **min** and **max** values of the slider are determined by the temperature range accepted by the selected model. For the Gemini 2.x family of models, this is from 0.0 to 2.0.

This adds the temperature slider to the sidebar, as shown in *Figure 16.17*.

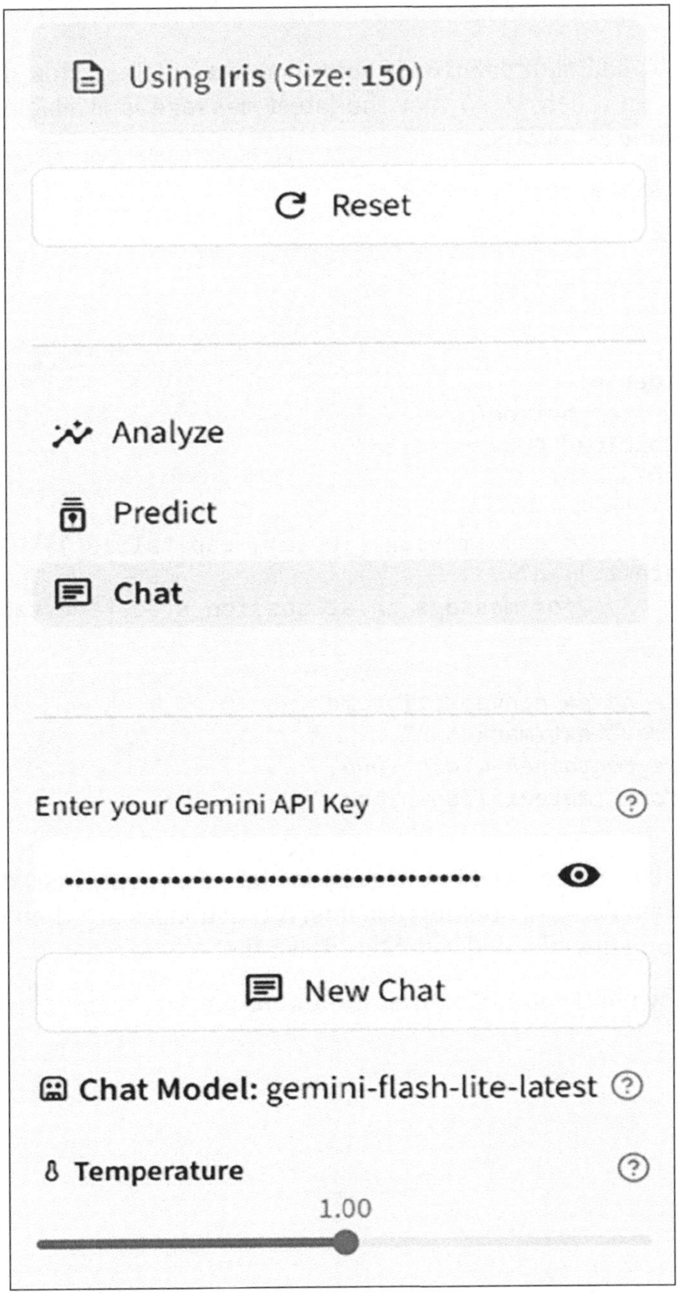

Figure 16.17: *Temperature Slider in the Sidebar*

The temperature can be passed to the model through the config, as follows:

```
response = st.session_state["chat"].send_message(
    user_prompt,
    config=types.GenerateContentConfig(
        temperature=temperature,
        system_instruction=SYSTEM_PROMPT,
    ),
)
```

Downloading the Conversation

Because the conversation is saved in the session state, downloading it is a straightforward process of exporting the **messages** session state to a file. Since we have instructed the chatbot to respond in markdown format, the conversation should also be downloaded as a markdown file for better *rendering.*

This can be done easily by adding a **download button** in the sidebar. This should be done after the chatbot response has been received, so that the latest **message** is available in the session state to download. This can be done as follows:

```
if st.session_state.get("chat"):
    ...

    if user_prompt := ...
        ...

    with st.sidebar:
        st.download_button(
            "Download Conversation",
            "\n".join(
                [
                    f"### {message[‹role›].capitalize()}\
n{message[‹content›]}\n"
                    for message in st.session_state["messages"]
                ]
            ),
            file_name="conversation.md",
            mime="text/markdown",
            use_container_width=True,
            icon=":material/download:",
        )
```

Here, we loop through all the messages in the session state and apply markdown formatting so that the role (**user** or **assistant**) is easily distinguishable. All responses are then joined as a single string separated by a newline, and downloaded as a Markdown file.

For the conversation shown in *Figure* 16.18, the raw and rendered downloaded conversation is shown in *Figure* 16.19.

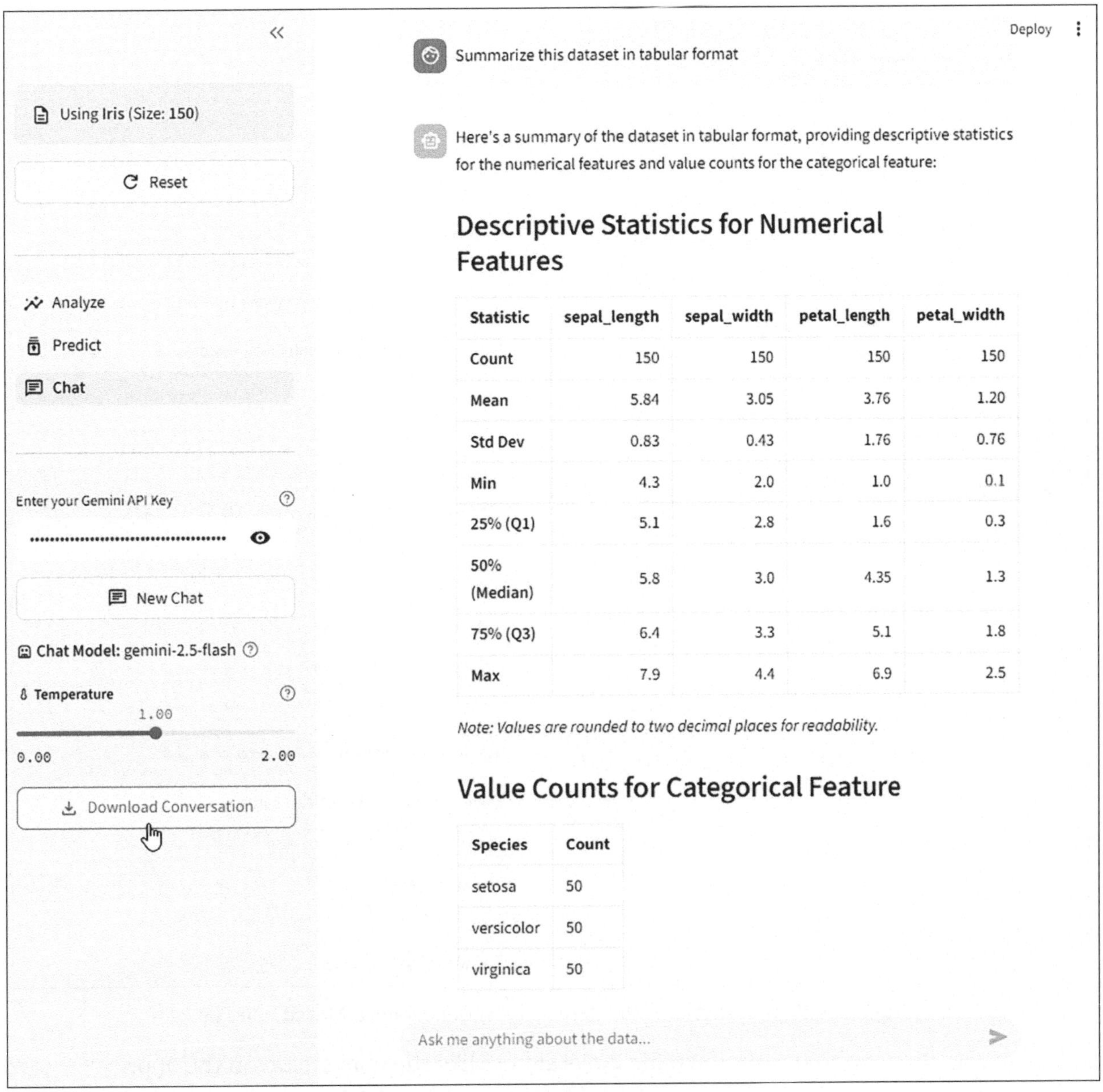

Figure 16.18: *Downloading a Conversation*

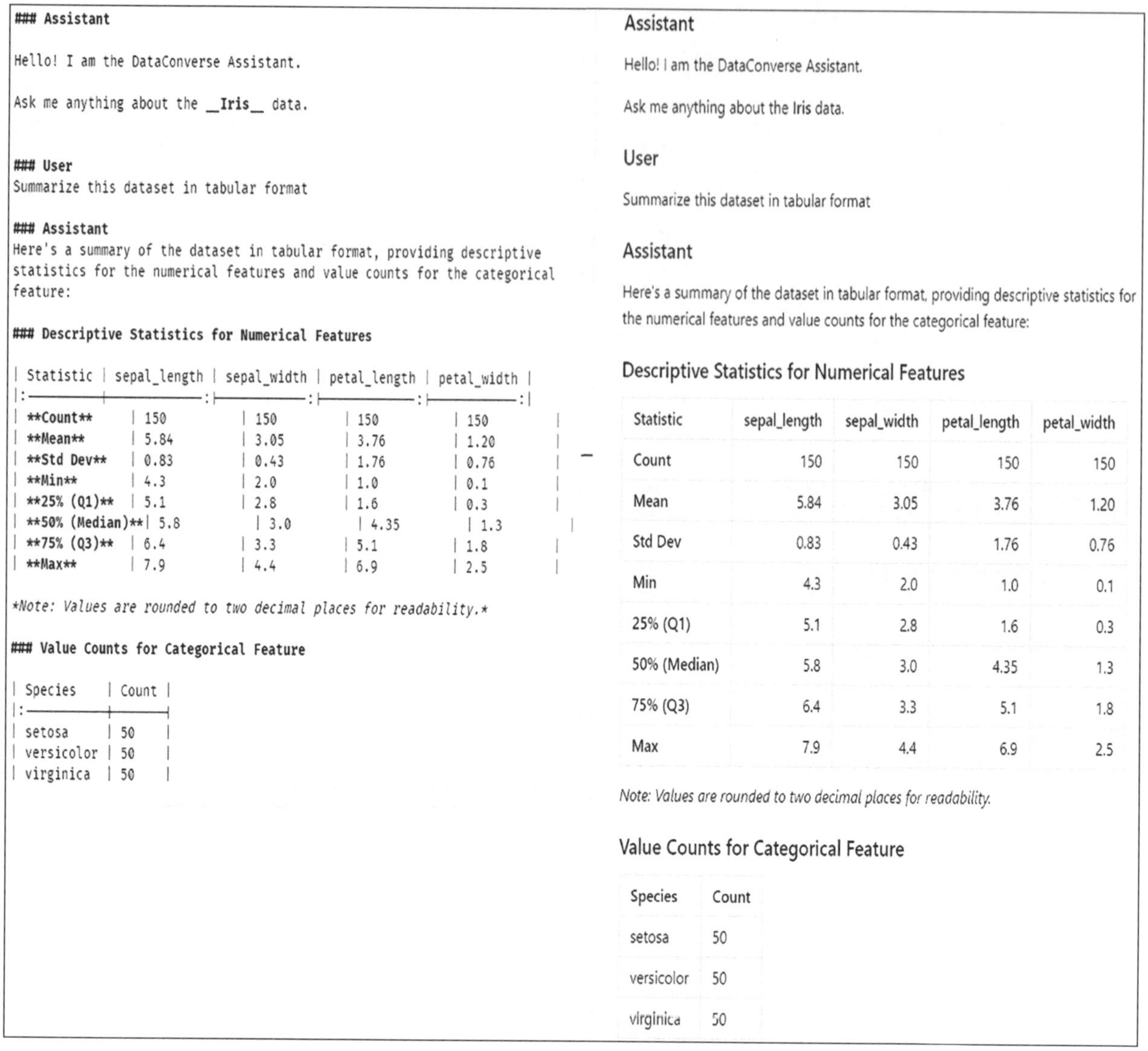

```
### Assistant

Hello! I am the DataConverse Assistant.

Ask me anything about the _Iris_ data.


### User
Summarize this dataset in tabular format

### Assistant
Here's a summary of the dataset in tabular format, providing descriptive
statistics for the numerical features and value counts for the categorical
feature:

### Descriptive Statistics for Numerical Features

| Statistic | sepal_length | sepal_width | petal_length | petal_width |
|:----------|-------------:|------------:|-------------:|------------:|
| **Count**     | 150      | 150      | 150      | 150      |
| **Mean**      | 5.84     | 3.05     | 3.76     | 1.20     |
| **Std Dev**   | 0.83     | 0.43     | 1.76     | 0.76     |
| **Min**       | 4.3      | 2.0      | 1.0      | 0.1      |
| **25% (Q1)**  | 5.1      | 2.8      | 1.6      | 0.3      |
| **50% (Median)**| 5.8      | 3.0      | 4.35      | 1.3      |
| **75% (Q3)**  | 6.4      | 3.3      | 5.1      | 1.8      |
| **Max**       | 7.9      | 4.4      | 6.9      | 2.5      |

*Note: Values are rounded to two decimal places for readability.*

### Value Counts for Categorical Feature

| Species    | Count |
|:-----------|------:|
| setosa     | 50    |
| versicolor | 50    |
| virginica  | 50    |
```

Assistant

Hello! I am the DataConverse Assistant.

Ask me anything about the *Iris* data.

User

Summarize this dataset in tabular format

Assistant

Here's a summary of the dataset in tabular format, providing descriptive statistics for the numerical features and value counts for the categorical feature:

Descriptive Statistics for Numerical Features

Statistic	sepal_length	sepal_width	petal_length	petal_width
Count	150	150	150	150
Mean	5.84	3.05	3.76	1.20
Std Dev	0.83	0.43	1.76	0.76
Min	4.3	2.0	1.0	0.1
25% (Q1)	5.1	2.8	1.6	0.3
50% (Median)	5.8	3.0	4.35	1.3
75% (Q3)	6.4	3.3	5.1	1.8
Max	7.9	4.4	6.9	2.5

Note: Values are rounded to two decimal places for readability.

Value Counts for Categorical Feature

Species	Count
setosa	50
versicolor	50
virginica	50

Figure 16.19: *Raw (left) and Rendered (right) Downloaded Markdown File*

As you can see, the rendered markdown file looks almost like the conversion on the app.

Streaming Responses

Currently, the application displays responses only after they have been entirely generated. This can lead to significant waiting times, especially for complex queries or slower models. Thankfully, the Gemini API supports streaming, and can be used to populate a placeholder markdown widget as and when responses are streamed, leading to a more fluid interaction with the chatbot.

To stream responses, update the code under the assistant chat message to as follows (the **Thinking...** spinner is not needed anymore):

```
if st.session_state.get("chat"):
    ...
        with st.chat_message("assistant"):
            placeholder = st.empty()
            response_chunks = []
            for chunk in st.session_state["chat"].send_message_stream(
                user_prompt,
                config=types.GenerateContentConfig(
                    temperature=temperature,
```

```
                    system_instruction=SYSTEM_PROMPT,
                ),
            ):
                response_chunks.append(chunk.text)
                placeholder.markdown("".join(response_chunks))

            st.session_state.messages.append(
                {
                    "role": "assistant",
                    "content": "".join(response_chunks),
                }
            )
```

Now, chatbot responses will be streamed incrementally as and when they are generated, leading to smaller wait times to get the response.

Full Code

The entire **chat.py** file is as follows, for reference:

```
import streamlit as st
from google import genai
from google.genai import types

SYSTEM_PROMPT = f"""
You are a helpful data analyst. Answer the user's questions in markdown format
based on the following data.

Data:
{st.session_state["data"].to_string()}
"""

WELCOME_MESSAGE = {
    "role": "assistant",
    "content": f"""
Hello! I am the DataConverse Assistant.\n
Ask me anything about the __{st.session_state["dataset_name"]}__ data.
    """,
}


with st.sidebar:
    st.divider()
    st.session_state["gemini_api_key"] = st.text_input(
        "Enter your Gemini API Key",
        type="password",
        help="API key will not be stored in the app.",
        value=st.session_state.get("gemini_api_key", ""),
    )

if st.session_state.get("gemini_api_key") == "":
    st.warning(
        "Enter your Gemini API Key to start chatting."
        " You can create a free Gemini API Key [here](https://aistudio.google.
com/app/api-keys).",
        icon=":material/warning:",
    )
```

```
    st.stop()


@st.cache_resource
def get_client(api_key: str):
    return genai.Client(api_key=api_key)


client = get_client(st.session_state["gemini_api_key"])


@st.dialog("New Chat")
def select_model():
    st.session_state["model"] = st.selectbox(
        ":material/robot: Select a model to use for this chat",
        options=sorted(
            [
                model.name.replace("models/", "")
                for model in client.models.list()
                if model.name.endswith("latest")
                and "generateContent" in getattr(
                    model,
                    "supported_actions",
                    [],
                )
            ]
        ),
        index=None,
        help="Details of all models can be found [here](https://ai.google.dev/
gemini-api/docs/models).",
    )

    st.info(
        next(
            (
                model.description
                for model in client.models.list()
                if model.name.replace("models/", "") == st.session_state
["model"]
            ),
            "Select model to see description",
        ),
        icon=":material/info:",
    )

    if st.button(
        "Start Chat",
        icon=":material/chat:",
        use_container_width=True,
        type="primary",
        disabled=st.session_state.get("model") is None,
    ):
        st.session_state["chat"] = client.chats.create(model=st.session_
state["model"])
        st.session_state["messages"] = [WELCOME_MESSAGE]

        st.rerun()
```

```
st.sidebar.button(
    "New Chat",
    icon=":material/chat:",
    use_container_width=True,
    on_click=select_model,
)


if st.session_state.get("model"):
    with st.sidebar:
        st.markdown(
            f"**:material/robot: Chat Model:** {st.session_state['model']}",
            help="""
The model to use for this chat. Start a new chat to change the model.

Details of all models can be found [here](https://ai.google.dev/gemini-api/
docs/models).
""",
        )
        temperature = st.slider(
            "**:material/thermometer: Temperature**",
            min_value=0.0,
            max_value=2.0,
            value=1.0,
            step=0.1,
            help="""Temperature controls the randomness of the model's output.
Lower values make the output more focused and deterministic, while higher
values make it more creative and varied.
Learn more about temperature [here](https://cloud.google.com/vertex-ai/
generative-ai/docs/multimodal/content-generation-parameters#temperature).

You can change the temperature for each message in the chat.""",
        )


if st.session_state.get("chat"):
    for message in st.session_state["messages"]:
        with st.chat_message(message["role"]):
            st.markdown(message["content"])

    if user_prompt := st.chat_input("Ask me anything about the data..."):
        st.session_state["messages"].append(
            {
                "role": "user",
                "content": user_prompt,
            }
        )
        with st.chat_message("user"):
            st.markdown(user_prompt)
        with st.chat_message("assistant"):
            placeholder = st.empty()
            response_chunks = []
            for chunk in st.session_state["chat"].send_message_stream(
                user_prompt,
                config=types.GenerateContentConfig(
```

```
                        temperature=temperature,
                        system_instruction=SYSTEM_PROMPT,
                    ),
                ):
                    response_chunks.append(chunk.text)
                    placeholder.markdown("".join(response_chunks))

                st.session_state["messages"].append(
                    {
                        "role": "assistant",
                        "content": "".join(response_chunks),
                    }
                )

        with st.sidebar:
            st.download_button(
                "Download Conversation",
                "\n".join(
                    [
                        f"### {message['role'].capitalize()}\n{message
    ['content']}\n"
                        for message in st.session_state["messages"]
                    ]
                ),
                file_name="conversation.md",
                mime="text/markdown",
                use_container_width=True,
                icon=":material/download:",
            )
```

Conclusion

This chapter completes the DataConverse application (or the name you have chosen for your project) that you have been building since *Chapter* 14, by adding intelligent chat capabilities.

You started with user authentication using the Gemini API key. This was followed by creating a new chat by selecting a model. The model selection process involved multiple cleaning steps to show only relevant models in the options.

Furthermore, you explored methods to ensure that your chatbot possesses the necessary context for delivering relevant answers, implementing this through basic prompt engineering with the system prompt. Additionally, you learned to leverage Streamlit's session state to store all conversation messages, and render them with accurately assigned roles.

Finally, you enhanced the application with additional utilities, such as configuring the temperature of the chatbot to control how focused or creative the responses are, enabling the download of conversations as markdown files and streaming responses as and when they are ready. These features improve the user experience, and contribute to a more comprehensive chatbot.

Throughout the implementation of this chat page, you were also introduced to several LLM concepts, such as the role of system prompts and context management, that will be beneficial as you work with other LLM applications.

This chapter also marks the conclusion of this book. You are now empowered to build and deploy your Streamlit applications for diverse use cases. The skills you have acquired throughout this journey will also prove valuable in other aspects of your career, whether in data analysis, data science, machine learning, or LLM application development.

The world of AI and web development is constantly evolving, but the principles of user-centric design, clean implementation, and iterative improvement you have learned here will remain timeless. We encourage you to continue experimenting, building, and sharing your creations with the world. The **`DataConverse`** application is not an endpoint, but a starting point for your own innovative projects.

Points to Remember

- Always treat API keys and other credentials as sensitive information. Never hardcode them directly into your application or commit them to public repositories. Using password inputs, environment variables, and **`st.secrets`** is the best practice.
- **Context is Crucial for LLMs:** LLMs require context to provide relevant answers. In this chapter, we used prompt engineering via the system prompt to provide data context. For larger datasets or more complex scenarios, consider exploring RAG or fine-tuning.

Multiple Choice Questions

1. What method is used to authenticate users using the Gemini API?
   a. API key
   b. Username and password
   c. Magic link
   d. Authentication code
2. Which of the following methods is primarily used in this chapter to make the LLM contextually relevant to a specific dataset?
   a. Fine-tuning the LLM on the dataset.
   b. Retrieval Augmented Generation (RAG) with a vector database.
   c. Prompt Engineering by passing the dataset within the system prompt.
   d. Using a specialized data analysis LLM endpoint.
3. How is the conversation history (user prompts and assistant responses) stored and displayed in the Streamlit application?
   a. In a temporary text file on the server.
   b. Using browser local storage.
   c. The Gemini **`client.chat`** object automatically manages and displays history.
   d. In **`st.session_state["messages"]`** as a list of dictionaries, then iterated and displayed.
4. In the chapter, how is the downloaded conversation formatted?
   a. As a JSON file.
   b. As a plain text file.
   c. As a markdown file.
   d. As a CSV file.

Answers

1. a
2. c
3. d
4. c

Questions

1. What is a system prompt in the context of an LLM, and how was it utilized in this chapter to make the chatbot's responses more relevant to the user's data? Provide an example of how you might modify the system prompt to change the chatbot's persona or task.
2. Describe the mechanism used to display the entire conversation history in the Streamlit application. Why is `st.session_state` crucial for this functionality, and what data structure is used to hold the messages?
3. The chapter mentions three ways to make a pretrained LLM more contextually relevant: Prompt Engineering, RAG, and Fine-tuning. Briefly explain each, and discuss why Prompt Engineering was chosen for this chapter's application.

Advanced Assignment

Using concepts from *Chapter 3, Creating and Deploying Your First Streamlit App* and *Chapter 10: Advanced Deployment Concepts*, deploy your app to the Streamlit Community Cloud.

Key Terms

- **Large Language Models:** Large Language Models (LLMs) are a category of machine learning models trained on large amounts of data to be able to understand and generate natural language. [3]
- **Application Programming Interface:** An Application Programming Interface (API) is a set of rules and protocols that allow different software applications to communicate with each other.[4]
- **System Prompt:** A system prompt is the foundational instruction that dictates an LLM's behavior. This prompt is generally not visible to the end-user.[5]
- **User Prompt:** A user prompt is the input provided by the end-user during their interaction/conversation with an LLM.[6]
- **Prompt Engineering:** This is the process of creating effective instructions that enable AI models to generate responses based on given inputs.[7]

[3] *https://www.ibm.com/think/topics/large-language-models* (Accessed: 15 April 2025)
[4] *https://www.geeksforgeeks.org/what-is-an-api/* (Accessed: 15 April 2025)
[5] *https://blog.promptlayer.com/system-prompt-vs-user-prompt-a-comprehensive-guide-for-ai-prompts* (Accessed: 3 May 2025)
[6] *https://www.nebuly.com/blog/llm-system-prompt-vs-user-prompt* (Accessed: 3 May 2025)
[7] *https://www.geeksforgeeks.org/what-is-prompt-engineering-the-ai-revolution/* (Accessed: 15 April 2025)

- **Retrieval Augmented Generation:** Retrieval Augmented Generation (RAG) is a technique to generate more accurate and contextually relevant responses from an LLM by retrieving relevant information from a knowledge base (such as a database or document set) and using this information to augment the generation of responses.[8]
- **Fine-Tuning:** Fine-tuning refers to the process of retraining a pretrained LLM on a specific dataset to make it more contextually aware.[9]
- **Temperature:** Temperature controls the degree of randomness in token selection. Lower temperatures are good for prompts that require a less open-ended or creative response, while higher temperatures can lead to more diverse or creative results.[10]
- **Streaming:** The process of sending or receiving data in a continuous flow of small packets (chunks) rather than waiting for the entire data payload to be available. In this chapter, it is used to display the chatbot's response incrementally, improving the user experience.

---

[8] *https://azure.microsoft.com/en-in/resources/cloud-computing-dictionary/what-is-retrieval-augmented-generation-rag* (Accessed: 3 May 2025)
[9] *https://www.geeksforgeeks.org/fine-tuning-large-language-model-llm/* (Accessed: 3 May 2025)
[10] *https://cloud.google.com/vertex-ai/generative-ai/docs/multimodal/content-generation-parameters#temperature* (Accessed: 13 July 2025)

Index

A

App Configuration Options 190
App Configuration Options, integrating 191-193
App Configuration Options, steps 190, 191
App Dependencies 144
App Dependencies, categories
  Non-Python 145
  Python 145
Application Reloads 47
Application Reloads, architecture 49, 50
Application Reloads, configuring 48, 49
Application Reloads, sections
  Nested Streamlit Buttons 53
  Script Reruns 50
App Resources 162
App Resources, integrating 162, 163
App Themes 172
App Themes, illustrating 172-178
AutoGluon 263
AutoGluon Attributes, illustrating 268-270
AutoGluon, configuring 263, 264
AutoGluon, integrating 265, 266
Automated Machine Learning (AutoML) 261, 262

B

Button-Click Counter App 64
Button-Click Counter App, illustrating 64-67
Button-Like Widgets 70

C

Cache Data 118
Cache Data, configuring 119, 120
Cache Data, steps 118
Cache Resources 120
Cache Resources, integrating 120-122
Caching 114
Caching, architecture 117
Caching, functions
  Cache Data 118
  Cache Resources 120
Caching, integrating 114-117
Caching, options
  Cache Duration 123
  Cache Size 123
  Clear Cache 123
  Custom Hash Function 125
  Input Parameters 124
Callback Caveats 108
Callback Caveats, integrating 108, 109
Chart Elements 79
Chart Elements, integrating 79, 80
Chatbot 279
Chatbot, concepts
  App Reruns 287
  Chat Dialog 279
  Conversation History 293
  Pretrained LLM 290
  Prompt Message 287
Chatbot, features
  Response Tuning 296, 297
  Session State 298
  Stream Responses 300
Chat Dialog 280
Chat Dialog, concerns
  Code Snippet 281
  Model Description 283
  Relevent Models 282
  Selection Dialog 285
Chat Dialog, ensuring 280
Cleanup Process 104
Client-Server Architecture 55
Client-Server Architecture, challenges
  External Actions 56
  Server Capacity 56
  Software/Hardware Access 56
Cloud-Based Development 17
Cloud-Based Development, advantages 17
Cloud-Based Development, disadvantages 17
Cloud-Based Development, terms
  GitHub Codespaces 27
  Hugging Face Spaces 28
  Lightning AI Studio 28
Community Cloud Logs 156
Community Cloud Logs, integrating 157, 158

Community Cloud Workspace 153
Community Cloud Workspace, illustrating 154-156
Configuration Options 166
Configuration Options, configuring 167-169
Configuration Options, illustrating 171
Configuration Options, methods
  Command Line Arguments 170
  Configuration Files 170
  Environment Variables 170
Customize Navigation 194
Customize Navigation, terms
  Dynamic Navigation 195, 196
  Navigation Link 198
  Programmatically Switch Pages 203
  StreamlitPage Object 194
Custom Plots 257
Custom Plots, ensuring 258, 259

D

Dash 7
Dash, configuring 7, 8
Data Analysis 250
Data Analysis, concepts
  Data Cleaning 252
  Dataset Code 251
Data Analysis Script 32
Data Analysis Script, implementing 33-35
Data Analysis Script, integrating 36, 37
Data Analysis Script, steps 32, 33
Data Analysis, tools
  Custom Plots 257
  Profile Report 255
Data Cleaning 252
Data Cleaning, foundation
  Missing Values 252
  Outliers Handling 253
Data Elements 78
Data Elements, illustrating 78, 79
Data Entry Section 270
Data Entry Section, integrating 270-274
Dataset Information 248
Default Widget Value 68
Default Widget Value, ensuring 69
Django 10
Django, configuring 10

E

Efficient Performance 246
Efficient Performance, configuring 246-248
Entrypoint 244
Entrypoint, configuring 244, 245
Entrypoint, terms
  Dataset Information 248
  Efficient Performance 246
  Page Navigation Links 250
  Reset Button 248
  Sample Datasets 245
External Data 125
External Data, terms
  MySQL Documentation 125
  Streamlit Connections 128

F

FastAPI 11
FastAPI, configuring 11
Flask 9
Flask, configuring 9
Formatted Text Elements 76
Formatted Text Elements, integrating 76, 77

G

Gemini API 277
Gemini API, configuring 277, 278
Git 25
GitHub 26
GitHub Actions 232
GitHub Actions, ensuring 232-237
GitHub Codespaces 27
Git, steps 25, 26
Gradio 7
Gradio, configuring 7

H

Hugging Face Spaces 28

I

Input Widgets 81
Input Widgets, integrating 81-84
Interactive Scatterplot 39
Interactive Scatterplot, implementing 40-42
Internal IDs 102
Internal IDs, steps 103

L

Layout Elements 85
Layout Elements, integrating 85-92
Lightning AI Studio 28, 29
LLM Providers 277
Local Development 17

Local Development, advantages 17
Local Development, disadvantages 17
Local Development, terms
- Git 25
- GitHub 26
- Python 20
- Steamlit Account 26
- Streamlit 24
- Virtual Environment 22
- Visual Studio Code (VS Code) 18

Login Page 210
Login Page, configuring 211, 212
Login Page, illustrating 212-215
Logout Button 221
Logout Button, integrating 221, 222

M

Media Elements 84
Missing Values 252
Missing Values, configuring 252, 253
Model Training 262
Multipage App 184
Multipage App, illustrating 204, 205
Multipage App, methods
- Page Directory 185
- Python Functions 187

MySQL Documentation 125
MySQL Documentation, issues
- App Performance 127
- Secrets Management 127

N

Native Testing Framework 209
Nested Buttons 106
Nested Buttons, configuring 107, 108
Nested Streamlit Buttons 53
Nested Streamlit Buttons, ensuring 53, 54
Non-Python Dependencies 145

O

Order of Priority 172
Outliers Handling 254

P

Page Elements 73
Page Elements, integrating 73-76
Page Navigation Links 250
Parametrization 218
Parametrization, configuring 218-221
Pre-commit Hooks 231
Pre-commit Hooks, integrating 231, 232
Pretrained LLM 290
Pretrained LLM, ways
- Fine-Tuning 291
- Prompt Engineering 290
- Retrieval Augmented Generation (RAG) 291

Profile Report 255
Profile Report, integrating 256
pytest 215
pytest, configuring 216
pytest, illustrating 216, 217
Python 20
Python Dependencies 145
Python Functions, section
- Customize Navigation 189
- Source Files 187

Python, implementing 21

R

Reset Button 248
Reset Button, configuring 249
Role-Based Access Control 231
Role-Based Pages 223
Role-Based Pages, integrating 227-229
Role-Based Pages, roles
- Bells/Whistles 224, 225
- Manage Users 223

S

Script Reruns 50
Script Reruns, ensuring 50-52
Secrets Management 133
Secrets Management, methods
- Configuration Files 134
- Environment Variables 134
- Hardware Security Modules (HSMs) 134
- HashiCorp Vault 134

Secrets Management, sections
- Global 137
- Project-Level 135

Session State 60
Session State, keys
- Automatic Key 63
- Python Dictionary 61

Session State, limitations
- Button-Like Widgets 70
- Default Widget Value 68
- Widget Value 67

set_option 170
Share Button 160
Social Forums 158
Social Forums, section
- Developer Permissions 158

Public Viewers 160
Status Elements 93
Status Elements, integrating 93-95
Streamlit 1, 2
Streamlit Account 26
Streamlit Account, steps 26
Streamlit, architecture 3
Streamlit Community Cloud 43, 138
Streamlit Community Cloud, terms
Advanced Deployment 138
Application, deploying 43, 44
App List 139
Git Repository 43
Streamlit, configuring 2, 3
Streamlit Connections 128
Streamlit Connections, illustrating 128, 129
Streamlit, domain
Dash 7
Django 10
FastAPI 11
Flask 9
Gradio 7
Streamlit, elements
Chart 79
Data 78
Formatted Text 76
Input Widgets 81
Layout 85
Media 84
Status 93
Streamlit, ensuring 5
Streamlit Hello App 183
Streamlit Hello App, configuring 183, 184
Streamlit, history 4
Streamlit, implementing 24, 25
Streamlit Script, executing 37-39

T

Testing Streamlit Apps 209

U

User Authentication 278
User Authentication, configuring 278

V

Virtual Environment 22
Virtual Environment, steps 22-24
Visual Studio Code (VS Code) 18
VS Code, steps 18-20

W

Widget Callbacks 104
Widget Callbacks, integrating 105, 106
Widget Keys 100
Widget Keys, configuring 100-102
Widget Keys, terms
Cleanup Process 104
Internal IDs 102
Widget Value 67
Widget Value, ensuring 67, 68
Workspace 145, 146
Workspace, sections
Limits 147
Linked Accounts 147
Support 148
Workspace, terms
Create App 152
Explore Public 151
My App 149
My Profile 150